MEETINGS, MANNERS
AND CIVILIZATION

MEETINGS, MANNERS AND CIVILIZATION

THE DEVELOPMENT OF MODERN MEETING BEHAVIOUR

Wilbert van Vree
Translated by Kathleen Bell

Leicester University Press
London and New York

Leicester University Press
A Cassell imprint
Wellington House, 125 Strand, London WC2R 0BB

370 Lexington Avenue, New York, NY 10017–6550

First published in 1999

Originally published in Dutch as *Nederland als vergaderland: Opkomst en verbreiding van een vergaderregime*, Uitgeverij Wolters-Noordhoff, Groningen, 1994, 1996.

© 1999 Wilbert van Vree

British Library Cataloguing in Publication Data

A catalogue record for this book is available from the British Library.

ISBN 0 7185 0123 3

Library of Congress Cataloging-in-Publication Data

Vree, Wilbert van
 [Nederland als vergaderland. English]
 Meetings, manners and civilization: the development of modern meeting behaviour/Wilbert van Vree; translated by Kathleen Bell.
   p. cm.
 Includes bibliographical references and index.
 ISBN 0–7185–0123–3
 1. Meetings—Europe. 2. Etiquette—Europe—History. 3. Europe—Social life and customs.
I. Title.
   AS6.V74   1999
   060—dc21   99–18363
                                                                          CIP

Typeset by Ben Cracknell Studios
Printed and bound in Great Britain by Cromwell Press Ltd, Trowbridge, Wilts

To Annie M.G. van Vree and
Pierre M.J.M. van Vree

CONTENTS

FIGURES

— • —

ACKNOWLEDGEMENTS

This book has been translated by Kathleen Bell with the financial support of the Norbert Elias Foundation. The index was made by Ansfried Scheifes.

—————— • ——————

FOREWORD

Wilbert van Vree's *Meetings, Manners and Civilization* is an example of the best kind of sociology, but one of the rarest: the kind that can be read with enjoyment by the general reader for interest and enlightenment. Anyone who can be described as a general reader is also quite likely to be a general attender at and general participant in meetings of every kind; and thus many of the fascinating questions discussed here will chime with personal experience. We take too much for granted in our everyday lives, and Dr Van Vree makes us think afresh about many aspects, large and small, of how meetings take place in modern society. Why, at least in the richer countries of the world, can we complacently assume that no matter how severely they may disagree, participants in a meeting are unlikely to come to blows or to draw weapons? What is the significance of the chairman's authority, and how was it established? What is the origin of the chairman's gavel? How does the problem of confidentiality relate to the rise of the meeting as a typical way of doing business? Or, indeed, what is the significance of men not wearing hats in meetings (unless, of course, they happened to be a British MP raising a point of order during a vote in the House of Commons, in which case, until 1998, they had to wear a top hat while remaining seated)?

The fascinating details with which Dr Van Vree's book is studded form parts of a larger picture. Dr Van Vree works on a broad canvas, and this is a work of major scholarly significance. The author shows how the rise of 'meeting regimes' is linked to many issues of central theoretical interest to historians and sociologists. He demonstrates, for instance, how the development of rules of order in meetings is tied to the long-term processes by which states were formed, how it was linked with religion, and with the intrigues of royal courts. He shows how meetings were themselves a means of instilling discipline, how Calvinists used them for this purpose, and how there thus emerged a 'Protestant meeting order'. The Dutch Republic is seen to be a 'game' of meetings, in which there was formed a 'meeting class' with its code of 'meeting class manners'. Moreover, as Dr Van Vree is able – like so many Dutch intellectuals – to draw on literature in several languages, his book is replete with comparisons of meeting manners in Britain, Germany, France and the USA as well as in his native Netherlands. There are quite marked differences in national styles of meeting manners, and many of them – for instance, the stridently adversarial debating style of the British House of Commons, which rather alarmed many overseas viewers when parliamentary proceedings were first broadcast on satellite television – are very long-established.

Meetings, Manners and Civilization is a distinguished product of the 'Amsterdam School' of sociology. Over the last three decades at the University of Amsterdam, under the leadership of Professor Johan Goudsblom, an outstanding group of sociologists has pursued an extremely varied and wide-ranging research programme. One distinguishing feature of its work is that, unlike a great deal of contemporary sociology, it is not 'hodiecentric' (Goudsblom's word) – that is, it is not preoccupied solely with present-day societies. Whatever they are investigating, members of the school always set out to explain how and why the way in which we live now has developed out of often very different human arrangements in the past: their concern is always with change and process. They have taken as their paradigm Norbert Elias's book *The Civilizing Process* (originally published in German in 1939). Although until recently British and American sociologists paid it relatively little attention, in 1998 this book was voted one of the ten most influential sociology books of the twentieth century by members of the International Sociological Association. Looking at more than 500 years of Western European history, Elias sketched the links between two long-term trends, towards the civilizing or pacification of manners in ordinary social encounters, and towards the internal pacification of territory in the course of state formation and the division of labour. As more and more people became enmeshed in ever more extensive webs of interdependence, as they were forced increasingly to live at peace with one another, their emotional make-up or 'habitus' gradually changed: from generation to generation they slowly developed higher standards of habitual self-constraint. In other words, as people became more and more interdependent with each other, and as power ratios between individuals and between groups and categories became somewhat more equal, a process of mutual pacification could be observed. These processes, as Dr Van Vree lucidly demonstrates, were very clearly at work in the formation of 'meeting regimes'. Today, as he notes, the conduct of meetings is often more relaxed in style than was once common. This is a reflection of an 'informalization' process widespread in western social life generally, which other Amsterdam sociologists have studied extensively. Paradoxically, though, it has been observed that the more 'informally' people behave in their dealings with each other in meetings – or in other contexts – the greater, rather than the less, the necessary degree of habitual self-restraint.

The less rigid the social rules, the greater the demands imposed on emotion management.

One might ask in conclusion why this imaginative and original book about meetings should come to us from the Netherlands. After all, meetings are a pervasive part of business and social life in all industrial or post-industrial societies. My impression is that most studies of meeting behaviour by English-speaking social scientists are either pragmatically concerned with helping businessmen or the parties to conflict to negotiate more effectively, or they focus on the microscopic linguistic details of behaviour in meetings. They take the very institution of meetings for granted. Perhaps Wilbert van Vree, almost in passing, shows why the Dutch should take a regime of meetings for granted only at their peril. In Holland, the sea posed a perpetual danger, a danger which could only be met collectively. The dykes and canals which kept the land from flooding could only be maintained by common effort. Such were the realities of Dutch everyday life, and a regime of peaceful meetings emerged there at a remarkably early stage. Meetings, one may reflect, are a social activity *sui generis*, and in understanding them there is little room for Anglo-Saxon gut reaction individualism of the kind that contends that 'there is no such thing as society'.

Stephen Mennell
Dublin, August, 1998

PREFACE

This book offers an enquiry into the development of meeting behaviour, that is: human behaviour during councils, assemblies, parliaments, conferences which increasingly represent more people, and other, both formal and informal, meetings to discuss and arrange the common future. The approach selected involved studying the history of meetings. However, it was the formulation of the problem from a sociological perspective which actually determined this approach. The theory which aroused my interest in meetings, and which appeared to offer many, sometimes surprising leads for a sociological study of meetings, was the theory of civilizing processes, the basis of which was laid by Norbert Elias (*The Civilizing Process*, 1994). Therefore, this is not a comparative history of meetings but a succession of 'case studies' exploring the genesis of meeting behaviour.

Initially, Elias developed his theory on the basis of the changes in behaviour of the French elite during the courtly phase of state formation. The following research is an exploration of an aspect of the civilizing process, which came into the open in Western Europe after the height of the court society, when the upper classes gradually altered from being nobles and courtiers to becoming parliamentarians, and from being entrepreneurs to becoming professional meeting holders. Attention is focused on societies and groups, which successively took prominent positions in the development of meeting behaviour. An attempt will be made to structure a theoretical model of the development of meeting behaviour, which may prove useful for further research into civilizing processes and the development of societies.

PART I

INTRODUCTION

CHAPTER 1

MEETING BEHAVIOUR
AND CIVILIZATION

Fighting, eating and meeting

Meetings are not covered in books of manners, the literary genre that Elias used in *The Civilizing Process* to trace the changes in the behaviour of the worldly elite of Western Europe.[1] Books of manners mainly concern what Elias terms 'elementary behaviours'; behaviours such as eating, drinking, sleeping, fighting, nose blowing, spitting, defecation, speaking and sexual activity, which appear in all human societies in one form or another and, because of their apparent individual character, had until then been studied only as psychological or biological phenomena.[2] The first lines of Emile Durkheim's *Les Règles de la Méthode Sociologique* (1895) were that 'each individual drinks, sleeps, eats and thinks, and it is to society's interest that these functions be exercised in an orderly manner'. He commented further that these facts should not be considered as 'social facts', because in that case sociology would have no exclusive scientific territory for itself as it would be confused with that of biology and psychology.

Elias paid particular attention to eating, because this activity had a central place in the process of socializing. When people gathered together, they often ate together. 'Eating and drinking then occupied a far more central position in social life than today, when they provide (frequently, but not always) rather the framework and introduction for conversation and conviviality' (Elias, 1994, p. 48). After tracing the development of eating from the etiquette books, Elias proposed that this development was to a certain degree a *pars pro toto* of a general behavioural change. Human behaviours are inseparable from each other: 'We may call particular instincts by different names according to their different directions and functions, we may speak of hunger and the need to spit, of the sexual drive and of aggressive impulses, but in life these different instincts are no more separable than the heart from the stomach or the blood in the brain from the blood in the genitalia' (Elias, 1994, pp. 156, 157). An entire complex of behaviours has been altered in a similar way and in the same direction; people have forced each other to behave in a more 'civilized' manner.

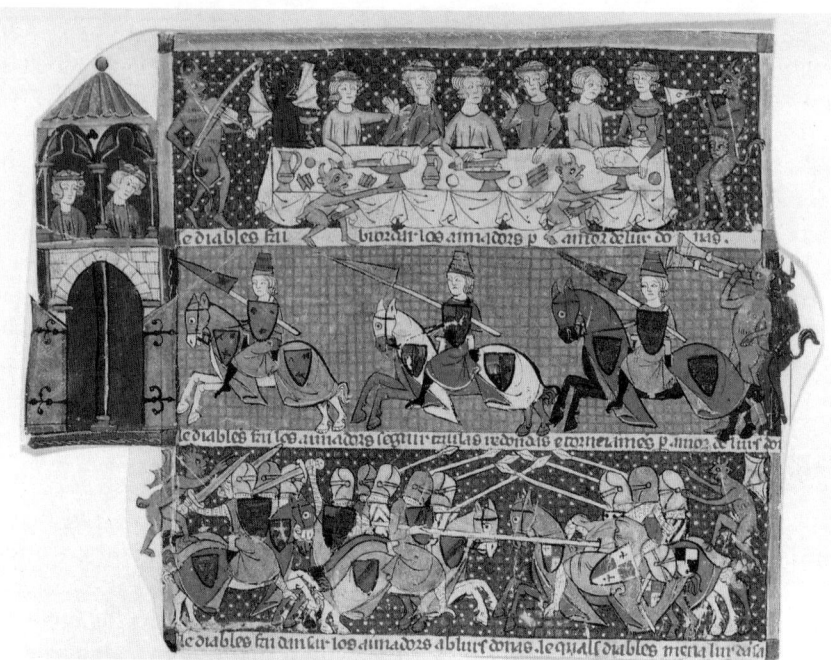

FIGURE 1.1   Medieval knights (thirteenth century) (© G. Dagli Orti)

Civilizing indicates the course of psychological processes in a certain direction. Characteristic of the Western European civilizing process of the last millennium is that more and more people have become dependent upon each other because of task division and the monopolization of organized violence, and have been forced to focus upon increasingly longer, more permanent and more specialized chains of actions and, while practising them, take the actions and intentions of an ever increasing number of others into account.

> Through the interdependence of larger groups of people and the exclusion of physical violence from them, a social apparatus is established in which the constraints between people are lastingly transformed into self-constraints. These self-constraints, a function of the perpetual hindsight and foresight instilled in the individual from childhood in accordance with his integration in extensive chains of action, have partly taken the form of self-control and partly that of automatic habit. They tend to a more even moderation, a more continuous restraint, a more exact control of drives and affects in accordance with the more differentiated pattern of social interweaving. (Elias, 1994, p. 453)

They work towards an all-round, continuous, equal regulation of behaviour and emotional life.

Elias has also established that, as an indicator of the civilizing process, the importance of eating behaviour diminished with the demise of court society and the courtiers, who were consumptive by nature to an unparalleled degree. Since then there were no changes in 'the essential basis of what is required and what is forbidden in civilized society – the standard eating technique, the manner of using knife, fork, spoon, plate, serviette, and other eating utensils – these remain in their essential features unchanged' (Elias, 1994, p. 85).

If table manners never did 'essentially' change after the demise of court society and, as far as these manners were concerned, the only thing that can be said is that the accepted standard filtered down to broader levels of the population, then one has to consider which other behaviour could be best used to research the course of the civilizing process. Meeting appears to be a most appropriate theme. Gathering together in order to talk and to reach decisions about the common future has become an increasingly important means of social integration. As a means of bonding and distinction for the elite, the stylization of meeting behaviour has replaced the stylization of eating and drinking.

In a lengthy process, deliberating and decision making have separated from communal eating and drinking and become an activity apart. Nowadays there is a tendency to consume something together after a meeting, thereby having the opportunity to air feelings and thoughts which could not be, or were not allowed to be expressed during the meeting. Although eating, drinking and meeting are sometimes combined nowadays, for example, as a working breakfast or lunch, the dominant trend seems to be in the direction of a continuing separation. Thus, in January 1997, at the instigation of the Dutch Minister of Foreign Affairs, Hans van Mierlo, the Ministers of Foreign Affairs of the European Community decided, henceforth, to restrict lunch to one hour after which the meeting was to be continued. Up until then, many councils of European Ministers, following the southern European custom, used extended lunches to go through the most tricky questions. As such, agreements were scribbled down on serviettes and later it was frequently unclear as to what had precisely been decided. Because Van Mierlo wanted to prevent 'eating during meeting and meeting during eating', he suggested dividing lunches into two parts: one part in which to make decisions and the other in which to eat. His suggestion was hardly followed. Representatives of southern European countries were strongly opposed. Apparently, the differences in meeting habits between national elites which have grown historically die hard.

In explaining the civilizing of behaviours such as eating, drinking, sleeping, fighting, Elias has pointed to the extension, the condensing and the differentiating of chains of interdependencies and the monopolizing of organized violence. If one approached the development of meeting behaviour by questioning who has mutually decided about whom and how, one would find the same conditions, but more obviously. After all, the topics discussed in (central) meetings often referred to aspects of these encompassing social changes.

The development of meetings has come about subject to a progressive pacification of societies within increasingly larger areas, which converged during the last millennium in Europe due to the extension of chains of actions and the formation of larger groups of people and stabler monopolies of violence. In *The Civilizing Process* and *The Court Society* (1983), Elias pointed out that the civilizing of behaviour in court circles implied that disputes were settled verbally instead of with weapons. In the absolutist courts of the late Middle Ages social functions developed in which physical violence gradually decreased and mutual conflicts had to be solved in a more peaceful manner than was previously the custom among 'free' warriors. Verbally fought trials of strength replaced armed trials of strength to advance one's rank and social success. '"Affaires", disputes over rank and favour, do not cease. If the sword no longer plays so great a role as means of decision, it is replaced by intrigue, conflicts in which careers and social success are contested with words' (Elias, 1994, p. 475).

In many of his later studies, including *The Germans* (1996), Elias observed that persuasion, argumentation, negotiation and compromise were forms of conduct which could only develop when the risk of actual physical attack or threat of attack with superior brawn or weapons had become socially unacceptable. In the introduction to *Quest for Excitement* (1986), he linked the emergence of modern sports among the governing classes of England to their simultaneous 'parliamentarization'. He designated the move from fighting with weapons to playing sports and fighting with words as a civilizing spurt: 'Military skills gave way to the verbal skills of debate, or rhetoric and persuasion, all of which required greater restraint all round and identified this change very clearly as a civilizing spurt' (p. 34). During the eighteenth century, one saw the transformation of the ancient estate assemblies into parliaments in the modern sense. Parliamentary factions gradually transformed into two parties, not radically dissimilar in social composition, competing with each other for the support of a relatively small electorate, but generally refraining from using violence against each other. The party that lost its majority came to hand power over peacefully to the other. 'The restraint of violence among the English upper classes in this period was, much more than among their French and German counterparts, a process of self-pacification. Restraints were imposed not by a king and his representatives but by members of a self-ruling oligarchy competing among themselves' (Mennell, 1992, p. 92). Less known is the fact that a similar process occurred in the Netherlands a century earlier.

As the monopolies over violence and taxation became more public, and the differentiation of societal functions and the related functional democratization progressed, meetings began to play a more central role, in which power and prestige accumulated. This is illustrated by the derivation of titles of address given to functions fulfilled in meetings, such as president, vice-president, chairman, general secretary, presiding officer and congressman. In the last few centuries, and frequently by force, the 'most powerful on earth' have gradually altered from being courtiers and entrepreneurs to becoming professional meeting holders and chairpeople. They developed the models for meetings to which an increasing number of people adhere.

The restraint of physical violence, at least locally and temporarily, was the *conditio sine qua non* of meetings. It is to be expected that the long-term development of meetings coincides with the organization of violence within basic entities, 'tribes', villages, towns, nation-states, confederations; i.e. within the increasingly large and stabler 'survival units' which 'have exercised comparatively strict control over the use of physical violence in relationships between their members. At the same time, they have allowed, and often encouraged, their members to use physical violence against non-members' (Elias, 1978, p. 138). One can regard survival units as 'meeting units'. The process by which 'survival units' grow and become more specialized can be more accurately studied by considering village councils, war councils, court councils, estates assemblies, parliaments and other central meetings, in which the actions of an increasing number of people need to be co-ordinated. The central meetings of 'survival units' may be considered as 'frontlines of civilization'.

It seems obvious, but should nevertheless be pointed out, that as more people became mutually dependent over extensive areas, the opportunities and needs to fight decreased, while those to confer and negotiate increased. People who previously competed freely with each other were compelled to set aside the use of force and to fight exclusively verbal battles in meetings. The primary function of these meetings was to discuss and make decisions about war and peace, about the preparation, organization, suspension and settlement of armed struggles against other groups, and about the use of physical punishment for rebellious members of one's own group. The line between verbal and armed combat remained precarious while the survival units were barely stable, frequently at war, and governed by small groups of well-established warriors.

With the stabilization of increasingly larger survival units, the differentiation of societal functions, and the centralizing and 'barracking' of arms and soldiers, more people were forced to consider the results of centrally held verbal battles and the decisions prescribing the 'dos and don'ts', to which they could be forced to comply by the use of organized violence. One of the resulting developments was the gradual standardization of manners in meetings or the diminishing of differences in the ways of meeting between groups within larger areas. This process accelerated when the balance of power was more equal between the controllers of a monopoly of force and the rest of the population. As more layers of the population, by means of their chosen representatives, took part in the battle for the control and the use of the organized violence, the more those central meetings became precisely those places where different meeting manners smelted together to become new standards of meeting behaviour.

Societal development in the last millennium is coupled with an increase in the number of meetings and levels of meeting, and with the development of a continually broadening network of mutually related meetings, in which manners and habits pass ever more quickly from above to below and in an increasing degree from below to above. As the contrasts in meeting behaviour between social groups diminished, the variations and nuances in the way in which meetings are held increased.

As stated previously, all this seems self-evident, but it begs several questions. We actually know very little about the exact course of events. Discussing, deciding, negotiating, deliberating are barely researched as behaviours which change along with the changes in the networks of interdependency and the balance of power between people. Frequently, implicitly or otherwise, people assume that present-day meeting manners are as they always have been. An overview of the way in which meetings have developed is lacking.

In a lecture in 1979, De Swaan suggested that in the last century a transition has occurred from command householding to negotiating householding: 'The variation in acceptable behaviour [has] enlarged within the new limiting conditions of mutual negotiation and consent' (p. 19). According to De Swaan, this move particularly occurred in, and spread from, modern organizations, such as welfare services and commercial service companies, in which the pressure to work and employees' wages were no longer sufficient to guarantee the required dedication, and pressure was put on the managers of the organizations to take employees' wishes more into consideration and, in a more subtle way, bind them to the organization.

Of course De Swaan's lecture should not be taken as a discourse about a process with an absolute starting and finishing point. The transition from command to negotiating, which De Swaan has observed in the last century within certain spheres of life, should be considered as the most recent phase in the development of meetings, characteristic of the European civilizing process. Likewise, Mastenbroek (1991, 1995) pointed out that this behaviour has developed very slowly. It was a process in which people have learned, with the aim of prolonging and thickening social networks, to avoid primary impulses in conflict such as fighting and instead transform and control them. In Europe the first books about how to negotiate appeared in the eighteenth century. They were written by diplomats of the French court and covered the modes of behaviour and rules of thumb that were usual in negotiations between state representatives, and what was desirable. On the basis of these books, Mastenbroek determined that, in comparison with the present day, the negotiating style of eighteenth-century Western European diplomats was 'more one-sided and more extreme, less differentiated, less varied and more whimsical', that emotional displays during negotiations were regulated less embracing and more unbalanced, and that 'interaction in a direct way was more dangerous, for example by displays of aggression and humiliation and sudden changes of mood' (1992, pp. 90–1). Similar comments reveal that the way of negotiating and meeting are extremely dependent upon the existing balance of power and dependency relationships.

These consideration lead to the proposition which serves as the backbone to this research: As larger numbers of people became mutually dependent over larger areas and/or differences in power decreased between people, an increased number of problems needed to be solved through talking and decision making in meetings which demand an ever increasing precise, more equal and more embracing regulation of impulses and short-lived affects; this 'compulsion to meet' was less well developed when the networks of mutual dependence were smaller and less stable, and/or the balances of power were more unequal.

This comparative research of the development of the act of meeting in the western world will depart from the holding of meetings within the process of state formation in the area roughly covered by the present-day Netherlands. This choice is prompted not only by practical considerations but also reflects the notion that the development of meetings in this area accelerated earlier than in the majority of the other European countries, where the restraint from violence among the upper classes was to a larger extent imposed by a king and his representatives and central co-ordinating functions were longer monopolized by aristocratic-monarchic court councils.

Instances that supplied valuable information concerning the nature and direction of the development of holding meetings were those in which manners were the subject of a societal discussion; those instances when people met to discuss the way in which meetings should be organized and managed and that, in reference to wider social changes, formulated and altered the rules and laws of meeting.

Instruction books about how to conduct and to hold a meeting provided another important source of information; a genre closely related to etiquette books, which appeared after the demise of court society in Western Europe. This literature particularly illustrates how, when, and which meeting manners were more widely adopted, or became lost when they were no longer necessary to accentuate or maintain differences in rank. Meeting manuals and textbooks reflect problems and difficulties which have occurred during the rise and expansion of 'a special sort of restrained aggression, measured hostility, adaptable to changing circumstances' (Elias, 1969, p. 411).

On the basis of lexicographic sources, the initial step will be to focus on the development of a number of Western European words which currently refer to (the holding of) meetings and the conduct within them. The changes in meaning these words have undergone give a first impression of the way and the direction in which meetings and meeting behaviour have developed and of the more embracing social changes of which this development is a part.

CHAPTER 2

THE DEVELOPMENT OF
THE CONCEPT OF MEETING

The contemporary Western European concept of meeting

In Western European language families, similarities can be observed in their concepts of meeting. The English word *meeting*, the German word *Versammlung*, the Dutch word *vergadering* and the French word *réunion* have the same meaning, and carry the same value judgements, in many respects. They are virtually but, as shall be demonstrated, not entirely, mutually interchangeable.

These words refer to the behaviour of people who come together to discuss and decide about future actions. They are words which distinguish more peaceful ways of conflict regulation from more violent ways, predominantly verbal activities from predominantly non-verbal activities, and more reserved and businesslike social intercourse from more intimate and personal social intercourse. They imply familiarity and acceptance of certain rules and norms of behaviour: the dos and don'ts.

The close relationship between concepts such as *meeting*, *vergadering*, *Versammlung*, and *réunion* is particularly evident if one compares these concepts to those by which communities with a lower level of integration refer to their own gatherings for communal talks and agreements. In an anthropological study of the Pintupi, a group of Australian Aborigines who, until recently, lived as hunters and gatherers, Myers (1986) observed that they had no word for meeting. Their concept of meeting had been adopted from the English after they were obliged to participate in self-government within the larger entity of the modern Australian state, and had to learn to assemble for meetings at village level.

> While the English term meeting is the marked form, it is not insignificant that Pintupi currently refers to all collective gatherings using both the loan word and the Pintupi unmarked form, *wangkinpa*, which means generally speaking. . . . Gatherings to discuss plans for initiation or other ritual matters, inquests relating to death, and the like are all described as meetings. (Myers, 1986, p. 434)

The concepts *meeting, Versammlung, réunion*, and *vergadering* are closer to each other than any of them are to *wangkinpa*. They reflect the long-term, common development of European societies, the still closer mutual interwovenness of these societies, and the correspondingly related increase in co-ordinated tasks at national, international, and supranational level. However, with deeper consideration, they do not appear to be completely synonymous.

For instance, the Dutch concept, *vergaderen*, and its derivatives and constructions, have exceptional and obvious emotional values. These values are difficult to define but they contribute to the meaning, nevertheless. For outsiders the impact of the concept of meeting is difficult to grasp as can be seen from the following quotes from a number of recent books by non-Dutch authors about the Dutch. Quote from an American book:

> The Dutch word *vergadering* is . . . difficult to translate accurately, because it imposes a specific and well-understood mode of behaviour not quite covered by the more vague meeting. . . . Typically the Dutch *vergadering* style is . . . somewhat dull and predictable, and seldom confrontational. (Shetter, 1987, p. 123)

Quote from a German book:

> *Vergaderingen*, although repeatedly the target of self-mockery by the participants, are weighty events. Nevertheless, the behaviour is unpretentious, not rigidly formal, does not indicate status as would certainly be expected in an authoritarian society, is experienced as correct and polite, and indicates immediately who is above and below in the political or bureaucratic hierarchy. (Zahn, 1989, p. 19)

Quote from a Portuguese book:

> *Vergaderingen* [are] in the main nothing more . . . than the solemn, pompous and boringly dreadful versions of our amicable pub chats. . . . These gatherings often take place on set evenings and at set times, and a Frenchman that I knew held the distinct opinion that this meticulousness served as a cover for night-time adventures, secret excesses. Because, so he said, it is incomprehensible that these people could be like that! But they are. (Rentes de Carvalho, 1982, pp. 82, 83)

In the book *Dealing with the Dutch* (1997) about Dutch lifestyle and etiquette, the anthropologist, Jacob Vossestein, quotes foreign businessmen (pp. 32, 33, 48):

A German:

> I wouldn't mind missing the Dutch meeting culture. If you phone someone, unavoidably the answer is: he is in a meeting, can you phone again? That disturbed me right from the beginning of my stay. They only meet here for the sake of

meeting. The positive side is that everyone is seeking consensus with one another, although often the opinions are fixed beforehand. It becomes a charade, a ritual, sponsored by coffee producers.

A Swiss:

In other countries conflicts easily escalate. Here people stay calm. The company council, the trade unions and the company directors take decisions in relative harmony.

An American:

In the Dutch company where I work, I exclaimed: for heaven's sake, let's stop talking about it and DO something!

In English, French and German there is no concept that refers simply to gatherings and behaviours of people who talk together and make agreements concerning their common future. The words *meeting*, *réunion* and *Versammlung* refer to a broader range of peaceful gatherings of people, including sporting and religious meetings. Nouns such as the German *Tagung*, the French *assemblée* and the English *assembly* have a more limited meaning than *vergadering*: they refer primarily to more formal meetings of relatively many people, such as parliamentary meetings, shareholders meetings, or synods. Other words, such as *conference, convention, congress* and *council* in English, *Konferenz, Kongress, Konzil*, and *Rat* in German, and *conseil, conversation, conférence* and *concile* in French, allude to a yet smaller part of the existing range of meetings. They correspond to similar words in Dutch. Moreover, English, French, and German lack the capacity to refer in one verb to the complete, accepted mode of behaviour during meetings as can be encompassed in the Dutch verb, *vergaderen*. In the other three languages, verbs are designated which represent a part of the meaning or allude to one particular way of meeting, such as *to negotiate, to consider, to confer, discuter, délibérer, besprechen, entscheiden*, and *tagen*. To obtain the same understanding as *vergaderen*, use must be made of a substantive, such as *to hold/attend a meeting, tenir une réunion, eine Versammlung abhalten*. The verbs *to meet, se réunir* and *sich versammeln* rarely mean *vergaderen*, but more usually a coming together.

It could be asked why there is a stricter demarcation in the Dutch language between those gatherings (and the behaviour therein) where people talk together and make agreements concerning their future, and other, non-verbal, and more intimate ways of being together. Furthermore, in Dutch, the limits are less defined between formal and informal ways of meeting, and between meetings with large and small attendances.

Distinct from natural scientific concepts, which represent a higher level of synthesis, concepts that are accommodated in words such as *vergadering* and *vergaderen* cannot be explained without knowledge of the society in which these words have acquired their meaning.[1] Such concepts express something that successive generations of a society, or initially certain social layers within it in particular, have communally experienced and endeavoured to understand. A brief review of the semantic development of these words in comparison with the English, French and German synonyms will clarify this.

The sociogenesis of West European concepts of meeting

By comparing the meanings of *vergadering* and *vergaderen* from the Middle Ages with the contemporary meanings, the initial observation is that these words have undergone a differentiation in meaning. From designations of all the possible usages of coming together and being together, these words have developed into terms for groups of people gathering together and being gathered together exclusively to talk mutually about their common future and to make agreements. The first changes in the use of the concept *vergadering* is noticeable during the transition from the first to the second stage formation of the state of the Netherlands. During the last phase of the Habsburg dominion in the northern Low Countries, and the formation of the Republic of the United Provinces (Dutch Republic) after the break with Spain at the end of the sixteenth century, the noun *vergadering* replaced a number of more specific nouns designating interlocal meetings. As designations of gatherings in the Provincial States and the States–General, the noun *vergadering* gradually became the mode from the end of the sixteenth century. The use of *vergadering* to specify the meetings of the highest boards of the Dutch Republic represented a break with the prevalent manner of talking together and decision making at a centralized level, which had been powerfully influenced by sovereigns and courtiers.

Before the secession of the Habsburg realm and the abjuration of the Spanish king in 1581, *vergadering* was seldom used in the sense of gathering to talk together and make agreements; apparently it was only really used in reference to municipal government. For designating committee meetings of farming communities, guilds, water boards and church groups, there were numerous special, local words in circulation. An indigenous concept that brought all similar gatherings, and not more than this, under one term was lacking. The noun *vergadering* had, like the verb *vergaderen*, a much broader meaning. Lexicographers have noted the following usages, among others, of these words in the Middle Ages: In the context of knights and courtiers *vergadering* often referred to a battle, a scuffle, a clash, the meeting of two armies, a showdown, a horde of warriors, an army, a contest or a sparring match. As applied to lovers and spouses, it usually meant the physical union, sexual intercourse or a wedding party. In a religious sense, it referred to a procession, a holy mass, a worship, a brotherhood or a cloister. Furthermore, *vergadering* was used for stampede, crowd, hospice, troop, multitude or mob. The verb *vergaderen* had the same broad spectrum of meaning: to come to blows, to have sexual intercourse, to marry, to flock together, to socialize, as used in the adage 'meeting is sweet, but parting is bitter'.[2]

From the same lexicographic sources, it can be observed that the increasing use of *vergadering* and *vergaderen* to designate governmental meetings at higher levels of integration was coupled with a limitation in the meanings of these words, which were less and less used to designate a scuffle, sexual intercourse, to fight, to copulate, and related phenomena, such as a sparring match, to flock together, a betrothal, a marriage, a commune, a cloister, to be associated with animosity, to meet for warlike purposes, and to have soldiers fall in and troop together.

This specialization of the meaning of *vergadering* and *vergaderen* is part of the development of a common Dutch language of (preponderantly town) representatives from the various regions, particularly the province of Holland. For those unfamiliar with the Dutch language, it is appropriate to point out what is understood by the term 'Holland'. Holland is the name of the coastal province of the Netherlands (nowadays divided into the provinces of North and South Holland) bordering the North Sea, and bound by Zeeland to the south. There is a long tradition of using 'Holland' as *pars pro toto*; initially, for the Republic of the Seven United Provinces, and later for the Kingdom of the Netherlands (now consisting of twelve provinces). In this book, the Dutch distinction is maintained, and the name 'Holland' refers only to the province.

In the Middle Ages, the populations of the various Low Countries such as Flanders, Brabant, Holland, Limburg, Friesland and so on spoke vernaculars and occasionally communicated in Latin or French. With the establishment of the Dutch Republic in the seventeenth century an accelerated development can be seen towards a common Dutch language with substantial extractions from Holland. It was a language spoken by the elite. Goudsblom (1988) wrote that intensive contact between the various provinces only existed via the municipal upper class and that the countryside and the common people took no part in it. The development of this common Dutch was powerfully stimulated by the meetings of the Provincial States, States-General, and the United East and West India Companies, as the need was felt for a communal means of communication.

Goudsblom has shown, in general, that characteristics are observable of a more encompassing civilization process in the Dutch language that was beginning to emerge during the last phase of the Burgundian-Habsburg dominion and during the period of the Dutch Republic. Among other things, he points out that this language excluded words 'which call up associations of the lower desires, those of the lesser man' (1988, p. 22). Examples of this are copulating and fighting, vulgarisms concerning the human body, basic bodily functions, sickness, death, instincts, and words derived from languages of lower class groups. Much later this development took another turn. With the narrowing of the mutual power differences and the emancipation of emotions in the twentieth century, there is greater appreciation of vernaculars, dialects, and regional accents (Wouters, 1990, pp. 111–17).

In the semantic specialization of *vergadering* and *vergaderen* during the first stage of state formation, similar characteristics of a broader civilization process are observable. After all, the activities which fell outside the area of application of these concepts, and which, therefore, were more clearly differentiated from talking together and coming to an understanding, included behaviours such as fighting and copulation. In *The Civilizing Process*, Elias demonstrated that, with the monopolization and centralization of organized force, 'vulgar' behaviours disappeared more and more behind the scenes of public life and became taboo. The semantic specialization of the Dutch concept of meeting is a part of the development of a more 'civilized' Dutch language that men from the large towns established in meetings, clubs, churches, and lobbies 'in order to facilitate the maintenance of incidental connections' (Goudsblom, 1988, p. 24).

With the stabilization of the Republic and the expansion of power and prestige of its leaders, the words *vergadering* and *vergaderen* began to be used by more and more groups of people. They were now understood as concepts which marked out more peaceful, more public, and more verbal activities from more violent, more personal, and less verbal activities. This concept of meeting was further refined through the centuries and eventually came into common usage.

The start of a new stage in the sociogenesis of the concept of meeting was marked by the replacement of the rather elitist and sectionalized States-General of the Dutch Republic by an elected national parliament during the Batavian Revolution at the end of the eighteenth century. This parliament was initially known as the *Nationale Vergadering* (National Assembly). With the subsequent gradual parliamentarization of increasingly broader levels of the population, *vergadering* came to refer more frequently to meetings for communal deliberation and agreement according to parliamentary rules. Other meanings of *vergadering*, such as religious practice, religious community, and mob, became more infrequent in the nineteenth century and, in the twentieth century, became redundant.[3]

At this stage in the development of the concept of meeting, jurists played an important part with their contribution to the basic, lawful definition of *vergadering* as a parliamentary form of assembly, and to the extension of the parliamentary rules of behaviour by compiling manuals of how to conduct and hold meetings for clubs, associations, political parties, local councils, and shareholders.

With the recognition of the constitutional rules of meeting in 1848 and the consequent Association and Meeting Law (1855), it was established that religious practices fell outside the realms of the meeting law. Likewise, amicable meetings and gatherings of armed persons, except for uniformed officers, were excluded. Thus the meaning of *vergadering* was limited to the communal deliberations and decision making at organized meetings. The following example demonstrates that at that time, this limitation was less obvious than it is in retrospect. In 1871 the Supreme Court of the Netherlands conducted legal proceedings to assess whether or not those councils determining the closing time for public houses were in conflict with the constitutional right to meet. The Solicitor General said: 'Meeting is, in my opinion, gathering together by means of appointment or summons for a communal aim.' The opposing solicitor argued: 'Every satisfaction of the need for amicability, all mutual gatherings, are protected by the constitution under the term *vergadering*.' In other words, this solicitor was of the opinion that those people who gathered together for recreational purposes in a society or public house were also a *vergadering* in the sense of the law and accordingly could appeal to the constitutional law of meeting. Nevertheless, the Supreme Court assumed an interpretation of the law of meeting in which the concept *vergadering* exclusively referred to the intentional assembling of people to enter into agreements about one or more subjects.[4]

At this time, the activities which were excluded from the range of meanings of *vergadering*, and which were more clearly demarcated from discussing and concurring, were comprised of behaviours which had the character of religious and amicable gatherings. This differentiation reflects a trend in the direction of a less fantasy-rich, and less personal, manner of speaking and concurring.

Furthermore, in this century, the meaning of the verb *vergaderen* has differentiated to become discussing and making agreements concerning the common future.[5] Thus the most accepted present meaning of *vergaderen* in one of the most authoritative Dutch dictionaries is: *The holding of or attending gatherings of people where various issues (from an agenda) are discussed and (possibly) decisions are made* (Van Dale III, 1984, p. 3141).

Particularly after the German occupation during the Second World War (when it was officially forbidden to hold meetings in the Netherlands) discussing and making decisions about the common future took an increasingly important place in the working lives of more and more people. With the expansion of labour organizations and the extension of more complicated and more vulnerable production processes, professional meeting manners developed which people increasingly adhered to in order to improve their chances of societal success. In this most recent stage of the socio-genesis of the concept of meeting, social psychologists have played a prominent role. They began to research meetings while they were in operation and wrote manuals on the basis of this research. Meetings were approached and understood as small group processes. They placed more emphasis on the informal rules and manners which people (should) employ if they were to discuss and decide about their common future than on the formal, parliamentary, judicial rules.

The societal development that is expressed in the history of *vergadering* and *vergaderen* was not confined to the Netherlands. Concepts also sprung up in other European languages which showed much similarity to the Dutch concept of meeting: *meeting, réunion* and *Versammlung,* and concepts for more formal meetings, such as *assembly, assemblée* and *Tagung.* A glance at the history of these concepts is sufficient to realize that they acquired their present-day meanings during similar state formation processes. However, these processes progressed at different rates. The French word *assemblée,* in the Middle Ages, had the same interpretation as the medieval Dutch *vergadering.* In court society, this French word fell into disuse as a designation for fighting and sexual intercourse. Later it came into use as a designation for a reception or receipt, and during the French Revolution it was chosen by the bourgeoisie as the name for the series of meetings in *and through which* they were going to rule France.[6]

The English *assembly* shows a similar development to the French *assemblée,* but from the seventeenth century it was already being used to designate national political meetings and national synods.[7] Nowadays *assembly* is little used. When *assembly* would have been used previously, *conference* or, more commonly, *meeting* are now used.

The word *Tagung* was taken from the Swiss-German and came to designate the more bourgeois, central meetings which had sprung up in various German towns in the nineteenth century (in Switzerland there was an earlier acceleration in meeting development). Later it was also used for the central meetings of the united German state.[8]

The other concepts, *meeting, réunion* and *Versammlung,* have mainly developed in the more recent political struggle for recognition and application of the freedom of meeting for all citizens of a state. The history of these concepts shows a gradual semantic specialization, but less advanced in comparison to *vergadering.*

In such a way *réunion,* which before the French Revolution meant reconciliation, became legally defined in the nineteenth and twentieth centuries as an organized grouping intended to exchange ideas together. This change occurred in the struggle for access to government functions by increasingly larger groups of the population.[9] At the same time *réunion* acquired and maintained the more general meaning of a gathering of people, animals, or objects.

The English *meeting* has undergone the same long and continuous development as the Dutch *vergadering.* It has gradually changed from a concept having the same broad meaning as the medieval *vergadering* and acquired the more specialized meaning of coming together for common discussion and decision making. This development reflects the history of a society which, since the latter half of the seventeenth century, has been governed by nobles, commoners and monarchs in and by meetings, and in which the commoners have gradually acquired the upper hand. A salient detail allows a glimpse at a noble past in the development of the meaning of meeting; in the nineteenth century this word was used as a euphemism for a duel.[10]

The word *Versammlung* is not only more recent than *meeting, vergadering* and *réunion*, but it also contains a more formal concept: this refers generally to a somewhat larger, mainly political meeting, which has to conduct itself according to constitutional rules. The concept *Versammlung* developed in a society which was governed longer by the military than their Dutch neighbours were. In the post-war legal settlement of the *Versammlungsrecht* (right of assembly) and the accompanying jurisprudence, detail was paid to various possible forms of force which should be avoided in a meeting (Weller, 1960, p. 46f). This echoes the more military character of the society in which this concept originally formed. In German, meetings of managers, employees, and company directors are more commonly designated by *Konferenz* or *Besprechung* than by *Versammlung*.

In summary, it can be said that English, French, and German have several words for the notion which in Dutch can be expressed by one word: *vergadering*. The more particular and formal concepts of *assembly, assemblée* and *Tagung* developed initially during a stage of state formation dominated by monarchs and nobility. The more generalized and informal concepts of *meeting, réunion* and *Versammlung* developed predominantly in the subsequent stage of state formation when broader layers of the population attained access (often with violence) to various governmental functions and were integrated into national states. The development of the Dutch concept of meeting was part of a less violent, more moderate, less interrupted, and more gradual process of state formation in which townspeople and bourgeoisie played a more dominant role.

In the following chapters the changes in meeting during the process of state formation in Western Europe will be further investigated. This research is intended further to strip the concept of meeting of its appreciative content, enabling it to be used for the study of a long-term process: the 'meetingization' of society or the development of meeting behaviour and activities in society.

PART II

MEETINGS IN MILITARY-AGRARIAN SOCIETIES

The rise of war councils as models for meetings

The long-term process, designated as the development of meeting behaviour, means that increasingly more people were compelled to adapt themselves verbally to others. This demanded an increasingly more accurate, more even tempered, and more encompassing control of the expression of emotions and a more distanced manner of speaking. A relatively strong compulsion to meet has anchored itself into the social habitus of the people in Western European countries and increasingly more parts of the world, although at different times and at different rates. The development of meeting obligation and meeting constraint is an aspect of the process of civilization that has come about during the formation of states. It is not suggested that people only began to talk and decide together on their common future after they had established states or stabler monopolies of violence and taxation. The capacity to speak to each other is a universal, human achievement. The genetically fixed potential for talking allows people to adapt themselves to each other and make agreements with each other. However, the use of this capacity relies on changes in power and dependency relationships. Changes in the ways of meeting (talking and concurring about communal activities) are, in the main, to be understood as survival strategies, as adaptions to changing social relationships.

It is unknown how people came to mutual agreement in the earliest phases of human development, when they were dependent upon hunting and gathering. In more recent, social scientific literature, the dominating (and the author's) view is that people in prehistoric times were subject to relatively strong pressure to discuss mutually during the lengthy period of dependence upon hunting and gathering. This view is in line with results of modern research on societies of hunters and gatherers.

In the study *Democracy and Despotism in Primitive Societies* (1986), Ronald Glassman gives an ideal-typical presentation (based on historical and anthropological knowledge of elementary societies) of how meetings might be conducted in prehistoric survival units. He strongly emphasizes that hunting and gathering demanded close mutual co-operation and that people became

A campfire meeting. A segment of a Pygmy band in the Ituri Forest, Zaire

greatly dependent upon the exchange of knowledge, fire, tools and food. Furthermore, people needed reliable ways of co-ordinating activities and regulating conflicts, which Glassman designates 'campfire democracy' (Part I, pp. 45–53). Conflict control and the consequential plan of action involved three stages. A problem or conflict, which compromised co-operation within the group, was first discussed by all the group members in family circles and between friends. Then the adult males would enter into discussions around the campfire to work out a final solution. The remaining group members, women and children, would gather around the men in a circle and were thus able to contribute to the discussion if they so wished. The actual decision, however, was taken by the men only and it had to be unanimous. The third stage concerned the re-establishment of group cohesion by discussions in which each member had to be convinced of the correctness of the decision. This stage could last days or even weeks. The decision was only acted upon when the entire group was unanimous. The necessity to work together ruled out physical force as a practical means of reunification. When arguments and disagreements continued to disrupt co-operation within a group, the group would split up.

Although the second stage of campfire democracy was to a great extent dominated by men, the other group members could also exert important influence on the course and outcome of the decision-making process. The relatively large predominance of men was based on their greater physical strength and their arms monopoly, created in the closely controlled, and differing, processes of raising boys and girls. In fact, except when hunting, use of weapons was rare. As long as the number of people in relation to the available open land remained small, and groups could avoid each other, aggression remained limited to skirmishes.[1] Presumably, previous to the assumption of a monopoly of arms by men, women played at least an equally important role in the plans of action.

Accepting that both the necessity and custom to fight out conflicts using arms were, in general, relatively limited, the degree to which people were pressurized to solve problems in meetings was particularly dependent upon their opportunities to break away and form a new group (thus avoiding troublesome meetings).

As the possibilities to flee became more limited, with the increase in the population and the population density, and the rise in the productivity or the standard of living, much suggests that the compulsion and the tendency to solve conflicts by armed combat increased and meetings became more precarious. The processes which limited the possibility to flee have been designated as extensive and intensive growth by E.L. Jones and other economic historians (Goudsblom, Jones, Mennell, 1989). In his study, *Fire and Civilization* (1992), Goudsblom suggested that the origin and spread of agriculture and husbandry, which brought about a quickening in growth rate of the extensive and intensive processes, were coupled with cultural divergence and social differentiation. Between societies, the cultural differences increased and, within societies, different social classes developed between which the differences in behaviour and power grew. The trend towards social stratification, or the dividing of people into higher and lower classes with respectively more and less access to power, possessions, and status, can be considered as a common characteristic of a settled agrarian society. Other converging trends mentioned by Goudsblom were the increase in the number of people, the concentration of people in permanent settlements, the specialization in an increasing number of skills and societal functions and the organization of people into larger economic, religious and political units (Goudsblom, 1992a, pp. 79–80; pp. 62–4). Because of these entwined social trends, society became more complex and different classes developed, each with its own societal functions and opportunities, such as warriors, farmers, craftsmen, traders and priests.

In practically all agrarian societies the possession of weapons, that had long been a monopoly of adult males, became monopolized by specialized warriors and they became the ruling class. Other social groups were usually insufficiently able to resist the organized force of the warriors. Their job or function made them vulnerable to physical force, and allowed them neither the time nor the means to defend themselves. They became dependent upon warriors who could protect them against other warriors (Goudsblom, 1992, p. 82). The domination by warriors formed a common structural character-istic of developed agrarian societies, which can then also be generally characterized as military-agrarian societies (Goudsblom, 1992; also 1988, pp. 104–32; 1992a, p. 87).

The social trends indicated by Goudsblom, which in individual societies sometimes stagnated for a while, or took a contrary direction, have commonly continued in the same direction for a very long time. They form the background against which meetings have developed in the time period when agriculture and husbandry were the most important means of subsistence.[2] Also, these trends had far-reaching consequences for the way in which meetings developed in Western Europe, where they continued from the early Middle Ages onwards without any great disruption. The main trends of this development can be summarized as follows.

The more people began to settle permanently, the more co-ordination problems occurred, which prompted people to hold meetings more often. The functions of meetings expanded from concerning the administration of the law, preparations for war and the establishment of peace, to controlling taxation, water boards, trade, industry, social services, and many other activities and problems stemming from the extension and differentiation of the chains of actions. With the concentration of people, meetings became centralized in special violence-free areas and separate buildings. The increase in the division of labour was accompanied by the arrival of more specialized meetings, in which various meeting styles developed, directed toward specific problems, functions, and possibilities of the various classes of farmers, craftsmen, priests and warriors. Within the larger military, religious, political, and economic associations people had simultaneously to learn to speak and decide about the future of more people. The stratification of people had the consequence that some people met more than they previously had done and decided for many, while others met less and were compelled to obey the decisions taken, usually outside their knowledge, by small groups of rulers.

The common structural characteristic of agrarian societies, the dominance of warriors, manifested itself in the development and spreading of formal, martial rules of meetings and manners. This development was initially due to the 'spiral of wars' through which larger numbers of people were compelled to act as one body. Waging war demanded, from the able-bodied men in particular, activities such as training boys for defence, the selection of leaders, the discussion and announcement of the strategy to be followed, the courtmartialling and punishing of warriors, deliberations about surrender or truce, and the division of seized goods and conquered land. For this purpose warriors issued commands and orders which they sanctioned by harsh physical punishment. Due to permanent warfare or threats of war, the martial meeting rules acted as an example for others.

Threats of war and waging war forced people to organize themselves into units of offence and defence led by warriors who could protect them against the organized violence of other warriors. Through pressure from above, by imitation, and due to habit, the meeting manners of warrior councils spread and the participation in meetings became strongly dependent upon military power and military considerations. In such a way, women, children, and initially also non-able-bodied men were excluded from the central meetings of survival units and from many other meetings. Until long after the Middle Ages, unrelenting rules forbidding women to take part in meetings of courts of justice, guilds, churches and towns remained valid (see Chapter 4).

The trend in the direction of the militarization of meetings was coupled with opposition from the non-military population. This opposition worked in the direction of a further differentiation of manners in meetings. The importance of warrior councils as a general model for meetings decreased.

In the following two chapters, attention will be paid to the changes in meetings in the Frankish and Burgundian-Habsburg regions, two influential military-agrarian realms of the Middle Ages.

CHAPTER 3

THE MILITARIZATION AND
DEMILITARIZATION OF MEETINGS

Farmers and warriors: 'Things'

The rather undifferentiated and small-scale agricultural societies of the early Middle Ages were ruled over by farmer–warriors; men who were allowed to carry arms and who owned land. They created armies, which were likewise 'political' entities, that is units of offence and defence, and 'meeting units'. These farmer–warriors were obliged to meet on fixed days and at certain times to administer 'justice'. They also had to assemble, when summoned, if war threatened, or for other calamities, such as fire, flooding, and for judging public criminal offences.[1] In all cases, the men had to arrive at the meeting armed. In Scandinavian, Dutch, English and German literature, this meeting is referred to as 'thing', 'ding', 'þing', although in English the term '(ge)moot' is more often used. For instance, it is supposed that freemen of the early medieval Anglo-Saxon tribes, while they were still living on the Continent, 'were accustomed to come together in the "Village-moot", to take "bye-laws" for their village, and to administer justice. These groups also chose men to represent them at the "Hundred-moot" of the district, which acted as a court of appeal and arbitrated inter-village disputes. Still higher in authority, and similarly constituted, was the "Folk-moot", which was also the citizen army of the tribe' (Robert, *Rules of Order Newly Revised*, 1970, pp. xxviii–xxix). The same institutions, it is believed, were carried into England during the 200 years after the first Anglo-Saxon invasions from the Continent. The Folk-moot became the 'Shire-moot' and a general assembly, known as 'witan' or 'witenagemot' arose in each of the separate early English kingdoms (Robert, *Rules of Order Newly Revised*, 1970, pp. xxviii–xxix). In this book the term 'thing' will be used to refer to assemblies of early medieval European 'villages', 'tribes', 'peoples' and other units of offence and defence or meeting units.

Fines were imposed for missing a 'thing'. For the administration of justice, participants did not only have to know about legal procedures, passing

FIGURE 3.1   Fragment of the Bayeux Tapestry. Negotiating in the 11th century
(Centre Guillaume le Conquerant, Bayeux)

verdicts, and enforcement of sentences, but also the reformation and
supplementation of the existing 'laws'; that is, the orally transmitted common
laws. At that time, no sharp division was made between matters of
government, legislation, the administration of justice, or its enforcement. The
'thing' was led by a justice, who was responsible for the judgement and the
implementation of the punishment. Judgements were 'made' communally by
the onlookers and, in later times, by a number of specially chosen or appointed
jurymen or aldermen. What we now call meeting (being together for
discussing and deciding about the communal future) became distinguished
from the administration of justice only during the period of modern state
formation. Therefore, reference to the administration of justice, in respect to
meetings, will be made less frequently in the following chapters.

Before Christianization, which coincided in North-western Europe with
the Frankish conquest, the 'things' also served as gatherings to practice rituals
led by priest–warriors. Here, in the name of brotherhood, or for inciting
fighting spirit, people practised bouts of drinking, made sacrifices (including
human sacrifices), and judgements, as it seems with a double-bladed fighting
axe, which had long been one of the most feared weapons of Frankish and
other Germanic warriors.[2]

Some of the pagan rituals of the 'thing' still exist in an altered form. Thus,
one can often read in the literature of the Middle Ages that warriors used
gathering together for communal meals as an opportunity to discuss and make

decisions. Holding a meeting was actually part of communal eating and drinking. Additionally, food and drink functioned in ceremonies of brotherhood and served to extend harmony, resolution and valour. Extensive and excessive eating and drinking was an expression of the predominance of the warriors in society. In agrarian societies, food was scarce for a good part of the year; only those in possession of much land, and those who could compel farmers to forfeit food, could get enough food and drink, and thus indulge in extensive meals (Mennell, 1985, pp. 41–7). As will be demonstrated later, non-military groups, such as merchants, imitated the warriors in this respect when they rose in societal esteem.

The ceremonial fighting axe may have been a forerunner of the chairman's gavel. When the old martial rulers' symbols, such as shields and spears, were replaced by less warlike symbols, including staffs or sceptres, orbs, and holy oils (originally symbols of bishops' authority), painters portrayed secular rulers holding a double-headed hammer-like tool as a sign that that person administered justice. Whether there were rulers in the Middle Ages who actually administered justice holding a hammer has not been established. A hammer-like tool as an attribute of a conductor of a meeting reappears in the guilds, where membership was initially only open to 'free' men – men who had the right to carry arms. The chairman's gavel, and the gavel ritual which opens and closes meetings, is most probably derived from the Germanic 'things' via the guilds of the Middle Ages (Akkerman, 1959, p. 128; 1961, p. 386; 1971, pp. 12–24).

The 'things' of the early Middle Ages were committed to unwritten, orally transmitted rules with a long, now untraceable, prehistory of wars, conquests, and occupations, in the course of which people, particularly warriors, had to adjust their actions to each other. The rules of the 'thing', as far as it is known, covered details such as the dates of meetings, the invitations, the opening, the seating arrangements, the participation in the discussion, the order of the speakers, the way of deciding, and the limitation of violence.

The dates of 'unordered things', usually in Spring or Autumn, were dictated by the pattern of warfare. After all, apart from juridically controlling tensions, 'things' were for war preparations in order to defend territory, and to capture cattle, goods and land, for the division of the booty, and for the finalizing of terms for a truce or peace.

In emergencies, those obliged to participate in the 'thing' were summoned by churchbells, by beacons, by town criers or (commonly) by sending round a weapon or another symbol of war. The latter was still prevalent in the late Middle Ages and is a reminder of the times when meetings could be the call-up for the united defence of land, cattle or harvest. While in some places in the Netherlands the representative of the ruler allowed a sword to circulate, in others, a peasant weapon (a cudgel) circulated as an announcement of a village meeting. In yet other areas the estate owners gave each other a small wooden sword with an inscription of an invitation to a local or regional meeting of free farmers (Siebs, 1933, p. 90; Gosses, 1941, p. 249).

The precarious character of the 'things' was particularly reflected by the way in which such a meeting was set up. The opening followed a fixed procedure, in which an order was imposed to refrain from violence in the meeting for its duration. A justice commenced the 'thing' by posing three 'security questions': whether the 'thing' was held at the appropriate place, whether at the appropriate time, and whether the appropriate people were present. Those unable to agree with the 'thing peace' because of a feud, first had to solve their differences. If that failed then both parties were obliged to leave the meeting. After the three questions had been answered in the affirmative by those present, the 'thing' was 'sanctified'; the area of the 'thing' was staked out with weapons, later on with poles and ropes, and a justice proclaimed the peace order, which included the commands for silence, to listen attentively, and to refrain from disorderly violence.

Families who had distinguished themselves in battle, who possessed the most land and had the most serfs and who had a retinue of young warriors, dominated the 'things'. The members of these warrior and landed nobility, from whom the leaders and justices were chosen, had the exclusive right to speak. In rank order of power and standing, they made suggestions about collective waging of war or making a truce, about potential leaders and potential justices, and about the application and reformation of the rules of law.

The co-operative of 'thing members' decided about the proposed plans and nominated candidates by groaning or clashing weapons: expressions of rejection and approval respectively.[3] This sacred way of deciding (originating from the domain of religion and magic) reflected the necessity of, and the tendency towards, harmony and consensus, which were particularly called for in times of war and threats of war. A collective endorsement counted as a revelation from God. Whoever held another opinion, and allowed it to show, was a threat to the unity, power, faith, and goal of the group, and was treated as one driven by 'evil powers'.

The acclamation rule functioned as a means to limit violence, but was often inadequate. Because both the notion and the practice of representation were lacking, the members of the 'thing', who had not taken part in the decisions due to absence, were not tied to the decisions taken. By staying away from the 'thing', one could avoid unwelcome decisions. However, absentees ran the risk that they would later be punished as deserters and be forced by more violent means into co-operating with the implementation of decisions.[4] The obligation to the 'thing', and the penalty regulation for absentees from 'things' and other meetings which one repeatedly finds in judicial literature, can be considered as steps against 'fleeing' and the use of violence. Initially, laws were virtually exclusively penalty laws for 'crimes against the community', such as disruptions during meetings, desertion, and surreptitious offences. In the restricted sense, jurisdiction had the character of a sacred lynch law: a number of people allocated by the justice proposed a judgement based on the current common law. This was then ratified by acclamation and implemented by the 'thing' community.

Disputes between people and groups, arguments about land or slaves, theft, assault and infidelity were generally 'solved' by the concerned parties, that is, by vengeance, revenge and negotiations between groups of families. Vendettas, and the fear of them, constituted the most important means for the regulation of tensions.

As the process of differentiation in power and standing between farmers and warriors accelerated through threats of and actual waging of war, and key leaders managed to extend their dominion, the existing 'private' regulations for solving conflicts were incorporated in an altered form within the regal law courts and tribunals.[5] In the course of the Middle Ages, everywhere in Western Europe, the position of farmers became subordinate to specialized warriors and later also to powerful towns.[6] There were a few exceptions, such as the northern part of the Netherlands and Switzerland, where farmers' republics with their own meeting rules arose after the disintegration of the Frankish Empire.

Priests and warriors: Councils

In order to temper centrifugal tendencies, the war lords sought the support of non-military groups to provide a counterbalance to the power of the warrior nobility, who were striving for independence. Thus, with the establishment of their dominion within the former West Roman Empire, the Frankish war lords sought support from the Gallo-Roman bishops, who had become autonomous regional power holders after the disappearance of the central Roman authority.[7]

After the Frankish royal house had converted to Christianity, the lords found an increasing number in the bishop nobility, who were prepared to co-operate and assist the central authorities with advice, delegations, mediation and participation in court judgements against, and research commissions into, clerical rivals. This assistance was provided in exchange for military protection and support regarding the preaching of the Christian belief (Hannig, 1982, p. 67). The later rulers bound the powerful Episcopal closer to them by arranging for confidants and 'clients', usually originating from the Frankish warrior nobility, to become bishops. Through a mutual interest in peace and order of the central rulers and the class of priests, there eventually developed a relatively close, but far from frictionless, co-operation.

FIGURE 3.2   Council of Clermont, 1095 (Photo Josse, Paris)

By this, the martial meeting manners of the warrior specialists were blended with the more ritual meeting manners of the religious specialists. It could be expected that, as long as they were subordinate to the warrior class, the bishops would be greatly influenced by military standards of behaviour in the development of their meeting manners. Likewise, it could be expected that the warriors would meet together in a less military manner when the bishops had achieved more social power and become more self-aware. Thus, a new, more modified standard of meeting behaviour finally arose from the fusion of codes and manners of both groups. In the remainder of this section, it will be shown how much the conciliar habits of the Frankish bishops, and the meeting manners in the Carolingian court and royal councils, reflected the periods of affinity and rejection in the relationship between the secular and church leaders.

The meeting manners of the Frankish bishops are known in particular through the *Ordines de celebrando concilio*, the regulations of state councils. The oldest maintained, *Ordo de celebrando concilio*, derived from the Visigothic domain in Spain, where the councils of bishops developed into a kind of parliament in the sixth century. This codification of the Visigothic council regulations, which was begun during the council of Toledo in 633, has since become the standard for the regulation of council behaviour of the Frankish bishops.[8]

At least 25 state councils were held within the Frankish realm from the beginning of the sixth to the end of the seventh centuries, in which the number of participants varied from 20 to 80. For about half of these councils, participation remained limited to the bishops from one or two Frankish territories (Weidemann, 1982, pp. 351–73; Loening, 1878, pp. 130–6).

These councils took place in a church, initially with the foreknowledge of, then by invitation from, and eventually by command of the Frankish kings. As a rule they arranged the agenda together with a number of prelates. In the course of the meeting the agenda could be supplemented with complaints from lower clergymen and laymen. Before the seventh century, the ruling monarchs were mainly absent from the deliberations. After a council meeting, a delegation brought the ruling monarch up to date with the council decisions, which the monarch would decree according to his own opinion. These decisions were not only related to religious questions, but also to secular questions, as far as this differentiation can be made for those times.

On the basis of the *Ordines*, other procedures during Frankish councils can be depicted as follows. At the start of a council, before dawn, nobody was allowed into the church; the doors were closed and the entrance guarded. First, the bishops entered and seated themselves according to seniority. After an opening ceremony which lasted for several hours, and consisted of alternating spoken and silent prayers, a three-day religious teaching session began, where the most important decisions from previous meetings and other practices of faith were read out and drummed in. On the fourth day the council moved on to the consideration of new topics. For this, the bishops were seated and the remaining groups stood. The meeting was chaired by an archbishop or some metropolitan bishops who, with the assistance of several priests and minutes secretaries, saw to it that the meeting progressed without tumult.

There was hardly any discussion. Officials read out proposals, upon which the bishops, in hierarchical order, gave their opinion, and likewise their vote. The first address came from the longest serving prelate. This was the most important and it set the tone. The speeches and related voting were sometimes accompanied or interrupted by acclamations, and assenting or deprecative cries.

A council ended after every bishop had given his opinion and complete agreement had been reached – *unanimous consensus* or *unanimitas patrum*. Differing opinions or minority views were inconceivable. The belief that a council was inspired by the Holy Ghost (the church's conscience) implied that a minority view would be interpreted as a manifestation of stupidity, malevolence or the influence of the devil; all the more so as the majority of the speeches were a repetition of rules of conduct taken from the Bible, or regulations which had been determined at previous council meetings.

All decisions were personally signed by the bishops. For these signatures, a double procedure had to be performed. First, the decisions were subject to another careful examination and, second, they had to be ratified by the non-participating faithful outside the auditorium by means of a collective *Amen*, or some other acclamation. After the archdeacon had summoned those present to a long silence of prayer, one of the bishops delivered the final oration and a *benedictio*. Finally, everyone rose and gave the kiss of peace to the metropolitan bishop seated on his throne, and to all others present.

The conciliar habits of the Frankish bishops, which can be observed from the middle of the seventh century, appear to be a result of the intertwining of Jewish-Christian rituals with the meeting manners of the Frankish warrior communities, the local and regional governing bodies of the latter Roman Empire (*concilia en ordines decurionum*), and the Roman senate (Batiffol, 1913 and 1919; Christophersen, 1969; Deininger, 1965; Gelzer, 1907; Sieben, 1979).

The late Roman influences which can be recognised are: the use of a building as a meeting place; the use of a preplanned agenda which used Latin for the preparation; the making and disseminating of decisions; the precise allocation of seating and standing places; and the making of decisions which, on paper, were determined by a majority vote but which were, in practice, usually made by one person. The latter was the case in the meetings of the community and regional bodies of the late Roman Empire, which undertook the notification and execution of imperial decrees and tax orders (according to Hannig, 1982, pp. 64–79).

The closing of the church doors prior to the entrance of the bishops is a reminder of the German habit of cordoning off meeting place with poles, weapons, or cords; the silent prayers and the kiss of peace, a reminder of the period of silence and peace at the start of a meeting, and the lifting of this injunction at the close of a meeting; the exclusive right of the bishops to speak, a reminder of the exclusive rights of the principal men to speak in a meeting; the collective *Amen* by the present clergy and the laymen gathered outside the church, a reminder of the bestowal of approval on a proposal through the rattling of weapons (according to Sieben, 1979, pp. 501–10).

From the Carolingian crown councils, and the more extensive royal councils that the Carolingian rulers held with their vassals and officials (the secular and clerical powers of the state) in one of their palaces at the times of important Christian feasts, it appears that the warriors, or at least their leaders, came to incorporate the more peaceful meeting manners of the bishops. These meetings comprised the supreme council of warriors, the highest court of justice and a forum for the discussion of 'home and foreign affairs'. With the increase in mutual dependence between warriors and priests, the councils became fora, where secular as well as clerical problems were discussed.

The following decisions of a Carolingian court council will give an impression of what could be discussed in such a meeting. Of the 38 decisions (*capitularia*), which were promulgated by Charles the Great during an important meeting in 805, sixteen concerned mainly clerical and 22 concerned mainly secular problems. The latter group included decisions such as the maintenance of peace; the right of protection for the church and the meek; the rights favouring the king; the regulations at times of food shortages; feuds; the arming of conscripts; trade with the Slaves and Awars; the administration of justice; oaths; conspiracies; perjury; custody; counts and other authorities; tollage; refugees; admission of free men to the clergy; the abuse of power at the expense of poor free men; churches established without permission; the recommendation of saints to the believers; counterfeiting; fines for the non-appearance of conscripts; levies payable to the king; robbery; marriages between free and non-free citizens of the royal domain (Ganshof, 1965).

The merging of the meeting manners of the warriors and the bishops into a new, more differentiated standard of meeting behaviour is clearly demonstrated in the following description of the procedure of the Carolingian crown council, a select assembly of a very small number of the highest nobility: the archchaplain and chancellor, members of the royal family and some bishops. The noted piece of writing, *De Ordine Palatii* (concerning the functioning of the court), by bishop Hincmarus of Reims (1980 [882]), who was for a long time attached to the West Frankish court, gives an impression of the manner in which the more select court councils around the Carolingian rulers used to discuss and decide about the entire domain.[9]

Hincmarus' idealized description of the election of the councillors is noteworthy. His summary of the 'exceptional' qualities which council members need to possess, indicated just how poorly developed meeting procedures were at that time. Loyalty was more important than knowledge of the facts. Hincmarus wrote that the monarch chose the clergy and the laymen as much as possible from people

who were so loyal that, apart from living for centuries, they preferred nothing above the king and his dominion; therefore not for friends, enemies, relatives, offerers of gifts, sycophants, uncouth orators, and not for people who had sophistic or cunning thoughts, or who focused upon pure secular wisdom.

In a society where all relationships between people had a highly personal character, holding a meeting like that of the crown council was a very exceptional activity, which demanded a relatively high degree of distance and self-control. Hincmarus stated that, in crown council meetings, a more distant future was considered than during the large royal councils. Questions were raised about topics which were expected to become urgent in the coming year. Complete confidentiality about the discussions was of the utmost importance, because

> It commonly occurs in a discussion about a particular person that the advancement, or the assurance, of the general interest is discussed in terms that would confuse the concerned person if he were to hear it or, what is worse, would bring despair to that person or, what is the worst, would incite disloyalty and, perhaps, instead of providing co-operation in various ways, becomes useless, while no damage would have resulted if he had known nothing about what had been said.

The meeting was held in a screened-off area, where the councillors could deliberate at length, usually in the absence of the monarch who was occupied elsewhere with state business or other affairs

> But as long as it was the wish of the confined counsellors, he could join them if he so desired. In complete confidentiality, in which the individual council decisions were taken, they reported the decisions to the king, and furthermore they informed him of the differences of opinion, wrangles, or friendly exchanges which had taken place during the making of their decisions.

The manners of the Carolingian crown councils represented an early stage in the 'courtization' of meetings.[10] Although the meetings of the Carolingian court, in comparison to those of the later courts of the territorial and absolute monarchs, were more disorderly, less tied to a set location and a set number of participants, less specialized, less differentiated, and limited to a smaller number of people, the initiation of a meeting discipline can be discerned that compelled the monarch and other courtiers to conduct discussions and make decisions concerning the future of the country.

The Carolingian courts were relatively peaceful enclaves in a social environment of near autarkic and little interdependent governmental and economic units. Central monarchs did not yet have taxation and an army at their disposal, as in the absolute stage of the court. For this, an adequate, specialized administrative machinery was lacking.

FIGURE 3.3 The 'treacherous' murder of the Burgundian duke, John the Fearless (Cliché Bibliothèque nationale de France)

The co-operation between the Frankish leaders and the ecclesiastical leaders did not result in a durable centralization of secular control. The bishops and the priests were usually insufficiently able to offer any resistance to the organized violence of the warriors (according to Prinz, 1971). When large-scale wars of conquest became impracticable and large-scale wars of defence were unnecessary, the massive Carolingian realm split into numerous small units of offence and defence.

In the subsequent eliminating rounds between warriors, the meetings of the previously 'big shots of the realm' increasingly acquired the character of precarious negotiations, as observed by Ingrid Voss in her research into the encounters of the East and West Frankish rulers from the ninth to the thirteenth century inclusively (Voss, 1987). Such negotiations often took place by, or on a river border. Each party was barracked in tents on either side of the river and spoke to each other across the water or on an islet, ship or bridge that, frequently, had been especially constructed for that purpose.

The choice of a river border corresponded with the precariousness and the safety risks of these types of meeting. The river separated the parties and offered some assurance against unexpected outbursts of violence, as well as the mutually held idea that they were gathering together on neutral territory. An added advantage was the limited opportunity for practising ceremonies which could be used, or misused, to one's own benefit.

In order to avert the danger of the talks spilling over into an armed conflict, prior to the talks the parties had to agree on stringent security regulations. One of these regulations, which reached its zenith in the fifteenth century, was the construction of a bridge with a fence separating the negotiators from each other.

Just how precarious such talks were is illustrated by an event which took place during negotiations between the French heir to the throne and the Burgundian duke, John the Fearless, early in the fifteenth century. For the talks, a bridge had been spanned over the river Yonne. In the middle, a fence, with bars as thick as an arm, had been built across the entire width of the bridge. In the divide was a gateway with a door which could be locked on both sides, such that it was only possible to cross the divide if both parties agreed to it. During the talks the duke opened the door of the gateway, either upon his own initiative or upon the suggestion of the prince. The door on the other side was also opened. As soon as John and three of his men passed through the door, they were murdered (Schneider, 1977, pp. 15–17).

This was not an isolated event. The murders on the bridge were the response of the French royal house to the murder of the French king's brother, twelve years previously, which snipers of John the Fearless had committed. The old jealousies between the houses of Orleans and Burgundy erupted into an open feud, which dominated the relationship between the principalities for a century. They were 'not aware of any other causes than the personal and the passionate' (Huizinga, 1973, p. 10).

Perhaps the most characteristic of the prevailing standards of meeting at that time was that John's contemporaries were of the general opinion that he had only himself to blame for his untimely death. It was their conviction that he had not complied to the rules of the game and had been too careless. Consequently, railings without gateways were constructed (Schneider, 1977, p. 17).

The incident on the bridge, and the subsequent reaction, typify the behaviour and emotions of people who were not directly dependent upon money, and who were mostly unfamiliar with any other standard than the sword. At the very worst, they were restrained only by the danger of being physically overpowered; by threats emanating from somebody clearly stronger.

Trials

In the Middle Ages participation in juridical meetings continued to be dependent upon the possession of land. Because, for the most part, land in Europe fell increasingly into the hands of warriors, the church, or the towns, the agrarian population's contribution to the 'political' and juridical decisions was drastically reduced. 'Things' became more formalized, through regulations made by centralized rulers, initially by the Frankish kings and later by the territorial lords, and through the church's involvement in trials. Local common law became codified, regularized and partially replaced by royal and clerical laws and regulations. Carrying arms was forbidden for everybody except for justices during a 'thing'. 'Thing' leadership fell into the hands of counts, sheriffs, and clergymen appointed by commanders-in-chief or lords. As justices, they came into opposition with the 'thing' community. With a retinue of horsemen, they journeyed through their official territory to chair court sessions. The farmers were obliged to offer them hospitality. At times of war, the justices called up the military aristocracy in their official territory, and led them into battle. From the farmers they demanded payment in kind.

The judgements of the municipality were adopted by a set number of royally appointed sheriffs or aldermen, usually large land owners, and recommended by the municipality. In order to break the spiral of revenge, the justices had the authority to summon the warring parties to court and demand a 'wergeld' (a sort of indemnity), part of which was intended for the government or justices.

At the start of a 'thing', all parties had solemnly to promise to comply with the rules, and to observe the decisions of the court. Backing out after the start of the case was not possible without the assent of the opposing party. Thus a social framework was created where the disputing parties were able to meet as outright enemies in a regulated contest, fought out under the authority of local leaders and in the presence of witnesses (Davies and Fouracre, 1986, p. 217). The assistance of the court was sought particularly in disputes about landownership as, through this, written proof of ownership or tenancy rights could be acquired. Such documents of evidence strengthened one's (legal) position. The courts usually made judgements based upon on-the-spot investigation, upon questioning of, and explanations from witnesses, upon written evidence where possible, and upon a 'discussion' between the judge, the adjudicators and the opposing parties.

Judicial arguments, which took the form of the swearing of an oath, the calling of blood brothers (compurgators) and the performing of a ritual of divine judgement, were characteristic of the administration of justice in the Middle Ages. The latter argument involved trials by water and fire and man-to-man combat, which was mainly (but not only) employed 'to secure a proof in circumstances where the normal modes could offer none' and 'certain knowledge was impossible, but uncertainty was intolerable' (Bartlett, 1986, pp. 135 and 33). Divine judgements were mainly employed in cases of surreptitious crimes and when there was an absence of witnesses, compurgators and documents. Public man–to–man combat during the 'thing' was one of the oldest and most widespread methods by which greater certainty was sought as to whether the accused and the witnesses spoke the truth, and also by which arguments and feuds between individuals and groups could be terminated or temporarily averted. Generally, only free men (those authorized to carry arms) and their families could make use of this procedure.

There were various types of man–to–man combat: a fight 'outside a state of war or feud', which was considered a crime; a fight 'during a state of war or feud', where both parties kept to certain rules, and which was dealt with more leniently or not punished at all; and a public man–to–man combat during a 'thing' which was determinded by strict rules as regards place, time, participation, and use of arms, and which formally terminated 'the state of war'. Juridical duels not only served to settle the differences between the parties and prevented the application of force on a larger scale, but also produced evidence of innocence or guilt in cases of surreptitious crimes. In these cases, man–to–man combat was 'an act of God' and the outcome was conceived as a divine judgement. The loser was executed and the winner could claim cattle, goods, or 'wergeld' from the loser and his family. Furthermore, free men could enter into duels with adjudicators or witnesses, in order to 'demonstrate' the impropriety of the judgement or the witnesses' statements. A juridical duel was a violent, grave and bloody occurrence, as is demonstrated in the following report of a duel in 1127 between two Flemish knights, Herman the Iron and Guy. Guy had been accused of being involved in a plot against the Flemish count, Charles:

> Both sides fought bitterly. Guy had unhorsed his adversary and kept him down with his lance just as he liked whenever Herman tried to get up. Then his adversary, coming closer, disembowelled Guy's horse, ripped him up with his sword. Guy, having slipped from his horse, rushed at his adversary with his sword drawn. Now there was a continuous and bitter struggle, with alternating thrusts of swords, until both, exhausted by the weight and burden of their arms, threw away their shields and hastened to gain victory in the fighting by resorting to wrestling. Herman the Iron fell prostrate on the ground, and Guy was lying on top of him smashing the knight's face and eyes with his iron gauntlets. But Herman, prostrate, little by little regained his strength from the coolness of the earth . . . and cleverly lying quiet made Guy believe he was certain of victory. Meanwhile, gently moving his hand down the lower edge of the cuirass where Guy was not protected, Herman seized him by the testicles, and summoning all his strength for the brief space of one moment he hurled Guy from him; by this tearing motion all the lower parts of the body were broken so that Guy, now

prostrate, gave up, crying out that he was conquered and dying. (Galbert of Bruges, 1978, pp. 166–7)

The warlike nature of these judicial processes corresponded to the concomitant societal level of violence control. Juridical duels are to be considered as a ritualized form of fighting; in the absence of a stable monopoly of violence, these were activities to which people were relatively rapidly inclined. Researching into the ways in which disputes were settled in the Middle Ages, Wendy Davies and Paul Fouracre (1986) pointed out that the judicial rituals of the early European societies:

> Derived precisely from a consciousness that this was the only way for legal institutions to make an impact on societies perpetually riven by antagonism and oppression. Ritual was the most effective way to channel off resentments in the direction of the ideal of renewed peace, through a close association with religious practice (as with the endless oaths in all courts, or, at the most extreme, ordeal) and through elaborate and lengthy procedures that could, in all senses of the word, be called dramatic. (1986, p. 240)

Reflecting the relatively low level of the societal and individual control of violence, the juridical procedures also included 'divine judgements' to which the unenfranchised, the perjured, the non-Christians, and the foreigners were exposed in cases of doubt. One of the oldest trials was the so-called trial by hot water. This trial, in which the accused had to scrabble with unprotected hands in a pot of boiling water for a small object like a coin or a ring, probably originated from the Frankish population, and it spread to large areas of Europe in the eighth and ninth centuries with the Frankish conquest and the accompanying Christianization. In this period other divine judgements made their appearance, such as the 'trial by iron', in which the accused had to take several steps holding a glowing piece of iron, and the 'trial by cold water', in which the accused was shackled and thrown into water to see whether he 'was taken by the water', that is, whether he sank. In the cases of trials by hot iron and hot water, the healing process of the injuries received during the trial determined the outcome. Rapid and clean (uninfected) healing wounds indicated that the accused had spoken the truth (Barlett, 1986, pp. 4–34).

The swearing of oaths on relics, or on the Bible, was the most popular means of proof in the 'illiterate' societies of the Middle Ages. Swearing oaths has been termed the cornerstone of justice in the Middle Ages (Barlett, 1986, p. 30). It was also some sort of divine judgement; it was felt that a perjurer would be punished in the hereafter for his evil deed. Using oaths in jurisdiction probably stems from late Roman law, which was the common law spread far and wide by the church (Wood, 1986, p. 17).

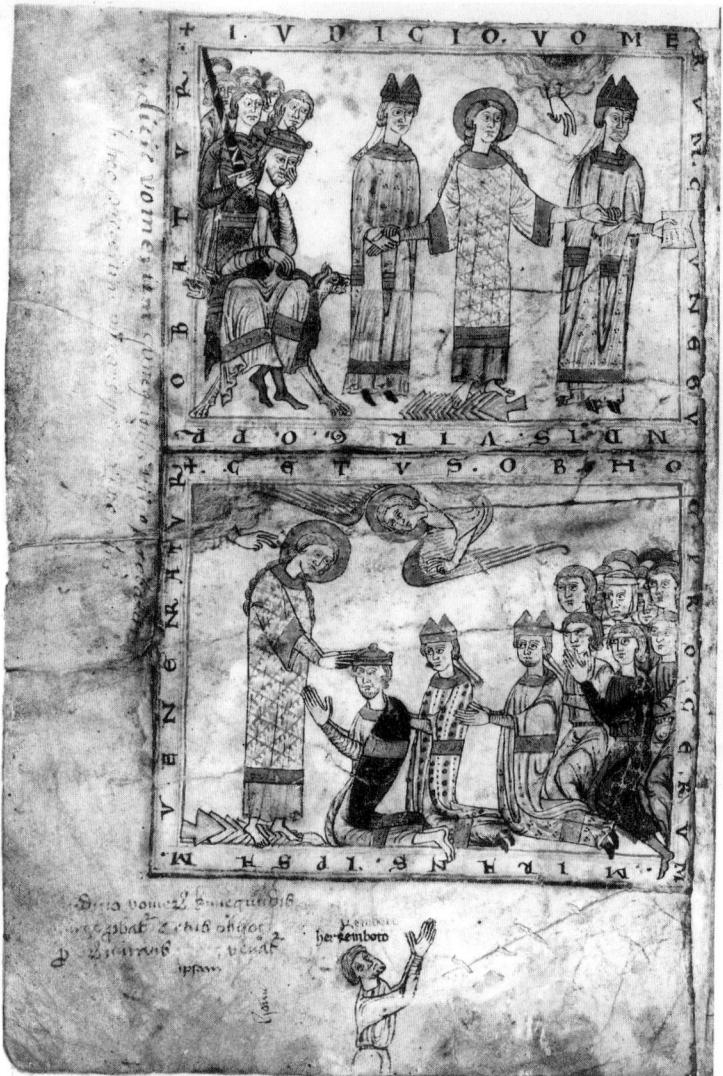

FIGURE 3.4   Twelfth-century depiction of the trial by fire of the Holy Roman Empress Cunigunde (Staatsbibliothek Bamberg)

Originally, the judge would ask a defendant to support his statement with an oath. If the defendant refused, he was found guilty; if he agreed, the complainant was then asked to swear an oath. If the complainant swore an oath, he won the case; if he refused, he lost the case and was obliged to compensate the defendant. Later it became the custom for witnesses and for other members of both accused's and accuser's families and compurgators to appear in court and swear oaths.

In general, monarchs were extremely sceptical of oaths as a proof. In their *capitularia* and decrees they often argued for a more frequent use of juridical duels and trials. The Merovingian and Carolingian monarchs decreed that anyone who claimed to know the truth and swore an oath in a case was not allowed to refuse participate in a man-to-man combat or a divine trial. Charles the Great has been registered as saying that he would rather have seen people fighting on the battlefield with cudgels than have them commit perjury (Wood, 1986, p. 16; Bartlett, 1986, p. 105). Ecclesiastical leaders were strongly opposed to the use of juridical duels, where 'Christian blood was spilt'. Initially, they were less opposed to water or fire trials to confirm or to substitute oaths as, in the period from 800 to 1200, it was actually through the church that these procedures were spread. Bishops and priests played an important role in cases of trial by water or fire:

> The ordeal rests on religious belief in the power and will of the deity to perform a miracle, takes place in church, with co-operation of the priest under the bishop's supervision, after consecration of the material, religious preparation of the proband and the surroundings, Christian oath and mass, involving the participation of the proband in communion, liturgical conjuration and biblical citation. (Liebermann, quoted in Bartlett, 1986, pp. 154–5)

The trials by water and fire gave priests and warriors an opportunity to dominate the farming population. The leaders of the courts of justice, priests, royal officials and lords decided about the healing process of injuries resulting from trial by fire, about the sinking of an accused and about the victor of a duel. 'Having the power to determine, they also had the power to defraud' (Bartlett, 1986, p. 41).

At the beginning of the thirteenth century a power shift occurred in the church, favouring those groups who were strictly opposed to the utilization of divine judgements. In the year 1215 the Pope forbade bishops and priests to continue practising trials by fire and hot water. As the use of divine judgement was virtually totally dependent upon the co-operation of the clergy, in practice, the papal ban was tantamount to abolition.

Building upon the remains of the Roman Empire, the church developed into an increasingly larger and more centralized organization with far-reaching influence. This organization made it possible to implement centrally issued regulations, such as the ban on seeking divine judgements. Furthermore, the church developed procedures on the basis of Roman law which replaced divine judgements. Alongside, and partially replacing, the secular administration of justice, an ecclesiastical jurisdiction originated, led by bishops. All 'clerical' and 'temporary' business fell into this category, such as the clergy, widows, orphans and public sinners, and other people as long as it concerned marriage, divorce, infidelity, incest, patricide, matricide, paganism, and testaments. Michael Schröter (1985) pointed out that the increase in the church's influence, manifested in making sacred all the important moments of a lifetime, including birth, marriage and death, was promoted by the process of state formation. Communities based on consanguinity and neighbourliness began to be part of larger political units, where geographical mobility increased and where opportunities for armed combat resulting from a conflict were limited. Local communities lost many of their governing functions to the church, which had at its disposal more adequate laws and codes of practice (more uniform and more general). No other organization was prepared, attuned, and available, to the same degree, for an ongoing pacification of society than was the church. Powerful monarchs and towns commonly allied themselves to the church in their attempts to curb the use of physical violence over larger areas. In this period of state formation, the social importance of the church as a co-ordinating and disciplinary authority greatly increased. As the monopolies of organized violence and taxation stabilized and the monopolies' administrative machinery grew larger and more intricate, the church had to relinquish to the state a large proportion of the tasks and functions that had been acquired in this period; particularly in Protestant countries, the church was shaped into an instrument of secular authority (Schröter, 1985, pp. 386–91).

The ecclesiastical legal procedure commenced with a written declaration, signed by the complainant. The two parties were no longer set against each other to duel and, from the thirteenth century, neither were divine judgements sought. Ecclesiastical administration of justice, like Roman law, focused upon confession of guilt and demanded other methods, such as the examination of suspects and witnesses, which were applied in doubtful cases instead of duels and torturous divine judgements. This was known as the Inquisition. In the end, the judge came to a verdict based on the guidelines of Roman and canonical law, which was drawn up in ecumenical councils and regional synods. With the ongoing centralizing and monopolizing of organized physical force and taxation, many procedures of ecclesiastical jurisdiction were adopted, and further developed, by royal and secular courts of law.

Meetings of farmers

In some regions covered by the present-day Switzerland and the Netherlands, which had been on the periphery of the Roman and Frankish Empires, no, or at least no powerful, sovereign authority was established after the demise of the Carolingian dominion. Tasks requiring a degree of co-ordination, including the division of the land, taxation, jurisdiction, and the regulation of the drainage system, were managed by local farming communities, and by officials selected from their own ranks. There were hardly any farm estates, controlled by, and for the benefit of, large landowners where serfs or slaves worked, and, as far as they were to be found, they disappeared in the late Middle Ages. Elaborating rather more upon the meeting manners of the farmer–warriors of the early Middle Ages than upon those of the Frankish monarchs and counts, in these areas the farming community developed a regional government (although somewhat vulnerable and unstable), where forms of conduct which could be termed 'agrarian-democratic' arose. This term (borrowed from Wichers) draws attention to a situation where participation in government and jurisdiction was associated with the possession of a certain acreage of land, and a large majority of the farming families fulfilled these conditions of acceptance (Wichers, 1965, p. 187).

In the tenth and eleventh centuries, in the northern coastal areas of the present-day Netherlands (Friesland), the sheriffs and the local Carolingian justices disappeared along with the Carolingian counts. Remaining were the judicial authorities of free landowners, who met regularly led by justices who were elected or rejected by cheering or hissing in the meeting. Raised 'wergelds' and fines were imposed for misdemeanours committed during a 'thing' (for instance, Beekman, 1907, p. 1731). With the ongoing stratification of the peasantry, it became the norm to have the function of justice performed in turn by more wealthy farmers and, finally, the function fell into the hands of several large-scale gentleman–farmers who dwelt in fortified farms and who had armed servants and horsemen at their disposal. In this period, there was an intensification in the struggle for the office of justice in the agrarian meetings. The farming communities banded together into alliances with the stated intention of counteracting feuds, and protecting themselves from both military attack from outside and the dangers of flooding. The most encompassing alliance was the *Treaty of the Upstalboom*, which came into existence in approximately 1200 in response to the fear of a desire for expansion by the counts of Holland. Annually, on the first Tuesday after Whitsun, the sworn judges from the Frisian areas assembled in the *Upstalboom*, an open area on an island. This alliance disintegrated in the fourteenth century with the outbreak of an armed struggle between two villages over a piece of land outside the dyked area. Eventually the Frisian areas fell under the control of sovereign authority.

One of the longest traditions of 'agrarian-democratic' government can be observed in the relatively isolated farming communities on the poor sandy areas of the present-day province of Drenthe (Gosses, 1941, pp. 162–243). The area is enclosed by marshes to the south and the population focused more on the forms of government of the 'free' Frisians to the north than on the (nominal) authority of the ruler, the bishop of Utrecht. For a longer period in Drenthe than in the Frisian areas (until approximately 1800), a larger proportion of the agrarian population could exert influence upon the local and regional government. In the sandy areas of Drenthe, land possession was more equally divided and the stratification process within the peasantry progressed more slowly than in the fertile clay areas to the north. Serious military threats from both inside and outside hardly occurred after the beginning of the thirteenth century, when a group of farmers defeated an army of noblemen led by the bishop of Utrecht in the Battle of Ane. In Drenthe, the nobility only took shape around 1600, but never had more than one of three votes in the Provincial States of Drenthe during the time of the Dutch Republic, while the remaining two went to the landowning farmers.

In the Middle Ages, Drenthe experienced various levels of government, of which the meetings were denoted by different names. The lowest level was that of the farming communities centred around carefully divided fields. Together, several farming communities formed municipalities. The subsequent, higher governmental level comprised the six parishes into which Drenthe had previously been divided. Within the framework of these parishes, formal 'things', and less formal meetings were held. The highest level comprised the annual conventions of all franchised farmers of Drenthe and the meetings of the annually elected central law court which functioned as a kind of day-to-day management. The law court administered justice and made regulations, assigned judges and representatives, determined mandates and made decisions regarding tax levies and the defence of the area. Every family in possession of a certain acreage of land had the right to send a male representative to each of these meetings. To begin with the central law court, for practical reasons it gradually became usual to elect or appoint representatives, the 'sworn' and 'authorized'. The central law courts, consisting of 24 sworn representatives, met on set days. For the annual general convention, the farmers were invited by the bailiff, the bishop's representative, who issued invitations by allowing a sword to circulate, as mentioned earlier. Likewise, 'things' were also called to assemble, led by the bailiff. They were held three, subsequently two, times a year on set days and in set places in a parish.

More informal meetings of municipalities took place at the request of one or several of the municipalities. They were chaired by an elected sheriff, who administered justice where the farmers required him to be, or were held without a set chairman on the village green, in a churchyard, or another central place.

The least formalized meetings were the meetings of the farming communities, where a relatively large degree of freedom was afforded to make laws and rules according to their own judgement. As the farmers had few sanctions by which they could actually enforce compliance to the rules, it was necessary to reach an agreement. Thus it commonly occurred that when someone had to appear before a higher court, due to infringement of one or other rule, he appealed that he had not been in agreement with the regulation or had not been present at the meetings of the community when that particular regulation was drawn up. In such a way someone would not consider himself to be tied to the agreement (Gosses, 1941, p. 189).

The most formal assemblies were the traditional 'things', to which the bailiff, previously the landowner himself, paid a visit a couple of times a year with a retinue of horsemen, horses and dogs. The farmers were obliged to offer hospitality to the bailiff and his retinue for several days; later this obligation could be bought off for money. The farmers disliked 'things', not only because they cost a lot of time and money ('things' were an important source of income for the bailiff), but because they were obliged to appear before their master to report misdemeanours and make pronouncements in personal suits presented by complainants. This typifies the relatively powerful position of the farmers in relation to sovereign authority; such that the 'things' were gradually replaced by meetings which were neither tied to a set time and place, nor to a formal language, and which were not enforced from above.

With the farmers' rise in power in relation to the sovereign, the meeting of the central law court was also 'deformalized'. Lacking was a set format of traditional dealings by which the assemblies were opened. A meeting was considered to be opened when the bell chimed and the bailiff, who functioned as the chairman, took his place. Until the end of the sixteenth century, the meetings of the court were open to the public, just as the similarly relatively informal convention, where the participants were appointed in rotation by the farming communities. During the meetings of the court, governing regulations were issued, general tax levies were determined, local meetings were arranged and treaties finalized.

During the time of the Dutch Republic, the convention's composition and manner of working was more regulated and it became a meeting of two social ranks. Every parish had one mandate and the number of seats for the aristocracy was determined, resulting in the meeting consisting of two-thirds farmers and one-third nobility. Replacing the irregular one-day assemblies an annual assembly of several set days was set up. Nevertheless, for a long time, one idiosyncrasy of the old convention remained: every landowner was permitted to appear and take part in discussions, but not in the voting. It was not until 1730 that the names of the 'authorized' would henceforth be registered, so that no confusion or lack of clarity could ensue about who was enfranchised and who not. It was ruled only in 1787 that the unenfranchised had to remain outside the meeting, behind the railing.

In not only the northern coastal regions and the relatively isolated Drenthe, but in all the low-lying parts of the present-day Netherlands, the nobility were in a weaker position than practically everywhere else in Europe. In explaining this, Jan de Vries (1973) pointed out that much of the land in these regions was only claimed from water from the twelfth century onwards, after the peak of 'feudalism' had passed. Furthermore, although it was often the nobility who stimulated the draining and settling of the land, with the increase in the use of money, it was no longer necessary, or possible, to follow the 'feudal system' and have serfs working on the new land to extract a profit. The desolate region was legally sold in tithes to monasteries, water boards or groups of settlers who, after the creation of the infrastructure to control the water, sold it on or leased it to farmers. In the society that developed on the drained land, warriors played no significant role, the farmers were less tied to local traditions, and both the leaders and the led had important mutual interests, which, in particular, found expression in the farmers' active involvement in the discussions and decisions about the construction, financing and maintenance of the water boards, characteristic of the Low Countries.

Meetings of water boards: Surveys and budget days

Responding to the threat of flooding and the draining and colonizing of marshy peat areas, water boards appeared during the Middle Ages as the population increased in stages in the lower areas of the present-day Netherlands. These water boards were 'unique in their organizational structure from a European perspective, and perhaps even from a world-wide perspective' (van Dam, 1989, p. 3). In the ninth century, people from the sandy areas in the west and the clay areas skirting the rivers began to reclaim the desolate peat regions. For agricultural purposes (sheep farming and subsequently grain cropping) the peat areas were drained by deepening and widening existing streams and the construction of ditches and wharves. This intervention in the landscape led to new, unforeseen problems which, in turn, led to a far-reaching control of nature, based on closer mutual co-operation between people. The land gradually became unusable for agricultural purposes as, due to the drainage, the land shrank from underneath and sank. People began to drain the land afresh and construct wharves on higher levels of ground. Gradually, on the highest points of the peat areas, these new wharves developed into artificially maintained watersheds and the former wharves developed into a system of connected dykes, which demanded continuous maintenance. Increasingly larger groups of people became interdependent on each other for the construction and maintenance of these works, and the necessity for holding discussions and making decisions increased.[11]

For each separate water drainage system, both in the sovereign and non-sovereign parts of the Low Countries, some kind of water board organization sprang up. In these organizations, the governing and judicial functions were fulfilled by local officials, a sheriff, or a justice responsible for legal procedures and the implementation of sentences, and a board of men (aldermen) who decided verdicts. With the expansion of the dyke system and the formation of interlocal co-operatives for water control, officials were eventually appointed by farmers and farming communities exclusively for the purpose of the survey by a peripatetic court of law, which adjudicated at local level matters concerning the fulfilment or neglect of the obligation to maintain the dyke system. In documents from the thirteenth century, originating from Holland, these new governing bodies were denoted as dyke boards. Usually the local sheriffs appeared to have worked themselves up into the position of head of the dyke board management.

In the thirteenth century, possibly even in the twelfth century, through the mutual co-operation of farming communities, parishes, monasteries, and large private landowners, the first organizations exclusively to regulate water levels (the first district water boards) arose. In particular the preparation, implementation and maintenance of compact and large-scale projects, such as damming rivers, regional drainage and extending dykes, appear to have advanced the development of these corporations with this specific aim (Van der Linden, 1978, p. 10). In sovereign areas, after large-scale floods, the monarch sometimes took the initiative to construct such regional systems. Making use of his right to call up his subjects in times of war, he was able to initiate advancement of water-controlling activities covering areas of operation on a scale larger than simply local. As a rule, these activities were then carried out and maintained under the auspices of a pool of water-controlling boards, established specifically for this purpose. Before 1250 the contact between water-controlling boards and central authorities was indirect and incidental; then the water boards in the sovereign areas were just as autonomous as they were in other areas (Van der Linden, 1982, pp. 14–15). Afterwards, the first to become more intensively involved with the regulation of the water were the Bishop of Utrecht and the Count of Holland. 'Frequent overflowing of rivers and floods due to storms compelled to evidently more powerful, more effective forms of organization, controlled by the count's representatives, who had at their disposal the most weighty sanctions' (Van der Linden, 1982b).

The involvement from above meant that the water-controlling boards acquired a more sovereign character. The administration of justice and the management of the water boards came to be dominated more by the regional justices; the stewards, who had been appointed by the Count of Holland, copying the Flemish count, so that he could administer justice together with the wellborn of the region. These stewards, receiving the title dyke warden, were entrusted with the position of dyke board judge and managed to bind the co-option of dyke boards for their approval. From this time onward, the initiative for new water boards practically always stemmed from the sovereign authority, and co-ordinated regional water boards or dyke boards were developed, managed by the wellborn of the district and having as chairman the dyke wardens, who had been especially appointed by the count.

Nevertheless, the management of the water works in the sovereign areas was rooted in local co-operation; likewise in the non-sovereign areas, where the formation of new dyke connections and water boards from below continued into the fifteenth century. For the carrying out and maintenance of works, the dyke board managements were dependent to a large degree upon the collaboration of farmers and farming communities. For important (financial) decisions, they were obliged to consult the farming communities, which had usually acquired the right to participate through representatives in discussions and decision making in the meetings of the dyke warden and dyke boards about how to divide finances for the maintenance and construction of new works, which required a raise in headtax. 'This trend of participation from below remained a rule throughout the Middle Ages in the dyke boards' (Van der Linden, 1978, p. 18). This can be seen in the charter granted by the Count of Holland in 1396, that the countrymen and farmers from every parish had the right to delegate two men to the committee meeting of the dyke board, where decisions were made about new constructions (*ibid.*, p. 18). Within a number of smaller water boards in Holland and Utrecht it remained the custom to call all the landholders together to discuss and decide about important issues and to elect officials for the water board (Beekman, 1907, pp. 879–80, 1534–35).

Following the drastic floods in the sixteenth century it became clear that many of the wellborn members of the dyke boards of Holland were not suited to their specialized task, and so the sovereign court in The Hague assumed the appointment of water board officials, and the landholders' right of participation was copied from the situation which had occurred on the polders (this situation is discussed later). In several places 'meetings of main landholders' developed: fixed representative boards with rights over the budget. Direct participation from the landholders spread further and, in the northern coastal regions, was preserved longer where, up to and into the sixteenth century, the property owners commonly gathered together. Here they made agreements about water management and could practice both active and passive rights of voting concerning the official and management functions within the local water boards. Attendance at these meetings was safeguarded against attacks and disruptions by strict rules, sanctioned by raised 'wergeld' (according to Beekman, 1907, pp. 1654–56).

In the northern regions, with the formation of larger, co-ordinating water boards and the establishment of a sovereign authority, landholders' direct participation in decision making was gradually replaced by indirect participation by authorized delegates. Long before this, the justices of the co-operating local water boards already used to gather together to discuss communal problems. As the interlocal co-operation intensified, these meetings expanded into regional governing centres, where the codes of behaviour were specified and recorded. Many of these rules were directed against cursing, fighting, injuring and killing during a survey or board meeting, and disrupting such a meeting. For example, from the beginning of the fifteenth century, there was mention of a cash fine if someone called another a thief or a murderer, or sat or stood without permission of the justice. Fines were set for whoever disturbed the meeting by quarrelling or fighting, appeared at the meeting armed and shielded, or failed to show up without sufficient reason (Beekman, 1907, pp. 1732–34).

From the latter half of the thirteenth century, with land reclamation resulting from the construction of levees bordering rivers and the sea, and the draining of dyked land with the aid of windmills, another type of water board appeared: the polder board. 'Just as the dyke board generally originated from co-operation between farming communities, the polder board stemmed from those entitled to land, from the landholders' (Van der Linden, 1978, p. 21).

In fits and starts, the land was gradually reclaimed. Meanwhile, in the already settled hinterland, groups of land users laid ditches criss-crossing farmland enabling more efficient drainage. These drainage activities received a powerful stimulus with the invention of the smockmill. By using these mills, water could be raised to higher drainage pools and, by so doing, the water level within a certain area could be regulated more accurately. Private initiatives by farmers and landowners resulted in a rapid increase in the number of polders. Following the example of the dyke boards, people co-operating in a polder would often institute one single management board, consisting of a neighbourhood sheriff and self-elected members of the board, who were named polder masters or windmill masters. Sometimes the managerial and judicial tasks were partially or entirely placed in the hands of officials from already established farming communities or dyke boards. Every type of organization appeared between the official and the grassroot-level organizations, and rose or fell. But around 1500 it was quite commonplace for polders to support themselves through their own cover charges, and they had to declare the daily financial charges of the polder managers during budget day, an annual meeting of polder landholders. At these assemblies, the landholders would elect the polder masters, board members or windmill masters, by majority vote from their own ranks. Furthermore, it appears that the landholders customarily organized food and drink during the budget days, as is shown by bills from these periods (Van der Linden, 1978, p. 21).

As drainage became more large scale during the sixteenth and seventeenth centuries, indirect participation took the place of direct participation in the polders also. To protect their own interests, the landholders changed to 'meetings of main landholders' for election of board representatives.

Other than in the farming communities and the district water boards which stemmed from them (where a certain minimum acreage was required for participation, and the management positions were monopolized by a small group of the wellborn) in the polders, it became increasingly common that all those who were eligible participated in decision making in proportion to their acreage ownership, and that they elected the management from their own ranks. 'There were no restrictions. Other than in the farming communities with established restrictive traditions, from the outset, a farther-reaching "democracy" could be imagined in the communities in question' (Van der Linden, 1978, p. 21).

The organization which developed during the Middle Ages in the land users' struggle against the water showed remarkable similarities to the sovereign organization which developed in the same period in the rivalry between warriors for land and control of land. Both organizations had a territorial basis and were led by multifunctional officials. They were authorized to make judgements and to pronounce the death sentence and, as disaster threatened, they could call up the population by the toll of a bell to contribute to the defence of the country (only adult males for waging war; everyone when floods threatened). Assembling for the guarding and defence of a dyke was indicated with the same term as assembling for the armed defence of the country, namely 'army'; the obligation to defend the country in times of armed attack and against the breaching of a dyke was also designated by this word. Furthermore, the term for weapon inspection could also refer to the inspection of instruments used for the maintenance of the drainage system. Similar problems of organization underlie these linguistic correspondences. In both cases, this organization was directed primarily at conquering and defending the land.

Along with similarities, important differences may also be observed. Water boards developed through the mutual co-operation of local communities and individual landowners and farmers. In many areas covered by the water boards, not only those who were in possession of a minimum acreage but all landholders in proportion to their acreage, were obliged to pay taxes, and they had the right to participate in decision making about their collective future. In contrast, the sovereign organization was directed from above, had a more authoritarian character, excluded larger groups of people from participation in decision making about their collective future, and had a differential, disproportional and ranked taxation system, which commonly, or at least clearly, better served the interests of the sovereign than those of the tax paying population (Van Dam, 1989).

For as long as technical development restrained the construction and maintenance of ditches, dams, wharves, dykes, culverts, locks, bridges, wind-mills and roads, people were dependent on the co-operation, and the labour of all the land users. This dependency relationship made it possible and necessary for an extremely large part of the rural population to be actively involved in decision making concerning the organization and financing of the drainage system.

As regards jurisdiction, clear differences can be observed between the sovereign and the water-controlling organizations. While sovereign juris-diction was based on the French legal system and Roman law, the jurisdiction of the water-controlling organizations, restricted to the Low Countries, was 'based on the principles of justice and reasonableness' for everyday administration of justice and, stemming from this, an extensive system of indigenous laws and customs developed (Van der Linden, 1982b, pp. 23–5). Proceedings, such as the survey of water courses, where the management of a water board could sentence a neglectful maintenance body on the spot, were part of this singular system. In the course of the fifteenth century, various regional water boards began to register those precepts and prohibitions in common use in lawbooks; these had close similarities. Similar problems apparently had led to similar solutions. Therefore, from the study of water board law by Beekman (1905, pp. 464–85), it can be concluded that, in the course of the Middle Ages, meeting manners ubiquitously appeared at survey meetings, and they concerned such matters as killing, injuring, cursing, quarrelling and contradicting.

As long as the majority rule was not, or, at least, not generally, accepted, there were regulations for the maintenance of dykes. In cases where drainage boards were unable to come to some agreement about required business, drainage boards from elsewhere attended to the business. For such cases, in some dyke laws, a singular remedy was prescribed. The drainage boards had to retreat into a hostel and were not allowed to leave until they were in agreement with each other (Beekman, 1905, p. 482). This remedy was more often applied in survey meetings. It was a generally accepted way of giving the negligent the opportunity, and indeed to compel them, to perform their maintenance duties. For this purpose, the inspectors suspended the survey and entered the nearest hostel, where they sat, ate and drank until the task was adequately dealt with. This was done at the cost of the negligent party, and the obligation to co-operate was fortified by having to pay the bill of the tavern, in excess of the fine and, naturally, the bill increased with the amount of time elapsing before work was begun (Beekman, 1907, p. 888). As a rule, such a survey meeting in a hostel lasted a certain maximum number of days (three) and was limited to a predetermined amount. The fact that the water boards' laws were often more severe than ordinary or sovereign jurisdiction, clearly demonstrates the vital importance of the maintenance of the water economy (Van Dam, 1989, p. 20).

Differing from almost everywhere else in Europe, the towns which developed in the late Middle Ages in the present-day Netherlands, were not juridical and fiscal enclaves in an agrarian society dominated by warriors. They developed in an agrarian society where mutual dependency relationships, stemming from their collective struggle against the water, were less asymmetrical. As the historian, Jan de Vries, comments:

> The weak seigneurial powers, the strength of the bonds of the free farmers, the autonomous rights of the drainage boards, and the capitalist organisation of the colonisation movement endowed the maritime region of the Netherlands with

taxing and property rights of a modern sort long before the sudden rise of Amsterdam and the other Dutch cities to economic supremacy. (1973, p. 202)

With the organization of water-controlling systems in the coastal and fluvial regions of the Netherlands, power and dependency relationships developed, which were favourable for the emergence and expansion of a meeting regime of a particular kind. This regime demanded from more people a more encompassing, more continuous and more stable self-regulation than the military-agrarian regimes that had established themselves, or were establishing themselves, over virtually the whole of Europe during this period. From this time on, participation from below has remained a characteristic of the organization of water-controlling systems in the Netherlands (Van der Linden, 1978, pp. 16–17).

Meetings of guilds and towns

Very early examples of processes of demilitarization, during which a meeting regime developed, can be found in classic antiquity in Ionic Greece, namely in Athens, and also in Republican Rome. For as far as it is known, over a lengthy period, broad layers of the male population acquired access to central meetings and brought to bear decisive influence on the prevailing meeting standards in their societies, for the first time in the history of an agrarian society. A powerful middle class, comprised of the wealthy, who also occupied important functions in the army, managed to limit the use of organized violence and systematic terror within the city-states by separating legislative, executive and judicial functions from each other, and by attaching specific regulations to the qualifications required to perform such functions and by specifying the periods of office. For this, general meetings, which were accessible for all free men, played an important role. These meetings selected and controlled the officials and leaders, and were consulted by the city magistrates for the most important decisions.

The Greek and Roman societies were, in fact, eventually conquered by warriors. The increase in the number of armed conflicts with other societies, and in the social tensions between the rich and poor within their own societies, provided the conditions under which military leaders were able to increase their power and use their military might to establish tyrannical and despotic regimes. Bearing in mind these later developments in Rome and Athens, Glassman (1986) has commented that, both a fairer division of wealth, and a more lasting legitimization of differences in wealth, are societal conditions required for the development of a 'democratic administration'. Such conditions first developed in commercial centres in early modern Europe where, with the progressive continuation of a differentiation between military matters and the economy, Protestant puritan religions emerged which, without question, legitimized private wealth as proof of divine selection (Glassman, 1986, II, p. 219).[12]

In the process of social division of labour, by which a wealthy class of merchants and entrepreneurs rose as trade, industry, and towns prospered, from approximately 1200, stabler and less vulnerable units of offence and defence appeared. This allowed the possibility for the development of meetings and meeting manners which went further than that of the ancient Greek and Roman societies.

In the elimination rounds between warriors, those who achieved ascendancy were those who had the greatest financial means at their disposal. They could pay mercenaries to contain rivals and compel towns to contribute larger tax payments. By having the groups play each other off (by first supporting groups from the nobility and then groups from the bourgeoisie) they were able to shape stabler monopolies of organized physical force and taxation. (The meeting manners which appeared in the centres of these monopolies will be dealt with in Chapter 4.) At this point, particularly the first stage of the development of urban meeting manners will be investigated; a stage in which merchants, artisans, and other burghers endeavoured to resist the organized force of the warriors by organizing themselves into guilds and confederations.

The organizing of guilds probably appeared in the early Middle Ages in the coastal regions of the North Sea by the collaboration of 'free' men who had the right to bear arms and who had started to practise trade.[13] Frisian 'merchants' played a prominent role in spreading this type of organization during their wanderings through the Carolingian realm. The guilds of free merchants developed meeting manners which can be considered as a intermediary step between the local communities of the early Middle Ages, based mainly on kinship, and the subsequent communities founded on occupation, residence and nation, such as towns, kingdoms and states.

The merchant guilds were voluntary organizations based on reciprocally sworn oaths. Originally these oaths were oaths of blood, by which, symbolically, a powerful, religiously inclined brotherhood was created that replaced family bonds. The sworn participants obliged themselves and each other to mutual assistance in times of feud and blood revenge, and for the payment and collection of 'wergeld'. For long journeys, the guilds acted as a sort of insuring body if occasions such as disagreements, legal actions, injury, sickness and death befell an individual.

Guilds regularly held general meetings, called morning talks, in a special meeting place: the guildhall. During the meeting the legal rules were read out, new rules were determined, new members were admitted, and transactions were completed. Furthermore, judicial cases concerning securities, loans, donations, buying and selling, and pledges were administered. The opening ceremony was a reminder of the original function of a guild as a collection for holding a sacrificial dinner, which, before Christianization, preceded a 'thing'. The morning talks began with offering peace in the form of a *potacio*, that is, a drinking bout where the participants drank to the well-being of deceased brothers, gods and saints, the king and other protectors. Communal eating and drinking sessions were the settings for mutual solidarity, and this created the ceremonial framework by which it was possible to discuss and to take all-binding decisions collectively. Whosoever disrupted the peace and broke the guild regulations during a meeting would be removed and punished.

It would be interesting to investigate how far the degree and manner of the drinking bouts of the guilds in the late Middle Ages were related to the return of the foot soldiers after warfare. From the eleventh century urban combat bands appeared in the more urbanized regions of Europe (starting in northern Italy and Flanders), each band grouped according to town district, and the guilds participated in the battles (Verbruggen, 1954, pp. 196ff). There is evidence that communal drinking increased with the active participation of the guilds in warfare and that it acquired a martial character (drinking contests). This gradually decreased with the appearance of mercenary armies.

In the late Middle Ages a guild meeting still consisted of two parts: the business–orientated meeting in the morning, the actual morning talk, and the drinking session, which also included eating, in the afternoon. The trading transactions took place in the morning talks, but:

> In the periods when there was no written documentation, they demanded a formal, that is, a ceremonial performance in the presence of witnesses in an atmosphere appropriate for the purpose. These judicial procedures apparently were not possible without the accompanying *potacio* and the drinking ritual contained within. From this the *potacio*, as it was regularly held in guildhalls, derived its significance for so many centuries. (Akkerman, 1971, pp. 40–1)

As trade developed and the number of transactions grew, the meetings became more businesslike. The eating and drinking and the guilds' religious activities fell into the background and majority decisions replaced unanimous decisions. This process developed slowly. The ceremonial residue of the drinking bouts could still be seen in the meetings of guilds, urban governments, and companies in the seventeenth and eighteenth centuries.[14]

The oldest guild statutes are those of the merchant guilds of Sint Omaars and Valencijn in Flanders which were only documented in the fourteenth century, but which stem from the eleventh century. In these, it was stipulated that the drinking session and the members' meeting were to take place on the same day and, in jeopardy of a fine, should be attended by all the guildsmen. At nine o'clock in the morning, all members were required to be seated peacefully for the obligatory business section of the meeting: litigations, business matters, announcements and determination of legal rules and admittance of new members. At the start of the meeting, women, children and staff were obliged to leave the room. The assembly was led by one of the annually elected guild masters. Twelve elected guildsmen administered justice; if one of the parties refused to acquiesce to the verdict, these twelve jurors elected a further twelve. Precise seating arrangements, a ban on sleeping during the meeting, and prohibitions on all types of disruption, such as fighting, shouting, drunken talk, knife pulling, glass throwing, and bearing arms, were part of the guilds' meeting requirements. Similar regulations were familiar to the subsequent craft guilds, for whom the organization of the merchants was an example (alongside the religious brotherhoods which had developed in the church). Thus, in the statutes of the fourteenth- and fifteenth-century craft guilds of Utrecht, it was laid down that the 'elders', who chaired the morning talk, were allowed to issue on-the-spot fines to the guildsmen if they spoke without permission, incited others, or spoke to others in a rebellious or indecent way (Overvoorde, 1897, p. LXXXIV). Likewise, at the start of the meetings of the guilds of Utrecht, women and children were required to leave. Furthermore, the guildsmen were obliged to appear appropriately dressed. During the meeting everyone had to remain quietly seated in his place and no more than three people at one time were allowed to stand up to take their turn to speak. 'The dealings of the morning talk had to remain confidential and the guildsmen were forbidden to reproach someone later because of what he had said' (ibid., p. C). Absence from a general meeting was punished by a year's ban, a punishment which was later replaced by a fine. Being late was likewise punished by a fine.

The free merchant guilds were structural models for burghers in the sovereign areas, who united in so-called confederacies in their struggle against feudal lords (Planitz, 1940; Van Uytven, 1980, pp. 214–17). The guild organization was somewhat indirect in its influence in the region north of the delta formed by the rivers Schelde, Maas and Rhine. Here urbanization began only after the blossoming of the free merchant guilds. Types of government and meeting manners, which the older towns of Flanders and Brabant had developed in a protracted struggle with sovereigns, served as models in the establishment of towns in this region.

Like the communities in the countryside, the oldest towns in the Netherlands were governed by a judge or a sheriff, and sentencers or aldermen, appointed by, or in co-operation with the sovereign. Jurisdiction and government did not differ essentially from those of the country 'things'. Gradually, the towns developed their own government and jurisdiction. With the aim of maintaining internal peace and to defend their trading and business interests from the sovereigns, the burghers in the sovereign areas often organized themselves into confederacies, modelled on the free merchants guilds.

Town dwellers bought their freedom and fought themselves free of manorial rights and taxes, tolls and stallage. As the manorial burdens lessened, land became transferable and suitable as security for business credit, and, in the towns, the right of participation in government and jurisdiction was disconnected from the possession of land and linked to residency. In the morning talks of the confederacies to which the members were called by the chiming of a bell, leaders were elected by acclamation (jurors, councils and lord mayors) who had the tasks of establishing peace, financial administration, the custody of orphans, the command of towns militia and the supervision of walls, gates and towers. The growth of the towns brought about many new problems and functions with which sovereign law was not designed to cope. Gradually sovereign law was substituted by by-laws, initiated by lord mayors or councils and aldermen, who had been elected by the burghers. Town governments began to administer justice which elsewhere was in the hands of lords. In meetings they determined by-laws concerning the maintenance of public order, taxation, the maintenance of roads and public wells, fire protection, control of the price of foodstuffs, the supervision of hostelries, the regulation of the sale of certain products and the settlement of weights and measures. Furthermore, the care of the poor, the sick, orphans and widows, and the management of poorhouses, hospitals, orphanages and almshouses obliged a notable increase in the necessity for holding meetings.

As a result of the specialization of urban government, the municipal morning talks were replaced by council meetings comprising a small group of wealthy merchants who, for the greater part, lived off their investments. Craftsmen sometimes managed to gain influence in urban government via their guild. By such means, after an uprising in 1304, the guilds of Utrecht obtained a decisive vote in the selection of magistrates and in important decisions concerning urban management. The guildsmen were subject to sometimes 'ruthlessly' strict meeting rules: To ensure that, during their periodical political meetings, the participants concentrated on the business for which they had assembled (namely the election of the elders and the urban councils), in 1457 the municipal government issued the order that those dealing with outside business during these meetings would be condemned to death (Overvoorde, 1897, p. XCVIII).

Throughout the fifteenth and sixteenth centuries, and due also to regulations of the Burgundian lords, urban government came to be more or less entirely in the hands of town councils comprising a set number of magistrates and ex-magistrates who co-opted new members from a limited number of wealthy or patrician families. These councils chose the representatives for the meetings of the provincial states and States-General, and had to be informed on all significant decisions made by the magistrature.

As municipal organization developed, the holding of meetings likewise gradually changed. Following a period of the merging of customs from the 'rural things' and the guilds from which certain elements, such as the toasting ceremony, long continued to be practised, urban meetings became more businesslike and more peaceful. This manifested itself succinctly in the appearance of more refined decision-making procedures, of which an impression follows.

Overview: Opening and deciding in medieval meetings

There is every reason to believe that, with the transition to agriculture, the holding of meetings became more problematical. It became more precarious, not only because of the necessity of harmonizing the dealings of an increasing number of people, but because the compulsion and the tendency to resort to force increased with the mounting tensions. Since many people were constantly ready violently to fight out feuds, arguments or conflicts, it was frequently impossible to reach reciprocal agreements without a stronger military presence or the enforcement of 'peace orders' issued and secured by them. The problem arose *in optima forma* when rivals or competing groups were compelled for one reason or another to negotiate with each other about peace, a truce or military co-operation. In the absence of a stronger individual or group who could impose a ban on the use of force by each side or an order to restrain from violence, there was a considerable chance that fighting would break out during the negotiations. A slight movement, a single word from one side could be interpreted by the opposing party as a sign for an armed struggle. There existed little mutual trust; every point of the negotiations could be a trap.

The meeting manners of the warriors reflected their reciprocal balance of power. The more powerful the leaders, the more the warriors' meetings acquired the shape of meetings where orders were dispensed. The more limited the leaders' authority over other warriors, the more warriors' meetings acquired the character of negotiations which could rapidly deteriorate into violent shows of strength. When violence appeared to be temporarily defused, the act of issuing orders and the act of negotiating were the two extremes of the 'continuum of military meeting'.

When warriors rallied around leaders as threats of war rose, war councils developed, led by supreme commanders. These meetings tended toward the dispensation of and the compliance with orders. As the warrior dominion disintegrated, the process took a reverse course and the central war councils were replaced by precarious negotiations and physical combat. A similar movement became more prominent after the collapse of the Carolingian Empire. The shuttling (which was mainly a result of war) between the three situations of giving/taking orders, negotiating and fighting ceased and, within larger areas, died down as the warriors became more dependent on upcoming non–military groups.

With the progressive division of labour in society and during periods of lessened warmongering, the martial meeting manners were changed by the formation of groups of priests, merchants and craftsmen, and sometimes also farmers, and adapted to their specific functions and problems. By this, meetings became more differentiated and more varied, and more peaceful styles of meeting developed. Priests developed meeting ceremonies, in which they maintained silence or prayed for hours, they celebrated mass, and they quoted from the Gospel. Merchants held more practical meetings concerning trade routes, mutual support during journeys to far-flung places, and transactions and prices. And farmers were responsible for the development of their own 'agrarian–democratic' meeting manners, particularly during the meetings of the water boards.

In comparison with later developments, the most striking characteristics of the meeting manners of the Middle Ages were the limited number of psychological nuances to be found, and their limited degree of complexity. Corresponding to the relatively short and little differentiated series of transactions, the high level of danger, and the large divisions in power in the society dominated by warriors and priests, the tendency to solve problems by discussion and agreement was, in general, relatively weak. Most people assembled infrequently, often only when they were directly threatened or forced by some higher authority. Meeting behaviour was regulated by a limited number of rules which permitted a reasonably large amount of elbowroom for the expression of either belligerent or excessively congenial emotions. In cases of tensions and conflicts, personal decisions played a large role – the more powerful the person, the larger the role.

The undocumented standards of meeting behaviour of agrarian societies gradually altered as the balance of power between members of local communities changed. This occurred more swiftly and more radically in times of war, uprisings, epidemics, floods and other events that made deep inroads into the social life of these local communities. The new or altered rules were part of an oral 'tradition', passed from generation to generation, which often differed widely between districts or regions. The rules of thumb used to regulate mutual tensions and co-ordinate actions were neither strict nor impersonal. Their application and functioning were both dependent upon the changeable personal emotions and decisions of the powerful. Prior to state formation, the legitimacy of the standards of behaviour were mainly determined by the degree of direct force that people exercised over each other in face-to-face situations; they changed faster and were more strictly tied to the power relationship of that specific moment (Schröter, 1985, p. 6).

It was only during the period of state formation, when organized violence was monopolized over extensive areas and a small number of monopolies came to dominate the rest, that sanctioned rules of conduct were created. These had a degree of generality and durability, which made it possible for people to accept them as 'objective' standards of behaviour: as 'laws' (Schröter, 1985, pp. 6–13; Elias and Dunning, 1986, pp. 181–2).

Both the prohibited and prescribed meeting rules were concerned with the abstinence from tempestuous violence for the duration of the meeting, until the appearance of rules which, in the pre-state and early state stages of co-existence in the Europe of the Middle Ages, were so widespread and generally accepted as to suggest a family resemblance between meetings. Surveys, 'things', feudal law courts and morning talks still had to start with three 'security questions' or variations of such, each posed by a judge or chairman. The questions demanded whether the place, the timing and the composition of the meeting were correct. In confirmation, the men present would shout 'aye'. Then the leader formally proclaimed the peace order or the proscription of the 'thing', after which it was forbidden both to leave one's seat and to speak without permission from the chairman. At the end of a meeting, the proscription of the 'thing' was officially lifted. For a long time afterwards, the peace order reverberated in the opening ceremonies of meetings. It could still be found in the regulations of eighteenth-century law courts and other official meetings.

It is remarkable that such an opening and closing ritual was preserved in many local and regional secular meetings for so long after the Middle Ages; in an ecclesiastical context, praying, and in court meetings and meetings of rank, a short welcoming address replaced the three security questions.[15] It illustrates the fact that the tendency, or the compulsion, physically to fight out differences of opinion was relatively strong for many people in a society that was both hardly centralized and strictly stratified.

As society became more peaceful, differences in power decreased, and reciprocal expectations of self-control increased, the opening formula was shortened to a single sentence, such as 'I hereby declare this meeting open' or 'the meeting will be in order'.

Compared to later developments, there was little discussion and argumentation. Before the Reformation, ecclesiastical meetings consisted mainly of praying and performing religious rituals. For the most part, many secular meetings consisted of swearing oaths, reciting 'thing' incantations, and indulging in bouts of eating and drinking. Activities used as a means to obtain decisive answers for the question of how to proceed were: trials employing bodily injury; man-to-man fights where men cursed, wounded or killed each other; dreams; loud screaming; collective hymn singing; communal catcalling; spontaneous flashes of the imagination; and other highly affective behaviour.

Agreements were infrequently documented, but were orally endorsed by sworn oaths, meals and prayers.

Little is known about the discussions that took place during meetings. Reports of meetings in the Middle Ages which consist of more than a list of decisions are non-existent. The only reports available are a number of personal eye witnesses, accounts found in chronicles and annals. From this limited material, it can be concluded that the margin of insecurity was broader than it was in the centuries following and that, in deliberating and deciding about the future, they referred to ideas which, by today's standards, can be considered as having insufficient empirical standing. As far as we can see, people were more powerfully in the grip of what Elias (1956) termed the 'double-bind process':

> On the one hand, they had little chance of controlling their own strong feelings in relation to nature and of forming more detached concepts of natural events as long as they had little control over them; and they had, on the other hand, little chance of extending their control over their non-human surroundings as long as they could not gain greater mastery over their own strong feelings in relation to them and increase their control over themselves. (Elias, 1956, p. 231)

Many events, such as war, famine, epidemics, conquest, floods, solar eclipses and earthquakes, which brought about anxiety and alarm, caused people to question themselves as to what they meant, what hidden scheme lay behind them. During meetings, dreams, apparitions, visions, the outcomes of sacred trials and ritual man–to–man fights, sudden thoughts, and especially spontaneous expressions of unanimity, were conceived and interpreted as revelations of God's intentions and plans.

The most common activity for decision making in ecclesiastical and secular meetings of the Middle Ages was that of acclamation. Chronicles and annals dating from the Middle Ages show that proposals and recommendations were adopted 'unanimously', and 'by common consent' by rattling weapons, cheering, hymn singing and applauding, or rejected by hissing, groaning and jeering (according to Maleczek, 1990, pp. 90–101). The employment of procedures which considered the expression of 'spontaneous unanimity' as decisive not only fulfilled the emotional needs for the relevation of God's aims and intentions, but also took into consideration the large differences in power and prestige between people. However, this way of deciding allowed those who were more powerful in society a rather large opportunity for manipulation, surprise attack, bribery and corruption, which has been commented upon by Gosses (1946):

> A meeting has but one voice, one collective voice. This is not indicative of approval or rejection; it is not considered as an indication of how the majority would be inclined in the event of a roll-call; but it is the single and indivisible

expression of the will of the meeting. Discussions, disputes, fights sometimes precede it. It could be that a small group of influential people (or even a single individual) have actually set up the whole affair. Yet the making of the decision is only achieved by acclamation; the choice is so determined. Whoever fails to agree, remains either absent or silent, or is shouted down, and more than once it has happened that the simultaneous noise rising from the meeting is not produced by the most, but by the loudest, voices. (Gosses, 1946, p. 36)

If no decision could be reached by acclamation, there often remained no other possibility but armed combat. Only in the church was there the possibility of remitting a case about which people were not able to reach agreement to higher echelons and thus preventing more violent 'solutions'.

As a result of extending, differentiating and tightening networks of interdependency, more refined methods of coming to agreement appeared, such as decisions requiring majority voting, which allowed the possibility for more discussion and argumentation and for more weight to be given to divergent opinions. Connected closely to the appearance of representational meetings, the (re)invention and extension of the majority rule (the ancient Greeks already applied the rule, see note 12, this chapter) was a lengthy process. In this process, urban and ecclesiastical groups and, in the Netherlands, also the water boards, led the way. Those terms deriving from the Latin word *maior*, like *majoriteit* in Dutch, *majorité* in French, *majority* in English, and *Mehrheit* in German, referred to adulthood in the vernaculars of European languages. Only in the course of the seventeenth and eighteenth centuries did these words begin to indicate majority regarding number, majority regarding votes.[16] Dutch was at the forefront of this development; the language of that area where both the water economy and trade more frequently activated more people to co-operate on prospective plans than in many other areas of Europe.

From the twelfth century onwards and, as far as is known, for the first time since classical antiquity, procedures appeared in meetings of guilds, towns, water boards and the church where decisions were made by majority voting. In the transition from the unanimity and acclamation procedures to the majority rule procedure, intermediate forms appeared, such as *arbitrage*, *scrutinium*, *maior et sanior pars* and combinations of voting and drawing lots. These methods can be regarded as attempts to reconcile the ideal of unanimity with the 'implacable' majority rule procedure. *Arbitrage* was tantamount to the choice of a small group of men who pronounced an absolute majority recommendation. The *scrutinium*, applicable in particular for religious orders, obliged those eligible to vote, one by one to declare their vote orally to three wise men. These would then present the opinion of the majority as the communal will. For *maior et sanior pars*, a procedure was instigated by which the vote of the 'most sensible' section of a meeting was the deciding factor.

Again, this procedure was initially developed in the church, where there was the possibility of appeal to more highly ranked ecclesiastical leaders for the well-nigh unavoidable and never-ending question of who were the 'most sensible'.

In the absence of such a possibility for appeal, and from fear of fraud and the formation of cliques, merchants and craftsmen in the relatively peaceful towns generally made an early transfer to using more refined ways of purely numerical means of making a decision. Initially, both complicated and, from a contemporary point of view, time-consuming secret and public voting procedures were applied, such as voting by placing various types of beans, stones and coins in various urns, or by marking a board with stripes; standing up and sitting; dispersing in groups; and staged elections. (These procedures were also intended to temper any animosity during the meetings.) Frequently, these methods were combined with drawing lots, particularly when the fraud-susceptible allotment of desirable office was concerned. In some towns the selection of high officials was done in several stages. First, there was a written or other kind of ballot of potential electors, who were then allocated by drawing lots. These electors co-operatively advised another group of electors, who were further allocated by drawing lots. These could then advise about further candidates and soon. The complexity of the election procedures was determined not only by the number of municipal groups and important families involved, but also by the importance of the vacant functions. In thirteenth-century Venice, the elections for a new doge took no fewer than fifteen rounds of votes, lots, electors' advice, allotment of candidates, lots, votes, etc. (Maleczek, 1990, pp. 127–34).

The meticulously detailed organization of elections and ballots in the towns of the late Middle Ages aimed at a kind of self-management which allowed people to suspend decisions, to make compromises, to direct discussions towards making proposals requiring a yes/no response, and to render the voting in such a way that the results were reflected in indisputable numbers. In the northern and southern towns of the Netherlands, the 'experimental' stage came to an end in the Burgundian period with the monopolization of town management by a limited number of wealthy families who, following certain codes, divided the offices of government among themselves. The stabilizing and limiting of the group of participants made the application of the majority rule easier, although decision making for a long time still followed a dualistic pattern. Until well after the Middle Ages, decisions were chronicled in reports accompanied by the comment, 'with the unanimity of and the majority of the votes'. In the latter half of the seventeenth century, townsfolk were apparently so used to the application of the majority rule that the alderman, Hans Bontemantel, mentioned merely as a curiosity in his description of the Amsterdam government that, in the city council, the clerk who counted the votes and noted them as stripes on a board had formerly been obliged to roll up his sleeves so as not to erase any stripes, accidentally or on purpose (Bontemantel, 1897, II, p. 12).

The development of the majority decision may be regarded as an expression of a gradually increasing interdependence, by which social relations lost their character of unrestrained enmity or congeniality, possibly in a rapid alternation. The codes of behaviour became more differentiated in the more broadly branched, and more finely meshed, interdependency networks that commercial farmers, merchants and townsfolk developed with each other. The increasingly longer and more complex trade relations required the tempering of congeniality and aversion in varying degrees and nuances. Increasingly, more people found themselves in situations where they were both each others' rivals and partners at the same time. In order not to disrupt the entire network of human actions and so jeopardize their own livelihood, people were more compelled to moderate their behaviour towards their rivals than in the previous societies of free warriors and small self-sufficient farming communities.

Considering the whole period thus far, the following may be concluded. When warriors became more dependent upon non-military groups who supported them in their rivalry against other warriors, units of offence and defence were created, within which the tendency and compulsion to control social tensions by discussion and agreement increased, to the detriment of the more martial strategies for controlling conflicts. The warriors were compelled to concern themselves with problems other than those of military co-ordination and had to adjust themselves to the meeting manners and customs of upcoming groups; first mainly the bishops, later urban representatives, sometimes farmers and, in the Low Countries, water boards. It has been demonstrated that, with the rise in social standing of the priests in the Frankish domain, and the development of the water boards and towns, the war council as a model for meetings became insignificant and the predominant meeting standards became more refined. Examples of this can be seen in the greater possibilities to express divergent personal opinions, the decision making by majority vote, and the signing and registering of decisions. With the continuing differentiation of meetings, and the merging of the meeting manners of warriors and upcoming groups, meeting standards arose which, in comparison with previous standards, prompted greater and more differentiated self-control, and allowed a more detached idea of the changing relations between people.

As long as the monopolies of violence remained vulnerable and unstable, holding meetings remained limited and it only obtained some degree of naturalness within small upper societal layers. As long as many people were strongly inclined to settle a dispute or difference of opinion by coming to blows or by armed combat, the necessity for holding a meeting was relatively limited and meetings maintained a highly ritualistic character.

CHAPTER 4

THE COURTIZATION
OF MEETINGS

Court societies

This chapter reviews the meeting standards achieved by the dominant groups in Western Europe on the eve of both a new stage in the monopolization of organized violence and taxation, and the formation of states. For most of Western Europe, the forthcoming states were centralized around absolutist courts. Elias uses the example of France to trace the process of state formation in the most detail. He uses France because there the monopolization of the means of violence and taxation took a less deviating course, and because, partly as a result, France was for a long time the foremost power in Europe and thus set the example for many other states (Elias, 1994 pp. 339–45; Mennell 1992, pp. 72–3).

In the Low Countries, however, where economic development and urbanization in the sixteenth century accelerated, the trend towards centralization and absolutism came to an end in the northern part during an uprising against the king, known as the Dutch Revolt. A consequence of this revolt was a segmented republic administered by town governors. Less than a century later, a similar development occurred in another economically powerful region of Europe, England. Here the alliance between land-owning gentry on the one hand, and urban interests on the other, was too powerful for the king to control. In the middle of the seventeenth century, during the Civil War, the English monarchy became constitutional and the government was brought under the control of a parliament, dominated by the gentry. In England at that time the centralization of government was more advanced than that in the northern Netherlands. 'The Norman Conquest, and William I's careful distribution of feudal holdings in such a way as to minimise the risks of lords acquiring consolidated territorial power bases, meant that for several centuries the English monarchy was unusually strong and centralized in comparison with its continental counterparts' (Mennell, 1992, p. 73).

FIGURE 4.1 King Louis XIV of France (seated) presides over a council meeting; other members must stand (1672) (© photo RMN, Paris)

In Chapter 3 it was shown that the development of meetings in military-agrarian societies was hampered by the dread of war, crop failure, being plundered, and other organized acts of violence. As long as towns and their feudal squires, and federations of towns and knights controlled the means to apply physical force, the social tensions between these groups constantly led to warlike actions. Furthermore, the feudal lords and princes did not have the capacity to bring these groups under enduring and effective control, thus restraining organized violence in the areas over which they ruled.

Elias has demonstrated how, from approximately 1200 onwards, in a long drawn-out elimination battle between warriors about land and land control, offensive and defensive units came into being, within which organized violence was more restrained (1994, pp. 335–440). A principal element in Elias' discussion of state formation processes is the 'monopoly mechanism':

> This term refers to intimately related processes: the gradual concentration of the means of violence and taxation (the two principal means of ruling) in the hands of a single ruler and administration in each territory; and the enlargement of the territory through competition with and elimination of neighbouring rulers. (Mennell, 1992, p. 66)

Through the intensification of trade and industry, the concentration of people in cities, the increase in the use of money, the improvements in communication and transport and other social processes, the competitive battle between warriors took another turn. The degree to which a warrior could depend on the moral and financial support of the towns began, in particular, to influence more and more his chances of being the most powerful in battle. Gradually dominance was gained by those having the greatest financial means to pay mercenaries for fighting their rivals and for compelling towns to pay larger taxes when necessary. These rulers became in the position to bring large groups of people under the control of one central authority and to pacify extensive regions.

In this stage of state formation a social phenomenon arose that Elias has called 'the royal mechanism': the internal balance of social forces within the developing state, by the presence of an 'absolutist monarchy' (1994, pp. 390–420). Such a regime emerged in many of the states of Europe. The archetype is French court society. Within larger and larger areas the use of verbal battles replaced organized violence, and the collection and spending of taxation money replaced armed battle for land and land control. In the expanding courts of the new 'territorial' lords, courtly figurations were formed, within which physical violence decreased, and mutual tensions and conflicts had to be fought out in a more peaceful manner than was usual for 'free' warriors. In Western Europe in the sixteenth century, this process had advanced so far that in areas as large as France, monopolies of force and taxation had developed which were governed from central courts by monarchs and their advisors.

According to Elias (1994, p. 476), more peaceful competition demanded from the French court specific characteristics and competencies such as weighing up the pros and cons, calculating in the long term, self-control, more precise and articulate regulation of one's own affects, knowledge of human and non-human nature, and insight into the social interplay of forces as a whole. The behaviour of the court's higher echelons gradually became more 'civilized'. This civilization process was greatly advanced by the process of social stratification. Because courtly habits, forms of conduct and fashions were imitated in a somewhat altered form by the higher middle classes, these habits lost their function as a means of distinction for the social upper crust. This obliged the highest echelons to refine their behaviour even more (Elias, 1994, pp. 499–513).

The courtly stage of the civilization process in Western Europe can be studied further by examining the changes in meeting activities and behaviour during the formation of states, such as those of the Burgundian dukes and the French kings. In the Low Countries until the Dutch Revolt and in France, monarchies comprised the most important centres for the state formation process. In the Burgundian kingdom, however, towns played a more powerful role (namely the towns in Flanders, Brabant and Holland) than they did in the French kingdom of that period.

In both areas, the royal monopolies of the means of violence and taxation expanded and the court councils developed into a differentiated entity consisting of 'wise assemblies enlightening the sovereign in his decisions' (Antoine, 1970, p. 629). The court councils were the most important places where the prince could validate his position of power vis-à-vis the courtiers both of aristocratic and bourgeois origin by playing those groups off against one another. In the meetings of the court councils, the monarch was central, even if he was not physically present. The words used in council meetings revolved around the monarch and were not permitted in any way whatsoever 'to offend the delicate ears of the king' (*ibid.*, pp. 27–8).

At the courts, not only eating manners and other bodily activities, but also the central council conduct became more stylized under the pressure of rising middle groups. At first, the monopolies of force and taxation centred around royal courts were relatively unstable and vulnerable. The central lords had to be constantly on their guard against the old aristocracy and the increasingly powerful towns, which possessed the capacity to destroy the unity of their realm if they chose to ally themselves. To finance wars, monarchs were extremely dependent upon taxation money which they had to bargain from the towns and the other estates in so-called meetings of the states, estate parliaments or other important meetings. Because the fixed incomes from the royal domains and taxation were totally insufficient to defray the costs of the wars that the monarchs had to, or wanted to fight, they were compelled to negotiate with their subjects. In exchange for authorizing extra taxation or 'aides' (pecuniary grants in aid to the king), the town governments, in particular, demanded a say in many areas of government. Before 1600, for varying periods of time, many European estate parliaments were able to exert influence in areas concerning jurisdiction, legislation, taxation expenditure, the appointment of regents and royal advisors, decisions regarding war and peace, foreign affairs, alliances, ascendancy to the throne, and currency (Meyers, 1975, p. 34).

In the Burgundian Netherlands, the influence that the urbanized provinces (Flanders, Brabant, and later Holland) could exert upon the central fiscal and military policies was relatively large. In these areas, the meetings of the states were dominated by the towns and both the military aristocracy and the clergy played a less prominent role than they did elsewhere. The urbanization of

Holland began in the thirteenth century partly as a result of the intiatives taken by the counts of Holland, who expected a financial advantage with the growth of the urban population. In the centuries following, this process continued to accelerate: between 1400 and 1500, the number of town dwellers doubled from 200,000 to 400,000. At the start of the sixteenth century, almost half of the population of Holland lived in towns. In every respect, the towns of Holland were able to profit from the experiences of the urbanized areas to the south, Flanders and Brabant, which had been urbanized earlier.

From the end of the sixteenth century on, the differences in social structure between France and the Netherlands and other countries became more apparent and the state formation processes began to diverge for some time. Mennell (1992) writes:

> In most countries there were struggles between kings and assemblies, with varying outcomes. Where 'absolutist' monarchies developed, assemblies tended to be abolished, or at least stripped of power. In France, the Estates General simply were not summoned after 1614 – until 1787, on the eve of the revolution. Many of the symptoms of the emergence of an absolutist monarchy were also evident in England under the Tudors and the early Stuarts, but there Parliament had always been a rather strong institution compared with most of the continental assemblies. Charles I did attempt for twelve years to govern without Parliament, but was eventually forced to call it again, setting in train the events leading to his defeat in the Civil War. (1992, p. 77)

While in England, and most of all in France, monarchs and court councils more or less succesfully monopolized the central co-ordinating functions, in the Netherlands, the states and town governments unexpectedly took charge. During the meetings of these boards, discussions and decisions about the communal future were conducted and made on a more equal level than during the hierarchical court councils of the French kingdom.

In the rest of this chapter, the development of the courtly and parliamentary meetings in Western Europe, especially in the Burgundian-Habsburg realm before the Dutch Revolt is examined. The initial investigation will cover how the monarch's councils ceremoniously gathered to meet in one of the wealthiest and most magnificent courts of that time. The meeting manners and problems of estate parliaments will then be investigated using a dialogue written by Erasmus of Rotterdam.

Court councils

The principalities which existed around 1200 did not usually cover one unbroken territory. The rural estates of the counts and other squires, which very gradually and in very different ways came under the control of one person (conquest, heredity, benefaction or marriage), were spread over a large area and were not easy to keep track of. The survival chances of the lords lay in manipulating the discord between the aristocratic landowners. This power game manifested itself more and more in the meetings of the councils (*curia*) in which the territorial lords initially made their appearance as *primus inter pares* (according to Coenen, 1986). These meetings had a relatively spontaneous character; there was little organization, as the medieval historian J. Buntinx (1950) has commented:

> The composition varied at every sitting. These *curia* sat at irregular times, whenever the lord felt the need. The sittings were composed of . . . those who for one reason or another at that time were in the vicinity of the lord; nobles and officials, usually from the area where the lord had taken up temporary residence, and several others, summoned as their presence was necessary for the handling of particular political or legal business. . . . The authority of the *curia* was extremely extensive; its task broadly encompassing. They covered the most wide-ranging types of subject: political, administrative, financial, and legal. Nevertheless, there was no division of labour, no specialisation, and no separate sections of the *curia* responsible for a well-demarcated assignment. One can scarcely call the consideration of legal questions on certain days, and the consideration of political questions on other days, a division of labour. . . . The same *curia* dealt with somewhat intermingled business of the most varying nature. (Buntinx, 1950, pp. 157–8)

The same has been written about the predecessor of the English parliament, the *Magnum Concilium* or 'Great Council'. This was the parliament of the Anglo-Norman kings of the twelfth and thirteenth centuries, composed of court officials, barons and prelates, of whom the number present depended on the importance of the business to be discussed. 'The council was obviously an elastic institution, as vague in its composition and as indefinite in its rules of procedure as was the cabinet in the first quarter or the eighteenth century' (A.F. Pollard, 1964, p. 29).

The court meetings became more frequent, more specialized, and more subject to rules, as people in the court centres of the increasingly larger and more stable monopolies of organized force and taxation had to take into account more links in the increasingly complicated interweaving of social relationships. This development could be observed everywhere in Europe:

> Ubiquitously, between the late Middle Ages and the middle of the seventeenth century, there was a distinct body for political affairs. This resulted mainly from specializations in the old '*curia regis*' or royal council, and sometimes from having been created by the royal cabinet (this variant seem to have appeared in a number of German states). In England it was the Privy Council, in France the *Conseil du*

Roi, in Austria, Brandenburg, and most of the other German states the *Geheime Rat*, and in Spain the *Consejo de Estado*. Initially these councils were fundamentally concerned with essential state business, particularly business of a political, military, and financial nature. They functioned as the highest advisory and, sometimes, the highest executive boards for internal and foreign affairs, and as the most important instruments for governmental centralization.

In the sixteenth and the seventeenth centuries, the differentiation process continued. Due in particular to the rapid growth in the number of state affairs, and through an almost natural process (Parkinson's Law), everywhere the royal council covered an increasingly broader range of business and began to specialize. Initially, ad hoc committees appeared. From these there subsequently developed more and more (semi-)permanent committees and independent boards for specific sub fields of work. (De Bruin, 1991, pp. 51–2)

In the Netherlands, these developments accelerated during the integration of territorial principalities in the Burgundian, and, subsequently, the Habsburg realm. The Burgundian-Habsburg court focused upon the rapidly growing number of governmental duties. These duties were fulfilled by court councils, comprising the sovereign and his advisors selected by the monarch from aristocratic families and families of bourgeois origin. The chancellor, several juridically trained councillors, and a majority of aristocratic councillor–chamberlains met almost daily to talk about various matters pending, under the supervision of the monarch or his representative. Initially there was hardly any division of labour, although the nobility tended to concern itself more with politics and the jurists more with jurisprudence. To a great degree, the actual governing was a personal concern for the monarchs. They envisaged neither a unified future, nor an integrated governmental apparatus. 'It was still in the first phase, with a view to directly wielding their power, that they issued decrees, enactments, and established boards' (Huizinga, 1973, p. 31).

Court councils developed into a differentiated entity of meetings which provided the sovereign with the information upon which he based his decisions. This process of differentiation occurred gradually, and developed with the establishment of departments and nuclei with different governmental, financial or judicial duties and functions. Nevertheless, the various court councils continued to operate in each other's field. For example, there was no division in legislative, executive, and judicial governmental duties, as in the *Trias Politica* (Montesquieu's doctrine).

The oldest known court decrees date from the latter half of the fifteenth century. They concerned summary decisions about at which times, and from which rank, which individuals were permitted or obliged to participate in the meetings of the central Burgundian court council. These decrees were announced shortly after the number of governmental and juridical duties had greatly increased due to the expansion of the dominion to include the regions of Brabant, Limburg, Holland, Zeeland and Hainault.

One of the oldest court enactments with interests in court deliberation dates from 1469. In it was determined that the court council had to meet morning and afternoon at certain times in a special chamber at the court of the duke, or in the chancellor's residence. Furthermore, it stated that the councillors had to attend the mass which was held every morning in the chancellor's residence, after which they had to accompany the chancellor to the council chamber so that everyone would arrive punctually. And last, it demanded that the court council discussed all petitions, and that the verbal instruction was immediately transcribed onto the petition (Van Rompaey, 1980; 1981, pp. 306–7). Court deliberation was one of the most important instances where the monarchs could demonstrate their position of power over, and their detachment from, the peerage and the bourgeoisie. As Elias (1969) pointed out: There was formed from among a minority of the old warrior nobility families and some families of bourgeois origin, a new court nobility increasingly distinct from the old landed nobility. Later, a new and separate hereditary elite of magistrates and officials, the *noblesse de robe* drawn wholly from families of bourgeois origin, rose in power (Elias, 1969, pp. 144–213; Mennell, 1992, p. 76). In the organization and composition of the court council, the monarchs endeavoured to induce the old warrior nobility and the new court nobility to play each other off, to advantage their own area of manoeuvrability. The monarchs were able to maintain the ascendancy over both sides by stationing independent, non-aristocratic, juridically trained courtiers next to their potential, aristocratic rivals.

After numerous 'experiments', the Burgundian-Habsburg court council was divided in 1531 during the reign of Charles V into three Collateral Councils: the Council of State, the Secret Council and the Financial Council. Twelve legists of bourgeois origin sat in the Secret Council. This council supervised the legal system and the home government, shaped regulations, issued edicts, and other governmental rules and supervised the execution of them. It played a large role in the process of political centralization. Members of the military nobility as well as the *noblesse de robe* sat in the Financial Council: they were collectively responsible for the general government of the dominions and 'aides', and controlled financial transactions (Baelde, 1965, 1967).

The most important council, the Council of State, was dominated by the old warrior nobility. This council advised the monarch with regard to war and peace, and in all the important matters of a military, diplomatic or political nature. The subsequent regents and governors of Habsburg kept attempting to disregard or bring this council, dominated by the landed nobility, under their own control by appointing members of the *noblesse de robe* to the most important council functions. In the 1560s this was successfully opposed by the military nobility, led by William of Orange. However, this success was short lived. The Council of State was totally dismantled with the arrival of Alva, the establishment of the Council of Troubles, and the murder of the dukes of Egmont and Hoorne. At a central level, there remained only the collective state meetings of the Netherlands (the States-General) as a political centre of power, following that of, and ultimately opposed to, the monarch and the court of Brussels.

Baelde's (1965) study, *The collateral councils of Charles V and Philip II*, provides an impression of how the council meetings were conducted in the court of Brussels in the last decades before the Dutch Revolt (in particular pp. 131–49). The monarch, his governor or governess called the council together and made the decisions. Meetings were called almost daily, mornings and evenings; the frequency related directly to the situation prevailing in the country. The councillors had to show the greatest courtesy towards the monarch and the governess/governor. One consequence of this obligatory courtesy was that they had to be present at the court council meetings – absence was considered an act of opposition.

At the start of a meeting the participants had to take their seats at table according to rank. The monarch or his governess/governor was seated on a raised armchair at the table head. The councillors had to attend the deliberations bare-headed; a condition later dispensed with by Charles V. Head coverings were a sign of distinction, by which an individual's social function and status could be recognized. The absence of a hat in the presence of another was a sign of subordination. It was an indirect message to the other that he need fear no usurping or, more figuratively, no opposition.

The meetings were conducted by the monarch, the governess/governor, or the head of the council, who was not necessarily the highest dignity but certainly the most powerful participant due to his function. Once the councillors were seated, the monarch or his representative opened the session with a short welcoming speech. This was followed by a brief summary of the first topic to be discussed; this having been chosen entirely by the monarch or the regent. The chancellor held consultations with them about the subjects to be dealt with and the order in which they should be handled. The chancellor could also participate in the discussions and the formulation of advice. The discussions were conducted in the following manner: The councillors were allocated in turn by the leader to expound their opinion about the subject under discussion or to indicate whether they were in agreement with previous speakers. If further investigation was required, this responsibility was given to one of the councillors who later would report his findings to the council.

Advisory decisions required a majority vote (*pluralité de voix et opinion*). However, votes were never taken. The councillors drafted the expressed opinions in such a way that everyone could determine the majority opinion.

After the chairman had conducted discussions with the 'opposition' if he so desired, the opinion of the majority was presented as definite advice to the monarch or governess/governor. It was obligatory to keep the discussed business confidential; decisions were transcribed in a secret code. The monarch or the governess/governor made the ultimate decisions on the basis of the advice given. They could adopt the opinions of the minorities but nevertheless, usually accepted the majority decision. A decision took effect once it had been documented by a councillor with legal expertise and then signed by the monarch or the governess/governor.

Reviewing the entire meeting procedure, Baelde (1965) concludes that the council's mode of operation was pragmatic and opportunistic:

> The business that was handled, was never actually dealt with systematically'. The issues discussed were never dealt with from the perspective of a longer term approach. Business was handled as it was presented; this was mainly by correspondence. Acute and serious problems would be given preference. Council business was tardy partly because councils were committed to exchanging letters for the announcement of many affairs and . . . sometimes it took a long time before the correspondence was received. Furthermore, it sometimes took a considerable amount of time before the councillors met to discuss the more important issues. (Baelde, 1965, p. 149)

In comparison to later periods, the pressure to meet in the Burgundian court could be seen as rather limited. The number of people who regularly met remained quite small, whereas the power of the monarch and the governess/governor remained quite large. In comparison to the way in which warriors in the previous stage of 'free' competition fought out their conflicts, verbal battles conducted by a central monarch or his replacement required a more constant restraint of momentary affects. The increased pressure on the central court to meet manifested itself in the obligation to meet practically daily at set times. Furthermore, the adherence to all sorts of detailed stipulations covering the order of taking a seat, the order of talking, the way of deciding, the listening to others and the maintenance of confidentiality, demanded relatively strict discipline from the courtier–councillors.

Estate parliaments

In 1920 A.F. Pollard wrote:

> Parliamentary institutions have, in fact, been incomparably the greatest gift of the English people to the civilisation of the world. Civilised man has drawn his religious inspirations from the East, his alphabet from Egypt, his algebra from the

Moors, his art and literature mainly from Greece, and his laws from Rome. But his political organisation he owes mostly from English conceptions, and constitution systems all over the world are studded with words and phrases which can only be explained by reference to the medieval English parliament. (1964 [1920], p. 3)

However

England was not the first country in which a parliament emerged. This happened in the kingdoms of Leon and Castile. . . . The constant struggles against the Moors had fostered both the importance and the subordination of the warrior aristocracy, and emphasised the duty of the king to make ceaseless war against the infidel. Successful war was almost a necessity for the king, not only to maintain his prestige but to provide territorial rewards for a land-hungry aristocracy; yet warfare on this scale was a serious drain on his resources. The constant border wars caused all towns to be fortresses, and their citizens to be trained to arms and granted special privileges to encourage them to resist the Moors. Townsmen too, therefore, had a spirit of independence, turbulence, and dignity. The king, in need of political and military aid and money, early looked to the towns for help in these matters and for support against the unruly aristocracy. In the first concilio of Leon to which representatives of towns were summoned, that of 1188, King Alphonso IX of Leon made concessions which seem to indicate an alliance between the clergy, aristocracy, and towns. (A.R. Meyers 1975, p. 59)

The common understanding that the English parliament was the cradle of the entire European parliamentary system ignores the fact that estate parliaments or meetings emerged all over medieval Europe, especially in the urbanizing regions along the trade routes. The meetings of leagues among towns in the Low Countries, for instance, are just as old, and have contributed just as much, to the development of parliamentary institutions and customs as the Anglo-Norman *Magnum Concilium*, the feudal council of vassals, from which the English Parliament emanates (Tracy, 1990 p. 34). In the Netherlands, the estate meetings of the most important regions, Flanders, Brabant, Holland and Zeeland, were dominated by towns. These towns exerted constant influence on central policy, and acquired and retained quite considerable political autonomy. The deliberations of the Burgundian-Habsburg court councils were under constant pressure from these regional meetings that held the purse strings without which the monarchs were practically powerless. Repeatedly the court had to negotiate about tax demands, or 'aides'.

Already by the fifteenth century the estate meetings in Holland became involved in areas such as finance, defence, foreign policy, jurisdiction, trade and home policy (Kokken, 1991, p. 276). By the sixteenth century the range

FIGURE 4.2 Meeting of the States of Holland in Dort, 1572 (Atlas Van Stolk, Rotterdam)

of activities covered by them was broad. The sovereign's 'aides' and the protection of trade and industry, as well as the solicitude about their privileges, demanded most of their attention (Koopmans, 1990, p. 86).

Several decades prior to the Dutch Revolt, the ruler's constant need for money led to the substantial expansion of the fiscal effectiveness of the states (Holland in particular). The states enlarged their position of power through the collection of taxes, giving and guaranteeing loans and the financial organization of defence. Under the activities of the latter fell the mustering, conscripting and payment of troops, and the provision of naval armaments, intended to protect the herring fishing and sea trade in particular. The towns had various alternatives for collecting money: excise duties, usually on basic necessities such as grain and beer, issuing loans, tax levies on wealth, capital goods and inheritance, and particularly the sale of annuities, a type of loan which appeared in the fourteenth century in the northern Netherlands and by the fifteenth and sixteenth centuries covered a broad area. Because the states had always played an active role in the organization and the control of taxation and state debts, they could continue to lay down conditions regarding the activities of the monarch in such areas as war and peace, foreign policy and diplomatic interests.

Due to the relatively strong position of the towns and the absence of a powerful aristocracy in the Low Countries, the setting of conditions on the granting of 'aides' was in operation in the 'Dutch' principalities before it was the custom in the English parliament and it continued after it had practically ceased elsewhere in Europe. In the English parliament, where delegates had full authoritative power from the fifteenth century on, it was well into the seventeenth century before negotiations first took place about an 'aide' and only subsequently about other issues. The reverse order of handling business in the Netherlands enabled the states to have greater actual influence. Tracy (1990) states: 'The provincial states, already distinguished by the structure that gave urban magistrates an unusual degree of influence in affairs of state, had fiscal responsibilities that made them even more indispensable to their ruler than similar bodies were in other territories' (1990, p. 41).

The power struggle between the states and the monarch was preponderantly peaceful before the 1560s and 1570s, the time at which the monarch attempted to enforce central taxation and started heavily to persecute the Protestants. Until the Dutch Revolt the estates of the Netherlands (designated as the States-General by taking the French as an example) were called upon to attend a communal meeting on 160 occasions at irregular times; on average three times every two years. These meetings of the States-General were attended by approximately 60–80 nobles, clerical and municipal delegates. The attendance could swell to more than 300 at important, ceremonial events, such as the abdication of Charles V. The institute maintained an ad hoc character for the whole of the monarchical period. The states were only consulted by the monarchs in times of crisis, and only received invitations to attend meetings depending on the nature of the crisis. Towns were usually dominant with regard to the number of delegates attending (generally about two-thirds of the participants) as well as with regard to their behaviour during the negotiations with the ruler. Furthermore, their interests were greater. In contrast to the nobility and the clerics, they themselves had to realize the taxes demanded by the monarch and they were not in a position to pass these demands onto others.

Knights and high clergy were invited as personal title holders and they represented themselves. Towns, however, were invited as collectives. Delegates who had been appointed in the meetings of the town governments were dispatched with mandatory instructions. In general those delegated were the elite of the town government: mayors or burgomasters, sheriffs, the city fathers or treasurers. They were accompanied by several civil servants and town pensionaries for administrative purposes. These municipal delegates were in a predicament. They were under simultaneous pressure from the monarch and from their mandators, the town governors, and also indirectly the remainder of the urban population who could express their dissatisfaction with the level of taxation through resistance and revolt.

The power struggle between the court (concerned more with warfare and diplomatic affairs) and the towns (concerned more with the extension of trade and industry) caused a division: political centralization or regional autonomy. A recurring bone of contention was the 'rights' of the states to call and organize their own meetings.

Already, in 1464, the Duke of Burgundy clashed with the states in the first collective meeting of the States of the Low Countries. This came about because the towns in Holland invited several towns from other regions to attend a meeting to discuss the regency during the Duke's crusade on the same day as Philip the Good had invited his northern countries to meet to assess an 'aide'. After a great deal of discussion, the states decided to attend the Duke's general assembly. By so doing they reconciled the situation. Subsequently, Philip wrote to the towns that only he, as monarch and ruler, had the right to invite others to attend a meeting (Koenigsberger, 1971, p. 149). If the states had been permitted to meet at their own free will, their autonomy would have been assured. This was a situation the central court wished to avoid.

During the dynastic crisis precipitated by the death of Charles the Bold in 1477, the States and the court of Brussels resumed their argument over the right to meet. Under threat of an uprising, a provision was granted in the so-called Great Privileges to several states by Maria of Burgundy. This provision stipulated that the towns and states had the right to meet whenever, with whom, about what, and as often as they themselves wished. Although the Great Privileges were set aside by Philip the Fair in 1494, the provision granted remained as an ideological principle up to the time of the Republic. In illustration of this, the states called upon this principle during their disagreement with the ruling authorities in the 1550s and 1560s, and during the Dutch Revolt (Kokken, 1991, pp. 91–102).

A meeting about meetings: Erasmus' *Senatulus* as a model and the opportunity for women to meet[1]

Until the end of the sixteenth century, no manuals or regulations about meetings had been written. Little more than the important decisions were documented in meeting reports. For an impression of the meeting manners and problems of the estate parliaments, manuscripts such as *Senatulus*, one of Erasmus' *Colloquia* or dialogues can be used. They were first printed in 1529 and had an immediate and enduring popularity, which was partially due to the fact that they were used as a Latin textbook in schools.[2]

The title *Senatulus* is a diminutive for *senatus* and a play on words on *senaculum*, a council chamber for women or a women's senate. The word appears in the *Scriptores Historiae Augustae*, a classical source which must have been on Erasmus' mind when he wrote the dialogues (Thompson, 1965, p. 442). *Senatulus* could be translated as 'small senate of women'. In *Senatulus*,

Erasmus writes about a meeting in which five women discuss and make decisions about the establishment and organization of a women's parliament that had to present a balance to patriarchy. Hence the dialogue is a meeting about meeting.

Senatulus has so far almost only been treated as a satirical document about women's emancipation, in which Erasmus 'attacks her talkativeness, her lack of shame, her ostentation' (Singels, 1912, p. 79). A letter written by Erasmus, about the use of his *Colloquia*, is often considered responsible for this interpretation. In it he comments that, in *Senatulus*, he was planning to banter about a number of womanly weaknesses, but that he had not been in a position to accomplish this as another dialogue had demanded his attention.

Craig Thompson (1965) comments that *Senatulus* differs from previous satires about women through the unheard of notion of allowing women a say in their own clothing fashions. He refers to this notion as a 'gentleman's joke', by which Erasmus ridicules both the moralists, who criticized the standard of clothing, and the estate parliaments, which issued strict regulations about the way in which women should dress themselves (1965, pp. 441–2).

Senatulus could also be viewed from another point of view, one as yet unconsidered as far as I am aware. Erasmus could have intended it as a satire about the meeting standards of the ruling men, their quarrelsomeness, and their inept meeting manners. As such he has his main character comment, with undisguised contempt, that kings, princes and ruling clerics sometimes spent three months wrangling about the seating order before they began their deliberations. She continues:

> Monarchs have for years done little else than wage war; theologists, priests, and bishops never agree with each other. So many heads, so many words. A more than womanly fickleness prevails amongst them. No state lives in peace with another, no neighbour with his neighbour. If the reins of government were but once placed in our hands, then the condition of man (I am so convinced) would be a great deal better.

One possible reason why *Senatulus* has not previously been approached as a satirical comment on then prevalent meeting standards could be related to the limited attention shown to the development of meeting behaviour. As long as there is no clear-cut conception of the way in which meeting behaviour has changed in the long term, and it is tacitly understood that the contemporary way in which meetings are held has essentially always been that way, then *Senatulus* will not be regarded as a literary statement about the actual meeting problems that accompanied living within increasingly large and more differentiated political units.

FIGURE 4.3 Erasmus of Rotterdam by Hans Holbein (1523) (Oeffentliche Kunstammlung Basel, Kunstmuseum; photo: Oeffentliche Kunstammlung, Martin Bühler)

Erasmus was not the first to write about a women's dialogue in the form of a meeting. A Latin poem has been handed down from the second half of the twelfth century, known as *The Council of Remiremont*. This anonymous poem concerns a group of nuns from the convent in Remiremont, who held a 'council meeting on the topic of love' at the beginning of Spring. After the meeting had been opened by reading 'the gospel according to Ovidius' and love songs were sung by the participants, the question as to whether women should give preference to knights or monks regarding love was discussed. The poem tackled courtly love in the form of a parody about clerical meetings where men talked about religious affairs (Warren, 1907; French translation in C. Oulmont, 1974, pp. 100–7). Besides this 'love meeting' poem, more 'meeting poems' can be found in Latin literature from the period 1100–1400 AD. In these, a topical subject was dealt with in the form of a meeting, usually a judicial meeting where ultimately a man-to-man fight or a vision provided the outcome (Walther, 1920; Oulmont, 1974). In these poems, use was made of the existing customs and manners in meetings, but they are not the actual topic as in Erasmus' dialogue.

It is an open question as to whether Erasmus was inspired by this medieval genre. A more evident influence was the play *Ekklesiazusai*, or 'Women's meeting', by Aristophanes dating from 392 BC. In the play, the Athenian women, dressed as men, hold a meeting and establish a dictatorship by deciding that all property, and men, are henceforth communally owned. The work criticized all the political blunders committed by men and their stupidity, and was a fanatical type of proto-feminism.

More important than the question of the literary influences upon Erasmus, and the degree to which he elaborated upon classical literature, is the innovative way he worked out the notion of a women's meeting. As in the case of much of Erasmus' work, when reading *Senatulus*, one has the feeling of having one leg in the Middle Ages and the other in modern society (Elias, 1994, pp. 56–66). Many of the meeting manners which appear in the dialogue were borrowed by Erasmus from court councils, estate parliaments, meetings of town councils and other meetings. These manners had been orally transmitted from generation to generation. The way in which Erasmus presented this legacy of meeting traditions deviated widely from what had been the custom until then. He chose, wrote about and commented on the contemporary meeting manners from the understanding and sentiment that these manners were no longer entirely satisfactory; more emotional restraint was necessary adequately to discuss and decide about the future of a large number of people simultaneously.

Senatulus appeared in a period of increasing mutual dependence between people from different estates and during the development of a new aristocratic–bourgeois upper class. Within this class, every individual was exposed to a degree of mutual social control, previously unknown. People became more sensitive to others. In comparison to earlier, there developed a more differentiated feeling about what a person should or should not do to avoid offending or irritating others, and the axiom of giving no umbrage began to be stringently applied (according to Elias, 1994, p. 64).

These changes also manifested themselves in meetings and what was written about them. In 1538, the afore-mentioned twelfth-century 'love meeting' was rewritten and became a comedy, entitled *Weiber Reichstag*. In it, a political meeting form replaced the council meeting form. The work was greeted enthusiastically. The appearance and the success of literary works such as *Weiber Reichstag* are to be considered as manifestations of an acceleration in the development of meeting activities and behaviour. This acceleration coincided with a decrease in the inequality of power between the physically strong and the physically weak, and with an increase in the social pressure to consider others and to curb one's more violent tendencies. In court society it became possible for women from ruling royal houses to participate in high state functions and central meetings. In *Senatulus* it was proposed that more women should occupy more governmental functions; at least those functions for which it was unnecessary to bear arms and which could be practised within the protective walls of a town.

Senatulus offers insight into a number of the problems and manners of meeting during the transition from a society dominated by warriors and priests to one governed by courtiers and aristocrats. The dialogue consists of a number of episodes. These coincide with the stages that existed in a sixteenth-century Burgundian court council meeting:

- introduction;
- discussion and decision making;
- implementation of decisions and closing of the meeting.

It is remarkable that hardly any distinction was made between discussing and deciding.[3] The monarchs strove either to keep any potential opponents from court meetings or to keep them well under control. Considering that the distinction between discussing and deciding is directly related to the prevention of differences of opinion, it is understandable that often no distinction could be made between these activities in the meetings of the court councils under the control of the monarchs. This distinction is mainly unclear in this particular piece by Erasmus.

The first stage of *Senatulus* comprises a word of welcome by Cornelia and an introduction in which she formulates the problem; women neither hold nor attend meetings. She goes on to suggest a solution to the problem by establishing a women's council. In the second stage, the practical problems regarding the composition and the organization of the women's council are considered: participation, use of language, seating arrangements, means of voting, maintenance of order, confidentiality of decisions and themes or items on the agenda. Cornelia closes the meeting with a brief speech in which she reiterates the most important points and makes a number of comments related to the settling of an agenda, the chairmanship, and the taking down of the minutes. Finally, she calls those present for genuine, not preparatory, deliberations.

The discussion that the five ladies hold about the composition and mode of operation of the women's council (the second and third stages) provides additional insight into the functioning of estate parliaments. Meetings like those held by the States of Holland, the Burgundian States-General, the English parliament and many other comparable meetings in Europe provided the blueprint for Erasmus' women's council, as shall be apparent in the forthcoming section. *Senatulus* is useful as a guideline for the investigation of the manners and problems of estate parliaments. Although Erasmus probably never, or perhaps but infrequently, attended such meetings, it is clear from his writing that he was well informed. Many of the meeting manners which are mentioned in *Senatulus* were undecided in the fifteenth and sixteenth centuries, and have led to quarrels and discussions between monarchs, states and members of the states.

Invitation and participation

It was customary for the delegates of estate meetings to put up at an inn the evening prior to the meeting. This not only made possible informal pre-discussion and sounding out of opinions, but enabled the meeting to commence at seven or eight o'clock the following morning, allowing optimal use of the daylight hours. Cornelia's remark, 'you have gathered together here today en masse and without tarrying' was no idle comment. Meetings frequently had to be postponed or cancelled due to excessive absenteeism or lateness. In this, apart from inadequate transportation and highway connections, tactical manoeuvres by the estates and the court's invitation policy played a part. The monarch, stadholder or his council usually had the invitations delivered two weeks before the meeting. This written invitation was in fact an order bearing reference to the monarch's mandate and it contained the most important 'points of convening'.[4]

Exactly which of the towns were invited for the meetings of the States of Holland was not fixed. Participation varied greatly, from two to about forty towns, but usually fewer than ten. However, the six largest towns tended to monopolize participation. If those summoned expected unwelcome decisions to be taken, they did not attend (absenteeism was simpler than dissension). Likewise, they remained absent if topics which did not concern them were to be handled. Furthermore, participation did not come cheaply. Mainly it was financed by the participants themselves. Regarding absenteeism from the meetings of the States of Holland and the States-General, in the latter half of the fifteenth century, Kokken (1991) remarked:

> Besides financial reasons, which mainly would have applied to small towns and individual members of the knighthood, it was generally opportunistic and tactical considerations which played a decisive role. (1991, p. 122)

Absenteeism remained high even when the ruler set heavy penalties for non-attendance, such as the withdrawal of privileges, the forfeiting of loans, and monetary fines; punishments which were never implemented anyway (*ibid.*, p. 123).

In general in the sixteenth century, only the towns of Dort, Haarlem, Delft, Leiden, Amsterdam and Gouda participated. Also attendant were members of the knighthood, who were supposed to represent the countryside and the smaller towns (Kokken, 1991, pp. 102–25). In exceptional circumstances, namely times of war, the smaller towns were invited to enable decisions with a 'broader mandate' to be made. In Flanders, a hundred years previously, the towns of Ghent, Bruges and Ieper had a similar monopoly position. Likewise, with the summons to the meetings of the States-General, the court initially followed no set rule for determining which regions should be invited to the assessment of an 'aide'. Moreover, those invited often failed to appear.

At all sorts of meetings, absenteeism and unpunctuality were often a problem. The regulations and penalties issued by the guilds have already been mentioned. Additionally, meetings of the city councils frequently set penalties for non-appearance and lateness. In 1482, for instance, the meeting of the city council of Leiden determined that members of the judiciary and the city fathers who failed to attend had to pay a fine and that, naturally, they should receive no attendance money. Given the considerable number of occasions on which such fines were set, it has to be presumed that they had little effect in practice. In the northern Netherlands, the problem of absenteeism was less acute after the states had developed into the highest political entity. With economic growth and an increase in the number of merchants and entrepreneurs living off their investments, there were more people prepared and in a position to fulfil the (honorary) governmental functions. In the seventeenth century, a 'meeting estate' emerged, which increasingly distinguished itself in lifestyle, means of existence and education from the merchant and entrepreneurial groups.

The ranking order of seating arrangements

From the end of the fifteenth century, the meetings of the States of Holland were mainly held in The Hague. If necessary, the twenty to forty participants were seated at table for their discussions. In the meetings of the States-General, which in the long term were held mainly in Brussels, the participants were regionally grouped and seated on benches along the walls and in the middle of the meeting chamber. The grouping differed from what was the custom in France, where centralization had taken place earlier; here members were grouped according to the estate they represented. The monarch and the remaining courtiers were seated on a podium on one side of the chamber.

Two lengthy passages in *Senatulus* tackle the question of who should participate in the women's council and in which order they should be seated. The criteria employed by the five ladies were: civil status, parenthood, age and social standing. These criteria are allusions to the standards which determined the seating arrangements of the estate meetings of the males. Usually the nobility was seated before the townsmen and peasants, and the clergy before the nobility. Within the nobility and clergy, possession of the highest rank or prestige gave precedence above civil status. For towns, a ranking order of reputed age or taxable wealth was in operation. Between persons within the individual estates, age was the decisive factor, after one's status and the ranking position of the town one was representing. However, both the interpretation and the application of these criteria proved to be very complicated.

The ranking order of the seating arrangements was frequently disputed which held up or prevented the meeting. For instance, in the early part of the sixteenth century, the aristocracy and the towns participating in the German *Reichstag* quarrelled incessantly about the seating arrangement. This resulted in 1529, in a violent confrontation between the representatives of various towns (Oestreich, 1972, pp. 225–6). In Spain, the towns of Toledo and Burgos fought each other extensively to achieve precedence in parliament, the *Cortes*. In 1506 it erupted into a fracas where the representatives from each town screamed so loud and long at each other and, by rendering each other's utterances incomprehensible, the sitting had to be abandoned (Meyers, 1975, p. 62). Sometimes problems arose with the ranking order at the meetings of town governments as well. For example, in Amsterdam in the sixteenth, and even the seventeenth century, the town government more than once wrestled with the question of who should take precedence in the meetings or committees of the city councils': the ruling sheriffs or the ex-mayors (Bontemantel, 1897, Part I, pp. 249–54; Part II, p. 32).

The quarrels about the order of summoning to a meeting and the seating arrangements therein can be largely explained by the fact that this ranking order also determined the order of talking and deciding. Whoever was seated first, spoke first, voted first, and set the mood of the meeting. Delegates were often instructed to take the same stance as those towns preceding them. Such politics stem from 'the understanding that unity strengthened the position of the states against the ruling authorities and, on the other hand, were caused by the fear that, by taking a disagreeable minority stance, they would incur the displeasure of the ruling authorities' (Kokken, 1991, p. 210).

In 1430 and 1508 Flanders and Brabant argued for the right to be seated and to speak first in a meeting of the States–General. As a dukedom, Brabant enjoyed priority, and demanded that their spokesman, the Pensionary of Brussels, should always be the first speaker of the states' meetings, everywhere. Flanders demanded the continuation of the custom in which their spokesman, the Pensionary of Ghent, should be the first speaker when the meetings of the States-General took place in their county. After an investigation instigated by the governess, the latter demand was accepted as the rule (Wellens, 1974, pp. 115–47).

The disputes about rank order in meetings were actually about opinion leadership. In estate society where power differences were relatively large, the relationships between people had a more personal character, and feelings towards each other had a more absolute character than in the present 'democratic' society. People were strongly inclined to consider each other as either friend or enemy. Differences in opinion, even 'businesslike' differences, would easily be seen as some kind of betrayal, while unanimity was interpreted as loyalty. Therefore, the first speaker not only set the tone, but to a certain extent established a claim on the meeting.

In the meetings of the states, nobody wanted to miss the opportunity to influence as many as possible by casting their vote as early as possible. The spokesman from the first town spoke first when each individual envoy had to announce his mandate. The other delegates had to announce their mandate to him. The position of the first, eldest and highest member to be summoned had a decisive influence on the stance of his subordinates. In actuality, the first town had the determining vote at its disposal. In the plenary estate meetings, when members of the clergy and nobility were present, these were allowed to speak and vote before the towns. Frequently, the significance attached to their opinions through this opportunity was out of proportion to their fiscal contribution (Blockmans, 1978, p. 247; Oestreich, 1972, p. 225).

Opening

Cornelia's opening words in *Senatulus*, 'Everything that is good, fortunate, and useful for this group and the entire community of women, we wish for you' is a paraphrase of a saying from ancient Rome. This saying was used in a meeting or another gathering in order to get the public's attention. That God is invoked only in the second sentence is not only typical of Erasmus' secular, civilian outlook, but it also illustrates the clergy's loss of function in the late Middle Ages. With the establishment of court society, the role of the bishops and priests became less prominent in secular meetings. In the sixteenth century, in the meetings of many (regional) estate parliaments, including those of Holland and Flanders, representatives of the clergy were no longer present. For the opening of a meeting, religious practices were less in evidence, less than in the thirteenth century for example. At that time the General Prior of the Dominicans, Humbertus Romanus, published a document entitled *De Eruditione Praedicatorum* in which he evoked his fellow brothers to preach at the start of each parliamentary session (Kluxen, 1983, p. 19). That Erasmus makes no mention of 'the three security questions' (mentioned in Chapter 3) reflects the changed circumstances. As society gradually pacified, these questions were omitted more frequently, particularly in the meetings of the court councils called by the monarch and the estate parliaments.

Generally, the meetings of the States of Holland began with a few introductory words from the governor or one of his representatives. He then proceeded to enlarge upon the letter of invitation in which the topics for discussion were mentioned. In meetings in which no court representative was present, this duty was fulfilled by a delegate from one of the towns, or by the civil servant appointed by the states in 1480 to assist them with executive duties.

The openings of meetings of the States-General were more ceremonial and usually distinguished by a brief speech by the monarch, his consort, or another highly placed member of court. Whoever opened the meeting also 'chaired' it: that is, he decided about the opening, adjournment and closing of the meeting. Following the opening words, the court representative (usually the chancellor) delivered a lengthy speech covering in detail the reason for the meeting, usually the matter of an 'aide'. Gradually this introductory speech or 'proposal' acquired a more definite character. One such acquisition was explicit reference to external military threats.

Ways of speaking and deciding

Ways of speaking and deciding were remarked upon several times in *Senatulus*. The ladies were apparently in agreement about the following four points:

- personal remarks should be avoided;
- decisions (by majority) should to be taken by spoken vote, and noted by clerks to avoid womanly chattering in the women's council;
- in order to prevent squabbling, no one should be permitted to speak out of turn, and otherwise should be punished by exclusion;
- whoever communicates council business to outsiders should be given a three-day oath of silence.

The meeting problems that the ladies hoped to prevent or solve with these regulations could be observed in the history of the estate meetings.

In the estate parliaments there were few discussions or deliberations as long as the delegates were strictly obliged to adhere to their mandates. As more freedom could be adopted by the delegates with respect to their mandators there was more room for discussion, and there was also a sharper distinction between decision making and discussing. Room for discussion was greater in the meetings of the States of Holland than in the meetings of the States-

General. Following the clarification of the 'specified points', the delegates expressed their viewpoints, one at a time, in the relevant order of rank. These points of view were then compared and the decisions made. In all affairs, except those concerned with the assessment of 'aides', decisions could be taken by 'outvoting', that is by majority. One way of avoiding being outvoted was to fail to appear. In practice, this was rather pointless, as the ruling authority generally acted as though the absentees had voted with the majority. More than once the states clashed with the ruling authorities about this. These disagreements nearly always involved the infringement of the custom that those opposing the ballot about contributions or taxation need not adhere to the majority position (Kokken, 1991, pp. 211–12).

Given that the ballot took place in hierarchical order and that the town governments tended to ally with the opinions of higher ranking towns, it can be said that (lacking facts to the contrary), in the fifteenth century, the States of Holland did not decide by statistical majority, as was already the usual practice in many of the town government meetings. In all probability, the mandates were less likely to be counted than assessed; this assessment was based roughly on the fiscal capacity of the participants. Therefore, the large towns had the determining vote. Later, in the sixteenth century, when generally only the six main towns and the knighthood met and everyone had but one vote, the statistical application of the majority regulation came into vogue.

The meetings of the States–General functioned more as an arena exclusively for the presentation of viewpoints than did the meetings of the States of Holland. The delegates could neither say nor do much without first consulting their mandators. The nature and the scope of the municipal mandates varied from meeting to meeting, but were generally described in such detail that meetings were often adjourned or postponed. On frequent occasions, the court insisted that the towns granted their delegates a somewhat wider warrant. But this had little effect. Only in obvious crises did delegates deviate from the procedure of following their strict mandate and, when necessary, consulting their mandators.

After the chancellor's introductory speech the delegates asked permission to retire for regional discussions. After several days, they would return to inform the monarch of the results of their consultations. Generally they returned to request the monarch's permission to go to their mandators and ask for a less compulsory mandate. Prior to the monarch agreeing to an adjournment, a date would be set as to when the sitting would be resumed. This procedure would be repeated until the court and the states had reached an agreement, even if this took weeks or months.

In principle, each delegation decided only about its own particular share of the 'aide'. The decisions of the various delegations could not commit the other delegations to anything. Nevertheless, the monarch compelled both the absentee and the intransigent estates to pay their share of the taxation. The court pressed for the application of the majority regulation only when it was advantageous to itself. Majority decisions first appeared in parliaments, such as the English parliament, where the members had a general mandate to vote as they saw fit on whatever issues might arise. In England granting of full power to deputies can be documented as early as 1295 (Tracy, 1990, p. 34).

In other European estate parliaments the pressure was great for an unanimous decision. Concerning the application of the unanimity regulation in the *Cortes* of Valencia, Meyers (1975) wrote: 'We find a rule of unanimity for decisions in the "brazo" or estate of nobles in the Cortes of Valencia; on at least one occasion, in 1645, unanimity was reached there by throwing out a recalcitrant member into the street and then proceeding to a vote' (1975, p. 32).

In respect of the way of discussing and voting, the position of both the court and the states was always equivocal. The states, which considered their regional autonomy to be of paramount importance, were not exactly enthusiastic about discussions and deliberations. In actual practice, they were compelled to talk with each other in order to be able to make compromises about the 'aides'. From the court's point of view, public deliberations during the meetings meant that decisions could be made more speedily. Moreover, a delegation that was persuaded to vote for a court proposition could act as an example for another. However, joint discussions could also be risky; one of the larger and more powerful states could reject the monarch's proposition and by so doing set a bad example. In 1473 Charles the Bold forbade joint discussions. Charles V feared them so much that he much preferred not to summon any meetings of the States-General. Court attempts to negotiate separately with the towns from the regions were totally rejected by these towns. However, on one occasion, in 1557, the monarch did succeed in persuading several states to send delegates with a free mandate. The meeting was intended to discuss the reorganization of the realm's deplorable financial situation, but the actual proceedings ended up not suiting the court. The delegates entered into discussions with each other and this resulted in an extensive list of grievances and requests to which the monarch was obliged to acquiesce in exchange for the granting of the 'aide'.

During the meetings, there was constant coming and going of delegates, which meant that the monarch, or his representative, had to grant an adjournment to allow the delegates the opportunity to deliberate with their mandators, who were strongly committed to not allowing taxes to be too high and certainly not permanent. One particular event, in 1476, illustrates the court's frequent irritation with compulsory mandates. When the delegates stubbornly refused to grant an 'aide' without consultations, the chancellor asked sarcastically whether the delegates had had similar strict instructions regarding their drinking habits. The irritated response was: '*Allez, allez, dites ce que vous voulez, l'on vous respondra ce que l'on vouldra avoir repondu.'* (Koenigsberger, 1971, p. 147). This anecdote focuses attention on the ceremonial remnant of the toasts by which decisions were ratified in older times. It was the custom in the meetings of the states that the host town's 'upper bailiff' served 'attendance wines', or offered every participating town a certain amount of wine (Prevenier, 1961, pp. 136–7; Kokken, 1991, pp. 206–7).

With the development of larger and more stable survival units, and the increase of interdependence within, an increased pressure can be observed towards milder ways of expressing any strong feelings towards each other in the unit's meetings. People were forced to use more impersonal terms when discussing their mutual relations. With this, there grew the necessity for concepts indicating the figuration of those people about whom, and in the name of whom, people spoke and decided about. For instance, throughout the fifteenth century, in the meetings of the towns and the States of Holland, terms such as 'the common land' and 'body' appeared to designate the inhabitants of Holland and that group of people who made binding decisions in their name. From an indication for a local entity as distinct from other local entities, the concept of 'body' developed into a concept which could be used to refer to the people represented by the States of Holland. As the states had to secure joint loans more frequently for collective warfare, the development of this concept was greatly enhanced.[5]

Huizinga (1982) remarked that even courtiers, at the highest level of integration of the Burgundian realm, sought a more impersonal nomenclature for the state in the process of formation. Designations such as 'the Burgundian party' (originating during the struggle against the French crown, in which John the Fearless was 'treacherously' murdered on the Montereau bridge) were replaced by somewhat vague, but impersonal, nomenclatures as 'hither lands'. The Burgundian succession states (as distinct from France and England) were initially designated by this name. The collection of countries belonging to the Burgundian dukes never had an unequivocal, definite name, as a total entity; not even when the Burgundian lands, with the exception of actual Burgundy itself (which became part of the French kingdom), were placed under the authority of the royal house of Habsburg (Huizinga, 1982, pp. 53 f.).

Confidentialities

It cannot be inferred from sources available whether disputes and brawls occurred between delegates during the meetings of the States of Holland and the States-General in the period of the monarchy. Very little is known about the proceedings of the meetings of the states as no formal notes were taken.

Only some lists of decisions and delegates' reports, written for the benefit of their mandators, are available. The notes of the meetings of the states, taken by the court, have been lost. The scarcity of written sources is partially due to the obligation to confidentiality, which was in force at that time for all political meetings. Initially this can be understood as being due to the vulnerability of internal and external security, and the concern for the misuse of information by both home and foreign enemies. In consideration of the rather permanent state of war, people were anxious that there were no leaks of the fiscal and military details and plans that had been discussed in the meetings of the states.

The maintenance of confidentiality was practically impossible, because the participant composition of meetings of the states continuously changed and the participants were obliged to both their charges and to consultations with their mandators. In addition, as no credentials had to be shown, as was usual in France, those not invited could mingle among participants in the meetings of the states. This was reason enough for the monarch to withhold information during meetings. The argument motivating Charles V's refusal to discuss 'state secrets' in the meetings of the states in 1545 was that 'in the meetings appear people who have not been summoned' (Gilissen, 1965, p. 290).

In *Senatulus*, a glimpse of yet another aspect of the confidentiality obligation was conceded by Erasmus. The fact that this obligation, and the regulation intended to prevent squabbling, were mentioned in unison indicates a connection between the two. There are many indications that the dominant groups endeavoured to keep their differences of opinion and discussions out of earshot of the 'common folk' from fear of taking sides, public fighting, and revolt. This topic is comprehensively covered in Chapter 5.

Agenda, chairman, minutes

At the end of Erasmus's dialogue, Cornelia calls upon those present to consider possible subjects for meetings and proposes the appointment of four clerks and two chairwomen. Again, Erasmus' clear and visionary observation of meeting behaviour is demonstrated by his comments. Meeting manners and customs, such as the appointment of a chairman and taking minutes (the reasons for which appear self-evident nowadays) were by no means apparent at the beginning of the sixteenth century. On the basis of changes in the ways of compiling agenda, the chairmanship and taking minutes, it is possible to draw up a picture of the meetings of estate parliaments.

As mentioned earlier, a written invitation to a meeting usually contained one or more 'points of convening'. These points were not a clear-cut agenda of the topics pending consideration, but were rather little more than an indication of the main points needed to be covered during the meeting.

In his study of the meetings of Holland during the last quarter of the fifteenth century, Kokken (1991) concludes that the talking began with a discussion of what appeared to be the most important subject. Afterwards, the remaining subjects were discussed in an arbitrary order. These subjects were partially advanced by delegates for the first time during the meeting. Decisions were neither formally noted nor centrally registered (Kokken, 1991, pp. 213–15). The setting out of agendas and handling them point by point, the taking of minutes and the registering of decisions became prevalent together with the development of a less ambiguous chairmanship and an official secretariat.

It cannot be discerned from available sources, how, or even whether, the chairmanship in fifteenth-century meetings in Holland was organized, or what its precise function was. Kokken (1991) surmises that the chairmanship was not tied to a particular person or function but, depending on the nature of meeting, to the host town, to a representative of the sovereign, to the 'first' town or the oldest aristocrat, or to the person who had called the meeting (1991, p. 209). Likewise, the chairman's function in the fifteenth century is unclear. Possibly the chairman took decisions about the commencement, adjournment and closing of a meeting, and supervised the adherence to the relatively few prevailing regulations, of which one of the most important was the ranking order of taking seats and speaking. Those tasks, which were later part of the chairman's function, such as the propounding of the topics to be discussed and the recording of votes, were usually performed by others. In sixteenth-century meetings in Holland, all these tasks were concentrated in the hands of one person, the government attorney. This function was instituted in 1480 by the towns to guarantee the privileges conceded to them by the Court of Holland in The Hague.

Initially the government attorney was a juridical councillor who kept a register of the resolutions and national matters, signed warrants, investigated and balanced state accounts and, as spokesman for the states, appeared in meeting of the States-General, in legal proceedings and in other meetings. As a result of his functions, his unlimited term of appointment, and his permanent presence in the meetings of the states and their interim commissions, the government attorney became the key figure of the states. He became more frequently referred to as Grand Pensionary. His position of power was reinforced by several conditions in his brief which were adopted by the states in the sixteenth century. For instance, the prohibition to hold other office except that of Pensionary of the knighthood and thus enabling him to devote all his time to the states; the obligation to be established in The Hague, considered as neutral territory sufficiently removed from the six main towns; and the maintenance of neutrality regarding differences of opinion between state members. The Grand Pensionary was assisted by a number of clerks to carry out his duties. They had the task, among others, of delivering copies of the resolutions to the delegates if they so desired (Koopmans, 1990, p. 94).

In the sixteenth century, the function of the Grand Pensionary developed from secretary to president of the meeting. This development has occurred elsewhere, for example, in communist parties where the secretary–general came to fill the highest position because of his familiarity with the party organization. As the function of the Grand Pensionary changed, the reporting improved, and the agenda was shaped and dealt with, more and more regarding his own perception. 'Officially the government attorney "only" had to chair the meeting and bring out a report of the transactions. In practice, this position allowed him the opportunity to raise certain matters, to postulate his own ideas and to influence the decision making' (Koopmans, 1990, p. 100).

The States-General were more loosely organized in comparison to the States of Holland. Throughout the entire period of sovereign rule, they never had their own government registry at their disposal, their own administration or their own archives. The chairmanship of their meetings was occupied by the monarch or a highly placed court representative. No reports were made – the participants maintained their own records for the benefit of their mandators (Van de Kieft, 1964, p. 15).

Meeting regulations

There was little structure in the meetings of states. Frequently, the starting time was postponed, and some delegates were either absent, too late in arriving or left the meeting early. As a result of this, and through the many adjournments caused by delegates adopting the procedure of persevering with their mandates and, on reaching an impasse, consulting their mandators, there was a constant shuttling of delegates.

Compared to meetings of the states, the meetings of the court council were more structured. Contrary to the states, the court councils met at fixed times and places, and had their own meeting area at their disposal. However, both types of meeting were still largely determined by traditional rules and by the personal decisions of the monarchs and other powerful people. The development and the deployment of impersonal meeting rules remained limited as long as the central co-ordinating functions of a state continued to be fulfilled by a monarch and his court council.

Prior to the Dutch Revolt, the States of Holland had only spoken a few times about the course of their meetings and the States-General not at all, as far as can be ascertained. In 1555 the delegates from Holland deliberated the high costs of the meetings, of which too many needed to be held because the nobility often left the meetings too early. Four years later it was determined that state members who did not behave according to agreement, and left a meeting before all business was complete, were charged a fine. It became increasingly the case that the level of meeting costs provided a powerful stimulus to find more efficient ways of conducting a meeting. In 1563, because the towns considered that the agendas were handled too slowly, and the numerous meetings left them with unnecessarily high costs, the Grand Pensionary was given the assignment to draft some articles 'for the advantage of the meetings'. The outcome was discussed by the states at the next meeting, but it remains unknown (Koopmans, 1990, p. 90). Before the Revolt, meetings were relatively informal and ad hoc, without many fixed procedures or clearly determined rules. There were no regulations for the meetings of the states. The Grand Pensionary's brief had to provide the order – he played a large part in the organization of meetings (Koopmans, 1990, p. 114).

In the second half of the sixteenth century, during the Reformation, more attention was paid to the regulation of meetings. In several European countries, including Germany, England and the Netherlands, the first documents appeared in which it was set down how the estate representatives met or should meet.

After the German realm had been divided into independent Catholic and Protestant monarchies in 1569, the archbishop of Mainz, as government chancellor, provided a first *Extended message as to how the Reichstag is usually held*. Subsequently more works appeared concerning the organization of the German *Reichstag* (Oestreich, 1972, p. 219). With the disintegration of the German realm, the *Reichstag* lost much of its significance.

Likewise, at around this time, the rules of behaviour in the English parliament were first documented. The initial outlines were written in the latter half of the sixteenth century by former parliamentarians. The oldest treatise concerning parliamentary rules of behaviour was written between 1562 and 1566 by Sir Thomas Smith, but was only published posthumously in 1583 as part of an extensive work about English government. The rules were relatively general and personally phrased (May, 1983, p. 211). The development of the meeting rules of the English parliament reached a peak in the first half of the seventeenth century, when parliament, under pressure from Puritan opposition, took greater distance from the king, and demanded the power of decisions over taxation and the military.

In 1689 Petyt published a manual, having made use of 35 previous works about the same subject. From Petyt's book, an impression can be drawn about changes in the meeting patterns of the English parliament in the sixteenth and seventeenth centuries. In 1581 it was determined that only one subject at a time could be dealt with. In 1592 it was ruled that a member wishing to speak against the last member to speak had priority over a member who wished to support the previous speaker. In 1604 a rule was applied by which the chairman also enquired about the negative votes. Also in 1604 it was determined that the chairman should take care that no personal attacks occurred, and that 'no reviling or nipping words must be used'. In 1610 it became established that a chairman could remove the privilege of speaking from a member who spoke in a shameless manner, estimated by the degree of 'hissing' and 'spitting' in the meeting chamber. In 1640 it was decided that a subject which, during the debate, appeared to consist of two parts, must be handled in two parts (Robert's *Rules of Order*, 1970 [1876], p. xxxi). Many of these old rules of practice are still in use today, and as to their function Erskine May wrote:

> The principal common characteristic of the rules of practice was to provide ample opportunity for debate and for initiative in choosing subjects for debate, and ample safeguards against business being taken without due notice so that decisions could not be reached without opportunities for full consideration being given. (1983, p. 211)

In Part III it will become evident that the period during the Dutch Revolt was also the period in which more impersonal and more detailed meeting rules were instituted in the Netherlands.

PART III

MEETINGS DURING THE TRANSITION FROM AN AGRARIAN TO AN INDUSTRIAL SOCIETY

State formation, Protestantism and disciplining

In the state formation processes in Europe from about 900 AD onwards, various mainstreams, with accompanying meeting traditions, can be observed.[1] In the areas where towns were dominant from an early period, in the districts where landowners were in control, and in the places where towns and large landowners more or less held each other in balance, state organizations existed which differed from each other in the ways in which the central co-ordinating functions were fulfilled and the central meetings were held.

In countries such as Russia and Hungary, where militarized landowners and the high clergy dominated a large rural population of farmers, the authority of the monarchs was but nominal. Actual power was in the hands of the regional lords who, in times of serious crises, were called to meet by the monarch, whose function was predominantly that of army commander. In these meetings only propositions about the main options could be voiced, and neither detailed consultations, nor executive functions were possible. The 'states' which dominated Europe until about 1400 were organized along these lines.

Another type of state organization came into being in those regions where trade and industry blossomed at an early stage and the populations became concentrated in towns. In these early urbanized regions, frequent informal meetings of representatives of relatively autonomous towns replaced the military 'control from above', and the incidental, mass-scale, and preponderantly ritualized meetings of bishops and nobles. The use of mercenaries to wage war replaced the traditional ways which had used conscripted vassals and farmers. The town dwellers' dependence upon food and raw materials from outside, and the sale of merchandise outside the region, compelled them to form all sorts of relationships with home and foreign authorities. (A town with a population of about 20,000 consumed the surplus of 150 villages.) For a considerable period, these contacts could develop independently from the monarch, who initially had little to contribute to these activities. The town governments of merchants and entrepreneurs were obliged constantly and concomitantly to hold meetings in different places at home and abroad so as to maintain their numerous commercial, diplomatic and legal relationships. Early examples of this type of organization can be seen in the North Italian city-states of the late Middle Ages, the North German Hansa towns, and in Flanders in the fourteenth and fifteenth centuries. They had the nature of 'constitutional republics'; characterized by urban or municipal independence, a high level of commercial development, and a 'rising' bourgeoisie. In the sixteenth and seventeenth centuries, these forms of organization reached a provisional peak with the development of 'decentralized or federally organized states, which combined effective government on the municipal and local level with parliamentary sovereignty at the centre' (Gorski, 1993, p. 272). Examples include Switzerland and the Dutch Republic.

In the United Kingdom, a related political model developed after the English Civil War from 1640 to 1660. In the subsequent two centuries this organization developed into a model example of a third type of state formation, a type that was particularly manifest in regions where there were both large rural and urban populations, for example Prussia and France. Initially, in these countries, co-ordinating functions were carried out in court and parliamentary meetings, which were comprised of the elite of both the nobility and the bourgeoisie. By strategically adjusting his stand, the central monarch could maintain a certain balance between these two groups. The phenomenon has been termed the 'royal mechanism' by Elias (1994, pp. 390–420). Monarchs succeeded in strengthening their position of power when they played rival interest groups off against each other, and so kept an even balance of power between these groups by placing their own weight in the balance. In France, for example, the rivalry between the central court and estate representatives heightened and, eventually, the central court succeeded in extending its opportunity for exerting power to the cost of the parliaments, which were summoned less frequently or not at all. The 'royal mechanism' did not work, or worked less effectively, if only one social class or group dominated, such as the gentry in England, or if various interest groups under the banner of the Reformation put on a united front against the monarch and were supported by foreign intervention (Koenigsberger, 1977, p. 314). In regions with both large rural and urban populations, after the 'royal mechanism' was ruptured and bourgeois groups gained the upper hand, a national state organization developed which, led by the United Kingdom, became the most dominant type within the complex of the European states in the nineteenth and twentieth centuries.

In the following two chapters the central meetings which took place during the formation and stabilization of the Dutch Republic are reviewed. This

A meeting of the German *Reichstag* presided over by Emperor Charles V, 1530
(J. L. Charmet)

Republic can be regarded largely as the unintended and unanticipated result of a complex struggle between various social interest groups who lent support to each other and who strove on the basis of gaining short-term advantages. Not one of the contending groups was in a position to procure a complete picture of the battleground, let alone to be in control of it. That a new state eventually unfolded, governed by representatives of the urban patriciate, was neither anticipated nor planned by anyone (Goudsblom, 1967, pp. 12–15).

The urban patriciate had power unexpectedly and unwillingly placed in its hands and the initial performance was somewhat hesitant. The uncertain performance was related to the fact that, at that time, government by civilians was unheard of and, therefore, unimaginable. For instance, the states first sought an appropriate representative of the upper aristocracy who could achieve military success in their battle against Spain and who could help suppress possible uprisings of the lower urban classes. On two separate occasions the States-General designated a 'successor' to Philip II: in 1583, Francis Hercules, the Duke of Anjou, and in 1586, the Earl of Leicester. But twice the elected monarch sought (unsuccessfully) to limit the power of the States-General by military means. Thereafter the administrators of the States-

General tacitly opted to let the throne stand vacant. In 1584 the vacuum of power at the centre was further exacerbated by the assassination of William of Orange. The patriciate was forced to govern the developing state. In the social power game between representatives of the upper aristocracy, the clergy, the provincial nobility, the urban bourgeoisie and the lower classes, the patriciate took a stance which determined its performance until long after the Dutch Revolt.[2] The increase in social tensions and conflicts during the reign of Philip II forced the upper class into a choice between the Catholic king, and a Protestant–military alliance of the lower aristocracy and the urban middle and lower classes. However, the patriciate was not in a position to enforce any decision as it had no weapons at its disposal. The social unrest, stimulated by the persecution of heretics and the Inquisition, provided the patriciate with an important reason eventually to opt for the insurgents.

The first manifestation of the increasing social tensions was the protest by the military nobility against the terminating of their role as the monarch's main advisor. In 1566 a section of the population demonstrated its dis-satisfaction with an outburst of iconoclastic fury: the 'Breaking of the Images'. The consequent intensification of the persecution of heretics forced the Protestants into mounting armed resistance. Gradually, the lower aristocracy affiliated itself to this movement. Of the higher aristocracy, William of Orange (then already known by his meeting nickname William the Silent) was one of the first and one of the few who affiliated himself to the reformers and the armed insurgents, the 'Beggars'. The town governments followed hesitantly. The tax reforms intended to provide the government with a fixed source of income without the mediation of the towns had, until then, turned many towns against the court, though it did not mean that they immediately took the side of the armed resisters. The impasse was broken by the military successes of the 'Sea-Beggars'. In the period from 1572 to 1578 the patricians of Holland, and later those of Flanders and Brabant, moved actively to support the opposition. This was a consequence of pressure exerted by the townsfolk, but sometimes it only occurred after the besieging and conquering of the town by the Beggars. Then the obstinate Catholic town governors were replaced by those more disposed to the reformers.

In around 1585 a new situation came into being in the Low Countries. Parts of the southern Netherlands had remained loyal to the monarch, which was due, in part, to the reconquering by the king's troops of some areas controlled by the Beggars. The states of the northern Netherlands declared that the Spanish king, Philip II, had forfeited sovereignty over the Low Countries and claimed that they were themselves in possession of sovereignty. Coopmans (1983) has pointed out that the declaration by the states of 'The Act of Abjuration' in 1581 was the first of a set of three comparable declarations, the other two being the English 'Charge against the King Charles Stuart' in 1649, and the North American 'Declaration of Independence' in

1776. These declarations showed 'striking resemblances' in their construction and content (Coopmans, 1983, p. 565). They all begin with the old doctrine of 'a monarch who is a tyrant, may be dethroned by the people'. Subsequently, the concrete grievances against the king were summarized, after which the right of secession was claimed and, finally, the actual process of secession was enacted. In the English case, the king was sentenced to death.

The parallels between the Dutch Revolt (1566–1585) and later political revolutions have been pointed out frequently. Van Gelder (1960) compared the course of events during the Dutch Revolution with those that took place during the English Civil War. This might seem odd, if one thinks that the Dutch Revolt only was a war against a foreign power, while the English Revolution was an internal or civil war. It is not that simple. There were no clearly limited, national states then. The Dutch revolted against their own king, who happened also to be king of Spain. Only after the abjuration did the armed conflict gradually acquire the form of an outward war. In both the Dutch and the English cases, the drama experienced an initial peak with a religious uprising: the 'Breaking of the Images' in the Netherlands, and the disturbances directed against the reformations by Laud in Edinburgh. In both cases, this was the start of comparable battles fought by similar sides: the Dutch states and the English parliament revolted against the church and the monarchy in order to obtain participation in the government, and in a more radical Protestant reformation. These battles produced essentially similar results: a government with a limited monarchical authority, actually led by representatives who were distinguished members of the public, and a church practising real Protestant worship, supported and controlled by the civil government, while all subjects, regardless of faith, enjoyed the same civil rights and freedom to choose which religious group they want to join (Van Gelder, 1960, p. 68).

The Dutch Revolt represented a stage in the lengthy process of the formation of nation-states. Subsequent important events in this process were the English Civil War, the American War of Independence, the French Revolution and the Italian and German Unifications (to mention only some). Together these events constitute a collective learning process. 'In the Netherlands, without much theoretical preparation, as far as resistance was concerned, what was aimed at, and what actually occurred, had theoretical repercussions in French writings. These were taken over by the English to theoretically justify, and provide the foundation of, their resistance' (Van Gelder, 1960, p. 71). American independence fighters and French revolutionaries further elaborated upon English political theory and practices. In Part IV, an attempt is made to justify the proposition that, as a result, meeting behaviour has experienced an accelerated process of parliamentarization.

With the establishment of larger and more populated monopolies of taxation and force, the contra-movements were likewise of broader scope. Thereby, religious movements have sometimes played a role of decisive importance. In a situation in which religion was represented everywhere, and the church and state leaders frequently maintained a close relationship with each other, many people realized their social ambitions in religious terms and practices. As such, Gorski suggested that the formation of states in early modern Europe (1517–1789) was also the result of 'a disciplinary revolution sparked by ascetic religious movements, the most important of which was Calvinism' (1993, p. 266). Protestant movements like Calvinism promoted discipline at three levels.

> First, they instilled an ethic of self-discipline within individual believers. Second, they invented a variety of institutional strategies for maintaining collective discipline within the church. And third, they promoted social reforms aimed at increasing popular discipline. Where such religious movements allied with rising political elites – in particular, urban burghers or centralizing monarchs – the result was a profound transformation of social and institutional life, a disciplinary revolution, with far-reaching consequences for state formation. (Gorski, 1993)

Gorski further worked out this thesis using research into two processes of state formation: the Dutch and the Prussian. The former occurred in the urbanized, economically developed region stretching from Northern Italy to the North Atlantic (the 'core' of world systems theory). The latter occurred in the sparsely settled, agricultural region of Central and Eastern Europe (the 'semi-periphery'). He compared the conclusions of this research to cases where a disciplinary revolution failed or was absent altogether. He concluded that 'successful disciplinary revolution led to the formation of republican states in the core region and made possible the strong, centralized, monarchical states in the semiperiphery' (Gorski, 1993, p. 267).

In his study *The Protestant Ethic and the Spirit of Capitalism* (1988 [1920]), Max Weber emphasized how Calvin's doctrine of the 'calling' harnessed the ideal interest of the believer to work and accumulation. Gorski pointed out that Weber paid insufficient attention to the fact that the doctrine of 'justification' also channelled the individual's energy into a refashioning of the self. He wrote that the Calvinist ethic consists not only of a work ethic but also of an ethic of self-discipline. Founded upon the old monastic practices, the Calvinists developed a variety of refined techniques to increase and maintain self-discipline. 'The Calvinist Movement provided the channel through which the discipline of the monastery entered the political world' (Gorski, 1993, p. 306). Given that the claim to self-discipline was simultaneously a claim to moral superiority, the Calvinists emanated a powerful attraction precisely upon the political elites for whom 'self-discipline could buttress or even replace birth as a sign of fitness to rule' (pp. 272–3). As is demonstrated in Chapter 5, this trend was indeed clearly present during the Dutch Revolt and during the formation of the Dutch Republic. The urban patriciate which assumed the central co-ordinating functions of the Court of Brussels could, in Gorski's words, be described as 'a "rising" career group that used disciplinary institutions to cement its status and dominion' (1993, p. 271). By researching the act of meeting in the Calvinist Movement and Church it is possible to elaborate this notion.

Meetings were important, if not the most important organizational technique by which the Calvinist minority maintained internal discipline, and acquired and preserved political power. In comparison to previous and other social movements, Calvinism was unique in the use of discipline as a means of politically organizing large groups of people. Calvinism was the forerunner of later revolutionary parties. 'At the same time, with its radical ethic of social discipline, Calvin anticipated the program of revolutionary republicanism (e.g. in the French and American Revolutions), which saw the voluntary subjugation of the individual will to common good (the internalization of virtue) as the foundation of the republican polity' (Gorski, 1993, p. 306). In conclusion to these theoretical speculations, it can be expected that research into the act of meeting during the Dutch Revolt and the Dutch Republic will throw more light on the relationship between civilization and the formation of states, churches and markets.

The period during the Dutch Revolt was a time of relatively rapid, societal fluctuations. Mutual tensions increased and various, new central problems and functions came into existence. The new rulers encountered problems of co-ordination and government, and problems with the regulation of internal and external organized violence. The states themselves were faced with both the organization of their meetings and those of other governing boards, and had to solve problems which previously could be averted by personal decisions of the monarchs or, in the interim, by other powerful persons. Meetings about 'how to meet' increased and many meeting rules were documented in terms of impersonal stipulations, which should be considered as standardized solutions to society's problems.

The meeting rules of the States of Holland, the most powerful province of the seven provinces forming the Dutch Republic, were documented for the first time shortly after the synod of Emden had determined the meeting rules for the Dutch Reformed Church. Many who, during and subsequent to the Dutch Revolt, obtained access to secular co-ordination centres, and many other inhabitants of the rebel provinces, had previously participated in meetings of the Reform Movement and had thus acquired a degree of meeting skill. For this reason, a chapter will be dedicated to the meeting rules and manners which developed during the Reform Movement in the Netherlands.

As soon as the Dutch conflict with Spain had been settled, the old tensions re-emerged not only between the former allies, but also between the towns, between the different urban classes and interest groups, between the town governments of Holland and the stadholder of Holland, and between Holland and the other provinces. Due to lack of direct authority over the use of organized violence, the patricians had to manoeuvre carefully during the Dutch Revolt. They continued to do so even after they had emerged as the ruling class. In regard of the deployment of military means, the patriciate remained heavily dependent upon others: the stadholder, who was commander-in-chief of the army and the navy, and the local militias who naturally did not want to do someone else's dirty work. A further consequence was that the patricians were forced into self-restraint as regards the use of (mutually) political violence during the period of the Dutch Republic. The patriciate was led to a considerable degree by its striving for internal peace and calm, particularly in institutions such as the church. However, this was without restraining themselves from force (juridical and police) directed towards individual 'criminals' and defenceless 'outsiders' such as gypsies. The Dutch Republic distinguished itself by the peaceful co-existence of different churches and religious sects, which, before and after the Dutch Revolt, had developed and established themselves in the Netherlands. The patricians had an aversion to weighty, public theological disputes, which they considered to be dangerous and improper (Spierenburg, 1978, p. 18). Derivations of the Latin concept *civilitas* were first used by members of the upper class of the Dutch Republic to indicate a more peaceful approach to religious differences and contra-distinctions, and only later to likewise designate 'good manners' in the sense in which the concepts *civilité* and *civilization* were used in France (according to Spierenburg, 1973). In an address to the patricians of Amsterdam in 1598, the Mayor, C.P. Hooft, pressed for the use of *civylheydt* against the old as well as the new religion; that is, relinquishing persecution in affairs of faith (Hooft, 1925, Part II, p. 67). Reacting on complaints from Lutherans from the town of Middelburg in 1606, the States-General requested the town governments 'to "civilize" these affairs and to treat them with discretion and assertion' (quoted in Van Gelder, 1947, p. 100). Originally, 'civilizing' was the opposite of using violence.

Within the upper social layer, the struggle for the authority to govern was mainly fought by using predominantly peaceful means. However, on two occasions the internal tensions became so great that a number of prominent statesmen met their deaths. In 1618 the Grand Pensionary, John van Oldenbarnevelt, was 'tried' and executed after a change of government which was normally free of violence. This change was made by the stadholder, Maurits, in the heat of the religious conflict between the Remonstrants and the Counter-Remonstrants. In 1672 the Grand Pensionary, John de Wit, and his elder brother, Cornelis, were victims of the conflict between the stadholder and the town governors of Holland. They were lynched in a people's revolt, which had been incited by both the fear of war threats emanating from France and England, and the anxiety regarding a drop in prosperity, which would have been caused by rises in taxation and the price of food. Both of these cases of political violence resulted in the strengthening of the position of power of the stadholder, who had his way with the town councils through so-called 'legal manoeuvres', that is, by replacing members of the (town) governments. However, the governmental structure of the Dutch Republic was essentially, in fact, not attacked. The urban middle class, which had supported the side of the stadholder in the hope of participation and co-leadership, found itself disappointed in these expectations. After a while, many patrician families, who were removed from government functions by the stadholder, re-occupied a position in the town government after the death of the stadholder or through changes in local power relationships.

The way in which government changes took place in the Dutch Republic was remarkably peaceful within the European context of that time. This can be explained by the fact that the central co-ordinating functions were filled mainly by commoners from a relatively homogenous upper layer, who controlled the monopoly of taxation, but who were heavily dependent on others if they wished to employ organized physical force, namely dependent on the stadholders. As a result of the more evenly balanced power and dependency relationships, which corresponded with the divided and decentralized military and fiscal structure, there came into being an upper layer of people who, more than the courtly, aristocratic upper layers in Western Europe, specialized in persuading, prevailing, debating, negotiating and similar, more peaceful ways of regulating tensions, and, in preventing conflicts occurring or worsening.

With regard to the Dutch Reformed Church, the patricians followed the same strategy as that of other social organizations, such as the militia. States and town governments maintained the right to approve or disapprove the appointments of the leaders of these organizations (captains, preachers) and they attempted, via the appointment of political commissioners to supervise the meetings of these organizations. Nevertheless, the 'ruling class' did not develop into a completely closed oligarchy. There always was some, although diminishing, social mobility of prosperous members of the broad middle class to the ruling upper layer (De Jong, 1985, pp. 90–4). And, because of their social position within the local community and their dependence upon civilian guards for the maintenance of public order, the patricians constantly had to consider public opinion, at least more than many other governments of European countries. At the end of the seventeenth century, the English ambassador to the United Provinces, William Temple, noted that the patricians maintained their authority, yet invoked little public dissatisfaction and jealousy, through giving considerable thought to the opinion of their townsfolk when it came to selecting magistrates (Temple, 1978, p. 97). The government was able to remain informed of public opinion. In the Dutch Republic, there was a relatively large degree of freedom to express opinions both verbally and in writing.

The Dutch Reformed Church played an important role in the movement from the lower levels to the upper levels of society. After the Synod of Dort in 1618/19, in which the doctrine of the Counter-Remonstrants was imposed upon the Dutch Reformed Church and the alliance between the secular and ecclesiastical governments, under the leadership of the former, was *de facto* reinstated, gradually, more members of the ruling families joined this church and (especially in the smaller towns and in the countryside) participated in the church councils. In the appointments by co-option, and the election of patricians, magistrates, and other administrators, the town governments showed such a strong preference to members of the Reformed Church, that at the demise of the Republic nearly all members of town and national meetings were likewise members of the Dutch Reformed Church.[3]

In church councils and welfare institutions, affluent commoners could participate in administrative activities and so prepare themselves for public governing functions. In a study of the church councils of Leiden during the Dutch Republic, Schilling noted that wealthy entrepreneurs and merchants forged close connections with members of the town government via their church activities. The meetings of the church council and the government of church institutions for the poor were opportunities for individuals to demonstrate to the self-appointed patriciate that they were suitable candidates for political functions and office (Schilling, 1980a, p. 443). However, this situation was not applicable to prosperous immigrants. Therefore, for the many Flemish refugees and their descendants, who commonly played an important role in church organizations, progression into government office was impossible.

In his study of uprisings in seventeenth- and eighteenth-century Holland, Dekker concluded that the violence was 'not too bad', compared, for example, to that in France. In Europe, both Holland and the Republic as a whole were oases of calm. Popular uprisings against a variety of situations were unexceptional: against religion, food shortages, taxation, and revolts by Orangemen (supporters of the stadholder). The patriciate was not overwhelmed by these insurrections and, when necessary, and if possible, subdued them by exerting their military and legal powers. During the revolts, violence led 'only exceptionally to serious injury to people, the number of fatalities in the course of two centuries could be counted on the fingers of one hand' (Dekker, 1982, p. 144). The degree to which this conclusion is applicable to the whole of the Dutch Republic cannot be determined due to the lack of a comparative study of popular revolts outside Holland.

Besides increased safety and social security, the development of a broad and extensively branched network of political, economic and ecclesiastical meetings was conditional for the channelling of many social tensions within the Dutch Republic. This was particularly the case in urban areas where there was relatively little internal political violence. This network of meetings was dominated by patricians, an elite which was specialized in governing and which originated in the urban population. Together with those of aristocratic origin they formed a social upper layer, which on the basis of its behaviour and activities could be termed a 'meeting estate' or 'meeting class', the first in Europe.

During the formation of the Republic of the United Provinces, many of the meeting habits and manners developed (or rather, they took on a more definite form) which outsiders have frequently referred to as 'typically Dutch'. Some recent examples: the German sociologist, Ernest Zahn (1989) writes:

> Meetings, although repeatedly the object of ridicule by the participants, are important events. Still the behaviour is not pompous, the formality is never rigid, and there is no behaviour implying status which is precisely what is expected as polite and correct behaviour in authoritarian societies, and which immediately shows who is more or less important in the political or bureaucratic hierarchy. (1989, p. 192)

As an explanation, Zahn highlights the urban tradition:

> In the Netherlands, the fraternal relations of the patricians have left their mark on forms of government and middle-class patterns of behaviour, and they have permeated to the lower echelons. (1989, p. 58)

The American sociologist, William Shetter (1987), writes:

> The society as a whole, in other words, shows a marked preference for creating a context for polite, urbane, discussion in which all are given equal opportunity to demonstrate familiarity with good manners. . . . Individual aggressiveness and open expression of emotion are not so highly valued, but high value is placed on group solidarity. . . . A certain polite reserve coupled with a broad tolerance of differences maintained by a well-developed set of social forms is a firmly rooted tradition in the Netherlands inherited from a city culture that reached a peak of development in the 17th century. (1987, p. 123)

In the latter half of the eighteenth century, during the Autumn of the Republic, the state formation process and the meeting norms of the Netherlands began to re-converge with those of other European regions. This coincided with the rise in power, and the economic success, of Britain and the spreading of the British parliamentary meeting norms across Europe and to other (colonial) areas of the world. Nevertheless, in Dutch society, the influence of the old republican meeting class was noticeable for a very long time, even up to the present day. One becomes aware of this all the more as one participates in European and global organizations and is confronted with the particular meeting habits of one's own nation and those of others.

CHAPTER 5

THE EMERGENCE OF A PROTESTANT MEETING ORDER

The Reform Movement

The Reformation spread across Europe from Germany and Switzerland where, 'the civic element of the Renaissance period and the new religion had joined forces for the first time' (Baron, 1970, p. 54). Particularly in the beginning, the Reform Movement borrowed its meeting manners from the North Italian and German towns.[1] The intermingling of reformatory and political ideas and practices were powerfully stimulated by the German imperial towns which, after the division of Germany into Catholic and Protestant monarchies, remained subordinate to the Catholic emperor Charles V. In Strasbourg the reformer, Bucer, first defended the opinion that a heredity monarchy was anti-religious, because it precluded God's will. Bucer argued for the election of kings in a way similar to how town magistrates were elected. Several decades later, in Geneva, Calvin put Bucer's political ideas into practice. Leading from the idea that unlimited power controlled by one person was an insult to God, the one and only Lord, the government of Geneva was placed in the hands of an elected board of magistrates.

During the expansion of the Reformation in France into a movement of national dimensions, new political ideas and ecclesiastical meeting practices developed, which were guided and canonized by Calvin and Beza.[2] There was a hierarchy of regional and national synods which was based on the model of the French provincial states and the States-General, which at that time were ruled by Catholics. However, with the militarization of religious disputes in France, the synods changed into mass meetings of armed men led by the lesser nobility (Koenigsberger, 1970, p. 57).

In the Netherlands, the Reformation was a late arrival because the Spanish king adopted strong measures against the movement's followers and persecuted its leaders. At the beginning of the sixteenth century, the Reform Movement of the Netherlands consisted mainly of clerks, schoolmasters, clerics, printers, educated workers and other men of letters, who took their inspiration from the German Reform Movement in particular. Charles V's persecution of the 'heretics' split the reformers of Germany and the Netherlands. In Germany, Lutherism was recognized by governments – not so in the Netherlands. Here counter churches developed relatively late and very slowly, as communal readings blossomed into religious services and field preachers became church ministers.

In the Netherlands, the Reformation had a polymorphous character for a lengthy period. Until the 1570s Calvin's influence was no greater than that of Luther and Baptist leaders. The subsequent Calvinist influence within the Reform Movement gradually increased. Prior to the Dutch Revolt, many French- and Dutch-speaking refugees from the Low Countries migrated to the East Frisian town of Emden, where representatives from various branches of the Reform Movement settled. Out of the various places where asylum was sought, including London, Emden became the most important. Before the Dutch Revolt, Emden had played a role in the organization of the churches of the Netherlands, similar to that played by Geneva in the French Reformation. Here Calvinism started to become influential (Duke, 1990, pp. 280 and 286). The consequence of Calvinism's illegality was that the members had to maintain a stricter discipline in order to gain entrance to Holy Communion than was necessary in places where Protestantism was recognized by the government. In the absence of secular magistrates, who (like in Geneva) could punish members if they showed insufficient discipline, locally chosen church councils or consistories checked for compliance to Christian rules for living. Due to the emphasis upon Christian discipline and the function of the consistories, the reformed churches in the Netherlands became more and more differentiated from the Protestant churches in other European countries.

After the Dutch Revolt, church discipline remained a matter for the church councils. It was based upon the establishment of peace, brotherhood and the reconciliation of the sinner with his church and his fellow men, in unity round the communion table. These disciplinary practices had little to do with the punishment of an individual but revolved around the community. The primary aim of disciplining those who strayed from God's path was the preservation of the church community (Van Deursen, 1974, p. 203). The members were in no way permitted to arouse the annoyance, disdain or derision of others. An individual who the ecclesiastical council thought had violated Christian norms (manslaughter, theft, resistance to the government, prostitution, preaching evil, drunkenness, indiscretion, dishonesty, or frivolity, all in the broadest sense of these words) was restrained from participating in the Holy Communion. Participation was withheld until innocence was proven or that the accused, after a period of restraint, had shown remorse and confessed his guilt. One of the tasks of the church councils was to get a sinner, through talking to him, to confess his guilt in the council's meeting, whereupon this meeting decided whether, and how, the confession of guilt would be read out from the pulpit. The sinner had offended the community which must be publicly appeased by words. If the 'censured' individual refused to confess his guilt, appeasement had clearly failed, and disciplinary measures were replaced by public punishment. The obstinate sinner was then publicly summoned for a confession of guilt, first anonymously, and then, if necessary, by name. Finally, on the authority of the classis, the church council could sever the sinful member from the church community.

The membership of the Calvinist Church grew relatively slowly after the Dutch Revolt. This can be explained largely by the fact that the ecclesiastical councils continued their disciplinary activities and so continued to draw a sharp line between 'secular children' and 'children of the church'. Initially, many could not or would not be reconciled with the Calvinists' church discipline (Duke, 1990, p. 273). The self-imposed isolation of the Calvinist Church contributed considerably to the development of a unique situation in the Dutch Republic, in which the Lutherans, Mennonites, Jews and even Catholics (unofficially) were permitted to practise their religions. In most European countries which recognized an official state church, such a situation was impossible and unthinkable.

In the Republic of the United Provinces, the church and the state were more strictly separate than in other countries. However, this did not mean that both the town governments and the states were unbiased regarding religious questions. Uniting a large part of the population, the Dutch Reformed Church was considered by the states as the official representation of the true Christian faith and had a preferential position in the Dutch Republic. Its churches and clergy were maintained by the state, its religious services could be held in public, and its prayers were used in political meetings.

In spite of the fact that the secular government could exercise control over the church by having the right of veto over such matters as the appointment of clergy and by the supervision by political commissioners, the ecclesiastical councils acted as fora where matters, such as marital and family laws, Sunday as a day of rest, holy days and education, could be discussed within certain limits. Many formal decisions concerning these topics were prepared in the church in close co-operation with the magistrates, who took the ultimate decisions. For this reason, also, it is important to investigate the Protestant ways of meeting further.

The synodal organization

The reformers rejected the Catholic proposition that one could be absolved of one's sins by the sacrament of penance. They preached a religion in which the relationship between God and one of his followers could only be restored by

God as a single and complete occurrence. Replacing the Catholic purification through expiatory rituals, they developed religious practices in which 'the moral faults and failings whether of the individual or the community were first sheltered under the promise of divine grace and then gradually rectified through instruction and moral discipline. Religious worship served to inculcate correct behaviour, not to make up for its absence' (Cameron, 1991, p. 418). The Protestant religious practices were directed towards restoring the proper relationship with God not by performing purification rituals, but by impressing one with the appropriate behaviour in relation to each other. Furthermore, these were the guiding principles shaping the institution and regulation of ecclesiastical meetings in which the communal future was discussed and decided.

Euan Cameron has pointed out that the success of the reformed clergy was largely a result of the invitation they issued for public debate. 'Where the old priests had retreated into their privileges and cloisters, the reformers went into the squares and council chambers and asked for lay support. Instead of burying dogmas in technical jargon, they translated it and insisted that any layman learn its tenets' (Cameron, 1991, p. 420). The Protestant Movement's attractiveness can be further explained by the ways in which the reformed clergy involved laymen. They asked the opinions of the laymen and treated them as guardians of the Bible's truth. According to Cameron, in the initial stages of the Reformation, large groups across the whole of Europe received ideological schooling for the first time. The Reformation was simultaneously a religious and political movement. 'In the sixteenth century religion became mass politics. Other ideologies ultimately more secular in tone, would take its place. The Reformation was the first' (Cameron, 1991, p. 422). On the basis of Cameron's study, it can be hypothesized that the Protestant churches played an important role in the organization of political debates during the formation of meeting units on a national scale.

In the following section, meeting rules will be investigated to demonstrate the reformers' contributions to the development and extension of the operational debating, discussing, and meeting rules in the Netherlands.

In 1571 a synod was held in the town of Emden on the initiative of Marnix van Sint Aldegonde, William of Orange's right-hand man. Here the structure of the organization of the Dutch Reformed Church was set down in detail. The 'Synod' of Wezel, an earlier meeting of refugees in 1568, provided the stimulus. The Protestants of the Low Countries could make use of the experience of their brothers in other countries as, by European standards, they were relatively late in developing. In the organization of their church, they were ultimately influenced more by the French Calvinist model than by the examples of Geneva or German Lutheranism. Geneva was a small city-state where the inhabitants and magistrates could, and had to be open about the Reformation. This situation was not the same as that in the Netherlands before the Dutch Revolt when the churches operated 'under the cross', that is, under a Catholic regime. The Lutheran model, which developed overtly in a number of German towns, was likewise unsuitable in the Netherlands for similar reasons. The Synod of Emden decided on a ecclesiastical order emanating from a collegiate and synodal government.

The meeting in Emden commenced by assuming the Presbyterian principle that 'no church above other churches, no servant above other servants, no elder above other elders, no deacon above other deacons shall assert preference or domination, but rather shall pause for all suspicion of it and opportunity for it' (Plomp, 1971, p. 89). The government of each church should consist of an elected board of clergy, deacons and elders: the church council or consistory. Neighbouring churches together formed a classis. A meeting of the classis had to be attended by delegates from the church councils every three or six months, and delegates of the classes covering a larger area had to meet annually for a provincial synod. Furthermore, delegates of the provincial synods had to hold a national or general synod every other year.[3]

In Emden, a meeting system for the Dutch Reformed Church was drafted along the same lines as that of the French Huguenots. This corresponded with the administrative tradition of the Netherlands, where town governments and states could assert influence upon the central authorities through their meetings. The consistories were comparable to the meetings of the town governments, the regional synods to the meetings of the Provincial States, and the general synods to the meetings of the States-General (Duke, 1990, p. 282).

The decisions taken by the Emden Synod regarding the organization of the Dutch Reformed Church had the practical consequence that numerous clergy and laymen had to meet regularly and frequently to discuss all sorts of religious and clerical questions. This was a new phenomenon: a behaviour that had to be learnt by the majority of the people. That the participants of the Emden Synod were aware of this is demonstrated by the fact that the stipulations for the organization of the church referred mainly to the way in which people should hold meetings. Most attention was paid to propriety for meetings of the classis and for provincial meetings. Only a few articles were devoted to the correct behaviour for church councils and for general synods (Plomp, 1971, pp. 91–4).

The church organization determined at Emden, instituted that, at the start of the meetings of the classis, the servants of the Word should preach in turn, and that these preachings should be judged by their colleagues. Then the servants had to choose a chairman from their midst. He was required to open the meeting with prayers, after which he was to ask several questions concerning the state of affairs in the local church community. These matters were then addressed and deliberated upon. Subsequently, topics that could not be dealt with in the church council, or topics that were relevant for all churches, could come up for discussions. Several of those present should then state some differences in opinion held by dissenters so as to sharpen everyone's perception. After a time and place for the next meeting had been settled, the chairman would close the meeting with a prayer of gratitude.

If the meeting of the classis was also intended as a preparation for a provincial synod then, after electing delegates, the participants had to consider whether the matters they wished to deal with in the provincial synod had previously been subjects of debate. A subject that had already been discussed was only allowed to reappear on the agenda if there were any doubt about the decision taken.

Regarding provincial meetings, the Emden Synod decided the following points. Delegates were obliged to bring with them both their credentials and the instructions from their classis. The only matters which were allowed to be discussed were those which could not be arranged individually by church councils and classes, and those which concerned all the churches. Every provincial synod should start with a prayer from the preacher who had chaired the previous meeting. After the election of a new chairman, a vice-president, and a minutes secretary (*praeses*, *assessor* and *scriba*), the chairman was obliged to say a prayer about the synod's forthcoming work. Subsequently, those attendant announced their presence in turn.

After the chairman had read the credentials and letters of instruction, and stated their contents, he requested the delegate's judgement and then, finally, announced the majority finding. The *scriba* transcribed this and read it out clearly 'so that it could be sanctioned with the approval of everyone' (Plomp, 1971, p. 93). When every matter had been dealt with, the *scriba* read the entire list of decisions once again. After being sanctioned by all present, the decisions were signed by the chairman and the minutes secretary. Every delegate was given a copy of this list to take with him. When the time and place for the next meeting had been settled, the chairman was required to close the meeting with a prayer of gratitude.

The Synod paid particular attention to the function of chairman. A chairman had to ensure that everyone spoke in turn, he had to order the 'quarrelsome' and 'embittered' to keep silent, and order them to leave the chamber if they refused, after which those present had to consider, as a body, the appropriate punishment.

Excepting but a few alterations, such as the relationship of the chairmanship to the function of the minister, the meeting guidelines instituted by the Synod of Emden remained valid until the end of the Dutch Republic. Individual consistories and classes worked out these guidelines in further detail.

Meeting rules of consistories and classes

The first rules for consistories and classes had already started to appear during the Dutch Revolt. Particularly striking was the strong emphasis upon regulations concerning the control of emotional behaviour, especially hostile behaviour, and the chairman's function in this. The concepts *moderamen* and *moderator* (the one who moderates), designations for the president and the chairman of ecclesiastical meetings, characterize their functions.

In 1573 the ecclesiastical council of Dort formulated more detailed regulations for its meetings where, among other topics, Christian discipline was discussed. This served as an example for the church councils of Delft, Amsterdam and probably other towns in Holland as well (Schotel, 1841, pp. 80–5; Evenhuis, 1965, p. 144). As far as it can be ascertained, the regulations of the various church councils, as well as their meeting practices, were broadly speaking similar to each other.[4]

The first five articles of the regulations of the Dort church council state that late-comers were punished by imposing a monetary fine. Moreover, that the preacher chairing the church council opened the meeting by invoking the name of the Lord, and praising and thanking God. He was obliged assiduously to examine what the brothers thought of all the matters under discussion and, as one man, decide according to a majority vote. This decision was then documented and announced verbally as the opinion of the consistory. It was his duty to maintain order in the consistory, using warnings and punishments when necessary. Furthermore, he had to collect the prescribed fines, and if failing to do so, risked a monetary fine himself. Monetary fines were likewise imposed if the chairman failed to document the decisions carefully. Other fines were imposed on those individuals who spoke without prior permission. The chairman was obliged to present the topic under discussion in a serious and sensible manner so as to enable the appropriate advice to be given by those present who, in reciprocation, were obliged to listen attentively.

The following three stipulations characterized in particular the Protestant meetings of that time. Article 5 stated that during a church council meeting a member who was 'engaged in swearing, larking around, quarrelling, dozing, chattering, lying down, walking around, etceteras would be punished on every occasion with a half a stiver fine'. In Article 6, it was formulated that everyone had to take it in turns to state his feelings and offer his recommendations and, if someone felt uncomfortable about certain points, he need not feel ashamed for going along with the soundest opinions receiving the majority of the votes, and should not 'stubbornly maintain his own opinion as the best'. Whoever 'resentfully, foolhardy, and vehemently wanted to impose their opinion' had to be treated in a way similar to that of disturbance of the peace. Article 7 goes into more detail about procedures and the ways of debating. This should be 'pleasant and edifying' and whoever 'spoke to another in an unseemly, derisive, or unedifying manner or erupted into swearing' was given a monetary fine.

The remaining articles concerned the obligation to document the decisions, the regular announcement of them, and the maintenance of confidentiality of the matters discussed, otherwise 'punished by a heavy fine' (Articles 8 and 9); the prohibition on personally opening letters addressed to the ecclesiastical council (Article 10); and the punishment of those who, for no serious reason, were absent or left the meeting prematurely without permission (Articles 11 and 12).

In 1581 the classis of Dort issued a regulation to assist the orderly and brief progress of a meeting (Tukker, 1965, pp. 22–4). The regulation had much in common with those formulated at both the Synod of Emden and the ecclesiastical council of Dort. It involved similar stipulations regarding meeting times, lateness, absence, premature departure, the election and the performance of the chairman and the appropriate way of making, and documenting, decisions. Moreover, it was stipulated that the points on the agenda had to be presented in written form, that everyone had to listen attentively to the proposals and the responses they invoked, and that they should keep their answers brief when it was their turn, so avoiding obstructing the meeting with unnecessary repetition and verbose reasoning. Interruptions were likewise forbidden: 'Nobody should interrupt another without prior permission from the chairman. If somebody is not attentive and talking to others, interjects with unseemly comments or, on the other hand, simply does not listen, he will be punished according to the opinion of the meeting' (Tukker, 1965, p. 23).

During the Dutch Republic several amendments were made to the regulations, such as the determining of the order of speakers, by which the clergy, according to seniority, were allowed to speak before the elders and the deacons (Tukker, 1965, p. 24; Evenhuis, 1965, pp. 145–6). Another alteration concerned the election of the church council. In 1618 the Synod of Dort determined that church members were no longer permitted to participate in electing members of the church council 'to avoid confusion which could arise from the election of common folk' (Evenhuis, 1965, p. 142). In this respect, as well as many others, the leaders of the Dutch Reformed Church followed the example of the secular government. However, this regulation was not applied everywhere. For example, in Friesland, all male church members, even beggars, kept the right to elect council members, although the candidates were sometimes nominated by the church council (Cuperus, 1920, pp. 8–9).

The number of church council members varied from three people in the smaller communities, to twelve in Amsterdam, the largest community. Whoever was chosen as an elder or a deacon could not refuse to take his place in the church council without risking being publicly called to order. This was equally valid regarding dismissal from the function (Van Deursen, 1974, p. 95; Cuperus, 1920, pp. 14–15). In a similar way to how a town's mayors and sheriffs regularly asked advice from ex-magistrates in the body of the patricians, many church councils adopted the habit of asking advice from ex-members of the church council when making important decisions. Such requests included decisions about the vocation of a preacher, the election of an individual for the purpose of consoling the sick, the expulsion of church members, and the preparation for classes and provincial synods (Van Deursen, 1974, p. 93).

Apart from church discipline, which took up a great deal of time, the church councils devoted their attention to caring for the poor; education and the diocese; protesting against fairs, Santa Claus and disruptions on the day of rest; lending financial support to friendly churches abroad; the organization of work in the diocese; and various questions of belief (Roodenburg, 1990; Van Deursen, 1974; Cuperus, 1920; Van der Zee, 1962; Gadant, 1904).

The larger meetings of the classis, to which participation was likewise obligatory for those who had been elected, had the last say in cases of excommunication and the terminating of church membership. Above all they concerned themselves with the examining of candidates for the clergy; the approval of the vocational callings of, and the dismissal of, preachers; organizational problems; and the practice of *censura morum et doctrinae*, in which the issues were the lives and learning of the preachers and those aspiring to become preachers (Cuperus, 1916; Van Deursen, 1974).

To what degree these meeting rules were adhered to in practice is hard to determine. There is not a great deal known about the course of ecclesiastical meetings; only that decisions were transcribed and the participants were obliged to maintain confidentiality about the subjects discussed. An attempt was made to give the outside world (that is, the rival religious communities) an impression of peace and harmony by keeping discussions and differences of opinion within the four walls of the meeting chamber. For the same reason, endeavours were made to make decisions unanimously, or at least to obtain as large a majority of votes as possible. Substantial argumentation intended to convince others was characteristic of the Protestant meeting behaviour. Majority decisions about important affairs were avoided as much as possible, as they increased the chances that discussions and differences of opinion would be taken outside the meeting chamber.

According to Cuperus, who researched Frisian church meetings of the seventeenth and eighteenth centuries, it was a fairly frequent occurrence for members of ecclesiastical councils to argue so vehemently that the act of meeting became practically impossible. Sometimes the secular government felt responsible to reinstate order in the church council, as did the town government of Stavoren in the Spring of 1665. At that time, the ecclesiastical council meetings in that town had become practically impossible due to dissension between elders and preacher.

Ecclesiastical meetings where mutual tensions and feelings ran high were to be seen in particular in the beginning of the seventeenth century. This was during the discord between the Gomarists or Counter-Remonstrants, on the one hand, and the Arminians or Remonstrants, on the other hand, about the question of whether belief stems from being chosen by God, or whether being chosen by God stems from one's belief.

The ecclesiastical politics of the states, drafted by the Grand Pensionary, Van Oldenbarnevelt, was aimed at fashioning a tolerant church with a sufficiently broad base so that no one, excluding Roman Catholics and Jews, need be segregated. The patricians aimed at a people's church under their control, which could 'render a meaningful contribution to the "treatment of, and the preservation of the tranquillity of, the multitude"' (Van Deursen, 1974, p. 225). For this reason many initially supported the Remonstrants, who were named after the remonstrance submitted to the States of Holland in 1610 by the followers of the theologian, Arminius, from Leiden. The remonstrance concerned five propositions of belief which related to the moderating of the Calvinistic doctrine of predestination. The followers of yet another theologian from Leiden, Gomarus, resisted these liberal propositions of belief and were known as the Counter-Remonstrants. They were the hard-core Calvinists. The states, which were governed by humanists, Erasmians and Mennonites, took various measures to oppose the appointment of Counter-Remonstrant or Calvinist clergy. An increasing number of Counter-Remonstrants detached themselves from the Dutch Reformed Church over this issue and established their own 'dissident' churches, the congregations of which were forbidden by the states.

In the thick of the battle between Remonstrants and Counter-Remonstrants, many had a great deal of difficulty keeping to the official meeting rules of the church, and thus these were frequently disregarded. In 1608, after a lengthy procedure, a Remonstrant preacher from the village Broek in Waterland, was discharged from service. Consequently, in the classis, four followers launched themselves into a formidable defence of their preacher 'by ranting and raving as if they were about to strike out'. Finally, the chairman had them leave the room. The delegates of the classis who gathered the following week in Broek to read out the act of deposition were waylaid by the church council and 'scandalously addressed and ridiculed' (Van Deursen, 1974, pp. 329–40). In 1611, during a classis administered by Gomarists in Dort, an Arminian was repeatedly made to hold his tongue and was dismissed from the room several times because 'he refused to heed the call for silence' (*ibid.*, p. 257). In 1615, when Remonstrant preachers challenged their examiners to a debate during an examination in a classis in the town of The Brill, the attendant public became so worked up that they incited the examiners with the words 'crucify him, crucify him' (*ibid.*, p. 251).

In places where the Remonstrants and the Counter-Remonstrants had separated and established their own churches, the controversy did not always remain limited to a battle of words (Van Deursen, 1974, pp. 330–45).

Frequently the use of the church building led to pitched battles as, for instance, in the town of Goedereede where, on the 19 January 1618 at eight o'clock in the morning, the Counter-Remonstrants took possession of a church occupied by Remonstrants in order to hold a service. After the Remonstrant preacher had appealed to his followers to fight for the church, they gathered:

> Armed with sticks, pitchforks and poles . . . to descend upon the churchgoers and strike them dead. After several stones had been thrown and some blows had fallen, the bailiff stepped in. Following the example of mutinous Spanish soldiers, the combatants chose their own leader or *eletto* and, led by him, presented their demands to the magistrate. They claimed that the sheriffs of the other denomination deserved to be removed from office, and demanded that the dissenters should be forbidden to hold meetings, that the Counter-Remonstrant schoolmaster should leave town and, furthermore, that the bailiff should henceforth always be of the Remonstrant church. The magistrate forbade the meetings and sacked the teacher. With this the Remonstrants were provisionally satisfied. They remained armed and formed four divisions, each of 22 men, who on command would also protect the town against government soldiers. (Van Deursen, 1974, pp. 330–1)

When the religious strife between Remonstrants and Counter-Remonstrants increased in ferocity, town governments issued decrees against assembling and debating on the street or in church, and against the use of threatening or abusive behaviour towards preachers at the end of a service (Van Deursen, 1974, p. 275). In many places, the Counter-Remonstrants, and, consequent to the Synod of Dort, the Remonstrants, were forbidden to congregate. The meeting ban, together with the government's application of it, sometimes contributed to the religious strife acquiring a more violent character, as demonstrated in this example:

> On the 24th of August 1621, the Remonstrants held a [forbidden] meeting outside Rotterdam. The dyke warden of Schieland, who had got wind of it, did not interrupt the meeting, allowed everyone to return to the town unhindered, but arrested the preacher, Simon Lucae, at the town gates. . . . The people attacked the soldiers, who were only able to escape their perilous predicament by firing their weapons. In consequence, four men lost their lives. (Van Deursen, 1974, p. 333)

Except during the turbulent years of the struggle between the Remonstrants and Counter-Remonstrants, ecclesiastical council meetings, where the official rules were no longer heeded, were usually concerned with discipline and decisions concerning vocational callings. Regarding the meetings of the Frisian classes in the period of the Dutch Republic, Cuperus stated that they frequently argued with hammer and tongs:

> It was not uncommon that members forced their way into the meeting uninvited; that a multitude of loiterers assembled outside the church or consistory room eager to be up-to-date on any small scandal within; or that the brothers came to blows, played schoolboy pranks such as leaving one's seat, haggling and talking, ripping pages from the book of edicts (particularly those pages about disciplinary affairs), removing the key to the cupboard of the classis, smoking tobacco, and other such things. Concerning the penultimate offence, the classis in Leeuwarden in 1708 even banned the sexton, Banga, to give tobacco and pipes in a special room to members of this Venerable meeting while the session lasts. . . . Even in 1776, it was considered necessary to give one's approval to the proposition of the treasurer, A. van Vliet, to always collect, before the end of the meeting, the fines for speaking prior to one's turn and other small misdemeanours. (1974, pp. 46–7)

The impression given by the books of edicts of ecclesiastical councils, classes and provincial synods, is that ecclesiastical meetings usually adhered to the stated rules, and that the rules were only violated incidentally. However, on the basis of existing research reports, it cannot be accurately determined if this were indeed the case. The previously cited study by Cuperus, although restricted to Friesland, painted a less respectable picture than many other researchers have painted. He states that certain meeting rules or stipulations, particularly those of the classes, were systematically violated and, although first codified around 1600, were determined afresh in resolutions. Some of these decisions are illustrated by the following examples taken from his book.

Both the prohibition of, and the fines for, absenteeism and lateness were commonly repeated. An extensive system of punishment developed in an attempt to prevent lengthy absences and indiscipline (pp. 37–8). Time after time, the discharging of both the chairman's and minute taker's duties presented problems and attempts were made to solve them by a system of rewards and punishments. In 1780, in order to prevent chairmen gaining too much power, the regulations were amended by stipulating that the chairmen were obliged also to implement the decisions of the meetings (pp. 39–40). Higher level meetings were frequently requested to interpret the rules in cases of conflicts about the ranking order in a meeting. This was formally determined according to the duration of membership of the classis, or according to the number of years of service (pp. 43–4). Measures were taken to hasten the drafting of an agenda (pp. 48–9).

The meeting regulations which were repeated frequently and gradually further developed were a good deal concerned with 'the maintenance of peace, decency and good order', what a Frisian classis termed 'the primary law of meeting' (p. 44). Apparently, meetings left a lot to be desired in this area. Some of the regulations repeatedly referred to in the books of edicts were: respect for and obedience to the chairman; removal of one's hat when speaking; allowing the chairman or another speaker offering his opinion the opportunity to finish; remaining seated at table (not walking around); refraining from interruptions; the prohibition on smoking and drinking and the avoidance of clique formation; and behaving in an emotional or passionate way during the voting (pp. 44–8). Regarding this latter point, it is stated: 'If someone behaves in a over-affected way during voting, the venerable meeting will assess whether such an individual is over-passionate and, when that indeed is the case, that person must leave the room' (p. 45).

Further research into the edicts of ecclesiastical meetings is necessary to identify which meeting regulations resulted from which difficulties and which were drummed in or documented, and only then could more general statements be made about the question of whether, and to what degree, formal rules of meeting were replaced by self-constraint. Studies such as that of Cuperus surmise that (part of) the lower framework of the church had a great deal of difficulty mastering the basic regulations of meeting, such as speaking in turn, desisting from noisiness and commotion, and restraining from threatening and powerful emotions.

The Synod of Dort

With respect to the biennial national synods, the Synod of Emden had determined that these should consist of preachers and elders who were delegated by the provincial synods. Moreover, these had to be held in the same manner as the provincial synods. During the Dutch Revolt and the Dutch Republic but four national synods had actually taken place. The provincial synods, which like the provincial states strove for as much autonomy as possible, had little need for national synods. Furthermore, the states expected nothing from these meetings apart from the unnecessary inflammation of feelings. The penultimate national synod was the Synod of Dort in 1618–19. This meeting was permitted by the states when the clerical battle between Remonstrants and Calvinists threatened to develop into a civil war between the states and the towns of Holland, and the stadholder.

In 1617, in various towns in Holland, riots broke out against the Remonstrants. The stadholder, Maurits, sided openly with the Counter-Remonstrants. The States of Holland responded with the Sharp Resolution, in which a national synod for settling ecclesiastical disputes was rejected; the sovereign authority of the states in ecclesiastical affairs was reiterated; and the town governments were advised to enlist their own soldiers to maintain order, replacing the regular troops which were under the jurisdiction of the stadholder. When the stadholder set off to restrain the town governments from following this course of action and to replace the most vociferous Remonstrant magistrates by those more disposed towards Calvinism, the States-General decided to allow a national synod to meet by a majority of four to three against. Through 'legal manoeuvres' or purging of the town governments, Maurits obtained the support of the States of Holland and the States-General. He was given complete authority by the States-General and took Oldenbarnevelt and several other prominent governors of Holland, including Hugo Grotius, prisoner.

Thanks to Maurits' 'legal manoeuvres', the majority of the enfranchised members of the National Synod, meeting in November 1618 in Dort, were Counter-Remonstrants. The invited theologians from the neighbouring Protestant countries had an advisory vote, as did the delegates from the states. A number of prominent Remonstrants were 'summoned' by the synod to clarify their opinions at the meeting. The synod reinstated the alliance of state and church, under the guidance of the former, and the synod imposed the Counter-Remonstrant principles, upon the Dutch Reformed Church. After the synod, Oldenbarnevelt was tried and sentenced to death by a special tribunal. Hugo Grotius and his fellow prisoners were sentenced to life-long imprisonment in the fortress Loevestein. Remonstrant congregations were banned and many Remonstrant prisoners were dismissed, driven abroad or exiled. As the ecclesiastical battle was decided and dealt with by the secular government the church remained formally free 'from complicity in the persecutions'. It could 'continue to speak the language of peace' and keep the way to reconciliation open for 'all the faint-hearted who refused to carry the cost of their convictions' (Van Deursen, 1974, p. 309). Within a decade of the synod some who had supported Remonstrantism had (re)turned to the Dutch Reformed Church and the ecclesiastical councils. Other Remonstrants instituted their own church, the Remonstrant Brotherhood.

The meeting regime employed by the Synod of Dort were largely borrowed from the States-General. The operating procedure was slow and time consuming. Particularly the English representatives complained about this. The states had issued seventeen 'articles or laws for conducting the National Synod', in which were laid down the composition, time, place and way of making decisions. Each province sent two delegates (church members) with an advisory vote. These 'political delegates' also had the task of 'ruling and guiding so that all confusion and chaos could be prevented' in the dealings of the synod (Brandt, 1704, Part III, p. 34). The synod was divided into 22 boards, which met separately, and which each considered the subject to be discussed in the plenary meeting the following day. If required, every board handed in a *judicium*, unless somebody on the board wished to cast their vote by roll call. If there was a radical proposition to be discussed, there were often eighteen or more judgements read out. These written judgements then went

FIGURE 5.1   Synod of Dort, 1618–1619 (Rijksmuseum-Stichting, Amsterdam)

to the *moderamen,* who produced a final *judicium* which was read out to the synod. After this, it was considered as accepted unless the president thought an individual vote was required (Kaajan, 1914, pp. 42–3). A remarkable stipulation in the regulations of the states was that whatever 'was accepted by majority vote would be valid as a decision of the synod, so that those who had voted otherwise should not be insinuated about, reprimanded for, or called to account for it' (*ibid.*, p. 34). The order for a reconciliatory attitude towards minorities is typical of the transformation from a society dominated by warriors to a society where civilians had the upper hand, and the requisite level of reciprocal self-restraint had increased in the upper classes.

In the Synod of Dort, besides the established meeting rules of the States-General and the regulations enforced by the states, use was also made of a discussion about the holding of national synods which had been written about 70 years previous by the German humanist and theologian Hyperius (Kaajan, 1914, pp. 43 and 45). In the middle of the sixteenth century Hyperius, who was attached to the University of Marburg, wrote a discourse about the way in which a synod should be held. In 1610 this treatise was translated into Dutch and published together with a thesis by Arminius under the title *Code book for organizing and conducting annual Synods*. With this publication, the publishers, supporters of the Remonstrant leader Arminius, hoped to inspire 'the High and Mighty States' to satisfy the religious quarrels 'with a Christian Synod, in which reasons would be compared with reasons' (Introduction, p. 7).

Hyperius's treatise consisted of a series of recommendations derived from the manners that the bishops employed in the ecumenical councils. The following points cover Hyperius's most striking recommendations.[5]

- The order of the speakers does not have to be the same as the ranking order of the seating. 'Often it happens that the best and soundest reasoning is heard from those seated at the back who, as such, are the last to be asked for their opinion. This is either because they have had more time to consider or because they have been assisted by all the opinions already voiced' (D 2 verso). The Synod of Dort did not take this recommendation to heart. As in the majority of meetings during the Dutch Republic they retained a strict order of speakers based on rank and status.
- After someone has been appointed to whom complaints and points of the agenda could be submitted, and everyone has put in an appearance by swearing an oath, the chairman should call those present to exercise 'belief, honesty, modesty, caution, and calmness' during the meeting. Nobody should be permitted to fail to appear or prematurely depart. God's priests should not 'through indiscreet noise create pandemonium, nor talk nor laugh idly nor, even worse, make a noise with obstinate contentions . . . there is no justice if silence is not observed and the din of loud shouting disturbs the judgement.' Whoever transgressed against these rules should be excluded from the meeting, because it is plainly apparent that nothing good could be expected from a synod 'where affairs are handled in turbulence and chaos by quarrelsome men hungry for honour' (D 4).

During the Synod of Dort there were frequent violent clashes, and the Counter-Remonstrant majority positioned the Remonstrants into being the complainers and finally ejected them from the meeting. This illustrates how both Hyperius's and the states' recommendations to respect differing opinions were hardly self-evident.

The seventeenth-century historian Gerard Brandt reported in his *History of the Reformation* that the Remonstrants were considered suspect from the outset. Already, after the first day, the Remonstrants complained about the unfriendly way in which they were treated: 'That on their entrance many did not remove their hats, that bias and bitterness could be seen on the faces of many of the men, and that the words used to address them were frequently as sharp as a razor's edge' (Brandt, 1704, Part III, p. 34).

Like the majority of the clerical and political delegates, the chairmanship (chosen by the synod) was well-disposed to the Counter-Remonstrant stance, and as such exerted additional influence in this direction. At 'indiscriminate' times in a meeting the chairmanship would have decrees read out from previous sessions for approval. This was not done 'in every session or in the following session when the details were still fresh in the members' memories', but sometimes ten or fourteen days later, and at times 'unexpectedly, at a moment's notice, when people were gathered to discuss other affairs, when people had partially forgotten it and did not have the notes they had made with them. All of a sudden a good impression was created and the decree hastily read out. Foreigners sometimes complained about this as such procedures came over as extremely suspicious' (Brandt, 1704, Part III, pp. 190–1). The summoned Remonstrants complained that the president, Bogerman, 'constantly interrupted them at whim when they were speaking about affairs in hand, in order to silence them or have them leave the room, thus creating the opportunity to blacken their reputations behind their backs without having to fear contradiction or accusations of bias' (*ibid.*, p. 302).

The chairmanship and the political delegates barely gave the Remonstrants an opportunity to bring their ideas into the limelight. The persons summoned were frequently not given a chance to establish a collective opinion by participating in mutual consultations, or only permitted to do so after lengthy implorations. Their opposers made attempts to keep these as short as possible. As a result some were not able to control their feelings of impatience, anger and animosity. In the 53rd session, when the Remonstrants refused to accede to the chairman's request to give the names of those whom they considered to be the church teachers, Bogerman became so angry that he began to suggest the names himself. According to witnesses the chairman uttered the names with such derision and in such a tone:

> That his face changed, and his limbs trembled, such that he could not express himself and spoke in a disjointed manner. When he recovered, he noticed that

several participants had taken offence and he ordered the Remonstrants outside so he could excuse himself to the synod. He put the blame onto the Remonstrants by entreating the political delegates and the synod not to hold his anger against him. (Brandt, 1704, Part III, p. 299)

According to the summoned Remonstrants some of the delegates of the states were even more forcefully against them than those from the church. The political delegates 'generally treated them extremely roughly, made many resolutions to their disadvantage and approached them in a very threatening way; those of them who were more modest could achieve nothing.' As the synod had made more than one pronouncement against the recommendations of the political delegates, the Remonstrants concluded 'that they could expect even less from the political delegates than from the synod itself' (*ibid.*, p. 303).

On various occasions, the political delegates and the Remonstrants had violent clashes. When the Remonstrants requested permission to discuss among themselves a question posed by the synod concerning one of the five doctrines to which the entire synod was orientated, they were initially refused. The chairman demanded a direct answer.

Sharp words were voiced. The then-president of the political delegates, a mild-tempered gentleman from Friesland, had his position repeatedly taken over by others. Mainly it was the secretary, Heinsius who, shouting and thumping the table such that the whole room resounded, repeatedly demanded 'you are commanded to be silent, will you comply or not?' (*ibid.*, p. 160)

Several days later tempers flared again when the Remonstrants refused to formulate their ideas about the five doctrines.

Many words were spoken regarding this, but whatever the Remonstrants objected to was in vain, and Heinsius, banging on the table, repeatedly called 'the Gentlemens' delegates of the States wish, command, charge, and compel you to silence'. Nevertheless, they continued to refuse. Then the president warned them that they should not behave as a board, but that they were each obliged to answer for themselves. (*ibid.*, p. 188)

In a separate meeting between the political delegates and the Remonstrants during the 56th session, members of the states accused the latter that they had 'brought the country to the verge of chaos; introduced a new doctrine to the church; split ecclesiastical communities; refused to submit to anyone; and refused to obey the commands of their government'. The Remonstrants defended themselves by referring to the freedom of conscience. They announced that they were prepared to accept the appropriate punishment for their disobedience. However, the political delegates demanded unconditional obedience. Brandt reported:

> For a whole hour, there was a bitter dispute about this. The Remonstrants said that the political delegates had constantly insisted upon obedience and had reproached their disobedience at every opportunity. As a result of this they were shouted at in such an indecently vehement manner that they did not know who to answer. The councillor Van de Honaert was not able to calm the gentlemen either with the use of words or by rapping the table. Therefore, embarrassed and cowed by all that turbulence, he remained seated for almost an hour without speaking. (1704, Part III, p. 291)

The final reason why Bogerman threw the Remonstrants out of the meeting was typical of the mood and the vehemence of many of the synodal sessions. The chairman said: 'Leave in the same way as you arrived. You began with lies, and you end with lies.' He concluded his speech with: 'Then I take leave of you in the name of the Gentlemens' delegates of the States and the synod. You have not succeeded. Leave' (*ibid.*, p. 299). Many of those present, even some Counter-Remonstrants, criticized Bogerman's speech because they took offence to his 'explosion into an excessive rage towards the Remonstrants during his last address. Moreover, he had neither control of his face nor tongue and, according to witnesses, he spoke faulty Latin on several occasions' (*ibid.*, p. 299). The moderate theologian, Crocius, from Bremen, who was present during Bogerman's speech, later wrote that for such an important question, more consideration and consultation should have been shown and, that for the synod's honour, it would have been far better if a calmer and less passionate speech had been delivered (Brandt, 1704, Part III, p. 301).

Not only did the discussions between the Counter-Remonstrants and the Remonstrants sometimes take a violent turn, but so too did those debates the Counter-Remonstrants had among themselves. The main advocate of the strongest interpretation of the doctrine of predestination, Gomarus, called his less rigid opponents 'stakes', 'blockheads' and 'donkeys' and got himself so wound up that, in his fury, he could not utter a single word. The chairman, Bogerman, 'saved' the situation by thanking the speaker on behalf of the entire meeting for his clever and virile speech (Romein, 1977, p. 315).

The Synod of Dort in 1618–1619, where the Protestant leaders sometimes had a great deal of difficulty in controlling their fury if their propositions and interpretations were challenged, draws attention to how slowly and laboriously meeting behaviour developed to become a more peaceful activity on a more equal footing. In this period, in which mutual tensions were mainly manifested in religious conflicts, emotional restraint during ecclesiastical meetings was not only a problem for the lower church officials but an equal problem for higher church officials and for delegates of the states.

One final example is taken from Brandt. After the Synod of Dort, a number of Remonstrants were allowed into the meeting of the States-General 'legally manoeuvred' by Maurits consequent to their requesting permission to arrange their financial affairs before their exclusion. Brandt writes:

> When making this request, the Messrs Muis of Dort and Pauw of Amsterdam frequently interrupted their address and effectively gagged them. The Remonstrants reported that the gentlemen let loose such stupidity and bitterness against them that president Ploos seemed ashamed and more than once rapped his gavel on the table in an attempt to be heard and regain order, but it was in vain. (1704, Part III, p. 696)

The Counter-Remonstrant majority imposed their interpretation on the church and, going against the decision-making procedures laid down by the states, 'accused', 'reprimanded' and 'aggrieved' the followers of the more reasonable interpretation of the Bible and church history – and the states, dominated by Calvinists, permitted it. In today's parliamentary society in which, concurrent with democratization, the reason for majority rule has become obvious, it is perhaps difficult for people to imagine what the application of this rule must have meant in a previous society as regards restraining from the tendency to denounce, threaten and eliminate minorities. Public accusation and condemnation of minorities with a differing viewpoint is a powerful parliamentary taboo. Regarding this point, generally, whoever is unable to control themselves in parliament is immediately called to order. The same is valid for majority rule as for many other present-day, self-evident meeting rules: their application presumes a certain degree of safety and security in everyday life.

More modest battles with words

The Protestant meeting rules were directed at a stricter and broader meeting discipline than had been until then required of people from the middle and lower classes, who were excluded from participating in official meetings of the towns, church and state. Absolutely forbidden were lateness, swearing, playing around, quarrelling, sleeping, chattering, lying, walking around, interrupting and imposing one's own opinion onto others. Individuals had to speak calmly, seriously, edifyingly, short and succinctly, in turn after permission from the chairman and without vehement, repetitious and circuitous arguments. They were also required to listen attentively to others. In comparison to previous writings about meeting behaviour, such as *Senatulus*, the Protestant meeting rules show a considerable increase in these types of regulations; this accentuates the politically educating function of the Reform

Movement. Large groups of people were educated in political skills as a result of the Reformation. Gradually they learnt to battle more modesty with words within a more pacified society. The course of the Synod of Dort and, as far as it is known, those of local and provincial ecclesiastical meetings, demonstrates that this collective learning process developed in fits and starts, without ever becoming finalized.

In some respects (for instance, the attention focused on sleeping, walking around and making a racket) the Protestant meeting rules are reminiscent of the guild statutes of the Middle Ages referred to earlier. This similarity can be explained by the comparable functions fulfilled by the guilds in the Middle Ages and the Reformed Churches in the early modern period. Both were institutions in which broad layers of the urban population were mobilized into, and educated in, the political power battle at respectively town and national levels. Probably the reformers elaborated on the meeting manners of the guilds of the Middle Ages. Many of the first reformers and members of the Reformed Church came from the class of artisans and could have been members of guilds and the civic guard.

The meeting rules of the Reformed Churches, within which more people from more differing levels and classes had to meet more often than in the guilds, as such presumed and demanded a greater and more differentiated self-restraint. While the guild statutes contained numerous stipulations referring to disruptions to order, such as fighting, shouting, drunken talk, knife pulling, glass throwing and bearing arms, the Protestant meeting rules were more concerned with regulating verbal battles, and made greater demands upon an individual's capacity for thinking and his 'conscience'. Although everyday social intercourse was still far from peaceful, the more violent aspects of society were excluded from the prescribed meeting behaviour more than they were in the previous period. The meeting rules were not formulated as worldly wisdom or practical requirements for social behaviour, but rather as ethical norms or laws of God, and learnt as 'semi-automatic functioning impulses of conscience'.

The lessening of conflicts and tensions within ecclesiastical meetings after the Synod of Dort provided favourable conditions for the individual learning processes of how to hold and attend meetings. Initially it was the custom to read out the prevailing meeting rules at the start of each church council meeting. Later this occurred less often – once or twice a year. This could indicate that the rules had become more self-evident for the majority of those present. However, sources of scarce historical research surmise that many were not always able to adhere to the church's meeting rules and that many would lose their self-control as tensions rose. From this, the falling into disuse of the custom of reading out the rules at the start of each meeting can be seen as an indication of decreasing tensions within the church and society, and a greater degree of safety and social security.

CHAPTER 6

THE FORMATION OF THE FIRST
MEETING CLASS IN EUROPE

The Dutch Republic as a game of meetings

The establishment of the Republic of the United Provinces was an unintentional and unplanned process. The borders of the Republic were largely determined by the course of the revolt and war against the Habsburg monarch. The government unexpectedly fell into the hands of an upper class comprised largely of patricians, after they had unsuccessfully sought for a member of the upper aristocracy to rule the country on their behalf. Hesitantly, the town governments undertook to lead the government of the country. Searching and groping, they shaped a new, relatively unusual state organization which, in the long run, they came to consider as something perfectly obvious and, finally, as something that should be maintained as it stood.

In contrast to the majority of other European countries of that period, where a long-term balance of power between the aristocratic and bourgeois upper classes afforded monarchs the opportunity to establish dynastic, aristocratic royal states, the relatively homogeneous, mainly urban upper class in the northern Netherlands organized itself into a political formation which was:

> Founded upon committees and boards in which the members sat as equal partners and through which the decisions were taken more as a result of persuasion than as a result of vetos or command from above. Unavoidably, behind these smaller committees were yet more meetings, not only the meetings of the States-General, but also those from every region, thus spread far and wide across the Republic, in regions, and towns. (Schöffer, 1964, pp. 77–8)

The network of political meetings on which, and through which, the Dutch Republic was governed was built from below. Town governments, boards of members of the knighthood and, in the north, farming communities too, sent

FIGURE 6.1 The Netherlands, 1550 (black and white) and 1648 (only black)

delegates to the provincial states who, in turn, delegated deputies to the States-General (who bore the responsibility for holding consultations). The highest governmental body of the Republic could accomplish little without the approval of the provincial states, the foundation boards of the town governments and the knighthood. Within the Republican meeting regime, the town governments of Holland fulfilled a pivotal function.

In the time of the Republic, a town government was comprised of between twenty and forty distinguished burghers or patricians, and boards of magistrates comprising a bailiff, seven to nine aldermen for the maintenance of order and the administration of justice, and two to four burgomasters [translator's note:

chief magistrates of a Dutch or Flemish town, equivalent to English mayors] for daily governmental affairs. The magistrates were chosen from the patricians, and usually by them. They filled their resulting vacancies by co-option. The patricians met on the suggestion, and under the leadership, of the presiding mayor about appointments, municipal finances, town defence, the care of orphans, the elderly and the poor and other affairs of the town. However, they spent the majority of their time and energy on the determination of the positions that their delegates should take in the meetings of the provincial and national boards, in which the enfranchised towns were represented in turn.

A taste of the way in which a meeting of the city council was generally conducted can be had from the following description. It was written by the historian, M. Prak, and concerns a meeting of the city council of Leiden in the eighteenth century. Prak's impression could be equally applicable to meetings of other town councils in Holland during the time of the Dutch Republic.[1]

> In the council chamber the burgomasters and the aldermen sat around a large, round table, together with the Pensionary and the secretary [author's note: in other towns the table was elongated, in Amsterdam it was L-shaped]. The remaining members had to be satisfied with a chair against the wall. Everyone had their own place, which was determined in order of rank. The meeting was provided with information in a verbal form only; no papers were circulated. After prayers and the opening by the president-mayor, the Pensionary read the report of the meeting of the states and announced the 'points of convening', a detailed agenda for the next sitting of the states. In response to all this, the burgomasters made recommendations about the position of the town. Then the matter was opened for comment, by which the councillors were allowed to make comments in the order of their rank. The youngest member was therefore the last to speak. Meanwhile, the gentlemen had to listen to lengthy monologues without having had the possibility to make any notes – after all, they were not seated at the table. Whoever wished to make a comment, had to restrain from doing so for a considerable time. Actually, the most important questions had frequently already been discussed by a small circle of burgomasters and ex-burgomasters, and too much discussion during the council meeting was generally not appreciated. Finally, the resolutions were decided by majority vote, and documented by the secretary. No report was made of the course of the discussions and the voting. (Prak, 1985, p. 33)

The admittance to the meetings of the city council and the fulfilment of a position as a burgomaster were the pivotal points in an official-political career, in a way similar to the key position that town governments held within the network of political meetings. Emanating from the town councils 'was a network of lines to practically everything that could be organized within a town, and to regional and national boards' (Prak, 1985, p. 30). Occupying a seat in council (for which no salary was paid) opened the door to all sorts of functions that were politically and financially attractive, such as chairman or steward of a board of trustees of a place of worship, captain of the citizens' militia, commissioner of the credit bank, church warden, alderman, tax collector, burgomaster and subsequently possibly bailiff, delegate at the provincial states and the States-General, member of a Standing Commission or the Council of State, auditor at an auditors' office, member of the Board of the Admiralty, dyke warden, or director of the United East and West India Companies.

The official positions at regional and central level were the most profitable in a financial sense; those at municipal level the least, with the exception of the bailiff. However, the fulfilment of a less lucrative municipal function was necessary to rise to a higher level. The holding of the position of burgomaster was a decisive point in a meeting career. In principle whoever was burgomaster, or had been burgomaster, had access to all other offices of state.[2] The number of official positions, which carried a lot of influence and were highly paid, was limited, and the competition was often fierce. 'Many regents had to wait a long time until they were able to secure such a position, others never had their turn' (De Jong, 1985, p. 44). After about 1650 the better official positions in most of the towns were monopolized by a small group of families.

In terms of a sociological game model that Elias described in *What is Sociology?* (1978), the Dutch Republic can be understood as a stage in the transition from an 'oligarchic type' into an increasingly 'democratic type' (pp. 87–91). During the transformation, in the latter half of the sixteenth century, from an urban court society into an urban republican society, the number of meetings in which a common future was discussed and decided increased considerably, and the power differences between the meeting levels decreased. Those who met at the upper levels were less independent than those at the lower levels; they operated more as the representatives of those who met at lower levels. Due to the mounting influence of the latter, the decision-making process became more complicated and differentiated. Every individual meeting participant was constrained and confined to a much greater degree, kept in check by the number of simultaneous interdependent meetings at lower levels and by people that were becoming less and less socially inferior.

The network of the interwoven meetings began to branch out further and could not be clearly surveyed even by the most gifted participant. It became increasingly difficult, as an individual or as a single group, to focus the decision-making process in the desired direction, although there was no lack of effort through manipulation and lobbying to do precisely this. As the distribution of the power weights became less unequal and more diffuse, the process that resulted from the interweaving of decisions of a large number of socially diverse participants, determined in its turn more strongly the thoughts and actions of every single meeting participant or group of participants.

In comparison to the previous courtly stage, the Dutch Republic represented a more democratic type of game in the sense that the most important decisions about the next moves in the social game (that is, those decisions involving the most people) were made in meetings of people who had received their directives from meetings taking place at lower levels of integration. However, this game had a heavily oligarchic character. The majority of the population (the players) were excluded from the meetings in which the important moves in the social game were discussed and decided and, as far as possible, they were kept ignorant of the considerations and discussions that had led to these moves. The limitations experienced by the meeting participants, when considering their decisions, emanate more from their relations with the upper levels of the countries against which they played, and from the relations between themselves and the ruling balances of power, than from the non-participants of the meetings. The latent strength of the latter was, in particular, indirectly demonstrated; in the measures that the meeting participants issued to keep them under control and out of the active game, and in the meeting manners that the active players developed under pressure from, and in distinction to, the rising group of meeting participants.

Further details of this 'urban republican game model' are described in the following section, based on regulations, reports, and descriptions of meetings of the States-General, the States of Holland, the town governments of Holland, the Council of State and the United East India Company, and on a series of meeting rules from an early seventeenth-century manual. For the proposition concerning the meetings of the states in the latter years of the Republic, particular use has been made of the study *Geheimhouding en verraad* (Confidentiality and Treachery) by G. de Bruin (1991).

Because of the risk of 'state affairs' being leaked to internal and external enemies, as little as possible was documented about the matters discussed in meetings and, consequently, the number of available sources is limited, although much greater than from the previous stage. The codes of order and the resolutions that the states deployed and determined in the last quarter of the sixteenth century are among the most informative sources.

The written regulation of meetings

During the Dutch Revolt when the leadership of the monarch and the court ceased, the town governments and the other foundation boards realized the need to fill all of the vacant supralocal co-ordinating functions in the communal regional and national meetings of the states. The lack of a governing centre, the great increase in the number of co-ordination problems, and the urgency of many of the decisions, prompted the states to regulate their meetings in a closer and more encompassing way. A large section of the rules to which the town and country representatives adhered, during the bicentennial of the existence of the Dutch Republic, for the meetings of the provincial states, the States-General, and many other secular boards, were developed or made explicit in this initial phase, and documented in regulations and resolutions. For this purpose, not only the existent meeting habits and traditions of political organizations were elaborated upon, but also ecclesiastical meeting rules were used, which the reformers had for the most part gathered from political meetings and councils.

Shortly after the States of Holland had broken with the royal government, they established a code of order for themselves. In September 1573 several of them were presented with the task of preparing a proposal for such a code. In February 1574 their first official set of regulations were approved. In 1581 and 1585 new versions appeared, in which the resolutions had been adjusted to the additions or alterations that the states had made in the meantime. Because the meetings did not progress 'as they should', it was also decided that every member of the states should get a copy of the code of order, so that every member of the board was informed of the way in which he was expected to transact business, deliberate and decide, and was aware of what he should comply to in consideration of the tranquillity, order and demands of the commonwealth (*Resolutien van Staten van Holland en Westvriesland, 19 February 1585*).

Likewise, the rebellious states that met together on their own initiative were, due to the absence of a ruler, faced with the problem of organizing their own deliberations. One of the first difficulties they had to tackle was the filling of the vacant function of chairman. It was decided to allow the chairmanship to be occupied for the period of one week by each of the different regions; a regulation which remained in force until the end of the Dutch Republic. With the replacement of the permanent monocratic leadership of meetings by a rotating chairmanship, the steep decline in power differences revealed itself most clearly.

The states developed their own registry for the determination and the registration of their resolutions and, on the 27 March 1577, shortly after the Pacification of Ghent, which heralded the spreading of the Dutch Revolt over the entire Netherlands, they approved their first official code of order *sur l'ordre à observer dans leurs assemblées*.[3] With the addition of several amending regulations, which were mostly dealt with before 1590, this code remained in power until the end of the eighteenth century, when broader layers of the population acquired access to the central political meetings.

The meeting rules and manners which were found out in practice, elucidated, and chronicled during the setting up of the Republic, served to determine where, when, by whom and in which way, deliberations and discussions should be carried out concerning the communal future. The demise of the monarch's authority, the increase in the number of co-ordination problems, the accelerated rate at which these problems occurred, and the changed status of the meetings, presented the states and other boards with the task of forging agreements about fixed times and places for meetings; about the distribution of co-ordinating functions; about participation, presence and absence, about seating arrangements, opening, speaking and decision making, documenting and registering decisions, and maintaining the confidentiality of the meetings.

Not all the operating or future operating customs and rules were documented. In the Code of Order and the resolutions about meeting order, there is little written about the application of meeting requisitions, yet important changes concerning this point took place during the Dutch Revolt. After the demise of royal authority, the use henceforth of a meeting table was characteristic of the new attitude of the States-General. In the monarchical period people used to be seated on rows of benches in the monarch's presence, while the court representatives were seated on chairs on a dais.

From using the regulations and resolutions of meetings as sources, just as little is known about the use of a chairman's gavel. However, from other sources, such as the previously mentioned book by Gerard Brandt, it seems that this requisite was used by the chairman of the States-General in the seventeenth and eighteenth centuries.[4] Precisely when this tool was introduced is unclear, but it could well be that it was copied along with several other customs, such as the use of a table, from the States of Brabant or the Brussels town government, which was heavily influenced by the traditions of the guilds. The states met in the town hall of Brussels, in the immediate presence of these bodies, until February 1578 (Japikse, 1916, p. 32).

During the establishment of the Dutch Republic, meeting regulations and meeting manners of other committees and organizations were also set down in writing. Not infrequently the states provided guidelines for this which they had taken in part from their own meeting practices. The restructuring of the Council of State and the structuring of the United East India Company are examples of this.[5]

In 1588, the States-General formulated a 'fluctuating' order for the Council of State, by which it was made totally subordinate to them. The Council was given two main tasks: to assist with the preparation and execution of the decisions of the states. In which particular instance the council had to perform these tasks was dependent upon the wishes and needs of the states at that specific point in time. Furthermore, the order contained a series of restrictions with regard to the Council's composition and its manner of meeting.

The meetings had to take place at an 'appropriate and safe' place; the exact choice of which was left to the Council itself. The Council chose the *Binnenhof* in The Hague, the former residence of the Count of Holland, now the meeting place of the States of Holland and the States-General (indeed, the Dutch Parliament still holds its meetings here). Furthermore, the order prescribed that the Council was to meet daily, in the morning at nine o'clock and in the afternoon at three o'clock, except on Sundays and public holidays. The vacant chairmanship was left for the Council to fill in its own manner. Imitating the decision of the States-General in 1566, the Council decided to allow the provinces to rotate the occupation of this function. One province was to chair the meeting for eight consecutive days. Moreover, the order determined that the chairman had the task of proposing the points of convening, to ask for the recommendations and to summarize, to reconcile deviating points of view to those of others, and to maintain supervision of the resolutions which were to be formulated in writing. Members had to request permission to speak from him, and nobody was allowed to speak or leave the chamber without his permission. Decisions could be taken by majority vote. The remaining articles of the order concerned the management, the signing and the sealing of matters concerning received and outgoing post and the salaries of the members of the council.

The organization of the states also served as a model for the structuring of the United East India Company (in Dutch abbreviated as VOC), which again served as an example for other business ventures, such as the West India Company (in Dutch abbreviated as WIC).[6] At the end of the sixteenth century in many towns of Holland and Zealand, companies were established for trade with Asia. These companies were organizations which co-operated for the arrangement of one shipment. The entrepreneurs accumulated the necessary capital to purchase a ship and muster a crew. Those who offered financial support, the stockholders, were termed 'participants'. Once the shipment had been completed, the commodities and the ship were resold, and the profits divided up among the stockholders and the entrepreneurs. Stimulated by sharp swings in the market, these previous local companies began to co-operate more closely together.

After several unsuccessful attempts at co-operation between the companies of Holland and Zeeland (the companies of Zeeland feared being financially dominated by Amsterdam), the States of Holland placed the co-operation problems on the agenda of the meetings of the States-General. In 1602, with the assistance of the stadholder, the Grand Pensionary, Van Oldenbarnevelt, succeeded in uniting the entrepreneurs of Holland and Zeeland into a common organization: the United East India Company. On 20 March 1602, following difficult negotiations with the entrepreneurs, the States-General confirmed that the Republic had issued the VOC with a monopoly for trade with the East Indies for 21 years.

The largest part of this patent was related to the organization of the VOC and it reflected the state organization of the Dutch Republic. One of the conditions determined by the patent was that a board of directors, to be known as chambers, should be installed in each of the six towns where companies already existed. Amsterdam was appointed a chamber comprising twenty directors, Zeeland (the town of Middelburg) a chamber of twelve directors, and Rotterdam, Delft, Hoorn and Enkhuizen were each to have a chamber comprising seven directors. When the States-General had financially to assist the VOC in 1610, the other provinces likewise demanded a say in the VOC. Consequently, 'extraordinary' directors were attached to the chambers. These had an advisory say in matters. Later, with the extension of the patent, several more extraordinary directors were attached, on behalf of, for example, the towns of Leiden and Haarlem and the knighthood of Holland.

The highest board of the VOC was the Court of Directors, the so-called *Heren XVII* (Seventeen Gentlemen), which met alternatively in Amsterdam and Middelburg; six consecutive years in Amsterdam, followed by two consecutive years in Middelburg. The highest meeting of the VOC comprised delegates from the different chambers: eight delegates from Amsterdam, four from Zeeland, and one from each of the smaller chambers. The seventeenth of the Court of Directors came alternatively from Zeeland and one of the smaller chambers. Kristof Glamann (1981) wrote:

> That the *Heren XVII* by nature must be considered the actual management of the company, its central organ, appears from the mere fact that its decisions were binding for the Chambers. True, it is evident that during the first years it was difficult for the *Heren XVII* to assert their authority as long as the directors in the Chambers were identical with those of the previous local companies [sic]. But gradually the Board gained ground and strengthened its authority. The procedure of the meetings was in advance announced to the Chambers by the so-called presidential Chamber, i.e. the Chamber in which the *Heren XVII* held their meeting and from where their president was elected. (1981, p. 4)

The creation of the VOC brought with it a new stage in the organization of trade. The VOC had ample military authority, the power of the stockholders declined in favour of the directors once they were obliged to invest their money for at least ten years, the organizers changed from being 'free entrepreneurs' to co-directors of an sustainable business with a large number of people in their employ: from several tens of thousands in the beginning of the seventeenth century to more than 125,000 by the middle of the eighteenth century.

The history of the Council of State and the VOC represents a development which can also be seen in other national and provincial governing bodies of the Dutch Republic, such as the Auditing Chambers, the Courts of Justice, and the Boards of the Admiralty. The latter was responsible for sea defence, jurisdiction about prices, and the levies on imports and exports. Characteristic of this development was the official subordination of these boards to the town governments, which were united in the meetings of the states. Through the issuing of meeting instructions and other guidelines, the delegation of participants and the appointment of supervisors or political agents, the town governments and the states attempted to obtain and maintain both dominance and an overview of the entire complicated 'decision-making process' of the developing state of the Netherlands.

More frequent and more regular meetings

During the establishment of the self-government of the states, merely the considerable increase in tasks was sufficient to prompt them into regulating for a firmer control of their meetings. The resolution of the Code of Order of the States-General begins with the words: 'Les estatz généraulx désirans donner accélération aux affaires survenans journellement en grande abondance.'[7]

During the Dutch Revolt, the tasks of the States-General extended to include the entire area for which the monarch had previously decided: conscription and payment of troops, instructing the Council of State, appointment of councillors and military commanders, issuing and imposing taxation, arranging loans and even choosing a governor. In the years following the Revolt, their tasks began to stretch to other areas, for example, legislation, jurisdiction and governing conquered areas, supervision of auditing chambers, the minting chamber, the trading companies, and the churches, the reception of foreign envoys and the concern for aliens (Schöffer, 1964, pp. 75–7).

Likewise, the sphere of activity of the provincial states was enlarged due to the Revolt. In addition to having to prepare for the meetings of the States-General by instructing the delegates in general, the States of Holland acquired important tasks in the field of warfare, such as the maintenance of reinforcements, the supply of munitions, and the determination of the strength and the placements of troops in Holland. Also regarding fiscal tasks, they found that the amount of work demanded of them increased while, at the same time, other activities also required their attention, such as the promotion of trade and fishing, the control of the water boards and the courts of justice, and tasks of legislation and jurisdiction. Entirely new was their involvement with the church, the University of Leiden, and the paying of preachers and professors (Koopmans, 1990, pp. 145–78).

The break with the royal government and the considerable expansion of governmental tasks had the consequence that the states began to meet more often. The annual number of days upon which plenary meetings were held in the decades before the Dutch Revolt and in the two centuries after the Revolt are summarized in Table 6.1.

Table 6.1   Number of annual meeting days of the States of Holland and the States-General before and after the Dutch Revolt

	Before Revolt	After Revolt	Percentage increase
States of Holland	< 70	> 210	≥ 300
States-General	< 45	> 330	≥ 730

Sources: Koopmans, 1990, p. 180; Gilissen, 1965, p. 275; Schöffer, 1964, p. 66

Before the Revolt, the states met at continually different times and places. Sometimes, the States-General met four times a year, as in the year 1505, but at other times, they did not meet at all for several years, such as the periods from 1537 to 1540, and from 1569 to 1572. They mainly met in Brussels, but sometimes they met in Mechelen, Ghent, Antwerp or in smaller towns in Brabant, Flanders or Henegouwen. Before the Revolt there was also variation in the place and times of the meetings of the States of Holland (Kokken, 1991, pp. 126–34; Koopmans, 1990, pp. 180–1). During the Revolt, because of the dubious situation resulting from the war, people were compelled to meet at irregular times and places sometimes distant from and sometimes close to the war front, as far as this possibility was allowed and demanded by the war. At the end of each meeting, the place and the time of the next meeting were agreed. It was only at the end of the 1570s that the states were in a position to meet in set places at set times.

In 1578 the course of the war enabled the States of Holland to choose a fixed meeting place. After some bickering, it was finally decided in order 'to avoid jealousy between the towns' henceforth to hold all the meetings of the states and the boards in The Hague, except when the stadholder had another place in mind. Both the stadholders' residence and the Court of Holland were also situated in The Hague (Koopmans, 1990, p. 182). From that time onwards they gathered together on average twelve times per year in a regular or special meeting which lasted between two to five weeks. At these times they met for several hours both in the mornings and in the afternoons. To deal with current business in the periods in between, they appointed from their number a smaller committee of delegates which gradually developed into an executive committee known as the *Gecommiteerde Staten* (Standing Committee). The uncertainty of the meeting place was thus solved in principle, but in practice, meetings were still frequently held elsewhere. This sometimes led to disorders in communication. Thus, it happened that for a meeting in 1587, the secretary and the Standing Committee sat in The Hague, while the nobles and delegates from Leiden, Amsterdam and Gouda had gone to Delft (Koopmans, 1990, p. 182).

Also, during the Revolt the States-General met each time in different places in the liberated areas and at irregular times. After the south was again placed under Spanish administration, the States-General likewise chose The Hague as the fixed meeting place. In 1588, they acquired a place in the *Binnenhof* so that Holland was in the same position as Brabant previously: close to the decision-making centre.

In the first years of the Republic, the States-General met only if they had been asked by written invitation. The meetings were only dissolved when the points of convening had been dealt with. The Code of Order of the States-General of 1577 determined that the meetings should take place from eight o'clock until eleven-thirty and from four o'clock until six o'clock. At the end of each meeting, the date of the next meeting was agreed. Soon there was so much to do that they had to meet throughout the whole year. As a matter of course, the meetings of the States-General became permanent fixtures. From 1593 onwards meetings were no longer adjourned and took place daily from ten o'clock in the morning to twelve-thirty in the afternoon. In cases of emergency, they also took place in the afternoons, evenings and even on Sundays after church service. In the eighteenth century the number of hours that the states met for plenary meetings diminished to between one and a half to two hours per day due to the expansion of the committee system.

At municipal level, administrative activities increased similarly. After the Revolt, the towns acquired power almost equivalent to that of a sovereign. The city council, that had to approve mandates of the municipal delegates in the meetings of the states, began to meet more regularly (generally once a fortnight), and the burgomasters much more often. In a middle sized town such as Gouda, they regularly met every Tuesday and otherwise 'if it was necessary'; however, this was the case almost daily.

> Moreover, the burgomasters were, as a matter of course, present at the meetings of the magistrates and city council and one of them attended the sittings of the States of Holland. In contrast to membership of merely the city council, burgomastership demanded pretty-well a full day's work. Through their many activities, they acquired an advantage over the other councillors, an advantage that they had no desire to part with. Many conflicts between the council chamber and the burgomaster's office could be traced back to the attempts of a section of the council to call a halt to these developments. (De Jong, 1985, p. 27; Kooymans, 1985, p. 29)

It was no different in the other towns. Everywhere the tasks and the power of the burgomasters increased noticeably after the Revolt.

The board of directors of the VOC met three times a year (later on it was twice) in sessions lasting for several weeks. Their meeting schedule was determined by the shipping schedule between the Netherlands and Asia. They met in the Summer and Autumn when the ships docked and in the Spring when the commodities were sold. The Autumn meeting was the most important. On this occasion the dates and the places of the auctions were determined; the 'equipage' for the following year was decided (the number of ships, number of crew members and goods); an estimate was made of the gold and silver to be exported and the goods to be imported; and the most important administrative matters and appointments were dealt with.

The meeting time of the board of directors could be relatively brief, as many co-ordinating tasks were prepared and executed by four committees which the board had assembled from its midst to check the accounts, to calculate the annual financial balance, to attend auctions and to correspond with administrations and civil servants in Asia. Besides this there were the local Chambers of the VOC with their own committees which had to implement the decisions of the central board, and be involved with the auctions and the construction of ships. They met throughout the whole year.

The regulation of participation

During the Dutch Revolt and the formation of the Republic, the criteria for admission to political meetings became more precise and formal.

The final size of the Republic and the ultimate composition of the States-General were predominantly determined by the course of the war against Spain. The regions of Gelderland, Overijssel and Groningen were the last to achieve full membership in the new association of states. The 'eighth province', Drenthe, where the state convention was dominated by free farmers, was excluded from participating in the meetings of the States-General. The extension of the number of enfranchised members in the States-General was restricted by the associated regions. The constant quarrels between the town of Groningen and the surrounding countryside was hardly viewed as encouraging (Schöffer, 1964, p. 69).

The provinces could appoint as many delegates for the States-General as they wished. Altogether they did not send, in practice, more than 25 to 30 delegates at the beginning of the seventeenth century, and between 40 and 50 in subsequent years. The actual number of participants in the meetings was generally lower (initially ten to fifteen and later 20 to 30), as not all of the delegates always appeared or were present for the whole of the meeting. Typical of the unplanned and unexpected character of the state formation process and its attendant meetings was that the number of participants in the meetings was restricted in practice, because there were only 28 chairs available in the meeting chamber.

The Reformation and the split with Spain were coupled with an increase in the power of the towns with regard to the nobility. Of course, in the political meetings of the Republic, members of the clergy and the court were no longer present. After the Revolt, the knighthood had a less influential voice than it had in the meetings of the sovereign states where, besides representing themselves and the countryside, they also represented many smaller towns. Even in the urbanized parts of Holland, they spoke for more than half of the population in the sovereign period. The position of the nobility weakened during the Revolt. Many nobles died in battle or on the gallows or, as supporters of Spain, were exiled, while both the standing and the welfare of towns rose progressively.

In the States of Holland after the Revolt, the nobility maintained its one and only vote, but its significance was lessened, because the number of enfranchised towns was extended from six to eighteen. A number of smaller towns, which previously were only summoned in situations of serious crises, were now a definite part of the meetings of the States of Holland. After a brief period in which the composition of the meeting was once altered, in addition to the six main towns of Dort, Haarlem, Delft, Leiden, Amsterdam and Gouda, other towns were admitted to the meetings of the states as enfranchised members. These were the towns of Rotterdam, Gorinchem, Schiedam, The Brill and Schoonhoven from the south of Holland, and the towns of Alkmaar, Hoorn, Enkhuizen, Medemblik, Edam, Monnikendam and Purmerend from the north of Holland. Furthermore, the towns attained a more powerful position in the other provincial states, with the exception of Friesland, where the free farmers had maintained an important say.

Robert Fruin has summarized the changes that the rise of the towns signified for the knighthood in the words 'in place of leading henceforth the knighthood had to follow' (1984, p. 35). The position of the nobility was in fact more powerful than suggested by the numerical relationship. H.F.K. van Nierop (1984) has pointed out that the nobles in the meetings of the States of Holland could exercise a substantial influence because both the mighty Grand Pensionary acted as pensionary and spokesman for the knighthood, and because the nobility was the only representative of the countryside and the first to make recommendations 'being the most senior, most distinguished, and most splendid'. Moreover, in the meetings of the states the nobles usually attended for a longer period than the delegates of the towns did. In addition, the nobles were allowed to sit on all of the state committees and in all permanent, provincial, and general governing boards, for which they usually also provided the chairman. 'The members (of the governing boards) originating from the knighthood usually had a greater continuity, antiquity, and experience which they, if they were competent, could translate into a larger political force' (Van Nierop, 1984, pp. 219). The changes in the position, functions, and behaviour of the nobility during the establishment of the Republic could be characterized as a symptom of the 'meetingization of society'.

Initially it was not obligatory to show 'credentials' from one's mandators, thus all sorts of other people could mingle among the delegates. In particular the first meetings of the States-General in Brussels suffered from these intruders. The majority of the participants were young noblemen who, both inside and outside the meeting, were noticeable by their 'studentlike' behaviour. According to witnesses not only did they regularly raise hell in the town, but were also drunk during the meetings; something that was likewise said about some municipal representatives (Japikse, 1916, p. 34).

On 2 February 1577, the states decided to counter the confusion stemming from the presence of a large number of people who had turned up without any sort of mandate. They appointed two separate committees of seven people to deal with incoming correspondence and the funds. A month later these committees were abandoned as there were sometimes only 30 people left in the plenary meeting for dealing with the remaining business. Finally, in order to combat the *désordres* which had led to the institution of the committees, it was decided to give the chairman the task of ensuring that all those who had not been sent by the states left the chamber at the start of the meeting (Gachard, 1861, p. 440).

For some time after the adoption of this measure all sorts of people, who had not been sent by the provinces, towns, or the knighthood, still turned up at the meetings. Until half way through the 1580s, resolutions were adopted in which the conditions for admittance were ratified or made more stringent. Thus it was decided, on 1 July 1577, that jobhunters, clerks, ushers and others, were not permitted to bother the states with requests or petitions before the end of the deliberations, so that the meeting was not constantly interrupted. The last time that this question was comprehensively looked into was in October 1586, when it was decided that 'nobody, in whatsoever capacity, would be allowed into the meeting unless he had previously shown and submitted his procuration, mandate or warrant of attorney' (Japikse, 1921, Part V, p. 234).

Moreover, the regulations of the States of Holland from 1585 determined that no one was allowed to be present in the meetings but the specified nobles and those who were commissioned to do so by the town governments. The delegates were obliged to show their letters of mandate on request or otherwise 'to depart from the meeting at the urgent request of the most senior of the nobles or the municipal delegates' (*Resolutions of the States of Holland*, 1585). In conjunction with the knighthood, the towns dispatched on average between 45 and 65 and later between 65 and 85 people to the meetings of the States of Holland. In the eighteenth century the number of delegates increased to more than 100 for important decisions.

In practice, the checks on the admission of participants were often omitted. The closing of the meetings at higher levels produced large problems which were connected to the decentralized governmental structure of the Republic. For instance, G. de Bruin states:

> Often in the (meetings of the) States-General and the States of Holland non-officially credited regents quietly entered, who were interested in the course of events or the nature of the council. For (meetings of the) States-General this was particularly true for delegates from Holland, who often attended the deliberations 'without an order or a mandate, but out of private curiosity'. In the meetings of the States of Holland this was the case for members of enfranchised town governments, particularly for ex-delegates to the States who, intentionally or by chance, graced The Hague with a visit. In addition, when the most important matters were dealt with, oustanding deputation from one or more regions would generally show up; Holland in particular had a tendency to do this. (1991, p. 233)

At all levels of government, the criteria for participation in the meetings became more exact, more stringent and more fixed. Several examples of this are illustrated by the following. In 1581 the States of Holland prohibited the town governments to consult the guilds and the militia about 'common national matters', that is, for the election of magistrates and for important decisions.[8] In the subsequent years, these organizations came under the authority of the town governments. Thus, the militias of Amsterdam came to be under the control of war councils comprised of captains appointed by the burgomasters; among the captains were several members of the city councils chaired by one of the burgomasters. Only in Dort, because of an old privilege, did the guilds maintain a say in the municipal government.

The number of members of the Council of State was fixed at twelve after the withdrawal of the English members in 1627: three from Holland, two each from Zeeland, Friesland and Gelderland, and one each from the remaining provinces. The members were appointed by the States-General, on the nomination of the provinces. They were required to choose 'qualified, competent men, familiar with state affairs, and adherents of the true Christian reformed religion' (Van Deursen, 1981, p. 50). The length of membership varied per province and, eventually, it was precisely determined to allow the different towns and other sections within a province to have their turn.

Initially, outsiders could enter the meeting chamber of the Council of State with hardly any formalities. It often happened that Van Oldenbarnevelt entered the room 'to forcefully let his opinion be known' (Fontaine, 1954, p. 46). In 1590 the conditions for admittance to the meeting were tightened. The ushers were informed to let in no one unannounced except the stadholder and the members of the States-General. As security against the attempts by Van Oldenbarnevelt and others to pressurize the council, not only the outer door, but also the inner door of the chamber was locked.

The regulations of the VOC from 1602 stated that the States of Holland and Zeeland were to appoint new directors from those who had deposited a certain amount of capital in the venture. In the same year that the states approved the patent, the burgomasters of the participating towns were also licensed to become directors. By this action, the number of burgomasters in the directorship increased at the cost of the number of operating merchants.

The regulations of attendance and absence

In regulating the participation in meetings not only were the criteria for admittance tightened, but measures were also taken to discourage absenteeism, lateness and premature departure. These measures should be considered as expressions of an increasing social control within the meeting groups themselves. Those who were admitted were also required actually to be present and to discharge their duties without disturbing the 'orderly' course of the meeting.

The Code of Order of the States of Holland from 1574 and 1585 stated that the knighthood had to send at least four (later three) delegates and each of the large towns at least two. To ensure continuity, these delegates had to be appointed for at least a year. Those who failed to appear were considered to be tied to the decisions that were taken in their absence and, moreover, were punished with a monetary fine. Those who arrived late at or who departed prematurely from the meeting also had to pay a monetary fine according to the Code of Order of Holland from 1585; 'six stivers' which the secretary had to transfer to 'the poor orphans of the town or the place where the meeting was held'.

Likewise, the Code of Order of the States-General from 1577 established that those who were too late, departed too early, or stayed away completely had to carry out the decisions that had been taken in their absence *and* pay a monetary fine. Between 1580 to 1584 at least fourteen resolutions were passed concerning meeting times and fines for absence or lateness, which were also to be made over to poorhouses.

The punishment of those who, without permission from the chairman, came too late, left early or did not show up also frequently appeared in meeting regulations elsewhere. Thus, at the beginning of the meetings of the board of directors of the VOC, it was customary to set a sand-timer of half an hour. Whoever arrived later than it took to empty one turn got a fine of a shilling, two turns a fine of two shillings, and whoever failed to turn up was issued with a fine of five shillings (Klerk de Reus, 1894, p. 42). In the Council of State, an hourglass was used to determine lateness. Hourglasses were used for the same purpose in the meetings of the classes and the synods of the

FIGURE 6.2 A meeting of the States-General of the Dutch Republic (eighteenth century) (Municipal Archives, The Hague)

Reformed Church where the meeting's start was announced by the chiming of a bell (Cuperus, 1920, pp. 13–14 and p. 42).

This latter measure is an illustration of Elias' proposition, 'the more differentiated the chains of functional dependency relations binding people together, the stricter the regimen of the clocks' (1985, p. 87). The use of timers such as clocks and hourglasses can be considered as an expression of the growing external, social constraint to attune the personal time control to the long-term social process of more precise time measurement and time control, which accelerated at the end of the sixteenth century. The social compulsion of time, represented by clocks, calendars and timetables, formed an increasingly finer mesh of relatively unobtrusive, moderate, even and non-violent, but omnipresent and inescapable social constraints.

In 1582 and 1583 the Julian calendar was replaced in Holland and Zeeland by the new Gregorian calendar which was better adjusted to the changes in the seasons. The other regions of the Netherlands followed this example, the last being Drente in 1701. The spreading and the improvement of instruments for the measurement of time (such as the invention of the pendulum clock by Christian Huygens) allowed for a more regular and more exact timing, so that human activities could be more carefully synchronized, even though the local clocks were somewhat discordant.

Until 1909, when a law took effect in which the mean time of Amsterdam was taken to be the national time, there were various local times in the Netherlands based on the different moments when the sun reached its highest point on the local sundials, upon which the local clocks were based. In the Netherlands, the local times differed from west to east by fifteen minutes at the maximum (Knippenberg and De Pater, 1988, pp. 77–82).

The afore-mentioned attendance rules and the punishments for unpunctual arrival at meetings reflects the struggle that the people of the seventeenth century had with 'the time', that is, with the increase in and the synchronization of appointments. The adjustment to the new 'demands of time' varied from group to group and from person to person. However, those who met at the central meetings belonged to the first group to feel an increased need for active timing and had to learn to live with more precise time measurement. They had to become more time conscious. Just as ancient Athenians used hourglasses in their meetings to measure the lengths of their speeches in order to curb them, the meeting participants in the Dutch Republic used hourglasses and other standardized time keepers to check the lengths of individual absence from meetings. The attendance rules scored a limited success. The meetings of the states were characterized in later years by the constant toing and froing of delegates and others. Lateness and premature departure remained standard problems. This chaotic course was intensified through some having to stand due to lack of seating, others walking around and falling into conversation if the official business did not interest them, and through the custom of regularly interrupting the discussions for regional consultations. Due to pressure from below, from the enfranchised members who were worried about losing power, it was practically impossible to take sufficient measures against such chaos. The doors of the meeting chamber were closed for one specific sitting at the most. It was not until 1723 that the States of Holland decided that no one was allowed to leave the meeting without first having informed the chairman (De Bruin, 1991, p. 234).

Absenteeism from meetings also remained a problem. For instance, the meetings of the States-General were only moderately attended in that period of the year when the provincial states met to fill vacant functions and offices, for example those in The Hague. However, a more general explanation of absenteeism from meeting must be sought elsewhere.

Because the States of Holland financed central expenditure by more than half, because they met in the vicinity of the administration of the States-General, and because their speaker, the Grand Pensionary, was the most important official in the government machinery, they had many opportunities to steer discussions and decisions in whatever direction they desired. The dominance of a certain number of delegates from Holland and the regional sectionalism (for example, the inland regions considered the fleet as something that concerned the maritime provinces alone) were additional reasons for the delegates from other provinces to stay away from meetings.

The establishment of the ranking order in meetings

A fixed ranking order of seating was employed in all of the meetings of the Dutch Republic which, at the same time, determined the order in which the participants could offer their opinions and recommendations. As previously mentioned, the regulation of speaking and deciding was an important function of the ranking order in the court period. It was the same in the time of the Republic. The first rule of the States-General states that a representative 'may only speak or make recommendations if it is his turn'. It was possible to ask the chairman for permission to speak in between, and if granted, take the floor but 'yet without interrupting the business under discussion'. The first rule of the States of Holland contains a similar regulation: 'That the nobles have the first word, followed by the towns, the first Dort and then following an old tradition the others, without interrupting each other'. In the relatively strictly stratified seventeenth- and eighteenth-century society, in which much significance was attached to differences in rank, the person to speak first had the chance to set the tone of the meeting and give a direction to discussions. In the meetings of the States-General the ranking order of seating was fixed according to the custom of the Burgundian realm. Before the states from the northern Netherlands had split off, people sat and spoke *selon le pied accoustumé*, as presented in the Code of Order of 1577. Moreover, this regulation stipulated that, during the announcement of the proposition by the registrar who was standing behind the seat of the chairman, delegates had to remain seated in their place, in rank order, or risk reprimand from the chairman for incivility.[9]

After some squabbling as to whether Friesland or Utrecht had priority, a ranking order was decided which was as good as identical to that in operation before the Revolt. Gelderland, as the only previous dukedom, was allowed to speak first followed by the counties of Holland and Zealand. Afterwards came the four manors of Utrecht, Friesland, Overijssel and Groningen. Within the individual provincial delegations, the nobles had priority over the towns; within the knighthood and within the towns antiquity and seniority were used as criteria.

In the eighteenth century, there were also several conflicts concerning the precedence of permanent delegates and appointed delegates of the States-General. Those 'who, salaried and in turn, represented their region in the States-General for a certain period' belonged to the former group, and to the latter group belonged those 'who only incidentally attended the meeting, particularly when exceptional events occurred; their attendance was generally of short duration and they received no salary, at most an attendance fee' (Gabriëls, 1989, p. 258). Although the majority of the regions made no official distinction between the standard and exceptional delegates in the determination of ranking order, in practice, the custom developed to allow the permanent members priority for taking their seats and in occupying the chairmanship (*ibid.*, pp. 263–6). Given the limited number of seats it frequently occurred in practice that both the appointed delegates and those non-accredited participants had to stand.

The members of the States-General sat for the meeting at a large, elongated table, covered by a green cloth. Round the table were 28 chairs, which the states had made for that purpose in 1590 (Japikse, 1923, Part VII, p. 7). Every delegation had a set number of chairs in set places: six each for Gelderland and Holland, three each for Zeeland and Friesland, two each for other provinces. There were thirteen chairs along each side of the table and one at each end. One chair in the middle and one at one of the ends had arms and were more decorative. The former was intended for the chairman and the second for the stadholder if he was present at the meeting. Opposite the stadholder was the chair of the registrar. The six representatives of Holland were seated to the left of the chairman; immediately to his right was a vice-chairman from the presiding region, followed by the representatives from Friesland and Groningen. Opposite the chairman, from left to right, were representatives of Gelderland, Zeeland, Utrecht and Overijssel. Of the seats appointed to each region, the one closest to the chairman was the first in rank (Schöffer, 1964, p. 80; Gabriëls, 1989, p. 253). Figure 6.3 illustrates the division of places around the table.

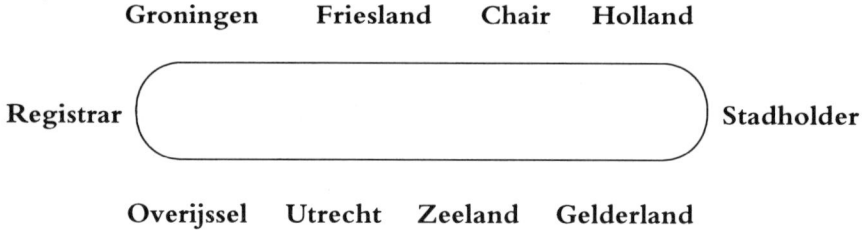

FIGURE 6.3   Seating arrangement at a States-General meeting

In the Amsterdam council the members were seated on chairs along the wall 'according to the seniority of their oath of office'. The presiding burgomaster, who sat at the table with other magistrates, began the rounds of polling by first asking the longest serving member and ending with the aldermen, who were also members of the city council, and the burgomasters 'from below, so that the presiding mayor voted last' (Bontemantel, 1897, Part II, p. 9). In 1663 this order was changed as a result of pressure from the councillor–aldermen who had complained that those sitting behind could never take the lead and, therefore, that the consultations were as good as clinched by the most votes before they could even offer their recom-mendations (*ibid.*, p. 11). Different from the burgomasters, who could wield great influence through their pre-meeting recommendations, their recommendations before every vote, or through manipulative activities such as the holding back of information, the aldermen, just like the majority of the other council members, had barely any opportunity to exert influence than by their single official vote.

The central board of the VOC settled the ranking order of seating and issuing recommendations in their meeting on 24 February 1603. If the meeting were to convene in Amsterdam, the chairman would have been chosen from the delegation from Amsterdam. The chairman was the first to speak, followed by the oldest delegate from Zeeland, who was followed in turn by one delegate from Amsterdam, one from Zeeland, one from Amsterdam, one from Delft, one from Amsterdam, one from Zeeland, one from Amsterdam, one from Rotterdam, one from Amsterdam, one from Hoorn, one from Amsterdam, one from Zeeland, one from Amsterdam, one from Enkhuizen, and finally by the seventeenth delegate from one of the small chambers. If the meeting had been convened in Zeeland, and the last delegate had been sent by the Chamber of Zeeland, the meeting was chaired and led by the oldest delegate from Zeeland, after which the oldest delegate from Amsterdam would take the stand. This was providing there were no burgomaster present in the delegation from Amsterdam and, if this were the case, the burgomaster would take precedence (Klerk de Reus, 1894, p. 40–1).

The ranking order of the city councils and the trading companies deviated from the usual ranking order in other political meetings. They made no distinction between members from noble origin and members from common origin. In the meetings of the town councils, an order ranked according to length of service was in practice, and in the meetings of the companies, an order ranked according to the financial capacity of the members of the chambers was used.

These new ranking orders show a displacement from below when they are compared to the ranking orders in the sovereign period. Financial contribution and length of service replaced hereditary, aristocratic titles as ranking criteria. These shifts were well under way, but were not particularly noticeable in the meetings of the states. Here the ranking order from the court period was anchored so much in the social behaviour of the members of the states that they even maintained 'the official ranking order of seating and issuing recommendations in confidential discussions between several enfranchised members in the inn' (De Bruin, 1991, p. 154).

Why did the states not replace the traditional ranking order after the Revolt with a ranking order based on the new power relationships? Internally, and between themselves, the states had to insist on reticence and care when confronted with differences of opinion and conflicts. There was no monarch or other higher authority who could separate warring factions or, if so desired, play them off against each other. Generally the stadholder did not occupy that position. As commander-in-chief of the army and navy, he was officially the servant of the states. Some old privileges, such as the right to appoint the members of the city council, actually gave him the opportunity to exert some power, but this was insufficient to place him above regional interest groups or sides in a conflict. On the contrary, he was often a faction or a 'side' himself. His powers were not as great as those of the European monarchs who were able to lean on a powerful aristocracy.

The risks attached to a possible conflict about the important ranking order were huge, especially in the uncertain, constituent stage of the Republic. They probably did not offset the disadvantages connected to the maintenance of the traditional ranking order. By the time the new power relationships had established themselves and a peaceful change was possible in the ranking order favouring Holland and the towns, a meeting practice had developed on the basis of the old ranking order. This order allowed the possibility to make decisions that met the requirements of the established power relationships.

The ranking order of the royal court was maintained until the end of the Dutch Republic. Its abolition, around 1800, was accompanied by replacing the co-opting of governors and the system of mandates and consultations, by elections and a system of free representation. With this, a sharper distinction was drawn between recommendations and voting, and between discussing and deciding. The order of the speakers, which became less important due to these changes, was now determined by the order of arrival, or by request, while the division of the allocated speaking times was related to the number of voters represented by a participant or group of participants.

However, these changes were not brought into effect unnoticed. In the first meeting of the elected Second Chamber of the States-General [translator's note: Dutch House of Commons since 1813] in 1814, the chairman from Gelderland wanted to begin discussions with the collecting of votes, 'as if the delegates were tied to a mandate and need not bother with the comments of later speakers' (Prins, 1964, p. 171). When Gijsbert Karel van Hogendorp, a delegate of Holland, took over the chairmanship several weeks later, he immediately adopted the rule that votes were only to be given after everyone had expressed their opinion and after there had been a chance for discussion.

A conscientious opening

In the Dutch Republic, every meeting began with a prayer, into which several meeting norms were impressed. This prayer replaced the monarch's or his representative's welcome address. The States-General decided in 1580 that members had to appear half an hour before the meeting in order to pray. A preacher would be present in the meeting chamber every day, 'to direct prayers to the Lord God to ask Him to offer His grace for the making of a good, definite, and united decision about the matters for which the gentlemen were gathered, and about any other matters which they brought forward' (Japikse, 1918, Part III, p. 34). Later, it became the habit for the chairman or the registrar simply to read out a prayer at the start of each meeting.

In 1587 the States of Holland decided 'that in honour of God, and for the benefit and advancement of matters of common interest and of interest for Holland, henceforth praying would take place every morning in the meetings of the States'. This daily praying included, among other things, praying to God by those present:

> That we, in our fear, piety, candour, honesty, and trust may acquit our tasks and may see, understand, perform, and decide what is the best for Thy honour and for the welfare, tranquillity and peace of the country, without being led astray by envy, hate, or other emotions, or forget to do what is decent and rightful, in order that we may appear unashamedly before Thee with a good conscience on the Day of Judgement. (*Resolutien van de Staten van Holland en Westvriesland*, 16 January 1587)

The content of this prayer coincides a great deal with that of the oaths which the delegates had to make at their inauguration into the meetings of the states, conducted by the most senior member. In 1586 the States-General determined that many matters had not been discussed in meetings or, if this were the case, with inadequate effect. On the one hand, this was due to a lack of a 'sufficient mandate from the delegates' and, on the other hand, because the matters which had been discussed 'were not kept properly confidential'. To avoid this problem in the future, it was decided that every delegate had to swear an oath, in which he promised to recommend, and to decide on, everything which 'according to his opinion and his conscience, served for the use, advantage, and prosperity of the countries, maintaining the true Christian religion, liberty, privileges, charters, laws, customs, salaries and contracts; and not allowing himself to be led by any particular emotion or feeling, and to maintain confidentiality about what had been discussed' (Japikse, 1921, Part V, pp. 234–5). The States of Holland had a similar oath which, likewise, ended with the promise to keep confidential what had been discussed. Everyone who participated in a town council, a provincial or national board, or the administration of a trading company had to swear a similar oath.

The prayers and the oath that the members of the states had to swear concisely express the changes that took place in meeting behaviour during the formation of the Republic. In the daily prayer and when making an oath, the delegates promised and swore that they would not judge by external appearance, be led by personal interests, hate, or other emotions, but that they would consider, exclusively, the prosperity, the tranquillity and the peace of the communal country so that on the Day of Judgement they would be able to appear 'unashamedly before God's throne'. In fact, God was no longer presented as a supreme being who demonstrated His will in the outcome of a ritual trial, a ritual man-to-man fight, or a ritual applause, but as a 'supreme judge, omnipotent, and omniscient' to whom one had to constantly justify one's statements and decisions. There developed an internal obligation to strive for the social ideals of peace, tranquillity, and prosperity, to moderate the expression of emotions and posturing, and to discuss and decide 'piously', 'candidly', 'righteously', and 'honestly' with each other; all this 'under the penalty of' shame and a bad conscience.

The changes in the opening procedure were part of a broader social development, in which large groups of people were more dependent upon each other, society was more peaceful, and 'internal' fears in the form of shame or a bad conscience were more usual in daily life than fears of overt physical violence, humiliation and threats from others. The prayer and the oath represent a new stage in the development of society; a stage in which more people were compelled to meet more often and more regularly, and to control more strictly all sorts of primary impulses. The principles, that were taught or impressed with the starting prayer and the oath swearing, forbade the 'outward expression' of hate, anger or other postures, and untrustworthy or misleading behaviour, and advocated the demonstration of friendly and righteous feelings.

During the extension and differentiation of the networks of social interdependency and the withdrawal of violence, those in the political and commercial centres were prompted to 'refine' their meeting behaviour by suppressing or negating some primary emotions and by the continuous expression of confidence-boosting feelings during meetings. This behaviour was characteristic of a certain stage in the social process of learning to manage one's own affects and emotions; a stage in which groups of people strongly differed from each other as regards to their ability for self-control. The exchange of formalities and the 'blatant' demonstration of the ability for self-control served to create a basis for the growth of reciprocal confidence in the restraint from aggressive impulses, the curbing of outbursts of anger, the ceasing of humiliations and rapid changes of behaviour and temperament (Mastenbroek, 1992, p. 91).

In the first years of the Republic, for example, in Groningen, conflicts between local leaders were fought out using weapons. 'Squires' governed these regions, and they maintained small, private armies and their residences were often genuine fortresses (according to Wichers, 1965, p. 56). As blood continued to be shed through the conflicts, it was decided, in December 1656, that weapons were not to be worn in the meeting chamber and that a guard would be attendant in the ante-chamber (Spierenburg, 1973, p. 36). It was only in the course of the seventeenth and eighteenth centuries that conflicts in the northern regions were channelled into ways of reaching a more diplomatic solution in the northern regions.[10]

In comparison to later, meetings were 'more ritualized'. During the Revolt and at the start of the Republic, the monopoly of physical force was certainly vulnerable and hardly stable. As long as social tensions could manifest themselves relatively quickly in the form of violent conflicts, and large parts of the population, through their exclusion from political meetings, had no other means to let their voice be heard than those of less peaceful means, meetings remained relatively ceremonial, class-ridden activities.

Certain Protestant rituals, which were introduced into the meetings of the states during the Revolt and the war against Spain, lost their significance with the stabilization of the internal power relationships, after the international recognition of the Republic in the middle of the seventeenth century. For instance, delegate Strik van Linschoten made the following statement in the meeting of the first elected people's representatives, the National Assembly of the Batavian Republic in 1796. During a debate about the opening prayer he stated that: 'He frequently saw the lofty members of the States-General drifting off in their meetings during the prayer, but that he had detected the opposite in other meetings, namely the utmost attention and deference while the praying was taking place' (*Dagverhaal der Handelingen van de Nationale Vergadering*, 1796, p. 91).

The National Assembly of 1796 finally decided with a small majority to maintain the prayer at the start of the meeting. A special committee fashioned the following prayer for that purpose for all faiths: 'Omnipotent, Omniscient, Omnipresent Being! Let Thy wisdom and love guide us in the faithful execution of our duty, for the furtherance of the salvation of the Fatherland and of our fellow men, Amen' (*ibid.*, p. 118). The custom of beginning each session of parliament with a prayer was only abandoned in 1814 with the establishment of the Kingdom of the Netherlands. The only part of this custom that remains to this day is the ceremony by which the king or queen opens the parliamentary year: 'That God's blessing supports your labour!' In the brief period of the Christian-Socialist cabinet led by Prime Minister Den Uyl (1973 to 1977), this prayer was replaced by the sentence: 'By expressing the hope that we will receive the strength for the purpose, I declare open this sitting of the States-General.' It was a somewhat peculiar statement in the sense that it was unclear to whom the request for strength was directed. The orthodox Protestant parties were up in arms against this quasi-humanistic prayer and attributed the 'Egyptian plagues' to the omission of the word 'God' from the crown address. The 'Egyptian plagues', which were affecting the Netherlands at that time, were actually a series of events including the oil boycott and various terrorist attacks. After Den Uyl's cabinet had collapsed, a prayer for guidance from above was quickly reintroduced into the crown address. At first, in 1978, this was rather indirect: 'May the work be carried out in the faith that many wish You wisdom and pray for Your blessing.' Several years later, the prayer was restored to its heavenly glory and the monarch again wished, as previously, 'that the blessing of God supports your labour'. The non–Christian, liberal–social–democratic cabinet led by Prime Minister Kok presented a compromise in 1994: 'From my heart I express the hope that You will fulfil Your responsible tasks also in this light, in the faith that many, along with me, wish You wisdom and pray for Your blessing.' According to the Prime Minister this ceremony is the most applicable to the pluriform society and accommodates the tradition and the parliamentary relationships of the Netherlands (Van Vree, 1994b).

The regulation of speaking, deciding and chairing

At every meeting, after the prayer, the chairman led the deliberations by a 'proposition', that is, by presenting information about the topic to be discussed, which was determined in response to incoming matters. For example, in the meetings of the states, these were letters from state envoys, memoranda from foreign envoys, reports from boards, committees and deputations, and written requests from individuals and boards. In the meetings of the states, in order to prevent vagueness, 'surprises' and manipulations, only written matters which had been handed in to the registrar or the secretary were dealt with, except in the secret committee meetings. This stipulation was already in the first Code of Order of the States of Holland.

There had been attempts to organize the agenda, and the drawing up and the determining of the order of the 'points of convening', according to general, impersonal rules, but this had had little success. In the Code of Order of the States of Holland from 1574, it is stated: 'That in the meeting what, in particular, should be resolved and dealt with were matters of common interest, followed by matters concerning the towns, villages, and boards, and finally matters concerning private individuals.' In general, these matters were dealt with in order of importance. The 'points of convening' were usually drawn up by the chairman together with the secretary, pensionary, or registrar. Prestige and power were bestowed upon these functions by such privileges. In the meetings of the States–General, the president for that week determined which matters would be dealt with. Each region attempted to arrange it in such a way that important matters were discussed in the week when they had the chair. In this, Holland had an advantage in that its pensionary had the permanent function of acting as advisor to the chairman.

The power attached to the chairmanship explains why the chairmanship of the meetings of the States–General was not permanent as it was for the meetings of the States of Holland. Here, this function was placed in the hands of the pensionary on behalf of the knighthood in 1586 and, likewise, in the meetings of the other states with the exception of the States of Friesland. The maintenance of the rotating chairmanship for the meetings of the States-General was the result of an impasse in the power relationships between Holland and the other regions. Neither of the groups was in a position continuously to claim the leadership of the meetings of the States-General. Neither wished the other to have the chairmanship; neither was powerful enough to insist on this function. In the absence of a superior 'player' manipulating the interest groups, the rotating chairmanship was an adequate solution, and a somewhat exceptional phenomenon in European relationships at this time.

The significance of the chairmanship in the States-General of the Republic was much greater than in the present-day parliamentary meetings. Nowadays, the function and the power of the chairmanship is limited to the surveillance of the prevailing meeting order based on the order regulations; the granting of the right to speak; the drawing up of the points on the agenda; the announcing of the voting results, and the implementation of the decisions. Previously, the chairman was also the one who made the proposals and often, as the first to speak, offered his prior recommendations, such as is now sometimes seen in a business meeting chaired by a director. The chairman's task of the meetings of the states comprised a large part of the tasks that in the present-day parliamentary meetings are the tasks of the government.

The current parliamentary chairmanship has developed step by step with the separation of the legislative and executive powers. An important moment in this development was the decision of the committee for the revision of the written constitution in 1814. This decision restricted the tasks of the chairman to the policy of the meetings of the Second Chamber of the Parliament. This committee dismissed the proposition of the committee member, van Hogendorp, to draw the chairman from outside the Chamber, and to give him both the status of a civil servant with the old official title 'Grand Pensionary', and the function of independent intermediary between the king and the Chamber (Seret, 1910, pp. 6–10).

In the meetings of the Republic, after the chairman's proposal, the relevant written pieces were read out. In the meetings of the states this was done by the registrar standing behind the seat of the chairman, while all the others present, according to the rule of 1577 *seront tenuz seoir et demourer en leurs places* (had to remain seated in their place). In fact, this rule was not strictly adhered to initially, because in 1584 the states decided once again that after the reading of the prayer nobody was allowed to walk around or leave his place, but had to 'sit or stand in his place' on the penalty of a monetary fine (Japikse, 1919, p. 360). Whether this ban was strictly adhered to is very doubtful. As mentioned previously, participants walking around and talking among themselves were activities characteristic of the later meetings of the states.

Considering that it was not possible to equip all delegates with the texts of all the items (copying cost a great deal of time), these were generally drawn up in a style which made it possible to read them out: 'Detailed and with many repetitions in the argumentation and with many examples, such as pointing out precedents and allegories from history and the bible' (Schöffer, 1964, p. 86). In the period of the Republic, in particular, meeting implied listening to items being read out by the chairman, pensionary, registrar, or secretary. A great deal of effort was demanded from the meeting participants due to the extensive reading out of items to which they had to listen attentively. Not infrequently would someone's attention be distracted.

In the Council of State 'a great deal of the time was taken up by reading . . . the incoming letters' (Fontaine, 1954, p. 43). Van Deursen wrote that whoever tried to suggest exactly how the Council met would become 'dizzy just thinking about the heap of paper that the secretary had had to read to members of the council in an endless drone' (1981, p. 63). De Bruin commented that, in the reading out by the town pensionary of reports, letters, and requests, the members of the city councils could 'only stoically allow it to flow over them without being in a position to develop their own initiative. . . . They were not presented with transcriptions of items read out, which seriously hindered the formation of an independent opinion (compared to the burgomasters)' (1991, p. 206).

After the reading out of the items, the chairman presented the matters for deliberation. This meant that the delegates gave their recommendations in turn. The Code of Order of the States-General determined that the chairman had to get *précise silence à tous* and had to attend to it that everybody should speak and make recommendations in turn and that only one person per province should have the stand. The Code of Order of the States of Holland from 1585 stated that the delegates had to vote on, make recommendations about, and answer all proposals, as the matter demanded, without interrupting each other or using, or answering back with, 'profligate words'. Those who did not keep to the rules would be called to order by the states in an appropriate manner.

This rule follows the ecclesiastical meeting stipulation that the chairman had to silence the 'embittered' and 'quarrelsome' and, if they refused, ask them to leave the chamber, after which those remaining had to discuss an appropriate punishment. In the regulations and resolutions of the States-General, the Council of State, and the VOC there is seemingly no such similar rule. It is possible that the States of Holland were stimulated to include this stipulation in their code of order due to the cutting performances of some delegates who originated from families who joined the states for the first time during the Dutch Revolt.

The procedure by which every member of a meeting in turn offered his recommendations or declared his vote (the rounds of polling) which, in practice, was current in all of the meetings of the Republic, also cost a lot of time. The Dutch historian De Bruin (1991) wrote:

> Everywhere the sessions were prepared by the day-to-day administration and the most important serving functionary, the Pensionary or secretary. . . . Everywhere, state business was submitted in a certain order, from important to unimportant. The deliberations began with the verbal and/or written report of previous business covered in the meetings of the States-General. Everywhere, those matters considered to be of importance were read out and the related problems were covered from beginning to end, with all the consequences emanating from this. Everywhere, the reading out of documents, reports, and decisions took the greatest amount of the time, and more time was spent on explaining one's vote than on deliberating. Everywhere, the unimportant and urgent matters were immediately dealt with and, increasingly, the remainder postponed for consulting mandators and/or referred to a committee, including the majority of the points specified on the agenda. This happened as much in spite of a strict mandate as well as a result of it. . . . Everywhere, decision making took place by the majority vote of the enfranchised members unless unanimity was insisted upon. Always included in this latter category was every matter concerned with finances, war, and peace-making although, in practice, the rule for unanimity was disregarded as a generality. Everywhere, in an almost identical fashion, minutes were taken of the motions, and they were, in a similar way, extended, summarised, registered and reproduced. (De Bruin, 1991, p. 152)

In order to accelerate this procedure, the States of Holland determined in 1585 that, for the delegates, it would suffice to read out or submit their mandate, and that they were not obliged to hold a speech on every point. Likewise, similar stipulations can be found in the regulations of other political boards, except in the meeting regulations of the churches. As such, the stipulation of the Council of State brought 'explicitly to the attention of the members that whoever wanted to endorse the words of the previous speaker had to keep it brief to avoid repetitions' (Van Deursen, 1981, p. 64).

After every member of every delegation had offered his recommendations, the chairman drew a 'conclusion' (a rendering of the drift of the recommendations) unless a member wanted to refer the matter to a committee for further investigation, or first wanted to speak with his principal or mandators. This was extremely common in the meetings of the States-General. Furthermore, a new round of polling was possible, but generally hardly anything was discussed and the chairman moved rapidly on to draw his conclusion. Everywhere, it was the custom that, if the chairman objected to drawing a conclusion, the most senior member of the meeting, or the penultimate chairman, took over this task.

More discussions and consultations took place in the committee meetings, in the pre-discussions of the chairman, the registrar, and the pensionary, and in the corridors and the inns. In the plenary meetings, members restricted themselves to presenting their recommendations and to criticizing texts, by which members paid particular attention to style, phrasing and vocabulary (elaborating upon the Calvinist tradition of criticizing Bible texts) (Schöffer, 1964, p. 86).

In the procedures that were current at the time, hardly any distinction was made between speaking and voting. The Dutch concept of 'recommending' had another meaning from that of nowadays. In the activity 'recommending' both an opinion was given and a vote was cast. The decision or conclusion was taken from the 'recommendations' by the chairman.

The conclusion had to be put in writing by the registrar, secretary, or pensionary, after which official approval could be granted. The conclusion could be rejected or adopted; motions or amendments were unheard of. Generally speaking, voting was not by call, but by using vote declarations. For all important decisions in the meetings at the central level, unanimity of votes was officially required; a rule which led to the development of complicated decision-making procedures. These procedures are dealt with later.

According to the Code of Order of the States-General from 1577, decisions had to be 'diligently' written down and be read out loud for their approval *en plaine audience de toute l'assemblée*. In 1637 it was decided that the definite text of an approved resolution had, henceforth, to be read at the start of the next meeting and officially approved as, according to the members of the states, it too frequently happened that the chairman and the registrar gave their own interpretation of the decisions when they were being put into their definite form. This habit, termed 'summarizing', was probably adopted from the meetings of the States of Holland, where it had been introduced in 1578 (Koopmans, 1990, p. 183). Thus, the consequent 'stipulated minutes' of the resolutions of the States-General were the only official reports registered. And thus it became in all of the meetings of the states, city councils, and companies; the decisions were registered, detailed, summarized, and registered.

More and more attention was paid to these tasks. The way in which the first registrar of the States-General registered the resolutions, 'reminded one sooner of a slovenly maintained merchant's journal than the daily register of the directives of the highest board of state' (Japikse, 1916, p. 32, 33). Through the appointment of secretaries and clerks, gradually the decisions were more neatly noted and registered. Because the number of resolutions steadily increased, the writing costs rose. In order to restrain this, it was decided in 1669 to have the ordinary resolutions printed.

On 7 March 1582 the States-General decided that, 'henceforth, the decisions will be in the language of the Netherlands' (Japikse, 1918, p. 320).

This decision can be considered as the first step towards the development of a national language, 'Standard Dutch'.

In the absence of a higher authority, the states were themselves compelled to formulate regulations with respect to the expression of feelings and, in particular, aggressive and hostile feelings, which hindered, disrupted or rendered the meetings impossible. The relatively equal power relationships within the upper layer allowed the possibility for more peaceful behaviour during meetings, and also made it necessary. A salient example of this was the seat-taking procedure in the meetings of the States-General.

Differing from the members of the earlier, courtly states and those of the House of Commons of the English parliament, the Dutch envoys to the republican States-General sat collectively around a table. In the English parliament, the delegates sat on opposite benches, separated by an area broader than two swords (to prevent fighting from the benches) and arbitrated by a president, appointed by the monarch. This type of arrangement, which dates back to the birth of the two-party system, seems more like that of the French crown prince and the Burgundian duke who, at the beginning of the fifteenth century, negotiated with each other through the bars of a fence erected on a bridge in order to keep the sides in the conflict apart. These arrangements represent different stages in the development of more peaceful ways of meeting and accompanying levels of reciprocally expected self-control.

In the States-General political or religious disposition, formation of parties or factions, or rigid class distinctions were not manifested in the procedure of taking seats round the table. For the most during the meeting, these remained 'under the table'. Political parties in the form of what currently is the case did not exist (with an impersonal 'ideology', a policy, an organization and rules for political loyalty).

> As far as 'parties' could be distinguished, the attachments were of a local or regional nature and, only in exceptional circumstances, had a national character. However, these latter alliances did not form a national party, but they were rather the sums of the local 'factions', as they were then termed. 'Party formation' was restricted to the social upper class of the towns and regions. (Tromp, 1993, p. 270)

It was considered 'inadmissible that factions in the Provincial States held pre-discussions and drew up outlines of decisions. Because in this way every town could not individually have their opinion heard in the real meeting' (*ibid.*, p. 271). The start of national party formation was observed during the religious conflict in the beginning of the seventeenth century, when towns of Remonstrants and towns of Counter-Remonstrants began to organize separate (pre-) meetings. Other than in the ecclesiastical sphere, where different organizations had been created, in the political sphere, this process was discontinued after the defeat of the Remonstrants in the Synod of Dort. The crisis, which was created in the conflict between the Remonstrants and the Counter-Remonstrants and which had offered the stadholder greater opportunities for exerting power, provided a warning for the municipal upper class. If they wished to maintain and strengthen their position of power, then they needed 'to compromise and conform'. Likewise, the decentralized form of government of the Republic was not stimulating for the development of more stable, national parties or factions.

Considering that the towns in the meetings of the provincial states and the regions in the meetings of the States-General only had one vote each, differences in opinion between groups or factions within local or regional entities could not be expressed at national level. Additionally, what still had to be taken into consideration was the possibility that an irritated opponent objected to a fiscal, military or other important decision requiring unanimity, and by so doing jeopardize the safety and the social security of everybody. With a more equal division of power within the upper class and the arrival of a corresponding higher level of self-control, which was reciprocally expected, developments appeared in the central meetings of the Republic which, in the context of Europe at that period, were characterized by peacefulness, care, prudence, and the striving towards consensus.

Many of these characteristics can be recognized in the way of meeting of the present-day Dutch parliament, where the tone, in comparison to the British House of Commons for instance, is calmer and more moderate. In the Netherlands, no political party has an absolute majority in parliament. To be in a position to govern, parties have to co-operate and establish coalitions and, moreover, the opposition which strives towards participation in government is compelled to restrain from posturing and delusions of grandeur. In the British parliament, the governing party and the opposition parties fight a more 'absolute' battle.

In a 'culturally historical' comparison of French and British parliamentary speeches, published in 1937, Oudendijk related one of the main characteristics of British parliamentary speeches, namely the great deal of attention paid to political personality, to the practical demands of the pre-eminently debating style dominant in the British House of Commons. The members of the House of Commons feel themselves compelled to defeat their opponents in any way whatsoever and, simultaneously, to elevate themselves, to captivate their listeners, and to win.

> All this, combined with the demand to refute all pragmatic arguments against in a decisive way, turns the parliamentary debate into a competition in ingenuity, ready wit, eloquence, and morality, upon which the public can raise its spirit. Often it even develops into a real tournament, which produces victors and defeated, and to which the listening and observing members, even though not

speaking themselves, can play an active part by their expressions of approval or disapproval. (1937, p. 113)

According to the more sporty character of the British parliament, the function of the chairman is that of referee, guardian of fair play or, if that is not putting it too irreverently, a barred fence. The differences between the Dutch and the British parliamentary traditions are clearly expressed by the position and function of the chairmen. In Britain the parliamentary battle is led in the House of Commons by a chair(wo)man, the speaker, who has more guarantee of impartiality than the chairmen of both of the Dutch parliamentary Houses. The speaker has a 'safe' seat, is generally re-elected, even if his/her party no longer has the majority; does not speak about proposals still pending; and only votes if the voting reaches an impasse. These guarantees developed over the centuries, in which the parliamentary debate acquired more the character of a competition between two parties. The speaker leads the battle as a referee who keeps the members under control.

The chairman in the Dutch parliament has another position and function. He is not automatically re-elected even though he does his work appropriately, is allowed to speak about proposals still pending, always votes and takes part in discussions in his faction and party. This position reflects a centuries-old tradition of a moderate, parliamentary battle of minorities, the form of which contained a stronger compulsion to the restraint of emotional expression.

Unanimity and majority

Typical of the nature of the power and dependency relationships within the Republic were those decision-making procedures based on 'persuasion' and consensus. Differences can be seen between the meetings of the Republic in the degree to which the majority rule was applied. These differences were closely connected to the position of a meeting within the existing order of the state and the degree to which the participants were tied to their mandates and consultations. Within the advisory meetings, such as that of the Council of State, the meetings of the VOC and the meetings of town councils, the majority rule was generally applied. Within the meetings of the provincial states and the States–General, the unanimity rule was dominant. In the course of the seventeenth and eighteenth centuries, the differences between meetings in the way of making decisions decreased. More differentiated procedures developed. Unanimity and majority became the two ends of a continuum of possible ways to make a decision.

In the meetings of the states, the participants were tied to mandates and consultations and could frequently do little else except maintain the stance of their principals (that is, those of the provincial states and the city governments), as all important matters were excluded from outvoting, that is, from taking the decision by majority vote. In Chapter 5, it was pointed out that the ways of making decisions in the sovereign period varied a great deal with the changes in the power relationships between monarch and states. Generally, the monarchs were more interested in the application of the majority rule than were the states, which were striving for autonomy. In practice, the majority rule was applied in the main (more often in the regional meetings than in the meetings of the States-General), but practically never when decisions were taken about taxation. During the formation of the Republic, the number of matters for which decisions could be made by majority voting was drastically curtailed. It was agreed at the Union of Utrecht (the treaty by which the northern provinces of the Habsburg realm united against the king) that unanimity was necessary in matters of peace, making a truce, war and assessment of taxation (Groenveld and Leeuwenberg, 1979, p. 33). Furthermore, from the text of the treaty, it appears that unanimity was necessary for the changing, augmenting, or ending of treaties and for decisions about the army and navy. Finally, to be able to make a decision in cases of disagreement about important matters, it was determined that a recommendation could be requested from the stadholder and that this recommendation would be binding. The stadholder was allowed to choose his advisors freely (*ibid.*, p. 34). This 'submission rule' was rarely applied, as there was frequently nobody fulfilling the function of stadholder, or it was undesirable to give such an assignment to him as it was feared that he would become too powerful.

The decision-making procedures requiring unanimity were maintained until the end of the Republic, but, in practice, they were often less stringently applied. For instance, matters were often passed to smaller committees, which used different procedures. On several occasions, the states deliberated about the changing of the decision-making procedure and the submission rule, because it was clear that the existing rules often led to obstructing, postponing, or cancelling decisions. No success was registered in structuring a regulation which was acceptable to all of the provinces (De Vrankrijker, 1938, pp. 115–18).

Meanwhile, other methods and techniques developed, of which one of the most important was the making of points on the agenda into matters for a 'committee'. Matters which could not be concluded immediately were delegated to other general institutions, such as the Council of State, the Boards of the Admiralty, and the Auditor's Office, or to a number of delegates designated for that purpose or a fixed committee, for the further investigation of the problem and for the making of recommendations to the plenary meeting. In practice, making points on the agenda into matters for a committee was often the same as the procedure of consulting mandators. In both cases the opportunity was created to consult one's colleagues.

The unanimity rule spread over the provincial states after the Dutch Revolt. In the meetings of the States of Holland until 1574, only taxation assessments were excluded from outvoting. When the policy areas of the states widened, the question arose as to how, in new matters, the obligation of the minority should be regarding the majority. The increase in the number of enfranchised members made this a controversial question. The greatest objection to the total application of the majority rule stemmed from the fear of the large towns that they would be outvoted by the small towns. In the decree on the meeting of the States of Holland in 1581, it was determined that not only taxation, but also matters of peace making, warfare and changes in the government would be excluded from outvoting. In the decree of the meeting of 1585 the areas still included were further curtailed by the exclusion of all important national matters. Also determined was that one side would only concede if two-thirds of the members had reached agreement. Furthermore, it was determined that the delegates, who previously could decide for themselves about unexpectedly presented matters, could henceforth only respond to matters on the agenda. That meant a serious delay in decision making, because henceforth, for all additional matters, a consultation had to be held. Not all members adopted the decree in total. Amsterdam, for instance, refused the concession rule, because it wanted to retain the possibility of preventing unacceptable decisions.

The only thing a minority could do in a case of outvoting in the meetings of the states was to register a protest in the registers of the states. This opportunity was likewise introduced in the Council of State in 1670, and the board of directors of the VOC decided in 1696 that it would be left to the outvoted minority whether they wanted their defeat registered in the minutes (Klerk de Reus, 1894, p. 41). Interestingly enough this custom, in a slightly altered form, has continued right up to the present day. For practical reasons, members of the Second Chamber of the Dutch parliament generally do not vote by division. Usually the chairman restricted himself to reading out the numbers of the bills, and proclaiming them one by one as official decisions with a slam of the gavel, unless a member wished a vote by division. It occurred repeatedly that a member declared no wish for a vote by division about a certain matter, but that he wished it to be registered in the official report of the meeting that he was against the decision.[11]

The custom of having a vote against registered in the report of the meeting originates from the time of the Republic, even though the registration was then already not a 'vote against', but a 'protest vote' in a meeting which preferably made decisions unanimously. The history of the origin of this custom also explains the fact that this procedure is unknown in parliamentary meetings of countries in which there is a powerful tendency towards a two-party system, such as in England (Rowen, 1970, p. 137).

The problem of settling internal conflicts was solved neither in the meetings of the States of Holland nor in the meetings of the States-General. None of the many proposals concerning this, which were presented in the seventeenth and eighteenth centuries, was taken on. The towns and the provinces continued to resist the broader application of the majority rule, in which outvoting was possible, and were against obvious submission rules, by which the power to decide was put into the hands of a third party. The foundation of this resistance lay in the very decentralized organization of the monopolies of taxation and physical force. Marjolein't Hart has pointed out that many military and fiscal functions were performed by lower, decentralized institutions:

> Naval warfare by the five admiralties, taxation assessments by the provincial civil servants, and also the loan politics moved from central to regional level. Alongside, there was a definite privatisation: excise duties were contracted out in the form of privatised bonds, also the fleet was familiar with managers who were outside the control of the state. Furthermore, in the army, military petitioners, the captains and the grand entrepreneurs of warfare succeeded in using state functions for their own profit. (1989, summary)

The army, the fleet, and the central official apparatus of the Republic were financed largely by taxation and loans, which had to be provided by the fiscally autonomous provinces. Frequently, the heartiest opposers of outvoting and the submission rule were Holland, which donated more than half of the states' expenses, and Amsterdam, which paid the largest part of Holland's taxes.

Based on consensus, the decentralized meeting figuration of the United Provinces, which corresponded to a highly segmented organization of the taxation assessments and the military apparatus, gave the Republic an exceptional position within the European family of states. Only Switzerland and Poland were familiar with similar 'decision-making processes'. In the Polish convention, the central meeting, which comprised mainly nobility, every noble had an unrestricted right of veto; a situation which led to a state of nearly total indecision, and from where originates the expression *a Polish convention*, meaning bedlam. In comparison to the Republic, Switzerland and Poland (both mainly agrarian countries) acquired a less prominent role within the network of commercial and diplomatic relations, which included an ever increasing number of people.

The insertion of the United Provinces into the diplomatic network dominated by monarchies, initially, did not go smoothly. The former rebels, during the struggle against Spain, had committed improvised diplomacy. 'It was certainly no easy matter, as representatives of a now-independent Republic, to find a suitable place in a fundamentally monarchical diplomacy, because diplomacy was, in the seventeenth century, mainly an activity that was played out at court, and also the ceremonies obviously had a monarchical tint' (Franken, 1980, p. 243).

Within the order of rank of the European states, the monarchies were higher in standing than the independent republics, even though, like the Dutch Republic, these were more prosperous and more powerful than many monarchies. After the Twelve Years' Truce of 1609, when the Dutch Republic became internationally recognized as a sovereign state, the country of the Netherlands was considered, following Venice, as 'a republic which possessed kingdoms'; the overseas territories were called kingdoms. Through this, the international status of the United Provinces rose and the leaders of the Republic could accept the existing monarchical order of rank without any loss of face.

As the highest representatives of the new state, the body of the States-General gave itself the title Noble and Mighty, and eventually, High and Mighty. The latter title, which was probably borrowed from aristocratic titles in which the words 'high' and 'mighty' were often used, was unique and reflected the exceptional position of 'the republic with kingdoms' within the European family of states dominated by monarchies (Heringa, 1961, pp. 265–9).

Committees, corridors and manipulations

The 'price' one had to pay for admission to, and enduring participation in, the status-boosting meetings, was the subordination of behaviour to the prevailing meeting norms and rules; that is, to a more 'democratic' pattern of control of emotions. Not everybody always managed to do this. Small groups continuously tried to force the decision making in a specific direction by lobbying, manipulating and coming to agreements in informal gatherings and in the corridors. Such less formal meeting activities are difficult to observe, but there are many indications that, particularly in times of war and crisis, for important military and diplomatic decisions attempts were made to avoid the formal, relatively public and protracted decision-making process and its accompanying risk of leaks of plans and intentions. Instead one used skills and cunning, by which delegates were put under pressure, hoodwinked, bought off or humoured with false promises. These contra-movements manifested themselves most strongly among those 'players' who felt the pressure of the international 'game of states' most forcefully, and who sought ways to decide more quickly and with more confidentiality about potential military and diplomatic steps than was possible using the general decision-making procedures. Among these 'players' were the stadholders, prominent members of the States-General, the States of Holland, and the Amsterdam city council.

A legal way to decide more quickly and with a greater chance of confidentiality was, as previously mentioned, by making a matter into a question for a committee. Throughout the seventeenth and eighteenth centuries, the number of committees increased enormously in the States-General, the provincial states, and the large towns in association with the mounting range and complexity of the co-ordinating tasks. Through this extension of the area of activity, the accelerated recurrence of subjects, and the need to make quicker and more confidential decisions, the ad hoc committees of the states gradually developed into set committees to which the states automatically referred practically all matters. Through this the specialization of meeting participants was promoted (De Bruin, 1991, pp. 141–2). The committees for foreign, military, maritime and financial affairs were the most important. The provincial states fixed the composition of these central committees quite specifically so that they themselves were always assured of participation. Throughout the seventeenth century, the participants in the committees of the States-General generally amounted to seven or eight delegates: one from each of the six small provinces plus one, and later two, from Holland (the pensionary and a member of the knighthood).

Usually the committee meetings took place in the morning before and in the afternoon after the plenary meeting of the States-General in the 'business-matters chamber'. Unlike in the plenary meeting, the chairmanship of the committee meetings did not rotate. The member from Gelderland remained the chairman. The way of meeting was broadly speaking similar to the way it was done in meetings of the states, with the difference that more matters were dealt with verbally and the delegates could express themselves more independently from their mandators in this preparatory stage. The deliberations were conducted just as much according to the same formal procedure as that of the plenary meetings. In a fixed order, every member could make his opinion known, after which the state of affairs was assessed and new rounds of questions could follow if necessary. Voting by division was avoided as much as possible, but it occurred more often than it did in the plenary meetings. In cases of wide disagreement, a recommendation was either not settled, or the committee issued dissenting recommendations. The result was presented either verbally or in documentary form to the States-General by the chairman. Mainly the resolutions of the states were identical with the issued recommendations (De Bruin, 1991, pp. 144–5). The growth in the bodies of committees meant that the discussions shifted from the plenary meetings to the committee meetings and the daily meeting of the states took less and less time; in the eighteenth century, not more than an hour.

The development of the bodies of committees in the States-General was accompanied by the formation of a small group of people participating in all important meetings. In the period when there was no stadholder, this group was led by the pensionary of Holland and the registrar, who were present at all committee meetings and, as such, were always well-informed. If a stadholder was in function, he comprised a similar informal meeting circuit together with several other trustees. In these top meetings all sorts of semi-legal methods were developed to guide the plenary meeting into a direction which was the most advantageous to themselves regarding the course of the inter-state relationships and their own position of power within these networks. As such, on several occasions, Holland presented the States-General with a fait accompli, having independently established negotiations with other countries.

Attempts to make important decisions without consultations were by far the most common methods and not always without the approval of the enfranchised members. Particularly in times of war, the latter were readily prepared to give their representatives greater authorization to decide according to their own opinion during confidential meetings. But moreover, particularly the deputation from Holland to the States-General had a knack of surprising the other deputations in the meeting with ready-made decisions, which could only be discussed with others after they had been made. This was only possible by keeping a section of the delegates from the discussions, by searching out poorly attended meetings, and by intensive use of the possibilities offered by the committee system.

> Before the discussions took place in the meetings, the Grand Pensionary, John de Witt, often first had talks with several influential regents of Holland, especially when important matters were concerned. When agreement had been reached, the question was presented in the committee meeting and then, in general, few difficulties were encountered. Weighty decisions were often actually taken in corridors, in offices of the Pensionary, or in inns where the deputies lodged, and they only required the formal endorsement of a committee or the States of Holland. De Witt often took advantage of this totally informal way of deliberation, which adopted such fixed forms in the eighteenth century that the term 'conclave' was used. (Franken, 1980, p. 147)

The following was a manipulation technique which the deputies from Holland led by the pensionary applied to avoid the mandates and unanimity rule in a complete meeting of the States-General. It was the rule that, if a resolution concerned a matter about which nothing had been previously discussed or decided, unanimity was required and, if a resolution was an implementation of earlier decisions, the approval of the majority was sufficient. This rule offered officials, such as De Witt, who knew the resolution registers better than the majority of the delegates, the possibility to place recalcitrant minorities out of the game. Several instances of this are known. Thus, in 1664, De Witt guided a conceptual decision, which could have led to a war with England, into the meeting by packaging it as a routine decision which he announced in a manner difficult to understand, while confidants of De Witt distracted several delegates so that they did not hear the content of the resolutions (Schöffer, 1964, p. 87).

The most efficient way to guide decisions into a specific direction was to restrict the circle of decision makers to a small group of meeting participants. The opportunities to do so were extremely limited within the republican configuration. The enfranchised members meticulously guarded their achieved positions of power, so that the best chances for having some control were in the preliminary deliberations, in the prevention of decisions with the help of private correspondence, in contact with foreign diplomats, in an intensive use of confidential committees of the states, and in secret meetings with confidants. In particular, the pensionary and the princes of Orange were extremely active in the corridors, in sending confidential correspondence, and in the holding of confidential pre-discussions. This was especially so during the Dutch-English wars, when De Witt was Grand Pensionary, during the Dutch wars against France and England, and during the stadholdership of William III, who spread his influence noticeably through 'legal manoeuvres'; that is by replacing members of the town governments. William III was lord and master in Utrecht, Gelderland and Overijssel and the 'delegates from these provinces were his political creations' (Franken, 1980, p. 255).

When the Dutch Republic arrived in calmer waters after 1713, the readiness of the lower meetings to trust a part of their authority to 'secret committees' decreased sharply, and there remained little interest for informal, confidential meeting activities (De Bruin, 1991, pp. 318–54).

Due to the exceptional figuration of the Republic, in which the central meeting participants were subordinate to the town governments, and the monopolies of physical force and taxation were under differing controls, for all important decisions, members were directed towards using negotiation, persuasion, informal discussions, sending delegates, threats with economic sanctions and buying others off; predominantly peaceful methods and techniques which offered Holland, as the wealthiest region, and Amsterdam, as the most affluent town, more possibilities and opportunities for guiding the decision making than the other towns and provinces. Under the guidance of the pensionary, Holland could make use of the elbowroom which the delegates from the other provinces had.

> This took place by manipulating them with the power of argumentation in committees, corridors, and inns, by surprising them with prefabricated papers, plans, argumentations, and manoeuvres in public and private meetings, by placating them with promises, positions, and concessions, and by directly placing them under pressure. Also, it was possible to drum up support from their sympathisers in other regions who were temporarily absent for the decision making. . . . In the remaining cases, warnings, threats, and delaying tactics seemed to work, although

the Standing Committees sometimes rendered assistance to the delegates from Holland and sometimes even the complete States of Holland showed up in a meeting of the States-General. Obviously an attack by fifty to eighty men placed pressure on the decision making during a meeting with ten to twenty delegates not from Holland. (De Bruin, 1991, p. 149)

By applying such methods, in the States-General and the States of Holland respectively, the State of Holland and the city of Amsterdam had more influence than would have been possible with majority or submission rules. Certainly, this was one of the reasons why these rules were not or not stringently applied at the highest meeting levels of the Republic.

In the provincial states, there was likewise a tendency for power to be concentrated in the hands of a small circle of delegates and top officials, although, more often here, the committees maintained an ad hoc character and a subordinate position regarding the plenary meeting. Here the development of a small circle of well-informed meeting participants was possible due to the rapid turnover of a large part of the members. A small number of the delegates who had participated in meetings over a longer period (often members of the knighthood) and the civil servants took the opportunity to monopolize certain information and to guide decisions into a certain direction (De Bruin, 1991, pp. 155–6).

The process by which more matters were prepared and arranged for reasons of internal and external security and for allowing more speedy decisions in small committees and inner circles, did not restrict itself to the States-General and the provincial states, but extended to the towns where a nucleus of burgomasters and ex-burgomasters controlled policy with the pensionary or secretary, and there was a decline in the influence of the remaining members of the city council. Cornelis Pieterszoon Hooft, who had held the position of burgomaster of Amsterdam on many occasions prior to 1610, but who was subsequently shunted into the sidelines, complained in 1616 that 'only the burgomasters were informed of the recommendations offered to the city and also what actually took place in the meetings of the States, thus the other members of the council could be easily misled through ignorance' (Hooft, 1925, p. 71). In the smaller towns, such as Leiden, the important issues were first discussed in a small circle of burgomasters and ex-burgomasters prior to being presented to a plenary meeting of the city council so that 'too much discussion in the council was generally not appreciated' (Prak, 1985, p. 33).

In the meetings of the central board of the VOC, where no matters were explicitly excluded from outvoting and the participants were not obliged to mandates and consultations, an attempt was made to guide the decisions in a certain direction from below rather than from above. Within the VOC, the lower administration boards were at the service of the highest representative board. The board of directors gave orders which had to be implemented by the chambers. In spite of the fact that in the highest meeting of the VOC the delegates were not tied to mandates and consultations, in the reports of the meetings of the chambers, there were frequent references to decisions in which the delegates were directed to 'conduct' the central board in one direction or another (Gaastra, 1989, p. 54).

Confidentialities

In the period of state formation, when the monopolies of physical force and taxation were relatively unstable and vulnerable, and the decisions taken by the central government affected more and more people, the confidentiality of 'state matters' was a bone of contention between the governors and the governed.

Out of fear of enemies from home or abroad, the government of the early-modern state strove to keep to itself everything that it did not have to make known, to comply with, or to warn about. In principle, speaking about and printing state matters and political news was not permitted if the government had given no order or permission to do so. Everywhere in Europe, governments denied access to the co-ordination centres for increasingly more people. In France, the *Etats Généraux* did not assemble from the beginning of the seventeenth century until the French Revolution, and other public, political meetings were forbidden as well. Central decisions were taken in the secret meetings of the court councils: 'The essential deliberations took place in the Royal Council and were kept secret' (Brasart, 1988, p. 12). In England, too, the court councils still had a dominant position in the national decision-making process in the early half of the seventeenth century. However, the English court councils found themselves more and more under the pressure of the parliament and eventually were literally beheaded with the execution of Charles I in 1649. In this battle between monarch and parliament, Thomas Hobbes wrote in *Leviathan* (1651), that:

A Monarch receiveth counsell of whom, when, and where he pleaseth; and consequently may heare the opinion of men versed in the matter about which he deliberates, of what rank or quality soever, and as long before the time of action, and with as much secrecy, as he will. But when a Soveraigne Assembly has need of Counsell, none are admitted, but such as have a Right thereto from the beginning; which for the most part are of those who have beene versed more in the aquisition of Wealth than of Knowledge; and are to give their advise in long discourses, which may, and do commonly excite men to action, but not governe them in it. For the *Understanding* is by the flame of the Passions, never enlightned, but dazled: Nor is there any place, or time, wherein an Assemblie can receive

Counsell with secrecie, because of their owne Multitude. (Hobbes, 1651, pp. 188–9)

Dutch scholars like Grotius and Spinoza, coincidentally, followed the same line of thought as Hobbes, namely that the governing power rests on the social contract of the people; that is, the rights of the people are rendered to a common government which has to ensure that the people cannot harm each other. However, they propounded more temperate opinions about the range and the autonomy of the state's power. Hobbes attributed the complete, exclusive power of the church and state to the monarch, as long as he did not go for 'that forbidden by God' and thus the social contract becomes one-sided. Conversely, Spinoza developed principles, according to which state power (analogous to the actual situation in the Republic) had to be exercised in a communal game of estate representatives. 'People only have to place the public interest above their own interests and the government has to rely on the persuasion of the subjects, not on fear or apprehension, as Hobbes wants' (Schmid, 1970, p. 7). In his last, unfinished and posthumously published paper *Tractatus Politicus*, Spinoza initially resolutely refused every independent government authority. In the last chapter of this political treatise, he suggested that a government of patricians was the best form of government, so long as they 'choose their fellow governors free from all passion and only guided by enthusiasm for the general good'. However, according to Spinoza, this was hardly ever the case in practice. Usually, after a short period, an oligarchy of patricians comes into being, who have a powerful tendency to stand above the law through the absence of rivals: they keep the best candidates out of the meetings and only look for colleagues to curry favour with them. Given these 'human weaknesses', Spinoza opted for a 'democracy' in his farewell essay, in which the governors were chosen from and by all native subjects who were financially independent and who led a respectable life. He excluded explicitly all women and slaves, who after all lived under the authority of their men and masters; children and orphans, as long as they were under the authority of their parents or guardians; and also criminals and those who maintained themselves in a unseemly manner.

Spinoza was ahead of his time with these principles, in which he explained the latent 'trend towards democratization' in the Dutch Republic. Only during the Batavian Revolution at the end of the eighteenth century did a similar, more 'democratic' government system come into being for the first time in Dutch history.

The trend towards the centralization and monopolization of the government apparatus into the hands of a small select group was most noticeable in the European monarchies, but it also made itself felt in the Republic. Thus, the administrators of the Republic continuously adopted regulations to serve the purposes of maintaining confidentiality about everything they had spoken and decided about in their meeting, and to distance and isolate themselves from the trading and entrepreneurial bourgeoisie and other layers of the population. Although, in practice, these regulations were not strictly adhered to, they contributed to the intensification of feelings of togetherness and exclusivity within the higher class of meeting participants and made access to the state government for potential 'rivals' either difficult or impossible.

The meeting participants of the Republic were prompted to make regulations for the maintenance of confidentiality of state matters due to the threats of war, which were practically continual until the beginning of the eighteenth century, and due to the internal tensions between higher and lower urban classes and between the different sections of the state complex; tensions which usually erupted with the outbreak of war and the accompanying tax increases. In 1586 the States of Holland decided to keep all state matters confidential and to request the same degree of confidentiality be respected by the members of the delegating town governments and knighthood (De Bruin, 1991, p. 229). In 1651, the States of Zeeland proclaimed that 'confidentiality is equivalent to the soul of the most noble part of state affairs' (*ibid.*, p. 42).

With the confidentiality of state affairs no distinction was made between what was said during a meeting and what was eventually concluded. Thus, the States of Holland demonstrated in 1586 that it 'would be unseemly if somebody's proposition, recommendation, or decision . . . would be made public; that it would also be against the liberty and prosperity of the country if somebody would be subject to something grave because of his proposition, recommendation, or decision, which he had candidly announced in the meetings of the States' (quoted in De Bruin, 1991, pp. 45–6). The currently accepted distinction between official secrets and state secrets, and between treason of the country, high treason and lese majesty (misdemeanours against external state security, internal state security, and the sovereign) first appeared during the process of political democratization in the nineteenth and twentieth centuries. In previous centuries distinctions were only made between very confidential and less confidential information, and between grave and less grave types of treason.

The meeting participants considered the confidentiality of everything that was spoken about in their meeting to be of crucial significance in view of the security of the state and the maintaining and strengthening of their own position within. They thought this so important that they linked the access to the meeting to a sacred proceeding by which the participants committed themselves to complete confidentiality regarding the matters discussed. Thus, at the start of his function, every member of a city council had to proclaim an oath in which he swore to keep confidential everything that was discussed in the council. Likewise, the delegates to the meetings of the provincial states were obliged to swear an oath of confidentiality. According to the regulations of the States of Holland of 1574, they had to swear 'to keep secret all matters discussed and decided in the meeting, and only to make these matters public if it was necessary and imperative'. Later the states adopted several resolutions in which the duty to maintain confidentiality was pointed out to the delegates.

On entering the meetings of the States-General, every member had to swear an oath 'to keep confidential everything that will be proposed, dealt with, recommended, or decided in this meeting, both the personal opinions of the delegates and the views of the provinces' (Japikse, 1921, p. 235). Later the officials, clerks, translators, and messengers were obliged to swear a similar oath. At the start of every political function, for membership of a national board, a committee or envoy, and at numerous of special events, a particular oath of confidentiality had to be declared.

For many reasons (detailed later), the sworn oaths did not have the desired effect and the states, the town governments and those participating in other meetings endeavoured to lessen the chance of leaks of confidential information. This was done by restricting the documentation of the matters discussed to a minimum by the introduction of ordinary and secret books for resolutions, by dividing and separating correspondence into more and less confidential, by the restriction of copying rights of the provinces and enfranchised members in order to restrain the circulation of state matters, and by the repeated enactment of decrees in which public discussion and documentation of state matters, and particularly the drafting, printing, and distributing of political and religious texts of offensive, subversive, and inflammatory nature, were forbidden (De Bruin, 1991, p. 228). Finally, there were the repeated attempts by some powerful administrators (mainly from Holland) and the stadholders to guide decisions about important diplomatic, military and financial matters into a certain direction, or to allocate them to confidential meetings of a limited number of delegates.

It was no different in the meetings of the VOC and the town governments. From fear of foreign competition and possible requests from shareholders to pay out higher dividends, the central board kept as much confidential as possible. Characteristic of the behaviour of the directors was the careful maintenance of the confidentiality of a manuscript by Pieter van Dam, who was employed by the VOC as a lawyer from 1652 to 1706. This document, in which the history and the organization of the VOC was set out in detail and which served as a book of reference for the directors, was carefully preserved in a locked cupboard in the meeting chamber of the directors from Amsterdam, to be seen by nobody but themselves (Gaastra, 1991, p. 151). The burgomasters of Amsterdam concealed extremely confidential state papers in a sealed box, which could only be opened in the meetings of the city council after confidentiality had been pledged by each member (De Bruin, 1991, p. 237).

In summary, it can be concluded that the acts of separately dealing with, transcribing and keeping ordinary and confidential resolutions, the confidentiality oaths, the ban on publication, the verbal business transactions which demanded drawing on one's memory more often, and the formation of inner circles enlarged power differences between meeting participants and non-participants and between the participants themselves, and resulted in meetings becoming more exclusive and more complicated.

However, this trend was subdued by the rivalry within the class of meeting participants and the relatively large need for urban middle classes to have political information. The number of people who had to be informed about state matters because of their profession or function was larger than elsewhere. There were many attempts, particularly by the pensionaries and the stadholders, to restrict the circle of initiates by discussing important (military) matters in 'confidential meetings' of delegates with unlimited authority, but the movement of the government of the Dutch Republic towards that of an oligarchy did not go as far as it did in the European monarchies. The secret meetings with unlimited powers of decision, which were instigated by the stadholders and grand pensionaries, under pressure from wars, rapidly lost power after the danger of war was over, because the members were again obliged to consult the provincial grassroots. The towns and provinces tolerated no lasting infringements to the system of representation which guaranteed them a large degree of autonomy. For the same reason, the matters which were discussed in the meetings of the confidential committees of the provincial states could not remain as confidential as in countries where the important decisions were taken by a small group of courtiers in the privacy of the council and royal chamber.

Confidentiality in the Republic was made more difficult because the different political branches thought it generally more important to fulfil their desire to be knowledgeable about all state matters and to give their opinion about them than to fulfil their obligation to confidentiality. Moreover, the rivalry between towns and provinces, and between factions within, was so large that state secrets were frequently made public if somebody thought that they could enhance their own position by so doing. The provincial states considered themselves almost as governments from separate states. Thus, in 1670, the States of Holland complained about the increasing leakage of state secrets 'to the regents, ministers, or residents of other states and provinces, yes, even to the enemies!' (De Bruin, 1991, p. 47).

Making state matters public was strongly promoted by the increasing demand for political information by the population. Particularly at times of crises, printers and retailers of pamphlets, books, and newspapers could barely keep up with the public's demand for political news. The great interest for political news can be explained by the extensive urbanization, the large degree of literacy, and the exceptional professional structure by which relatively many people were dependent on information concerning wars, dangers from the sea and land, prices, and other such matters.

The government was not in a position to hold back or control the stream of political and religious literature. They limited themselves generally to seizing the worse 'outcrops', 'if the internal and external security and their own position were part of the discussion, and the protests from the enfranchised members, the prevailing church, and the foreign powers and diplomats were not to be ignored' (De Bruin, 1991, p. 417). The confidentiality regulations of 'state matters' and their limited success represent the two trends between which the republican-urban 'game' oscillated: a dominant trend in the direction of democratization and the further development of meetings, and a contra-trend in the direction of 'oligarchization' and the reduction of meetings. Both trends can also be observed in the terminology used to talk about society.

Towards a more distanced meeting language

The replacement of a monarchy by a government of a relatively large group of mandated and, in principle, equal, meeting participants promoted the depersonalization of thinking and speaking, as individuals were obliged to talk and decide on behalf of many. As the chains of actions became longer, more enduring, and more differentiated, and the decision-making process became more complex, concepts developed in the national meetings which made a sharper distinction between the meeting participants or the meetings, and the society about which individuals met. The need for concepts, which were directed towards the relative autonomy of social processes regarding the motives and plans of individuals or groups of people grew very gradually.

This process of depersonalization progressed extremely slowly. It has already been mentioned that, when precisely what had to remain confidential was determined, no distinction was made between 'matters of state' and 'the general government'. Just as a French king could equate himself with the French state (*l'état c'est moi*), the governors of the Republic of the United Provinces often saw the developing Dutch state as their own common enterprise. This view can be found, for example, in a school textbook from the period of the Republic in which the reader was urged 'to love and revere the High and Mighty Lords States, so that they remain a loyal subject to them and the fatherland' (De Bruin, 1991, p. 584). Apart from the notion of the Republic as a matter for the Noble, or High and Mighty Lords, there was a much broader notion by the clergymen who considered the Reformed religion 'as the soul of this state, the basis upon which this flourishing Republic is established, and the predominant, yes only connection by which the provinces have remained united, in a communal state government' (De Bruin, 1991, p. 589).

For much of the population, the feelings of mutual solidarity did not really extend further than the borders of their place of birth and habitation. This, for instance, appears indirectly from the stipulation in the meeting regulations of the States of Holland, that not only did the delegates themselves have to live with the decisions of the meeting, but likewise these would be enforced upon the remaining townsmen and inhabitants. The middle classes from the more prosperous regions, who during the Republic became more involved in provincial administration, showed a powerful preference for their own province. Thus, in the disastrous year of 1672, Pieter de la Court argued for the withdrawal of Holland from the Union and for the independent defence of the province by constructing an enormous canal.

Particularly by means of meetings, other, more impersonal concepts came into circulation, such as 'province', 'state', 'republic', 'United Countries', 'United Netherlands', and 'the Netherlands'. As terms for the social unity represented by the states, these concepts gradually replaced terms referring to an individual such as 'dukedom', 'county' (under authority of a count) and 'manor'.

The varied scale of terms for (part of) society was characteristic of a stage in the lengthy process of state formation and the development of meetings, in which initially individuals worked and fought for a person or a distinct group of people, but who began to feel its inadequacies once they began to discuss and decide on the future of tens of thousands and sometimes hundreds of thousands of people. They discovered that life had become more complicated and it was no longer possible to bring things down to personal denominators (according to Fontaine, 1954, p. 188). The concepts that were used continued to oscillate between the notion that society had transformed itself and become concerned with the dealings and decisions of individual people or groups of people, on the one hand, and the notion that society was a phenomenon apart from people, on the other.

In the Republic, meeting instructions and manners developed which demonstrate that differences between 'private interests' and 'public interests' had begun to become sharper. In 1583 the States of Holland decided that a delegate had to leave the meeting if the discussion was to be about him or a member of his family (Koopmans, 1990, p. 185). On entering the Council of State, individuals had to swear to distance themselves 'from all private correspondence whether it was with the provinces or towns, or whether with private individuals in so far as these would be objectionable for the common good' (Van Deursen, 1981, p. 51).

The increasing social pressure towards a less personal and more businesslike manner of discussion in meetings was a problem for many, as seems apparent from the meeting instructions documented in a seventeenth-century manual.

Meetings and conversations: books of etiquette and the first meeting manual

In 1623 a type of book of manners written by Godefroy Boot appeared in Amsterdam. In it, comprehensive attention was paid to 'what the person going to and appearing in state meetings should do'. As Boot deals with the unwritten codes and the manners of meetings, his recommendations will serve to supplement the picture that can be gleaned from the official meeting regulations, resolutions and instructions. Also, Boot's lessons indicate that people had to focus upon the state meeting manners and codes in order to rise socially. At the time Boot's book appeared, the formation of a social upper layer of meeting participants (a meeting estate), through the mingling of individuals originating from the settled bourgeois and aristocratic groups and the rising middle classes, was still in process. The relatively rapid progression of individuals from the bourgeois to the higher class of meeting participants can explain Boot's attention to meeting behaviour and the public interest in meeting etiquette which he had assumed.

Godefroy or Godfried Boot was born around 1570, the offspring of a noble family. During his youth, he served seven years under the banner of his uncle, Willem van Zuylen Nijeveld, Lord of Heeraertsberg, and toured through France and Germany. After his marriage in 1595, he settled in Utrecht where he participated in the town government. In 1599 he received from the state the function of receiver of convoys and licences in Gorinchem. In 1608 he resigned to apply himself to literature. He translated *Batavia* by Hadrianus Junius. Three years later he was prosecuted for having relations with the enemy and was imprisoned in The Hague. After he was set free, he wrote the book in question. What further is known of the man is that he was subject to extravagant fantasy, demonstrated by the 'fabulous genealogy' which he had constructed for his family. He died in London in 1625, where he had just moved.

The full title of Boot's book was *A civil instruction or termed otherwise: Polite advice, consisting of many different necessary, pleasant and delightful lessons, stern warnings and very commendable teachings*. It was the first manual in which comprehensive attention was paid to meeting together and reflected as such the exceptional 'meeting culture' of the Republic, where the central co-ordinating functions were fulfilled by a relatively large number of people, based on equality. In as far as Boot's book can be called a manual on manners (there was little attention paid to behaviours such as eating, nose blowing, sleeping, and other such things), it is to be seen as something new and unique in the European genre of books of etiquette. In accordance to the greater degree of confidentiality by which meetings under monarchies were shielded, as far as speaking was concerned, one found in the books of courtly manners only instructions for 'conversing'; a more personal way of speaking in 'good company'.

The number of copies issued of Boot's book is not known. Probably only one edition appeared. It received little recognition when it was issued since the only thing noteworthy about the book is the attention devoted to meeting activities.

Boot wrote his meeting lessons from a secular perspective. His prescriptions actually agreed strongly with the Protestant meeting rules which were covered in Chapter 5, but the arguments which he advanced differed strongly from those of the Reformers. He hardly ever appealed to God or the Bible, but rather pointed out the consequences of someone's 'incorrect' meeting behaviour for their social position and social standing. Boot's instructions were practical lessons about life, borrowed not only from his own experience, but also from classic literature, like the works of Aristotle and Cicero, and probably also taken from descriptions of meetings of royal councils. He tried to apply this knowledge to meetings in the Republic, where 'many people are found, who together undertake the same business, having equal power' (Lesson 160).

Boot's meeting lessons illustrate the transition from court to early-bourgeois etiquette viewed from the aristocracy's perspective (an aristocracy in a predominantly bourgeois society), and they form a summary of the prevailing meeting standards in the Republic. Boot did not cover so much the formal rules of meeting, such as the opening, closing, chairmanship and ways of deciding or taking minutes, but instead covered the 'correct' ways of presentation, speaking, treatment of co-participants and other, more 'psychological' aspects of meeting. Many of his recommendations were related to problems of 'involvement and detachment' (Elias, 1987).

The first of Boot's meeting lessons was, according to him, also the most important: when a decision had to be made in a meeting, participants first had to ask themselves whether the 'reasons they hear submitted are good or bad, with respect to the matter for which the Council has gathered'. Participants should not allow themselves to be distracted from the business of the meeting by considerations of whether the one who had spoken was good or bad, because the council had not convened to study someone's goodness or badness, but to make decisions 'for the good fortune, blessing, and prosperity of the rich country and the town' (Lesson 118). This lesson reappeared in various forms. In a meeting, those individuals who forwarded proposals that others disagreed with were not to be attacked in personal terms. Above all, participants should 'never abuse the council or the opinions of another member, who is not in agreement'. To do so would have given cause for quarrels and disputes. This was damaging, because it undermined the authority of the meeting and its decisions (Lesson 136). Meeting participants had to listen patiently, imperturbably and calmly to the recommendations, opinions and decisions of others, regardless of how awful they may have been.

A good meeting participant did not permanently contradict, seek arguments, chatter or keep silent. Meeting required a continuous control of one's own impulses, moods and feelings. A good assessment was only possible if the first burning lust had cooled a little (Lesson 125). Of all the expressions of the affects, becoming angry was the worse because it hampered the understanding and clouded the judgement (Lesson 153). 'Passions' and 'tendencies to anger' could be held in check by considering matters calmly, by actually preparing them and by dealing with them one at a time, in a specific order (Lessons 127, 131, 132, 143 and 144). The majority of the shortcomings and the greatest mistakes committed by people during deliberations and decision making emanated from the problem that people were too easily led by short-term considerations and by the mistakes of the day (Lesson 134). A good meeting participant sought a middle position between silence and obstinate adhesion to an already-held point of view, between constantly making objections and changing one's opinion (Lessons 128, 135, 149 and 152).

The early bourgeois character of the organization of the state of the Netherlands in the seventeenth century was clearly expressed in Boot's instructions that one always had to place considerations of income above those of expenditure, and that the military were not allowed to be part of national meetings except if requested to make military recommendations, because meetings were not there 'to display a man of honour', but to investigate the pros and cons of the proposals and plans in complete peace and tranquillity (Lessons 158 and 141).

Boot's way of treating meetings had no following in the Republic. This could have been surmised because of the stagnation due to the rise of the middle classes in the seventeenth and eighteenth centuries. Later books did not take up the theme but were directed towards foreign court models in which another way of speaking was considered: conversing, or rather the art of speaking in drawing rooms, at court and during other court company.

In the European monarchies, the meetings, where the most important military, diplomatic, financial and religious decisions were taken, were only accessible to a small group of the monarch's trustees and they had a strongly hierarchical character. In these countries, speaking about politics and religion was strictly taboo. This situation was reflected in the books of etiquette which blossomed during the absolutist period and in which no attention was paid to the 'secret' activity of holding and attending meetings.

Absolute monarchies were not fertile ground for the growth of the art of meeting. This was stated by the author of a study of the national assemblies during the French Revolution: 'The sort of rhetoric through which decisions are made about a nation, and which determines the public will . . . does not exist in an absolute monarchy' (Brasart, 1988, p. 7). The 'essential' deliberations were the domain of the court council and they were kept confidential (*ibid.*, p. 12). In France, just as everywhere else, there were textbooks and courses in which the beginnings of classic rhetoric were set down, but this genre was directed towards speaking in public and the holding of speeches and arguments about some subject. It contained only a part of what individuals were meant to know, and should be capable of, if they met with others to talk and decide about the communal future. It was only in the latter half of the eighteenth century in France that the first 'meeting schools' arose: literary drawing rooms, academies and patriotic clubs which practised a manner of speaking with the intention of coming to common decisions or choices. This was done by means of discussions about mutual and more general problems, like judging each other's work, research programmes, elections, and the government (Brasart, 1988, p. 11; Heilbron, 1990, pp. 119–24).

In the world of the court and the drawing room, through which the courtly standards of correct behaviour were spread, a way of public speaking was cultivated by which the subjects of religion and politics were avoided as much as possible. There

> Reigned an atmosphere of refined and graceful entertainment. . . . In this atmosphere of decadent gallantry and subtle battles for status, there was no place for lectures and lengthy considerations. A sharp play on words was more successful than a well thought-out argument, a surprising paradox was better regarded than a stringent rationalisation, a light-hearted recital more desirable than an erudite manner. . . . Short, sharp ways of expression (aphorisms, maxims) enjoyed exceptional popularity, particularly when these were related to human behaviours and desires. (Heilbron, 1990, p. 46)

This manner of speaking appeared in the books of manners in the court and post-court periods under what was termed 'conversing' or 'speaking in company'.

It is remarkable just how much the rules for conversation in manners books and Boot's meeting regulations agree with each other concerning the restraint of aggressive tendencies and other expressions of the affects. Just as would be expected from Elias' theory (courtiers no (longer) fight each other with the use of weapons, but with the use of words), all of the books of court etiquette concern speaking, body posture during speaking, polite phrases, forms of address, both desirable and undesirable topics for discussion, choice of words and pronunciation. Likewise, one comes across speaking instructions again and again which mark the border between fighting with the use of weapons and battling with words. The following examples have much in common with Boot's instruction never to scoff at other opinions.

In the book of etiquette from which Elias frequently quotes, *Galateo* (c. 1558), by Giovani della Casa, it is stated that perpetual objectors were unbearable people who were not familiar with human nature and were not aware that 'everyone loves to win an argument and dreads just as much to be conquered by words as by weapons' (p. 63).

To speak politely, and with good manners, in company required that 'people had to use modest and mild words, which had the minimal harshness. Far preferably, people should say, "I could not express my opinion clearly enough", rather than, "it is your fault if you do not understand me". It would be far better to say, "just let us consider that, just let us see if it is as we say", rather than exploding into words' (della Casa, Dutch translation, 1715, p. 92).

According to the well-known manners book of Antoine de Courtin, entitled *Nouveau traité de civilité* (1672), individuals who constantly contradict in a conversation are 'difficult people, who make it quite clear, that they do not know human nature, do not realize that everyone loves to win, even in intimate company. People dread to be won over by words just as much as by deeds'. Courtin wrote that people should not constantly argue, 'but if one was forced by chance to choose sides and to argue about a subject when in the company of others, then one should do it genially, and not be so fired up to win the fight that not an inch is given to the opposing party' (Courtin, Dutch translation, 1733, pp. 197–8).

At the end of the eighteenth century, when broader layers of the European and North American populations acquired access to the political meetings of their countries, a particular genre of meeting training books developed. The authors of manners books continued both to avoid the theme of meetings and to advise their readers against discussing politics or religion in company. The following quotations taken from Dutch books of manners from the past 50 years are illustrative:

> In general, a prohibited topic is politics; . . . Religion is also a topic which had better not be broached in large groups of company. (Olga van Haeften, 1936, pp. 115–16)

> Particularly with the subjects of politics and religion, one must be extremely careful not to offend others. (Amy Groskamp-Ten Have, 1945, p. 83)

> Religion and politics are treacherous subjects in large groups of company in which one does not know everybody else equally well and, therefore, unintentionally, could tread on the toes of others in a quite impolite and painful way. (Lidi Luursen, 1964, p. 64)

Horst-Volker Krumrey, who studied German books of manners from the period 1870–1970, established that in those books no directives were given for speaking about 'central social matters', such as political and religious questions (1984, p. 283). It can be noted from these quotations that this is just as relevant for Dutch manners books, at least until about 1965.

The spread of the meeting class manners

The development of meeting activities in the period of the Dutch Republic indicates a close connection between changes in behaviour and changes in power and dependency relationships. During the Republic, frequent, regular, orderly and peaceful meeting activities, which were held on equal terms as regards the participants, were a means of power and distinction for the social upper crust. Many of the meeting rules and manners which developed during the Republic can be explained as the means by which a particular group of people distances itself from other groups and extend their power. Like the rules of etiquette in general, meeting rules serve 'to define the boundaries between those who belong and those who do not belong; they function to hold outsiders at bay and to set standards of sensitivity and consideration which preserve the (feeling of) purity and integrity of the group, group-identity and group-charisma' (Wouters, 1995). The state meeting manners had the same 'double function of communicating and distancing' for the upper class as had the standard Dutch language, which had been developed by them. In reference to this, Goudsblom has commented: 'Where the social distance was relatively great, the differences in rank not directly clear, and the integration "incomplete", people will base their behaviour upon standardised rules, which allow social relations mindful of commonly accepted reserves' (1988, p. 24).

Meeting manners make possible a closer co-ordination of more actions and serve as the means by which the rulers distance themselves from the lower classes in order to strengthen and maintain their positions of power in the towns, the state and businesses. Through presence and absence, the opening, the order of rank, and closely organizing and formulating the discussion and decision making in meetings, the upper class could increase its internal cohesion, its identity and its superiority, and could present itself as a 'meeting class'.

As the patricians could not decide autonomously about mobilizing the army, which was under the leadership of the stadholder, they were forced to take measures by which disorder and revolt in the towns could be nipped in the bud to a greater degree than the aristocratic upper classes could manage elsewhere. For example, the town governments built up stocks of grain to keep the price of bread low and, by so doing, reduce the risk of revolts over food shortages. These and other rules indicated that they and many others had to meet more often and on a more organized basis. Attempts were made to avoid social unrest by establishing houses of correction and almshouses, and by appointing political commissioners, or members of the administration, to manage the church councils, guilds, civil militias and water boards. These attempts led to a further branching away and condensation of the meeting network, within which many people performed tasks of co-ordination by order of, or under the supervision of, the town governments and the states.

The etiquette of the meeting class functioned as a model for the middle classes of merchants and artisans, intellectuals and church leaders. This can be illustrated in more detail by the local and interlocal meetings which developed with the organization of the textile manufacturing, a trade which acquired a more capitalistic character during the Republic (Van Dillen, 1970, p. 197). Co-ordination problems developed with the increase in scale of the work places, the ongoing division of labour and the stratification within this branch of business. These changes prompted the application of the traditional meeting manners which had been developed in the guilds.

In the middle of the seventeenth century the doyens and heads of the textile manufacturing guilds in the Dutch towns and the textile merchants who were settled there and who operated a private manufacturing firm, started to organize biennial, communal meetings, which were jokingly termed 'dry-shaver synods'. In 1638 the States of Holland issued a decree, in which the masters of the textile manufacturing guilds were obliged to deliberate with each other in the event of 'mutiny' by the dry-shavers (the labourers who had to cut the rough textile smooth) about the way in which they could end the workers unrest, and prevent it in the future. At their first meeting in 1643 in Leiden, the textile manufacturers decided that henceforth they would meet for several days in July every two years, although the decree did not oblige them to such regularity. Between 1643 and 1793, the textile manufacturers met 61 times, initially biennially, but quadrennially after 1737, when this branch of industry was still declining.

The meeting places changed according to the towns' order of rank and age of establishment. The meetings took place with the permission of the burgomasters of the host town. One of the secretaries from that town had a place of honour, conducted the round of polling and took care of the minute taking. The meals which closed the meeting days were at the cost of the host town and, generally, were attended by several magistrates. Travel expenses were paid by the delegates' home towns. Generally, two leading figures from every town participated, but from the host town, the entire board of deans and merchants were present. There was always a number of the patricians or the burgomasters present.

Apart from the differences between employers and employees, other subjects were discussed in these meetings, such as opposing the importation of foreign textiles, improvements in the methods of the firm, the exclusion of industry from the countryside, the establishment of uniform conditions regarding the testing of labourers and masters, the level of the wages, the

FIGURE 6.4 *Syndics of the Cloth Hall* by the seventeenth-century painter Rembrandt van Rijn (Rijksmuseum-Stichting, Amsterdam)

number of labourers and apprentices that each master should be allowed to have in his service, the duration of the employees work and overtime. As the textile industry declined, more time was spent on the question of how to prevent the collapse of the entire branch of the industry. Recommendations were presented in the same order that was employed in the meetings of the states. It was the rule to decide according to the majority of the votes, but considering that approval by the town governments was necessary for the implementation of many of the decisions, a minority of affluent ship owners and textile purchasers could often get their own way in the end by pressurizing their own town governments (Kernkamp, 1894, pp. 85–132; Van Dillen, 1970, pp. 294–9).

The directors of the textile manufacturing guilds started their meetings as a reaction to the repeated restlessness of the dry-shavers, who formed a workers' elite in the seventeenth century. This was due to the fact that they were relatively well-educated and better paid than the labourers in many other branches of industry. From about 1600 onwards the dry-shavers began to organize themselves locally, and sometimes regionally in the so-called 'court meetings'. Rudolf Dekker (1988) wrote about this phenomenon and a large proportion of the following details have been taken from this article. Although officially forbidden to do so by the town governments, the dry-shavers organized meetings to discuss work and wages. In Amsterdam, they met on the Old Bridge, which had been designated by the government as a place where employers and those seeking work could meet each other. In Leiden they met in public houses.

In these meetings, which were usually held on Sundays, any conflict between the patrons and the workers, or between the workers themselves, was settled informally. Both sides of a conflict selected 'good men', who functioned as judges and, as such, proposed a judgement which could be approved of, or dismissed, by the workers in their meeting. The fines sometimes amounted to three times the weekly wages of a labourer. The patrons contributed to these meetings and the government turned a blind eye to them.

However, this was not the case for the meetings where the dry-shavers deliberated and decided about petitions and other activities for the protection of their economic and political interests, such as striking. Strikes were a continuance of an older type of action in which the workers stopped work, left the town, and remained away until their demands had been granted. This older form of protest lost its effectiveness when the towns developed closer links with each other. By informing each other, the town governments and manufacturers could prevent workers who had left one town getting work elsewhere. The dry-shavers were the first to hold strikes. The meetings they held to prepare for these strikes were strongly suppressed by the government as 'complots'.

The dry-shaver labourers, who were for the large part immigrants, probably partially borrowed their meeting rules from workers' organizations which had developed in regions of Europe where large-scale manufacturing was more developed than it was in the Netherlands (Dekker, 1988, pp. 16–19). Their meeting manners were part of a more encompassing, European, pre-industrial workers' culture, which developed in the seventeenth and eighteenth centuries in the large places of work and in the working-class districts of the large towns (Lis and Soly, 1992, 1993).

Labourers from other pre-industrial companies employed similar activities and meeting manners (probably copying the dry-shavers). Thus, in 1744, the cotton printers of Amsterdam chose six strike leaders. 'They were chosen because they had "somewhat more understanding" than the others, and because they could read and write better. The elections were conducted "by voting", as was emphasised by the labourers, and not "by lottery". Amongst other things, a voting procedure guaranteed that all labourers carried part of the responsibility' (Dekker, 1988, p. 11). Also the hat makers in Amsterdam frequently held meetings about their grievances, on Sundays in particular, 'which was strictly forbidden by the judicial authorities more than once' (Van Dillen, 1970, p. 300).

These labourers meetings show strong resemblances to the neighbourhood meetings in the towns of Holland during the Republic. From the late Middle Ages onwards the inhabitants of the towns organized themselves into neighbourhood units with the intention of ensuring peace and order in the direct residential areas, helping each other with births, marriages and deaths, and organizing festivities to strengthen friendships (Lis and Soly, 1993, pp. 6–7). The family heads in these neighbourhood organizations chose a doyen and several leaders who had the task of guaranteeing the observation of mutual right and duties, and in the case of disputes to act as negotiators. In the sixteenth century the social and territorial division of higher and lower classes led to neighbourhood groups losing a large part of their governing autonomy. In the course of the seventeenth and eighteenth centuries with the reinforcing of the government of the towns, monopolized by the patriciate, the possibilities for the neighbourhood groups to take action were restricted to the informal settling of conflicts and a number of more formal tasks, such as the registration of foreigners and the poor (Lis and Soly, 1993).

Nevertheless, the neighbourhood organizations in working-class districts often continued to, or started to, fulfil functions extending mutual solidarity and militancy. Thus, during a people's revolt from 1747 to 1749, a meeting took place in Haarlem in the meeting house of the spinners and weavers where petitions were drawn up. The revolt had ten to twelve leaders and chose four men to represent them to the outside world. During this revolt, and also later during the Patriots' Revolt (1780–1787), the people's influence was particularly noticeable in Amsterdam and Leiden, those towns where traditionally the informal workers' organizations were the closest knit. For instance, in Leiden in the 1780s 'in all districts of the town "speakers" were chosen and the central leadership was in the hands of ten "chief speakers"' (ibid., pp. 15–16).

To put it briefly, the lower classes employed meeting manners, which could be characterized as 'informalized' guild rules. These covered areas such as voting about activities, choosing leaders and the use of inns as centres of activities.

After the middle of the eighteenth century, many branches of industry, where the labourers' militancy was the greatest, fell into decline (including the textile industry). Initially, at the end of the nineteenth century, a new wave of industrialization took place. Because of this break, a gap exists in the Netherlands between the eighteenth-century neighbourhood and labourers' organizations and the modern workers' movements that is greater than in many other European countries, where industrialization occurred in a less disjointed manner. The industrial stagnation in the eighteenth and nineteenth centuries can help explain why, in the nineteenth century, Dutch workers were originally organized along church lines in particular. With the disappearance of the pre-industrial workers' culture and the abolition of the guild system in about 1800, there frequently remained only the church for many from the lower classes as the most encompassing social network in which they could be engaged and meet.

While the workers and labourers, for whom originally a meeting and strike ban was in force during the Republic, were forced to discuss and make agreements with each other clandestinely, the patrons of the textile industry adopted the meeting manners of the upper class and thus distanced themselves from their labourers. The pressure and the possibility for adopting and imitating the etiquette of the meeting class by upwardly mobile burghers differed during the two centuries of the Republic's existence. There are indications that the upward movement of members of the urban middle class to town and state meetings, the higher realm of the meeting class, stagnated after the Republic was recognized by the European monarchs, and the patriciate had become firmly in charge and thus felt less threatened from above. From the latter half of the seventeenth century most of the governors of Amsterdam's detention centres were wealthy merchants, entrepreneurs, clergymen and those with a profession such as a notary, solicitor or pharmacist. Only a few of them were able to winkle their way into the government of Amsterdam (Spierenburg, 1991, pp. 107–8). Likewise, after the constituent stage in the sixteenth century, the administration of the Dutch Reformed Church communities was increasingly left to prominent members of the middle class, from which group fewer and fewer were admitted to the city council. The town government of Amsterdam was, like the administrations of other towns, monopolized by a small group, frequently from related families. A relationship to these governing families and/or good relations with the court of the stadholder were increasingly important criteria for admission to the meeting class and a career in it. For those who satisfied these criteria, some meeting experience still remained necessary, however, to be able to rise in power, status and income.

In the latter half of the eighteenth century, the pressure from below increased on the meeting class, culminating in the Patriotic Revolt and the founding of the Batavian Republic. The contrasts and tensions between the meeting class and the upwardly mobile middle classes became stronger. Finally, as the balance of power between both groups became more equal, both in waves of attraction and rejection, and in waves of smoother and stricter regulation of meetings, a new, parliamentary meeting standard developed in which elements merged from the codes of behaviour from both classes. Middle-class clubs played an important role in this process, as will be shown in the next chapter.

Differences between European upper classes

The formation of an upper class of meeting participants was possible because of the way in which the inhabitants of the northern Netherlands unintentionally came to be tied to each other and through the opportunities for power provided by this. This notion can be further clarified by comparing the Republic with other European societies from this period. The Republic was administered by a relatively large and complicated network of urban administrative boards and provincial states, rising to boards of the generality and the States-General, which continually met. This political network was closely tied to the administrative meetings of the Dutch Reformed Church, the water boards, the trading companies, the textile industry and the universities. Several thousand people from a population of about two million were obliged to meet regularly due to their membership of the Republic's governing and administrative board; an unusually large number in comparison to other European countries at that time.[12] This governing system, with the corresponding meeting manners, developed within a state organization which was strongly decentralized and financed in an exceptional way.

Similar to elsewhere in Europe, on average 70 to 80 per cent of the state's expenditure was for military purposes. In contrast to the governments of many other European countries, the States-General did not actually have at their disposal sufficient opportunities for financing state expenditure from their self-controlled income from taxation or elsewhere. The financial problems fell largely onto the shoulders of the fiscally autonomous provinces or they were shunted into the future by borrowing money. The taxation duties in the Republic were distinct from those in other European countries particularly through the large number of voluntary, internal private loans from all classes of the population, namely those emanating from prosperous Holland ('t Hart, 1989, pp. 155–9). State expenses were more than half financed by loans and taxes collected from Holland, which, as such, was given a determining vote in the central meetings of the Republic. Due to the decentralized tax and lending systems, the central official apparatus could remain smaller than in those countries like France, where the military apparatus was financed mainly with the assistance of centrally controlled sources of income, and the state was organized in a more bureaucratic way.

In countries where trade and urbanization lagged behind and a wealthy middle class did not develop, the governments continued to co-operate with the large landowners, who transferred the tax levies onto the farming population. This sometimes led to revolts by the farmers, but with the defeat of these revolts, the military was frequently able to further extend its influence on the government of the country concerned. Prussia, and later Germany, were the prototypes of a similarly strongly militarized state organization, in which the central meetings often had the character of warrior councils.

The degree of militarization of the country's government was also determined by the sort of army that was necessary for a successful war campaign. In those states where their geopolitical position sooner gave rise to waging war on land, the army generally played a more active role in governing the country than in states which mainly fought their wars at sea. This can be explained by the fact that a land army can be mobilized more easily than a navy to suppress any uprisings and force payment from those unwilling to pay their taxes. This is not only a logistical but also a social fact. Land armies were generally under the command of people originating from the nobility. Maritime commanders more often stemmed from lower social classes, as the more specialized knowledge demanded by war at sea was more usually found in the common population than in the nobility (Mann, 1988, p. 477; Elias, 1989, p. 18).

In the Republic a good part of the military command at sea came from common stock. Land engagements were fought by mercenaries under the command of the stadholders of Orange. The stadholders were popular with the lower classes and the population of the provinces, who feared the power of Holland, but they were totally reliant on the co-operation of the towns of Holland for performing their military functions.[13] In the Republic, mercenaries were used to suppress uprisings and insurrections among the urban population, but these soldiers left once the job had been completed, leaving the control of authority once more to the burgomasters and the town councils.

The controllers of the taxation monopoly, the states, could not autonomously decide about the monopoly of physical force. They were forced to share power with the stadholders. The latter had practically nothing to say about the levying and spending of the taxes, which mainly served for maintaining a standing army of mercenaries. On balance, the burghers had the edge over the military. The military was permitted no political function and had no access to the national meetings unless asked to make recommendations in the capacity of its particular function. Participation in town government and in meetings of the states was denied the military so that matters 'could be discussed confidentially and candidly' (*Resolutions of the States of Holland* 1583, quoted in Koopmans, 1990, p. 185). The stadholders still had a purely advisory function in the meetings of the States-General. If a stadholder were to be present, an armchair was saved for him at the meeting table. He made use of this only occasionally and usually only on ceremonial occasions. Then the ceremony of the meeting was not heightened by his presence. He was not met officially at the door, but was acknowledged simply when he entered or left the chamber. The stadholder Frederik Hendrik took care of his own ceremony. He was escorted by his halberdiers and several of his courtiers and officers across the courtyard of the states buildings from his own residence to the door of the States Chamber. They were expected to leave him at the door (Schöffer, 1964, p. 84).

The fiscal and military organization of the Republic brought with it an upper class more concerned with 'refining' its meeting behaviour than with stylizing eating, conversing, playing games and other behaviours, in which the courtly aristocratic upper classes from other European countries specialized, and were imitated. In the eighteenth century the Frenchman, Duclos, noticed something similar with respect to the difference between France and England, 'manners do in Paris what the spirit of government does in London' (Mennell, 1985, p. 121). In France and other countries, the court was the centre of the *Grande Monde*, a social upper class within which the observation of others and the interaction with others was raised to a complicated art form, and which became one of the means of distinction for the upper class. Within the court figuration, etiquette functioned as a royal means of control, as a 'method' by which the monarch tried to keep the aristocracy and the commoners under control and play off against each other. Knowledge and the application of the rules of etiquette was indispensable to be able to rise within court society. The court council was one of the arenas in which the absolute monarchs could validate their position of power and distance regarding the courtiers of aristocratic and common descent. In the middle of the seventeenth century a reorganization of the court council was carried out, led by Colbert, the General Secretary to the Treasury of Louis XIV. This reorganization served to play the military nobility and the nobility of bourgeois origin off against each other (the *noblesse d'épée* and the *noblesse de robe*) thus enlarging the elbowroom of the king. The *noblesse d'épée* was practically exclusively admitted to the councils which deliberated about the use and the organization of the monopoly of physical force. The *noblesse de robe*, however, was only admitted to the councils concerned with financial, fiscal, administrative and juridical matters. The court council was the king's confidential advisory body and the king made the final decisions: 'The composition, the convocation, the meetings, the discipline, the procedure were entirely in the hands of the monarch.' Louis XIV impressed upon his expected successor: 'Listen to and consult your Council, but decide yourself' (Antoine, 1970, p. 30 and 334). This was the reason why the French kings subjected the meetings of the court council to observing a strict etiquette.

In the Republic, a *Grande Monde,* or high society, developed around the States-General, the centre of a network of town governments, provincial states, and central boards, like the Council of State, the Admiralty and the large trading companies of the VOC and WIC.[14] Whoever wanted to penetrate the 'better circles' around the States-General did not only need to come from a respectable origin, but also had to have the capacity to talk and decide, on an equal footing with others, about a common future and in a calm and peaceful manner. Knowledge and confidence with the specific republican 'meeting etiquette' was necessary to rise in society.

The Republic was considered as a second-class state in the ranking order of states headed by absolute monarchs. The exceptional proficiency of its representatives in negotiating nevertheless frequently pulled the attention of the representatives of the absolutist states. The Marquis de Torcy, a minister to Louis XIV, and France's negotiator during the international peace talks of 1709–1710, said about the Grand Pensionary, Heinsius: 'His presentation manner was cool, he was not rough; his conversation was civilized. During debates, he did not get heated' (Murris, 1925, p. 238). These impressions corresponded with the picture that many French had about the Dutch at that time, and was thus expressed by a traveller: 'They do not like argument, are not quickly irritated, hate insults, cursing, swearing, and duelling' (De Parival, *Les délices de la Hollande*, Amsterdam 1685, quoted by De Vrankrijker, 1934, p. 50).

These comments must be seen against the background of a development in the direction of more regulated contacts between European states. Mastenbroek pointed out that, in France at the beginning of the eighteenth century, educational books appeared about the negotiations between state representatives (1992, pp. 82–103). One of the first to publish on this subject was François Callières (1716). He recommended his readers to avoid arrogant behaviour, to show no contempt, to not take recourse to threats immediately, to allow no animosity to show, not to submit to foul moods and not to brag or show off (*ibid.*, p. 82). The type of self-control recommended by Callières was precisely what Torcy remarked about Heinsius' behaviour. Furthermore, Heinsius' behaviour is noteworthy if it is compared with the performance of the Heinsius in the Synod of Dort one hundred years earlier, when he constantly thumped the table in anger and impatience so that 'the whole chamber shook'. During the Republic, the members of the upper class learned to meet in a more civilized manner.

In the eighteenth century the French enlightenment philosophers looked in admiration to the Dutch 'meeting culture'. According to Diderot, the constitution of the Dutch Republic was better than that of England. The highest meeting of the Dutch Republic could not finalize any decisions without the approval of the mandators, while the English constitution 'gave unrestricted power to the members of parliament'. He called the meetings of the States-General of the Netherlands 'the most exalted meetings of the world. Here one can see traders, burghers with the weighty tone and the majestic attitude of kings'. According to Diderot, the registrar's reading out of items at the start of meetings lent these meetings an 'imposing and religious appearance'. For him, the Republic was the closest to 'pure democracy' (1982, pp. 47, 48, 49 and 58).

A stable regime of meetings developed in the Netherlands earlier than it did in England. Before the latter half of the seventeenth century changes in the English government generally were coupled with violence and it was more or less never certain that 'once in office, one's opponents . . . would not use the resources of government in order to impeach the former office holders, harass and use threats against them, force them into exile, or prison and kill them' (Elias and Dunning, 1986, p. 28). Until the Glorious

Revolution of 1688, armed struggles over royal power and royal succession continued for three centuries (Tilly, 1990, p. 155; 1993, p. 114). England frequently provided the background for a violent battle between parliamentary and court factions. During the reign of the Stuart, James I, at the beginning of the seventeenth century, there were constant conflicts between king and parliament. The succeeding Stuart, Charles I, dismissed parliament in 1629 and only had it reconvened when, after eleven years, it was clear that he could not reign without the finances that only parliament could provide. Subsequently, two sides developed which carried the country into civil war. This turned out to be the decisive stage in the lengthy struggle between the Crown and parliament. After the Battle of Naseby of 1646, the king succumbed to the Scottish army. Negotiations to hand the king over to the English failed. Then, parliament broke with the king. A 'second' civil war started, in which parliament came to stand against troops under the command of Oliver Cromwell. The king fell in the hands of this army, which 'purged' parliament. What remained of it, the so-called 'Rump Parliament', appointed a committee which was referred to as the High Court of Justice. This unlawful court condemned the king to death. In 1649, Charles I was executed and the monarchy and House of Lords were abolished. England became a republic under the name of 'Commonwealth of Free State'.

Parliament was replaced by an assembly appointed by Cromwell's council and the power of state came into his hands. His government was a remarkable mixture of theocracy and military dictatorship. Cromwell died in 1658, leaving behind a political vacuum. The son of the last king, Charles II, tried to reinstate the monarchy. However, his work was suffocated during the short reign of his younger brother James II (1685–1688). James was openly Catholic, sent parliament home and tried to establish an absolutist regime after the French model of Louis XIV, who actually sponsored him. In 1688 the country revolted. Leading revolutionary groups summoned the help of the Protestant Dutch Stadholder William III, who was married to James' daughter Mary Stuart. To avoid a new civil war, James fled to France. His place was filled by Mary Stuart and her husband. These were the beginnings of a constitutionally restricted monarchy in Great Britain. This bloodless coup is called the Glorious Revolution. It marked the victory of a more public regime of meetings and the establishment of an upper class of (semi-)professional meeting holders.

In the seventeenth century, English burghers were often highly interested in the state construction of the Dutch Republic, where, according to William Temple, everyone's competence was clear in the meetings and discussions of its boards and councils. Temple also pointed out that the Dutch were not clever enough to get into pleasant and congenial conversation, but that they did not lack the healthy common sense to scrutinize and look after their own business, both public as well as private, because it was a talent of an entirely different nature than the former.[15]

The Dutch historian, G.J. Schutte, has pointed out that British and American writers' assessments of the Dutch constitution changed in the latter half of the eighteenth century. Some connected federalism to freedom and viewed it as the best weapon against despotism. Others emphasized the inconvenience resulting from the sovereignty of the provinces and 'the slow and inefficient administration and decision-making process'. American rebels wrote 'we may derive from Holland lessons very beneficial to ourselves', but also criticized the Dutch system. They saw little that was democratic in it, because a small town like Purmerend could put just as much weight in the balance as Amsterdam, and because the large degree of autonomy for each town, 'promoted inertia and endless delays, and so paralysed the process of decision-making' (Schutte, 1985, p. 115).

Along with wealth, origin, and family the capability for holding or attending a meeting was a criterion for admission to the upper class and for rising within it. The importance of this criterion for the chance of social success was limited in comparison with later. Nevertheless, compared to the previous sovereign period and the court societies elsewhere in Europe, the opportunities for rising in the Dutch Republic were more determined by possessing meeting capabilities and meeting experience. The upper class of the Dutch Republic was the first 'meeting class' of Europe.

PART IV

MEETINGS IN INDUSTRIALIZING AND INDUSTRIALIZED SOCIETIES

Parliamentarization and professionalization

During the process of industrialization in the last few centuries, many societies have developed into differentiated, multi-layered meeting units which, in turn, are constituents of continental and global units. The number of meetings and meeting levels in the areas of politics, economics, culture and almost everything else, has increased enormously. More than ever before, opportunities for societal success are dependent upon an individual's competence and experience in talking and decision making concerning lengthy and differentiated chains of actions. The upper level of industrialized society was, and increasingly is, shaped in and by meetings which require a relatively large, precise, constant and flexible self-regulation of expressions of affects and emotions.

The development of meetings during the process of industrialization was largely an unintentional and unplanned process. It was maintained by the necessity to solve the complex problems of co-ordination which arose during the unprecedentedly powerful, extensive and intensive growth, and the accompanying processes of task division, urbanization and organization of people into larger and closer political, economic and cultural units, in which the power differences became smaller and smaller or, at least, became less pronounced (Goudsblom, 1992a, pp. 198–9; Wouters, 1990, pp. 257–80). Likewise, forces against these developments constantly manifested themselves. At the most, in the shape of revolts, authoritarian intervention, and wars; at the least, in the shape of the lament that meetings were dreadful, boring, and time consuming. Having to meet has become the fate of 'civilized' people. It is the price that has to be paid for greater security and a higher standard of living.

Two stages can be distinguished in the development of meetings during the start and spread of industry; they are the sign of two consecutive, dominant trends. From the latter half of the eighteenth century to the middle of the

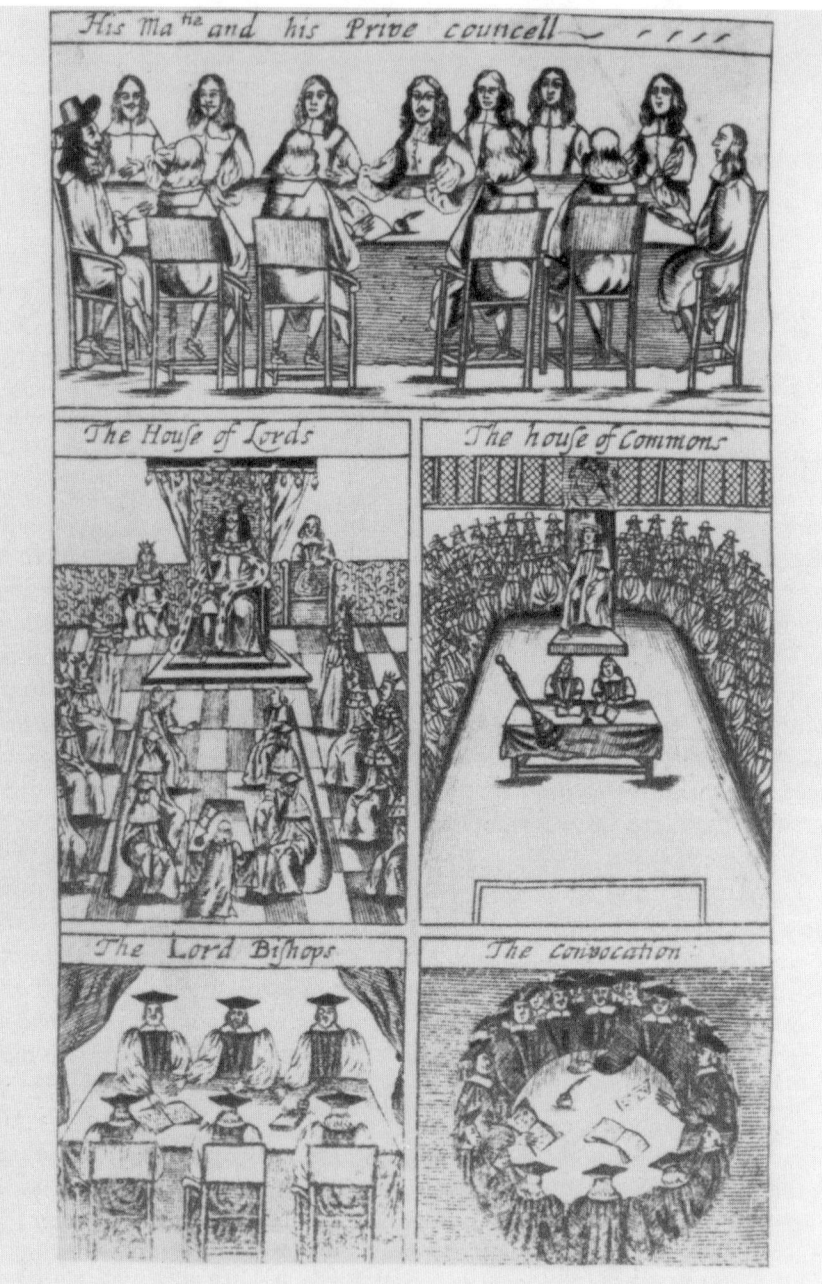

The birth of modern England as a regime of meetings. Frontispiece of *England's Glory*, 1661 (Collection Frits Lugt, Institut Neérlands, Paris)

twentieth century, there has been a dominant trend, which could be designated as the 'parliamentarization' of meetings. The trend which later became more prominent could be designated as the 'professionalization' of meetings. Elias concluded in *The Civilizing Process* that the courtization of the warriors was a 'key event' in the Western European process of civilization: 'Not only in the Western civilising process, but as far as we see within every major civilising process, one of the most decisive transitions is that of warrior to courtiers' (1994, p. 467). Elaborating upon this, it can be said that a subsequent decisive event in this process of civilization was 'the parliamentarization of the courtiers' (Van Vree and Bos, 1989). Initially, in the parliaments, which took over the co-ordinating tasks from the royal courts, many courtiers were given a seat next to people originating from common stock.[1] The more peaceful, more differentiated and more businesslike etiquettes which developed in parliaments functioned as examples; a function similar to that of court manners in the previous societal stage. Phrases such as 'to express oneself in a parliamentary way', which means to express oneself politely, and 'an unparliamentary expression', which is used for an expression not complying to accepted standards of politeness, indicate that parliaments played a central part in the development of the standard of politeness or 'civilized' behaviour.

The regulation of discussions, namely discussions about changes in the relationships between people, has become more prominent and received more emphasis in the post-court stage of the Western European process of civilization. For the development of the rules and codes of behaviour in discussions, the extension of meetings and the pressure to meet in a national context have been of great importance. In parliamentary meetings, models were developed to enable discussions about many people en bloc.

The 'parliamentarization' of the inner-state competitive struggle between people developed under conditions precipitated by an increasingly faster growth in trade, in lines of transport and communication and in industry. In the competitive struggle between states, success and failure became more dependent on the means and support, which governments had to request from commercial and industrial groups. While the production process, with the increasing use of fossil fuels, became more extensive, more complex and more vulnerable, and more and more people became dependent upon each other as producers and consumers, opportunities arose, which made possible a continuous parliamentarization of the social competition within states.

In all Western European states, and in many other countries discussing and deciding about the monopolies of physical force and taxation, sooner or later became more public and also centred in elected national parliaments. The continuous competitive struggle between states forced groups within these states to close ranks and take each other into consideration to a greater extent. While increasingly more people became more strongly tied to individual states with the introduction of national duties, such as military service, tax obligations, compulsory education and obligations to social security and national systems developed for the registration of the population, jurisdiction, the police, education, social and medical care and social security, the competitive struggle for power, possession and status within states acquired more the character of a regulated battle of words or a parliamentary struggle.

This 'parliamentarization' of the population occurred in waves. With every change in the composition and the position of power of the national parliaments, the rules were altered, adjusted or newly stipulated in the regulation codes. These regulations acted as an object for study for juridical specialists and served as models for the legal regulation of meetings and meeting practices within companies and corporations, societies, associations and other social organizations, with whose help, large groups of outsiders were integrated into society.

During the extension of voting rights, a rapidly growing number of manuals appeared for establishing, managing and running the meetings of associations and companies. These manuals (penned in particular by lawyers) can be considered as vehicles by which parliamentary etiquettes were passed 'downwards'. Together with the parliamentary code of regulations and the juridical literature which covered them, these manuals were an important source of information about the changes in the meeting standards that occurred during the formation of united nation states and the national integration of the middle and lower classes.

The trend in meeting behaviour, which has gradually become more prominent since the 1930s in the Unites States and after the Second World War in Western Europe, can be termed 'professionalization'. This trend became dominant together with the integration of national states into continental and worldwide meeting units, and accelerations in the processes concerned with the division of functions, the enlargement of the scale of institutions and functional democratization. Particularly in professional life, more people were more frequently obliged to hold discussions with each other, and to negotiate about the implementation, division and payment of functions, and the acquisition, management and spending of capital. In everyday social intercourse meetings acquired a central position. As far as meeting behaviour was concerned, competence and knowledge became essential ingredients for a successful societal career. One author of a manual of meeting etiquette put it like this:

> Meeting together is an activity in which people participate more and more, the higher they are placed in the hierarchy and the further they rise on the societal ladder. This means that participation in meetings and conferences has become a

status symbol. Whosoever participates is taken seriously. 'Sir is in a meeting' sounds weightier than 'John is in the store-room'. (Luijk, 1966, p. 4)

Whoever wishes to rise in present-day society has to climb the meeting ladder. Every rung upwards carries with it the consequences of holding discussions with others and making common decisions more frequently and more regularly, about lengthier, more enduring and more differentiated chains of actions. Little or no participation in meetings is characteristic of an outside position in society. This is neatly illustrated by the fact that people placed outside normal society for punishment, are not allowed to hold meetings.

Nevertheless prisons, at least Dutch prisons, nowadays appear unable to function without regular consultations between the warders and their wards, and among the prisoners themselves. Several years ago, detainees in an Amsterdam prison demanded in summary proceedings that the prison governors should allow the chosen 'detainees' committee' to meet daily for half an hour and weekly for three hours. Where the dependency relationships between people are less asymmetrical, the societal pressure for mutual consultations increases. Thus, in the last decades, the number of pupil and student councils in schools and universities has increased; as has the number of works councils and consultations about work in general in companies and other employment organizations.[2]

The extension and improvement of the means of transport and communication provided an important impulse for meetings. Getting together for consultations has become easier in many cases. Furthermore, it has become possible 'to meet at a distance' through telephone connections and computer networks, the so-called video-conferences, by which people in various places in the world take part before a camera and video screen, and enter into consultations with each other. These types of meetings appear to have developed rapidly because, particularly for multi-nationals whose managers as good as live in aeroplanes, meeting through a video screen can demonstrably lead to lower costs and higher productivity. The use of such techniques makes consultations and negotiations within companies, and between representatives of companies, states and other organizations simpler; so much that it can be expected that in the future they will be further extended. In their study, *Managing Language. The discourse of corporate meetings* (1997), Francesca Bargiela-Chiappini and Sandra J. Harris referred to a particular piece of research, according to which:

Video-conferencing has not lessened the importance of meetings in organisations, including companies in their various forms. Whether two-party or multi-party, internal or cross-organisational, intra-cultural or cross-cultural, face-to-face meetings continue to provide a forum where participants can arguably expect 'total commitment to the interaction, . . . maximum degree of urgency exerted by the parties and no technical problem . . . as an excuse'. (p. 6)

Furthermore, they quoted from a recent book for managers and by managers, which reported that studies commissioned by the Industrial Society and the Confederation of British Industry (CBI) showed that 'by far the most common, and highly rated channel for communicating with employees is team briefing. Electronic media, such as e-mail and video, came low on the scale' (p. 29). The authors remarked:

> Meetings are not simply an anachronism or dysfunctional in the quasi-perfect cyber-space criss-crossed by ethernet links. Ever faster information highways are not likely to make face-to-face events redundant, *pace* video-conferencing. Most organisations exist and will continue to exist in so far as individuals come together *to talk* them into being during meetings. (1997, p. 6)

Meeting manners have spread to family life with the increase in power opportunities for women and young people. Family members are obliged to discuss and negotiate their relationships more often and more regularly. By using marriage guidance publications, Regina Mahlmann demonstrated in *Psychologisierung des Alltagsbewusstseins* (1991) that since the 1960s a shift has taken place in Germany of the image of an ideal marriage and of actual marriage. With the entrance of more women into the labour force, marriage has developed from a male-dominated institution towards an institution composed of more equal partners, who largely have to negotiate their personal interaction rules themselves, more frequently have to discuss their problems, and are more inclined to 'linguistic conciliation' (*sprachliche Verständigung*). Bram van Stolk and Cas Wouters had previously noted a similar development in the Netherlands (1983).

At many levels in all sorts of organizations, both men and women of all ages and of all classes gather more often and more regularly in order to talk and decide on increasingly more aspects of their common future. Learning how to participate in meetings has become an important part in the rearing and education of the young. Whoever wants to participate in society with some chance of success needs to know and be able to apply the elementary meeting rules, and to have mastered the type of language spoken in meetings. This recent societal development is the background against which those manuals developed which approached meetings from a social-psychological angle. What is mainly expressed by these books is that meetings have become more varied and more informal, and that the meeting manners, which were developed at higher levels of co-ordination in companies and other employees' organizations, have mainly taken over the exemplary function of the parliamentary manners.

In the following two chapters, the development of meeting behaviour during the industrialization of economies and the emergence of inter-state organizations will be outlined. Much attention will be paid to meeting manuals. These publications provide a continuous series of detailed information about the problems, ideals, precepts, prohibitions and customs of meetings. They can be considered as a rich source of information about changes in the behaviour and self-control of people at that stage of society when meeting, with the increase in mutual dependency and the decrease in power differences, became a central and everyday behaviour.

CHAPTER 7

DEVELOPMENT AND SPREAD OF
PARLIAMENTARY MANNERS

Development and significance of the British parliament

Two stages can be discerned in the processes of parliamentarization in Western Europe, North America, Australia, and Japan (Spoormans, 1988, p. 73). In the first stage, from approximately 1770 to 1870, national parliaments, parliamentary governments and restricted voting rights emerged. The forces driving these developments were the urban populations and the commercial farmers. In the subsequent stage from about 1870 to 1970, pressurized by organized labour movements, the franchise was extended to include all adults. In each of these countries both stages have developed at different times and at different speeds. The general outcome was an elected parliament consisting of one or more houses, chambers or assemblies with three major functions: representation, decision and control over the executive. However, the way this is organized differs from country to country and has gone through considerable changes during the last 200 years.

Huub Spoormans distinguished four routes or trajectories which ultimately led to the same (interim) result, namely to a more democratic, parliamentary regime. The first route, followed in Germany, Austria, Japan and Finland, was characterized by a relatively late and abrupt parliamentarization, and a subsequent, temporary regression in the form of an authoritarian regime. The second route consisted of a slow and gradual parliamentarization, and was followed by Belgium, Denmark, Great Britain, Norway, Sweden and the Netherlands. The third route, characterized by periods of construction followed by periods of demolition, occurred in France, Greece, Italy and Spain. Parliamentarization began relatively early in these countries, progressed slowly and, encountering numerous obstacles, regressed and accelerated, and ended relatively late. The fourth route, which initially developed rapidly but endured an extremely lengthy second stage, is characteristic of the process of parliamentarization in Australia, Canada, New Zealand, the United States and Switzerland (Spoormans, 1988, pp. 31–73).

FIGURE 7.1 William Pitt addressing the House of Commons on the French declaration of war, 1793 (National Portrait Gallery, London)

With the processes of (de)colonialization and globalization, parliamentarization spread over larger and larger areas of the world by imitation and force (see Valentine, 1976). In 1889 two parliamentarians, Frédéric Passy from France and W.R Cremer from the United Kingdom, founded the Inter-Parliamentary Union (IPU). Initially, members of the Union came from approximately 25 different countries mainly in the western world. Currently members come from about 125 different countries all over the world. Almost every country has a parliament or something similar.[1]

The presence of a parliament does not necessarily mean that in a country, the 'most powerful collective decision makers are selected through fair, honest, and periodic elections in which candidates freely compete for votes and in which virtually all the adult population is eligible to vote' (Huntington, 1993, p. 7). Many states have parliaments which do not meet these 'democratic' criteria. For example, their parliaments are dominated by an autocratic ruler or a privileged upper class. However, the establishment of a parliament often turned out to be a step in a more democratic direction, an initial stage of a whimsical long-term process of political power sharing. In practice, political democratization mainly comes down to parliamentarization. Parliamentarization is the way in which democratization displays itself. Democracy is the dream, meeting the actual practice.

In his study *The Third Wave*, S.P. Huntington (1993) observed three 'waves of democratization'. The first wave occurred from 1828 until 1926. It 'had its roots in the American and French revolutions' and was mainly European. From 1922 until 1945, the democracy trend was tapering off and reversing. 'The reversals occurred largely in those countries that had adopted democratic forms just before or after World War I, where not only democracy was new but also, in many cases, the nation was new' (p. 17). At the end of the Second World War a second, short wave of democratization started, including a number of old European and Asian states and new states in decolonalizing areas in Asia and Africa. In the 1960s and early 1970s there was a global swing away from democracy. 'One-third of 32 working democracies in the world in 1958 had become authoritarian by the mid-1970s' (p. 21). The third wave, which is still going on, started in 1974 with the final phase of European decolonization. 'Democratic regimes replaced authoritarian ones in approximately thirty countries in Europe, Asia, and Latin America' (*ibid.*). At the beginning of the 1990s, about 45 per cent of the 130 existing states in the word were 'democratic', i.e. central decisions were parliamentary controlled. The long-term process of democratization promoted the expansion of meeting regimes to continental and global levels. As Huntington observed: 'From the early nineteenth century down to the 1990s . . . democracies did not, with only trivial of formal exceptions, fight other democracies. So long as this phenomenon continues, the spread of democracy in the world means the expansion of a zone of peace in the world' (p. 29). He did not say that this 'zone of peace' in fact is where meetings replace wars. Thus, in the European Parliament, the European Council of Ministers, and in the Assemblies of NATO, national states more peacefully compete with each other according to mutually agreed rules. The development of these meeting regimes may be seen as an 'extern' aspect and product of parliamentarization of an increasing number of national states in the nineteenth and twentieth centuries.

In general, it can be said that the competitive struggle for power, property and status between social groups acquired and maintained a more democratic or parliamentary character when none of the competing sides was sufficiently powerful to deny others permanent access to governmental positions; when the established power holders were prepared to forfeit some of their privileges; and when the rising groups were satisfied with a part in the decision making. The time at which these conditions prevailed was decisive for the route followed to parliamentarization (Huntington, 1993, pp. 274–8). In Great Britain, especially England, these conditions developed steadily after the Civil War and the Glorious Revolution.

England, the core of the United Kingdom of Great Britain and Northern Ireland, took a front-rank position in the process of parliamentarization, especially in the eighteenth and nineteenth century. The emergence of parliamentary government in this European region was part of a state formation process, in particular, a shift in the balance of power between king and landed upper classes. Different from in France and many other Western European countries, from the Middle Ages onwards, the monarchy and aristocracy in England were involved in a power struggle in which neither of them succeeded permanently in excluding the other. Gradually parliament developed as a meeting place for the monarch and the representatives of interest groups, mainly from the nobility. Although many violent struggles were waged and a tendency in the direction of absolutism was observable during the reigns of the Tudors and early Stuarts, the government in England did not develop into an absolutist regime like that in France.

Under pressure of continuous warfare at the north end of the country France was powerfully centralized at the cost of the regional nobility, while in England the power of the Crown and the loss of power of the regional nobility remained limited. Because the English territory was less difficult to defend, there was no need for such a strong central command as in France. The position of the nobility remained relatively strong, as is evident from the Magna Carta of 1215 and the old right of parliament to grant or refuse a taxation request by the government. The English kings had the position of *primi inter pares* and acted without the grandeur of their French colleagues.

In comparison to France the process of integration and centralization in England started earlier, passed off more quietly and gained a less hierarchic and more democratic character. This was expressed in the emergence of the House of Lords and the House of Commons. Parliament was not so much a place for representation of local interests vis-à-vis a strong central power, but rather an arena for negotiations between equals. This does not mean that the English state had an efficient civil service and an effective parliamentary control at the end of the Middle Ages. On the contrary. 'Armed struggles over royal power and royal succession continued for three centuries, until the Glorious Revolution of 1688' (Tilly, 1990, p. 155; 1993, p. 114). The tensions between king, aristocracy and middle class were high. Due to wars against Spain, the Netherlands and France, the position of the Crown was even strengthened in the sixteenth and seventeenth centuries. The Stuart kings were associated with attempts to create an absolutist regime on the French model, and with leanings towards Catholicism. Eventually the relationship between Crown and Parliament was defined in the Bill of Rights of 1689, which declared, *inter alia*, that 'the pretended power of the suspending or dispending with laws, or the execution of laws, without consent of Parliament, is illegal, and that levying money for or to the use of the Crown, by pretence of prerogative, without grant of Parliament for longer time or in other manner than the same is or shall be granted, is illegal' (May, 1983, p. 4).

In the 1670s and 1680s the exiled king:

James II, and the Jacobites still formed a continuing focus for political rebellion. On the other side, the defeated Puritans, now called Dissenters, were subject to various legal disabilities including exclusion from Parliament. In the eyes of many members of the upper classes, in the early eighteenth century, they were still associated with rebellion and dictatorship. Between the two – the monarchy and the largely lower and middle class Dissenters – stood the great bulk of the country's most powerful social group, the landowners, who dominated both Houses of Parliament. (Mennell, 1992, p. 91)

However, the landowners were not a united group, and the terms 'Whigs' and 'Tories' were introduced to distinguish the two main factions. The Whigs were led by immensely wealthy aristocratic families of relatively recent descent, whereas the Tories had in their ranks a larger proportion of the untitled gentry, who were the descendants from longer, distinguished, family trees, but who were generally in possession of smaller estates. The Whigs took a firm stance against the Stuart pretenders, but were more lenient towards the Dissenters. In contrast, the Tories were totally opposed to the Dissenters, but were favourably disposed towards the Jacobites. The two factions were frequently engaged in a relatively ruthless struggle from the time of the Restoration onwards and into the eighteenth century.

In the course of the eighteenth century, 'cycles of violence calmed down and conflicts of interest and belief were resolved in a manner which allowed the two main contenders for governmental power to settle their differences entirely by non-violent means and in accordance with agreed rules that both sides observed' (Elias and Dunning, 1986, p. 26). The main political cleavage was not rooted in an antagonism between different social classes with a different style of life, different social aims and economic interests. This was in contrast to France and the majority of the countries of Western Europe, where strong and open divisions existed between urban middle classes and the landowning nobility. Furthermore, the untitled English gentry comprised an intermediate group, which stood between the urban middle classes and the nobility. This was in a manner totally different from that of the French 'office nobility', *la noblesse de robe*; there was no distinct line to demarcate them from the nobility, and members of both groups enjoyed the status of 'gentlemen'. These circumstances, among others, facilitated the 'parliamentarization' of political conflict.

Up until about 1722, when Robert Walpole gained control of the government, the heritage of seventeenth-century turbulence was still very much alive. 'Robert Walpole began to steer the boat away from violence. He possessed in considerable measure the diplomatic and manipulating skills needed by the leader of a parliamentary government and gave an strong impetus to the development in that direction' (Elias and Dunning, 1986, p. 33). Parliament or the ancient estate assemblies now transformed into something like a parliament in the modern sense.

The factions were gradually transformed into two parties not radically dissimilar in social composition, which came to justify their political struggles in terms of rival 'principles' or 'philosophies'. They competed with each other for the support of a relatively small electorate, using bribery as well as arguments, but generally refraining from the use of violence against each other. And when one party lost its majority in Parliament, it came to hand power over peacefully to the other. (Mennell, 1992, p. 192)

Elias called this transformation of the English upper classes a telling example of a civilizing spurt. 'As both sides gradually lost their distrust of each other and gave up relying on violence and the skills connected with it, they learned instead, and in fact they developed, the new skills and strategies required by a non-violent type of contest' (1986, p. 34).

Before the Glorious Revolution, most elementary parliamentary regulations were already established. An instance is the rule passed on 5 May 1641, that 'if any man shall whisper or stir out of his place to the disturbance of the House at any message or business of importance, Mr. Speaker is ordered to present his name to the House, for the House to proceed against him as they shall think fit' (May 1983, p. 440). Other remarkable examples are given in *Roberts Rules of Order Newly Revised* (1970, p. xxxi):

One subject at the same time: 1581. When a Motion has been made, that Matter must receive a Determination by the Question, or be laid aside by the general sense of the House, before another be entertained.

Alternation between opposite points of view in assignement of the floor: 1592. It was made a Rule, That the Chair-man shall ask the Parties that would speak, on which side they would speak . . . and the Party that speaketh against the last Speaker, is to be heard first.

Requirement that the chair always call for the negative vote: 1604. It is no full Question without the Negative part be put, as well as the Affirmative.

Decorum and avoidance of personalities in debate: 1604. He that disgresseth from the Matter to fall upon the Person, ought to be suppressed by the Speaker . . . No reviling or nipping words must be used.

The emergence of these rules and other basic codes of parliamentary conduct (other examples have been given in Chapter 4) expresses the granting of equal rights to all members of parliament including ministers. Together with the right of initiative, the practice of committees and the system of the two 'readings', which developed in the second half of the sixteenth century, these rights and codes of conduct served as the basis for modern parliamentary rights and proceedings including the process of debate as a fixed part of the deliberation by analogy with jurisdiction, the privilege of freedom of speech, legalization of the opposition, protection of the minority against the majority and an increasing number of 'standing orders' or written parliamentary rules.

From the eighteenth century onwards hostile factions united by a 'gentlemanly' code of sentiment and conduct learned to trust each other sufficiently for the emergence of a more peaceful type of contest in parliament. Parliament became to be considered as the first 'club' of the country, 'the best gentlemen's club'. In an atmosphere of fair play a man could be gentleman among gentlemen; 'natural', independent, worldly, and in an Erasmian sense Christian, as described by Locke in *Thoughts on Education* and *Thoughts Concerning Reading and Study for a Gentleman*. However, it should not be forgotten that in eighteenth-century England, the political decision-making process was rather a system of accommodating each other by means of patronage, bribery and corruption. This tradition continued well into the nineteenth century. Limited suffrage, a non-secret ballot, the exclusion of all women, rotten boroughs, electoral corruption and pressures exerted by the existing authorities were the rule (Yves Mény, 1994, p. 188, p. 227). The responsibility for government was only transferred from rule by a government of the aristocracy and the monarch to parliament with the Reform Act of 1832. Then the franchise was slowly extended to include the upper echelons of the bourgeoisie and it continued to be extended in stages: to the middle layers with the electoral reform of 1867, to men over 20 and women over 30 years old in 1918 and finally to women on the same terms as men in 1928. In 1948 the last remains of the plural voting right were abolished, and in 1966 the right to vote was lowered to the age of 18. During the extension of the suffrage, parliamentary behaviour became more conciliatory and the codes more detailed and more sophisticated. The way in which the legislative work was organized can serve as an example.

Because plenary sessions of the House of Commons proved to be ill-adapted to the delicate work of drafting and redrafting laws, committees were set up, which exercised two essential functions: to gather information, and to amend and revise the drafts that were submitted to them. The first committees date from the latter half of the sixteenth century. The practice developed, in which the House of Commons debated in the course of two 'readings' only those general problems presented by a bill and decides 'whether or not to pass the text on to a specially created standing committee. The committee thereupon undertakes the real task of legislation, discussing the text, article by article, line by line, with the opposition systematically attempting to substitute its own proposals for those of the government' (Mény, 1994, p. 198). Committee debates are not public, so it is easier for members to collaborate and there is less pressure from party whips. Standing committees are neither permanent nor specialized. Each committee is composed of eighteen members appointed by a selection committee. 'The chairman is appointed (in the case of each separate law) by the Speaker on the recommendation of what is known as a "chairman's panel", a group of about ten Members of Parliament who are themselves endorsed by the Speaker, on the recommendation of Government and Opposition whips, at the beginning of each parliamentary session' (Mény, 1994, p. 206). Since 1907 the chairman of a committee has had the right to close debates, and since 1934 also the right of choosing which amendments to table (*ibid.*).

In order to control amendments and limit obstructionism, the House has adopted firm procedures. Thus, a member is not allowed to speak more than once on a subject. And when the House discusses a text that has been amended by the relevant standing committee, the government can force the majority to accept either its own amendments or, alternatively, the elimination of the amendments adopted by the committee. To avoid obstruction by filibusters several instruments have been devised. Bringing forward a motion to close the debate is one of them. This method, which was first used by Gladstone in 1881 to counter the filibusters of the Irish Nationalists, implies that a member can request that a motion to close the debate be put to the vote. If the speaker agrees that there has been sufficient debate, the motion is proposed. Another means of preventing possible blockages in the work of legislation is constituted by the so-called 'kangaroo technique': 'selecting for discussion only the most important of the amendments in cases where it looks as though debating every single one will take too long' (Mény, 1994, p. 210). The third instrument is the 'guillotine procedure', which was also introduced in 1881. This rule allows the government to close the debate on any individual item in a bill. When the government considers the debate over a bill drags on, it can move an 'allocation of time order'. In that case, it allows a limited period of time for the discussion of each item of the bill still to be debated. When this period has elapsed, the debate is closed and the House must vote on the bill. Parliament is forced to make a drastic choice: 'Either to slow down the process at the risk of debating only a small part of the bill, or to co-operate with the government by debating only the most important points and persuading their supporters to speak briefly or not at all' (*ibid.*, p. 211).

During the development of a parliamentary government the chairman of the House of Commons, the speaker, rose in power and significance. Without the speaker the House could not sit. He had to maintain order and watch and interpret the customs and rules, except when the House decided to set up a 'committee of the whole House'. In that case the speaker had to leave his seat and place his mace under the table, indicating that the procedures that usually apply, have been suspended. For instance, in these circumstances, a member was allowed to speak more than once on a subject. 'It is a procedure that is used particularly when the problem under consideration is too extensive for a single committee to handle on its own and, above all, when the government commands only a small majority that would be further reduced by the few members engaged in standing committees' (Yves Mény, 1994, p. 205). But even in that case the speaker was obliged to be on stand-by in the gallery of the House or in his room. One of the most remarkable and influential Speakers was Arthur Onslow, who held office from 1728 until 1761. His precise maintenance of the proceedings and manners according to the custom of the House gave him a good deal of respect. As a model of devotion to duty, fairness and impartiality he lent high prestige to the function of speaker. He carefully handed the floor over to government and opposition alternately so as to avoid giving the appearance that the opposition was directed against the Speaker. Gradually the function of speaker acquired the features of an arbitrator and a judge. The speaker became the spokesman for the whole parliament and the guard of the constitution (Kluxen, 1983, pp. 96–102).

With the development of more impersonal and more detailed meeting regulations and the crystallization of the function of the speaker, the parliamentary struggle took the form of a game of two teams competing with each other without being after each other's blood. However, for a foreigner a parliamentary debate could be frightening. When Montesquieu visited the British parliament he believed the country to be on the eve of a civil war, until the opponents started to compliment each other at the end of the debate. Sharp debating in the form of a match has continued until today. This tradition produced a lot of snappy remarks, acerbic expressions, honourable insults and a literary series of collections of such sayings. Greg Knight has composed two compendia of 'wicked wit, barbed comment and downright parliamentary cheek'. His repertory starts with Robert Walpole: 'A Patriot? Patriots spring up like mushrooms – I could raise fifty of them within twenty-four hours. If I refuse to gratify an unreasonable or insolent demand, then up starts a patriot' (1993, p. 3). It ends up with Northern Ireland Minister Robert Atkins commenting on Labour's Dr Jeremy Bray: 'He behaves like a headless chicken', whereupon a Tory back-bencher said: 'He is living proof that there is life after death' (p. 112). This sort of literature can be very helpful to trace trends in the standards of (un)parliamentary language.

In the relatively long parliamentary history of England, rules and manners emerged which served as examples for the establishment of centralized national meetings in other countries. This was particularly in the period when England held the most powerful position in the family of states and its constitution was often imitated. As a result 'the practice of Western parliamentary systems generally is . . . broadly comparable with that of the "mother" of them all, namely the British Parliament' (Mény, 1994, p. 196). Judging from parliamentary manuals the borrowing from the British parliament started at the end of the eighteenth century.

As previously mentioned, the first (proto-) parliamentary manuals appeared in the sixteenth and seventeenth centuries in the Dutch Republic and

England. The book by the Dutchman, Boot, was discussed in Chapter 6, and in Chapter 4 reference was made to old English parliamentary manuals, which were characterized by a personal approach and a general nature. At the start of the nineteenth century, resulting from the problems of meeting which became apparent during and shortly after the American War of Independence and the French Revolution, there appeared more detailed and more impersonal manuals for parliamentary conduct.

In 1801, in the United States of America, a parliamentary manual emerged, compiled by Thomas Jefferson during the period when he was chairman of the national meetings. The author composed this work, known as *Jefferson's Manual*, 'considering the law of proceedings in the Senate as composed of the precepts of the Constitution, the regulations of the Senate, and where these are silent, of the rules of Parliament' (quoted in *Robert's Rules of Order*, 1970, p. XXXIV). In other words, the content of *Jefferson's Manual* was borrowed, *inter alia*, from British parliamentary practice and the meeting experience which the colonists had built up since about 1600:

> Into each legislature – into county, town, and parish meetings – the colonists trans-planted the rules and costums of Parliament, as far as these rules and costums were applicable under the particular company charter, proprietary grant, or similar instrument by which the colony was established. This new type of self-government, through general parliamentary principles operating under specifications contained in a written basic document, represented a phase in the development of parliamentary law that was peculiar to America, since in England the constitution was unwritten. Thus, each colony acquired the beginning of a body of experience later to go into the framing of individual state constitutions. (*Robert's Rules of Order*, 1970, p. XXXII)

Shortly after its appearance, *Jefferson's Manual* was accepted as the official code of order by the American Senate. It was the forerunner of a long series of more popular American manuals for 'parliamentary practice'.

In his manual, Jefferson refers to about 50 English works and documents on parliamentary law and related subjects. The book most referred to was published in 1781. It was entitled *Precedents of proceedings in the House of Commons* by John Hatsell, who was clerk to the House of Commons from 1768 to 1820. This book served as the best authority on eighteenth-century procedures in the House of Commons. The authoritative work about the British parliament was compiled by Erskine May. It first appeared in 1848 and many new editions have been published since. It is still used today as a reference book.

An older compendium of mainly British parliamentary rules and customs appeared in 1816. It was written by the English philosopher and lawyer, Jeremy Bentham, and the Genevan politician, Etienne Dumont. They published a parliamentary manual which was entitled *An Essay on Political Tactics or Inquiries concerning discipline and mode of proceeding proper to be observed in political assemblies: principally applied to the practice of British Parliament and the constitution of the National Assembly of France*. From now on in this text, this will be referred to as *Parliamentary Tactics*.[2] This treatise was an extended version of an excerpt from the regulations of the British House of Commons that Bentham had written in 1789 on the request of his friend, Mirabeau, the chairman of the first French Constituent Assembly. Bentham and Dumont's parliamentary manual had great influence in Europe. It was translated into French in 1816, and into German the following year. It served as a model for many parliamentary codes of order for the European mainland and for many parliamentary manuals intended for a broad public. It has been reprinted several times and is referred to, and criticized, in numerous other books (Coopman, 1939, pp. 33–4).

Parliamentary regimes remain vulnerable, likewise in those countries which already have been administered in a parliamentary way for a longer period. Actually, every new generation has to familiarize itself with parliamentary rules. That is to say, in a short period, they must learn what previous generations have devised. The success of these individual learning processes, and therefore the continuation and stability of a parliamentary regime, are extremely dependent on the degree to which older generations succeed in communicating the existing parliamentary rules and norms. Parliamentary manuals belong to the conscious attempts to emphasize to upcoming generations and other relative outsiders that they need to control their behaviour and emotions in line with the relatively peaceful and more democratic way of tussling that characterizes parliamentary regimes. Constantly reiterated in parliamentary manuals is the precept that, in a battle of words or debate between parties, one should exercise self-control and express oneself politely or in a parliamentary manner. This chapter will therefore be concluded by considering these aspects of parliamentary society: the formation of political parties and parliamentary use of language.

Sudden and unsteady parliamentarization in France

For Bentham and Dumont the initial shapeless course of the central meetings during the French Revolution had been the stimulus to write their parliamentary manual. 'There was no subject for discussion, no order whatsoever . . . the delegates spent the day waiting, debating minor incidents . . . they considered themselves more members of a club than members of a political body' (Dumont, 1951, p. 47). When the French States-General reassembled in May 1787 after more than 150 years, they were faced with drafting their own meeting procedures. During the French Revolution, procedures developed which came and went. Sometimes meeting manners and habits, which had developed in England over several centuries, were detailed, (re)discovered and supplemented at a staggeringly rapid rate. This occurred in the presence of many interested parties, from both France and outside France, including Dutch democrats who were exiled to France. Undoubtedly, they would have encountered many ideas, which they later applied in the directly elected national assemblies of their own countries.

In *Paroles de la Révolution* (1988), Patrick Brasart investigated how a more organized and regulated national meeting procedure was arrived at, by trial and error, in the years of revolution. To give an impression of this learning process, there follows a sketch of the way in which the French Estates sought solutions to the problems which occurred in their meetings in the first months of the Revolution.

On 12 May 1789, a week after the first sitting of the French States-General for 150 years, the first rules of order appeared. It was decided to allow the chairman, the oldest member, and his six assistants, the following six oldest members, to draft a list of delegates, and to appoint people for leading committee meetings and for acting as ushers.

These first attempts to organize the meeting and the occupants of the meeting chamber made it possible to speak to each other in a more ordered way and to employ parliamentary techniques, such as presenting motions and amendments. Nevertheless, every motion and every amendment were debated for hours.

Dissatisfied with the lengthy and tumultuous course of the debates, after a few weeks, Mirabeau suggested the installation of a special committee to set up a code of order. He felt that strict rules were necessary to maintain order, to ensure freedom to make decisions, and to protect the integrity of the voting (ibid, p. 29). This suggestion was accepted.

While the committee was still working on the framing of a conceptual code of order, regulations were already made, which served to distinguish more clearly the delegates from the public, and to put an end to the continuous comments and exclamations of approval and disapproval from the onlookers. These regulations had little effect. In order to shorten the voting time, it was also decided henceforth to vote by counting those sitting and those standing instead of voting by call.

On 6 June 1789 the committee submitted a provisional code of order which, alongside those regulations already mentioned , contained stipulations regarding the use of an agenda and the function of the chairman. An hour before the arrival of the meeting participants, the executive office should withdraw in order to determine the order of the day. No one should be allowed to have the word without permission from the chairman, and debates should be terminated on the suggestion of the chairman (ibid, pp. 31–2, p. 198).

On 17 June 1789 the delegates of the third estate proclaimed themselves the only representatives of the nation and formed the National Assembly. On 29 June, this meeting approved a regulation based on Bentham's excerpt. This regulated the right of participation; the way of opening and closing; the keeping and approving of minutes; the granting of turns to speak; the authority of the chairman to call a digressing member back to the subject, to call for order, and to reprimand a member; the seating of the delegates, speakers, and the public; the way to submit and discuss motions and amendments; the way of making decisions; and the allocation of speaking time. Much still had to be arranged and, initially, many rules were either inapplicable, or hardly applicable.

Parliamentarization in France occurred relatively early, but experienced an unsteady development. 'France has been a sort of experimental garden: there is no constitution which has not been applied in France' (J.J. Vis, 1989, p. 28). Between 1789 and 1875 France experienced three monarchies, three republics, two empires and two short periods of popular governments (Jacobin Convention and Commune of Paris). These governmental changes took place in two similar cycles: a monarchy was transformed into a republic, which turned via a military dictatorship into an empire. The first cycle started in 1789 with the gathering of the States-General. Two years later, an aristocratic revolt provoked a popular revolt. The estate assembly changed into a national assembly, elected directly but by a restricted group of the population. After a short revolutionary interlude there were again restricted elections for a national parliament. The unsteady and precarious balance of parliamentary factions opened the door to a *coup d'état* in 1799 by the popular general, Napoleon Bonaparte, who changed his military dictatorship into an emperorship in 1804. The second cycle started with the restoration of 1816 and ended with a *coup d'état* and the emperorship of Louis-Napoleon from 1851 to 1852. A new cycle seemed to start in 1871, but was broken off by a laborious and difficult compromise between monarchists, bourgeoisie and landowners. The parliamentary system has mainly remained intact since then, although the democratic balance was unsteady for a long time. 'The origin of political democracy in France has been a turbulent event. Popular classes continuously intervened but remained outsiders. The mutually strongly divided upper classes repeatedly tried to escape from popular influence' (Spoormans, 1988, p. 56).

The present constitution dates from 1958–1962. It was strongly inspired by Charles de Gaulle and his Prime Minister Michel Debré. As most other western States, France has a bicameral system, consisting of the Assemblée Nationale and the Sénat and an elected president. As upper house or upper chamber, the Senate is a remnant of the country's constitutional past, just like the British House of Lords, and it is not a product of a federal or regional structure, such as is the case in the United States. However it has more real power than the British House of Lords, but is less powerful than the US Senate, which is in some ways even more powerful than the House of Representatives. French senators are elected by universal suffrage for a period of nine years. 'Their major electors are themselves elected locally, but the rural areas are over-represented' (Mény, 1994, p. 189).

The twisting French route to parliamentary government can be explained by the particular trajectory of the French state formation process, which took place almost entirely according to the model of the competition–monopolymechanism, described by Norbert Elias in *The Civilizing Process*. In a long series of violent struggles, from the disintegration of the Frankish realm in the ninth century onwards, an increasingly larger and stabler unit of offence and defence was formed. The formation of France was completed with the defeat of the English Normans in the west and the Burgundians in the east in the fifteenth century, and the conquest of the last pieces of territory in the north and the east in the sixteenth and seventeenth century. The French state was organized from the centre, Paris. Government and administration were and are characterized by a relatively centralist and hierarchical structure. However, the real power of the central state is tempered by strong regional counterforces. Nevertheless, the French governmental system can be characterized as hierarchical centralism. 'On the one hand the state demands respect but on the other it is regarded with suspicion' (Kapteyn, 1996, p. 22–6, cit. p. 25). The recent parliamentary history of France reflects this state of affairs.

Under the Third and Fourth Republic, the National Assembly and the Senate were supreme. For instance, they were responsible for determining their own agendas, which facilitated obstruction of the legislative machine and placed the government in a weak position. In 1958, in the Constitution of the Fifth Republic, it was laid down that the government was to decide on the agenda of the parliament, that sessions of parliament should be limited to 170 days a year, and that the legislative power of parliament was restricted to a series of constitutionally determined matters. Furthermore, the right of amendment was strictly controlled. The government could reject all amendments as a result of which funds would be depleted or public expenditure increased. On rejecting amendments parliament could request its majority to adopt the law as drafted by using the 'blocked vote' procedure. To create a law, agreement between the two assemblies was necessary. This was effected by means of shuttling the proposed text between the two for repeated examination. The government can block a text proposed by one of the assemblies by manipulating the other so as to avert a compromise; the proposal would then founder. Only the government had the power to unblock the situation when the two assemblies fail to reach agreement. The prime minister could convene a mixed committee of seven deputies and seven senators. This committee had to try to elaborate a compromise, which the government could put to the vote in both assemblies. If agreement over this compromise text failed:

> The government is empowered to request the National Assembly to pronounce definitively either upon the text produced by the committee or upon the latest version adopted by the Assembly. . . . This mechanism is ingenious, for it makes it possible for the government to block and unblock the process at will, choosing, according to the prevailing political circumstances, either to give the Senate parity with the National Assembly or to make it subordinate. (Kapteyn, 1996, p. 213)

Despite the restrictions imposed on the parliament by the latest constitution, in actual practice, the French governmental system tends towards a stable parliamentary regime. In the last few years, this has particularly been promoted by *cohabitation*: the co-operation precipitated by the electorate between a president and a parliamentary government of different political colour. This situation forces government and parliament to have more consideration for each other and to co-operate.

Clubs and parliamentarization

In the primal period of parliamentarization in Western Europe, literary, artistic, scientific, political and other societies or clubs played an important role. They embodied the organizational framework of the emancipation of the middle classes and promoted parliamentarization in the eighteenth century. Thus, the dominant standards of meeting behaviour adopted a middle-class outlook. In academic fellowships, reading societies, patriotic clubs and other popular societies, the Enlightenment was shaped and more democratic meeting manners developed, less value was attached to class differences, every member received one equal vote, discussions increased, the majority rule became dominant, and deliberations and decisions were separated more distinctly. In talks about societal problems, more account came to be taken about a larger number of social groups. Fellowships, clubs and societies were the 'proto-parliamentary teaching schools' of the rising bourgeoisie. As will be shown later in this chapter, the nineteenth-century sequels of these middle-class societies had similar functions for the lower classes; such as workers' associations, brotherhoods, unions, political parties (Dann, 1981, pp. 253–74).

Everywhere in Europe, societies sprang up with the increase in opportunities for power for the middle classes in the pre-industrial period. These prepared the way for the adoption of middle-class attitudes in government. In a comparative study of the eighteenth-century literary societies and book circles, Otto Dann concluded:

> The modern bourgeoisie in Europe had not only been successful as the new leading class, but also as a cultural upper layer, as a reading public. As such they organised themselves from scratch; they formed themselves into circles, clubs, and fellowships. Transcending classes, these democratically organised forms of association, which were connected to the Enlightenment, made an important contribution to the modernisation of society. (Dann, 1981, p. 9 and p. 23)

The first fellowships emerged in sixteenth-century Italy and consisted of humanistic scholars and naturalists. From the beginning of the seventeenth century, societies spread all over Europe, first in the centralized kingdoms where governments founded societies in honour and glory of the monarchy. So, the French Académie des Sciences, the English Royal Society, and the Berlin-Prussian Academy were established. In the history of the societies of the Enlightenment, three stages can be discerned:

1 fellowships of scholars and academies on behalf of the state;
2 patriotic societies and clubs for the common good including secret societies such as Freemasons;
3 literary and popular societies, from which sprang the Jacobin clubs during the French Revolution (Reinalter, 1993, p. 7).

The meeting manners of the eighteenth-century societies can be considered as strongly secularized descendants of the meeting manners of the Protestant churches and synods, where the clergy took the leadership and decisions were made more frequently by referring to the Bible. In Protestant countries, especially the United States and Great Britain, the first autonomous societies put down roots in wider layers of the population. A reminder of this is the international spread of the English word, club, to indicate a society not instituted for governmental purposes.[3] The meeting problems, meeting regime and meeting behaviour of Protestant churches of the sixteenth and seventeenth centuries show striking similarities with those of the societies and clubs in the 'Age of Reason'.

In a study of the literary societies in eighteenth-century Liverpool, Kay Flavell pointed out that the meetings of these clubs functioned as a basis for practising democratic manners, because all members possessed equal rights and their goal was in the public interest. Furthermore, meeting with people of different denominations and political convictions demanded a rather tolerant attitude (Dann, 1981, pp. 124–5). Scholars of eighteenth-century club life in France and Central Europe reached the same conclusions. For instance, Marlies Stützel-Prüsener wrote that the statutes of the literary societies in Germany and France only differed in details. The basic ideas were the same everywhere: equal rights for all members, and the general right of consultation about the main interests of the club. All important decisions, including the admittance of new members and the changing of the statutes, were being taken in regular meetings, in which every member had one vote and the majority decided. Committees were used for the settlement of current affairs and the performance of special tasks (1993, p. 46–7).

Meetings became more important as societies increased in number and became politicized. This was particularly the case during the French Revolution.

> In 1789 the attitudes of Frenchmen changed. Citizens, exhilarated over their newly won freedom, but fearful of isolation and counterrevolution, began to meet regularly in cafes, tennis courts, salons, public buildings, chapels, and convents. Although these groups normally purchased and read periodicals, they differed from pre-Revolutionary reading circles in their preoccupation with politics. They gave ordinary citizens a chance to discuss current issues and to gain a sense of participation in the Revolution. The title *Société patriotique et littéraire*, which they frequently adopted, underlined their widened interests. (M.L. Kennedy, 1982, p. 10)

Thus, deputies from Breton to the Estates-General had the habit of meeting nightly in a café near Versailles. Their 'salon' or 'club' became a rallying point for reform-minded deputies such as Mirabeau, Barnave, Robespierre, Pétion and Sieyès. In November 1789 about twenty of them founded the *Société de la Révolution*, in part, inspired by the Revolution Society of London. At first it consisted exclusively of deputies to the National Assembly, but non–deputies soon joined in large numbers. The club rented a hall at a Jacobin convent and changed its name into Society of Friends of the Constitution. 'By then, however, royalist pamphleteers had already christened it the "Jacobins", the name by which it lives in history' (*ibid.*, p. 4). This society served as a model for many revolutionary or patriotic clubs, of which the number grew rapidly, especially after the National Assembly's decree on 13 November 1791, which declared that 'citizens have the right to assemble peacefully and to form free societies'.

The meetings of the patriotic and Jacobin clubs were more clearly organized along parliamentary lines and were held mainly for political reasons including electing and supporting deputies. The clubs had no standard code of procedures but imitated their neighbours and the 'mother society' in Paris. Basically, they were debating clubs with a parliamentary organization and parliamentary ambitions. 'A speaker is recognized, makes a motion, defends it, yields the floor, sees his motion referred to committee, passed as a resolution, or defeated. Rules govern recognition of speakers, order of debate, and the other details of procedure. Set speeches are almost always made not from the floor, but from the tribune, a sort of pulpit usually raised opposite the president's desk' (Brinton, 1930, p. 21). The presidency was usually held for a month. Presidents were ineligible for immediate re-election. 'Their responsibilities included opening and closing the meeting, moderating debates, signing official documents, welcoming guests, appointing commissioners and members of ad hoc committees, convoking extraordinary assemblies, and representing the society at public events' (Kennedy, 1982, p. 34). At first societies met behind closed doors, later they instituted public assemblies serving as a medium of propaganda. 'Spectators normally sat in the rear of the assembly room, separated from members by a wooden balustrade or ribbon. The rostrum stood at the front, with chairs and rug-covered tables for the president and secretaries and, perhaps, an armoire to store minutes and records' (*ibid.*, p. 37).

A closer picture of the meeting regime and behaviour of the revolutionary clubs emerges from Kennedy's study *The Jacobin Clubs in the French Revolution.*

> By 1791 the average society met two or four times weekly, and a handful of clubs held daily conclaves. Meetings might be a few minutes or several hours in length. They usually commenced between 5 and 7 p.m., save for Sundays and holidays. . . . When the president rang the bell calling the assembly to order, those in attendance were expected to go directly to their seats to hear the reading of the minutes. Then, secretaries read excerpts from letters and recent newspapers. Committee reports and the induction of new members customary followed. . . . An 'order of the day' was posted in the hall before the sessions; however, motions from the floor caused repeated diversions. Rules of decorum forbade sarcasm and abusive language during debates; but catcalls and murmurs, not to mention the rustling of papers, disputes over whether windows should be open or shut, late entries, early exits, and yes, even snoring, were recurring sources of irritation. Certain people could always be counted upon to express their options. . . . To control those who spoke often and said little, the clubs adopted rules limiting the times that one could comment on a given subject. . . . Many sessions commenced or ended with acclamations such as 'Long live the Nation, the Law, and the King'. . . . Delegations of schoolchildren, women, constitutional priests, electors, soldiers, national guardsmen, and officials showed up frequently at the halls, adding a festive note to the meetings. (Kennedy, 1982, pp. 39–41)

Preserving order in the meetings often was a big problem, especially when children and other lively spectators were present. Michael Kennedy quoted from a letter of 6 November, 1790, written by a member of the *Friends of the Constitution* in Lorient:

> Wednesday, I entered a hall where sixty to eighty people spoke at once, where one rose only to abuse another in the most rude and indecent manner! . . . I witnessed a protracted discussion on a proposed locale (for the sessions of the club) which led into a scientific digression on air in which two members spoke in a

fashion incomprehensible to everybody. I was astounded that during the whole meeting the president totally failed to fulfil the responsibilities of his office. (Kennedy, 1982, p. 40)

According to Brinton (1930, pp. 33–5), the records are full of mention of disorder. So, in the rules of the club of Chablis it is provided that 'as republican brothers and as brothers sufficiently friends to be above politeness, the members will keep their hats on, except that the president shall remove his, if need be, to bring the assembly back to order.' At Lille, it was suggested that, to restore order in debate, the president should place his hand on the bust of Marat which stood on the presidential desk. However, this proposal was rejected in favour of the decision that the president should place his hands on a copy of the Declaration of Rights which was hung at the back of the desk. Sometimes there was a great deal of disorder in club meetings. Members would call to one another, move their chairs about (sometimes chairs had to be nailed down), hurry in and out, and hang about in the entrance. Often there was difficulty with drunken members. Therefore the rules of the Jacobin club at Dieuze include the proviso: 'Members shall recall that the first attribute of the free man is the complete exercise of his reason, that therefore none should present himself to the assembly in a state of drunkenness, nor trouble its order by improper acts.' Moreover, the president had to call members to order using this formula: 'Citizen . . . you forget your dignity, you have outraged the decencies; the respect due the sovereign people requires that you leave this hall.'

Speeches were punctuated with references and quotations taken from the Bible. This should not be interpreted as proof that Jacobinism was, in essence, a religious movement. According to the historian Peter Gay, 'the alleged religious endeavours of the Jacobins "reflect no more than the depths of poor taste reached by obscure and uneducated men", and that "the widespread use of religious connotations proves no more than the ease with which the revolutionaries used familiar metaphors"' (quoted in Kennedy, 1982, p. 43). The Jacobins also liked to bring historical analogies to the fore, especially if they came from the Spartans and the Romans of republican times. In order to manipulate public opinion in an age of widespread illiteracy, the Jacobin clubs used pageantry and the fine arts on an unprecedented mass scale. 'They refined the art of visual and oral indoctrination to a high degree, producing thousands of services, banquets, parades, festivals, and dramas' (ibid., p. 46).

As the Revolution developed, the clubs showed remarkable changes in their way of holding meetings and elections. In the beginning, election to membership took place by open vote and was based on the majority vote. During the Terror it was, theoretically, still based on the majority vote but, in practice, unanimity was demanded. In some clubs one voted with the use of white and black balls. 'If there was a single black ball, the candidate had to leave the room, and those who voted against him were obliged to acknowledge the fact, and to explain their reasons. If the society approved of these reasons by a majority vote, the candidate was excluded. If the society failed to approve these reasons, the original black balls were counted out, and the candidate "unanimously" elected' (Brinton, 1930, pp. 24–5). Another, more frequently used, method was the institution of a 'committee on elections with secret proceedings, to examine rigorously into the political past of a candidate, and to turn him down or to accept him. The public vote of the club itself thus became a mere formality' (ibid.). This change from majority into unanimity rule, and from open to secret proceedings, are merely two examples of the regression into military meeting manners, which took place in the period of the Terror. Another example is hymn singing, which became very usual as the revolution went on, and the clubs fell more and more into the control of an active minority of their members. 'The characteristic method of exercising that control was the committee. In this, the clubs followed the same course as French government during the Revolution' (ibid., p. 27).

Another European country where societies played a decisive role in the process of parliamentarization was the Netherlands. Here societies could elaborate on a relatively long-standing meeting tradition and they were tolerated more than clubs almost anywhere else in Europe, excepting Great Britain. It led to a relatively early but suppressed middle-class upheaval, the so-called Patriot Revolt of 1781–1787, and with the help of the French army, to a more successful revolution in 1795. On this occasion the first, directly and broadly elected, national assembly of the sovereign Dutch people was established.

In the barely centralized Dutch Republic, the foundation of societies was a private matter. The movement started in the latter half of the eighteenth century. According to the historian W.H. Mijnhardt, four generations can be distinguished in the development of societies in the Netherlands. The earliest societies functioned as semi-governmental maecenas. They were established by patricians and important townsmen and administered by directors recruited from the patriciate and the nobility. Generally the members were recognized men of letters. Acknowledged by the state, the societies mainly concerned themselves with publishing learned discourses by members and holding competitions. Their autonomy in respect to the meeting class was quite small and they held their meetings according to the model the upper class presented.

The latter was less the case for the more locally organized societies of the second generation. These were established and administered by members of the middle class: intellectuals, professionals, clergymen, small merchants and people of independent means, who were excluded from the traditional university culture and the official church and political meetings. These people organized themselves into clubs concerned with physics and literature, into freemasons, closed societies, and particularly into reading clubs. They did not seek any acknowledgement from the government for their societies. The establishment of such societies was strongly stimulated by 'moralistic' publications, which carried the message that townsmen could only lay the foundations for knowledge, virtuousness and happiness, by voluntary getting together in friendly circles, company and societies. In a society 'the townsman can learn to control his passions, to free himself of prejudice, to practise virtuousness, and to develop his natural talents with the help of "civilizing" and "useful" sciences' (Mijnhardt, 1983, p. 83). In these societies the basis was laid for the development of a pre-political, bourgeois ideal of emancipation. The second-generation clubs were distinguished from the first by striving for demarcations in a world of equals. In comparison with drawing rooms, which were thinly spread in the Republic, speaking in society's meetings was more controlled: 'Replacing drawing-room conversation was discussion determined by rules, replacing the spontaneous and rapid exchange of subject was the pre-reading of a previously written discussion' (Mijnhardt, 1983, p. 84). Members meetings decided about the most important questions by majority vote.

In the 1770s a new type of society arose; it was organized nationally and more directed to the outside. These clubs of the third generation strove for the development and enlightenment of all townsmen through the spreading of knowledge and the promotion of virtuousness; for the passing on of the societies' procedural rules and principles to the entire population. The establishment of such societies can be considered as the first attempts by middle classes to take the responsibility for tackling societal problems, in competition to the controlling meeting class.

Not only the disastrous course of the war against England, which exposed the political weakness of the Republic, but the escalation of economic and financial problems, and the increasing polarization of incomes, provided the background against which societies with a more overt political character arose in the 1780s. Initially, these societies were particularly directed against the ruling patronage system dominated by the stadholder. They formed a coalition with members of the meeting class, who were excluded from participation by the stadholder, against those sitting in power. In the course of the struggle, this 'patriotic' union of townsmen and opposition leaders from the meeting class disbanded and, in the main, the political societies gradually turned against the government of the Republic. The struggle of the (book) clubs of the fourth generation societies was in the end completely directed towards the formation of a united state, administered by members of a national assembly who were elected by all townsmen. Members of this assembly could decide without mandates and deliberations, and by majority vote. At the start of the 1780s the patriotic societies took the leadership in the organization of townsmen into volunteer corps and militias. These corps, militias, clubs and other societies joined forces and became regional federations, which turned to drafting political programmes. It was thought that these could be implemented, with support from the oppositional leaders from the meeting class by compelling the town governments to 'democratize' the composition and procedures of their meetings. The method used for this aim was always the same; armed townsmen gathered around the town hall and held the town government hostage until they were prepared to admit patriotic representatives to their ranks. In this way, townsmen expected to gain entrance to the meetings of the states and to reform them in a democratic sense. As the movement operated within the decentralized framework of the Republic, the established meeting class was in a position to remain in office. Town governments made concessions when social unrest manifested itself in their towns, but rescinded these once the storm had blown over. Opposition leaders tended to distance themselves from the patriotic movement after they had achieved their own aims; their own return to the meeting benches. The struggle reached an impasse, at which point, the stadholder restored the old order with the help of the Prussian army in 1787.

The restoration of the stadholder's authority was but brief. In the winter of 1794/95, the French army attacked the Netherlands, and in its wake the exiled leaders of the democracy movement returned. There were sporadic, local uprisings and elected townsmen gathered in political meetings. Initially, the French mainly left the reformation of the state apparatus to the home political powers. Without bloodshed, the Batavian Revolution unfolded (Te Brake, 1988).

Just over a year after the departure of the stadholder, the provinces and the various sides in the conflict reached an agreement about the framework of a nationwide government and a legislative national assembly, elected in two stages. The first stage consisted of so-called 'basis meetings', from which women, children, beggars, bodyguards, servants and followers of the stadholder were excluded. During these meetings, representatives were chosen along with civil servants for various organs of state and electors who, in district meetings, appointed delegates for the national assembly by secret ballot. In order to avoid a return to local and regional autonomy, the electors were not permitted to appoint national representatives from their own midst. The representatives at the national assembly and the national government authorities were to represent the entire nation without mandates and deliberations (Spoormans, 1988, p. 102).

On 1 March 1796 in The Hague, the first National Assembly of the 'representatives of the Batavian people' was convened with the primary aim of drafting a constitution. Those elected were predominantly from the higher bourgeoisie: lawyers, merchants, manufacturers, professors, clergymen and priests. Of the 127 delegates, only 34 had held public office during the time of the Republic (Schama, 1977, p. 246). One of the first acts taken by these meetings was the setting up of a committee for drafting a code of order. A fortnight later, the committee offered a proposal which, after a few changes, was approved (*Dagverhaal der handelingen van de National Vergadering*, 1796, pp. 65–7, 90–4, 98–9, 115–18). The Code of Order of the National Assembly consisted of 46 articles of regulations, which were largely distilled from the customs of the meetings of the republican states, with the remainder stemming from the meeting practices of the societies. A number of rules, such as the way in which to present or alter law proposals, were taken over from the French national meetings by the bourgeois representatives. These, in turn, had been mainly borrowed from the practices of the English parliament. In other words, the Code of Order of the National Assembly was an amalgamation of procedures from the old meeting class, the rising bourgeoisie, and the English parliament.

Included in the regulations which were taken over from the meeting class were: the obligation to hand in the propositions on the agenda in writing to the chairman prior to the meeting, the opening of each meeting with a prayer, and the reading out of the summary minutes of the previous meeting. Also included was the use of an agenda containing a set number of points: incoming missives, petitions, day-to-day business, and reports from the committees.

Included in the rules and customs which were previously used in bourgeois societies and the English and French parliaments were: the distinction between deliberations and decisions, the granting of a turn to speak when it was requested instead of according to rank or class, the using of the absolute majority rule as the accepted procedure for making decisions, and the free and secret election of officials, such as the chairman and the secretaries. These new rules and the public nature of the meetings were functions of the extension of the right to vote, the centralization of the government, and the abolition of regional authority with its accompanying obligation to have a mandate and hold deliberations. For the first time in Dutch history, central meetings were open to outsiders. Newspapers could write freely about what was said and decided. The population was informed daily about the assembly by a specially written journal.

In comparison to the dominant meeting standards during the Republic, the new obligations and the prohibitions were more embracing, more detailed, and more concise. More consideration had to be given to a greater number of people and the tendency towards self-promotion had to be curbed. Here follow several examples of this. Whoever wished to speak had to ask permission to do so from the chairman and could not simply rely on their personal rank or class:

> Every member with business to propose should ask for the right to speak from the President, and not begin to speak prior to this, and the same person should not be given the word on the same subject more than twice. (Article 15)

One had to control one's tendency to interrupt and digress,

> Whoever is speaking should not be hindered or distracted; the President should ensure that the member speaking retains the word and should hinder any participation or individual talks. (Article 17)

> Whilst a member is making his recommendations, the President may not interrupt him except to prevent him digressing. (Article 20)

The participants of the National Assembly had to take into greater consideration the feelings and sensitivity of more people from more layers of the population. Particularly the expression of feelings of aggression and animosity needed to be avoided. This is apparent from the stipulation that a speaker always 'should employ modest means of expression' and the president was obliged 'to call to order' a speaker who used 'any discourteous words' and 'compel silence if disobeyed' (Pippel, 1950, p. 120).

The increasing interdependence between social and regional groups, and the appointment of representatives using an electoral system with an extended franchise, are clearly manifested in the rule stating that all decisions should be taken by majority vote. This rule hampered possible attempts by anyone to get their own way by means of manipulation, bribery, blackmail or intrigue. As noted in the previous chapter, such practices formed an integral part of the style of meeting, based on unanimity, of the meeting class of the ex-Republic.

The new style of meeting made greater demands on the meeting participants, on the chairman in particular. The regulations made the chairman the guardian of the new parliamentary rules. He became the 'personification' of the social constraint towards self-control. His function rose in power and status. According to the regulations, the chairman was obliged to 'wear a distinguishing mark of his rank everywhere he appeared in public, and guards, in particular those stationed in the building of the Parliament had to afford him the greatest military distinction' (Article 26).

After the approval of the Code of Order, the National Assembly erupted into a verbal battle concerning matters such as the separation of the church and the state, the equality of tax assessments, the modernization of industry, free public education, the regularization of the right to vote, and the tasks of the executive government. Gradually, the talks about these problems focused upon the matter of the 'unity and indivisibility' of the sovereignty and the centralization of the national government. By degrees, two trends became more polarized. The fiercest supporters of the idea of an indivisible unit state were found among the representatives of the outlying regions and the rising bourgeoisie, who were attempting to strengthen their position of power in relation to the upper echelons. For this matter, a minimalist view was taken by the representatives of, and sympathizers to, the meeting class, whose potential position of power was closely tied to the continuance of a large amount of local and regional autonomy. A third trend of pragmatists, designated as 'moderates', who depended upon bankers from Holland and important merchants, attempted to bridge the gap between the 'Federalists' and the 'Unitarians'. After about a year of meetings, a conservative proposal was made which was rejected in a plebiscite in the elementary and district meetings.

It is not possible to investigate how the meetings were conducted, to what degree the participants adhered to the meeting regulations, and how the rules were applied in practice. It is sufficient to say that frequently there was a fierce contest between those for and against unity and indivisibility. The historian Simon Schama, who researched this period of parliamentary history in detail, noted that as the discussions became polarized, the chairmanship became a tennis ball for party quarrels and the debates were characterized by 'intense acrimony' and 'acerbity' (1977, p. 247). He typified the meetings as a 'spectacle of a tawdry slanging match' (p. 271).

It can also be established that during the meetings it never came to a scuffle; that the main points of the regulations were applied and honoured. Furthermore, no one was disparaged and dismissed, such as happened in the Synod of Dordrecht. Until the final vote about the conceptual constitution, members continued their discussions and talks with each other on the basis of equality, regardless of how bitter and fierce they sometimes were. This cannot be said for the second National Assembly, the participants of which were even more divided than the first. They disbanded after several months when radical groups seized power with the assistance of armed French troops. Neither this, nor the coup six months later by more moderate members, provided the peace and order which the French considered necessary to engage the population of the Netherlands in its war against England. In 1801 the French government seized power. With a firm hand, they centralized the government, by which the representative boards were reduced to a rudimentary appendix of the executive power.

The parliamentary process, which had accelerated relatively early in the Netherlands, thus received a setback from which it slowly recovered in the course of the nineteenth century. This recovery can be described as a process in which an important part of the repertoire of behaviour of the old republican meeting class was extended to broader layers of the population, and was applied to more and more areas of society, resulting in specific changes. These changes included the introduction of the use of motions and amendments, the recording of what was said in stenographic reports, the allotment of speaking time, and other customs and rules which made possible a more precise way of discussing and deciding about increasingly more people simultaneously, and which required of the participants a tighter control of behaviour and emotional outbursts. Several of these newly introduced meeting techniques, such as the use of motions and amendments, were taken over from other parliaments, namely from the then leading nation in Europe, England.

The first historical study of the regulations of the Dutch parliament appeared in 1838. It was written by J.L.W. de Geer, the clerk of the Dutch parliament at that time, and it provides a summary of the code of order of the States-General and its application in the period 1815–1837. The next summary was written in 1925 by the clerk of the Dutch parliament at that time, J.G. Pippel. This sizeable and more encompassing work has since been revised and reprinted several times. It was used in parliament as a book of reference. Apart from those people directly involved, others, namely lawyers, have also written about, compared, and criticized the rules of the Dutch Parliament (for example, Couturier, 1914, Coopman, 1939). Nowhere in this literature is there any elucidation as to which of the rules and procedures were borrowed by the Dutch from the British parliament. As far as imitation is concerned, it has been rather creeping. In any case, the Dutch could build on their own, long tradition of parliamentary behaviour. Unlike that of Britain, the dominant meeting behaviour in the Netherlands did not have the character of a debate or a contest between two parties, but that of public game of confrontation and coalition between many factions and parties.

Parliamentarization in the Netherlands has been part of a process of state formation in which the bourgeoisie played a decisive role. Centralist tendencies were weak and the relationships within and between the components of the federative Dutch state had a fairly egalitarian character. In that respect the process of state formation in the Netherlands differed from that in France and many other regions of the European continent in a remarkable way. Large contrasts in interests, and tensions, between large aristocratic landowners and urban capitalists, which elsewhere often led to violent conflicts and lengthy breaks in the process of parliamentarization, were absent in the Netherlands. Already, the central co-ordinating functions had been performed for centuries by a mainly urban upper class which did not identify itself with the state to the same degree as the aristocratic upper classes did elsewhere. The members of this meeting class were used to adjusting themselves to government changes and showing reserve when they themselves were in the position of government. They reacted to the arrival of these new commercial and industrial groups from this traditional stance, and transmitted to them the skills of government by negotiation and holding meetings. During the latter half of the eighteenth century, the differences and tensions between the governing meeting class and the rising middle classes were rather strong, but gradually, in the waves of attraction and rejection, as the balance of power between both groups became more equal, new (parliamentary) standards of meeting behaviour developed in which elements of the codes of behaviour from both layers merged. During the Napoleonic period, the federative structure of the Republic was replaced by a more centralized organization, which was maintained after the regained sovereignty in the nineteenth century. The Dutch state changed from a bourgeois republic into a bourgeois monarchy, which developed further in an egalitarian-centralist direction (Kapteyn, 1996, p. 41). After the parliamentarization process accelerated during the Batavian Revolt in 1796, there have only been two brief intermissions. On both occasions, foreign military intervention was the cause: the French occupation from 1797 to 813 and the German occupation during the Second World War.

These Dutch and French examples draw attention to how closely changes in the standards of meeting behaviour are connected to fluctuations of more embracing processes such as division of functions, formation of states and (de)militarization. The development of meeting behaviour, just as civilization in general, is not a linear process. Thus, meetings adopted a more martial character in the course of the French Revolution and were forbidden during the foreign occupations of the Netherlands. Furthermore, French revolutionary leaders, just like Dutch Protestant leaders before them, often were hardly able to control their emotions when social tensions and conflicts increased and their propositions and interpretations were challenged. This again draws attention to how slowly and laboriously meeting behaviour developed to become a more peaceful activity on a more equal footing. The rules of the clubs demanded a stricter and broader discipline than what was, until then, required of people from the middle classes, who were excluded from participating in official local and national meetings. Adapting new and higher standards of meeting behaviour often was a lengthy and difficult learning process with both accelerations and regressions. This is most obviously shown by the relatively late and jerky processes of parliamentarization in Germany and Russia.

Parliamentary perils

According to the authors of *Parliamentary Tactics*, the greatest danger threatening the progress of parliamentary meetings were violence, hastiness and fraud (1822, pp. III–IV). All three dangers emanated from insufficient control of aggressive impulses, feelings of hostility, passions and passing impulses. To prevent parliamentary battles degenerating into violence, which could have easily escalated into civil war, a code of order and a chairman were needed; the chairman being 'someone who was authorized to apply the regulations in order to immediately stop difficulties which hindered the transaction of business' (1822, p. 60). 'Attack the words of your opponent, and not the opponent himself', Bentham and Dumont advised their readers:

Demonstrate that what the opponent wants, has the most disastrous of consequences, but never throw in their face that they had wanted or foreseen these consequences. Just as in warfare, you must employ no means in a political debate which you would not wish to be used against yourself. Do not accuse the opposition of malicious intentions, because you will no longer be heard and the debate easily will degenerate into party formation based on resentments and personal hostilies. (*ibid.*)

For the same reason, bitter or vehement expressions should not be resorted to. Bentham advised his readers to speak to each other via the chairman because the chance for a discussion to end up with personal comments was greater if the members directly spoke to each other (*ibid.*, pp. 165–7).

The central problems covered in *Parliamentary Tactics* are characteristic of the transition from a military-agrarian to an industrial society and from a monarchy or dictatorship to a parliamentary system. In the early part of the twentieth century, such problems were also encountered in Germany, and more recently in Russia and other East European countries, where a one-party system was in force until recently.

The timing and rate of the process of parliamentarization in Germany differed widely from that of England, the Netherlands, the United States and less widely from that of France. It was only after the Second World War that a stable parliamentary regime was instituted in West Germany. The tardy parliamentarization of Germany was the outcome of a practically continuous waging or threatening of war, which this central part of Europe had engaged in since the Middle Ages. From nearly all sides the country was exposed to hostile invasions. Thus warriors had more chance for power than in the European coastal areas. Warrior dogma, based on orders and obedience, made a great impression upon ways of conduct. Behaviours such as persuading, convincing and discussing was little valued, at least in government circles. This remained so for a long time. In the Weimar Republic, the words *Schwatzbude* (nonsense chamber) and *Quasselbude* (drivel stall) were popular tags for the German parliament. Members of parliament were distrusted. 'They only fight with words, but do nothing. They do not really fight with each other' (Elias, 1969, p. 411).

Germany has only been united since 1871. It had become a patchwork of states and polities during the disintegration of the Habsburg empire and the Thirty Years' War which ended with the Peace of Munster in 1648. In the words of Metternich, Germany was 'merely a geographical concept' for a rather long time. In the seventeenth century reintegration started with military expansion from the Prussian area around Berlin. Social relationships became characterized by large distances between the military and landowning aristocracy, and the rest of the population. In the very beginning of the state formation process under Prussian leadership, the nobility had put an end to the various types of town self-government, which had developed. As has been stated in the previous chapter, exactly the opposite happened in the Netherlands at that time. The German bourgeoisie was as fragmented as the German Empire itself. It was only after the French Revolution that, in several German states, cautious attempts were made to restore civilian self-government by instituting parliaments often led by (patriot and Jacobin) societies. In the majority of cases, these attempts were doomed. Many Jacobins emigrated or were prosecuted and condemned. Some went underground and founded secret societies for the promotion of democratic and national ideals (Reinalter, 1993, p. 110).

Inspired by the Paris Revolt of 1848, the humanistically orientated civilian population of Germany instigated the formation of a parliamentary administered nation state. Everywhere in the country elections were being held for a general German parliament, which gathered in Frankfurt am Main. This parliament decided, after a year of discussion, to establish a hereditary German Empire without Austria. The crown was offered to the Prussian king, who refused to accept it 'out of the mud', as he remarked. The civilian initiative to unite the German countries failed and the national unification occurred during a series of short domestic wars easily won by the Prussian army, and a war against France. A German empire was established in 1871 with the king of militarist Prussia at the head. The warrior nobility around the emperor's court monopolized the highest functions of state, and smothered any instigations to parliamentarization from the start. Chancellor Otto von Bismarck, who detested the 'muddy wave of parliamentarism', said: 'The great questions of our time will not be solved by majority decisions and resolutions – that was the mistake of the men of 1848 and 1849 – but by blood and iron!' The power of the *Reichstag*, which was already extremely limited, decreased further during the time of Bismarck. As a result, those politically interested individuals stepped down from public life. A political career was unattractive to educated men. Also, the administration saw much in keeping the academic youth out of politics for as long as possible. Finally, all opposition movements were outlawed. The *Reichstag* was dominated by the warrior and landed nobility. The demonstrative applause which broke out after the following statement by a member characterized the atmosphere of this parliament. 'The king of Prussia and the German emperor must always be in the position that he can say to a lieutenant: "take ten men and rifle the *Reichstag!*"' (Tumin, 1982, p. 35). In the meetings of the *Reichstag* prior to 1918, it was not exceptional for members to punch each other or throw inkpots at each other.

In 1919 the German emperor was exiled and a national elected parliament came into being, which was authorized to choose a government. Alongside this parliament was an elected president. An article of the constitution allowed the president exceptional authority in times of internal or external threat. In 1933, by referring to this article, President Hindenburg cleared the way for

Hitler to become Chancellor, even though his party occupied only 248 of the 584 parliamentary seats. During Hitler's regime, the *Reichstag*, comprised of delegates dressed in *Sturmabteilung* uniforms, was little more than an applause machine. Voting was exclusively by acclamation. It was a total regression to military codes of behaviour. The national anthem was sung so many times that the *Reichstag* was scornfully referred to as 'the most expensive singing society in Germany'.

In Germany, the transformation from a military to a parliamentary regime was a lengthy and whimsical process. Only after the Second World War, with the integration of West Germany into NATO and the European Community, did this process accelerate. The *Bundestag* has been characterized as a mingling of the British 'debating parliament' or a political forum, and the American 'working parliament' or legislative body. It devotes most of its time to committee work rather than to plenary meetings, and most of its energies to drafting and amending laws rather than, strictly speaking, monitoring the administration. Germany's strong juridical tradition makes parliamentary monitoring less essential. (Steffani, 1967, p. 241; Mény, 1994, p. 225). Particularly at the start of the 1950s, although the meetings of the German Parliament were stunned by both extreme right and extreme left interventions, these remained mainly limited to verbal violence. In the years between 1949 and 1953 the chairman had to call a speaker to order on 156 occasions. After 1953 the German parliament gradually became calmer, and the chairman only needed to call a member to order on average 23 times each sitting (Floehr, 1984, p. 10). The ear boxing and inkpot throwing were replaced by verbal battles and swearing, involving the use of words such as upstart, warmonger, drunkard, unashamed clodhopper, neofascist, head-hunter from Formosa, sheep's head, villain, quibbler, Hitler, Goebbels, dumbo, pleb, uncouth lout, muckraker and malicious gossiper (Pursch, 1980). The most vehement debates, in which members were threatened verbally, mostly took place when actual political force between Germans, or the organization of the monopoly of force, were on the agenda. This is a connection which actually can be more frequently observed elsewhere.

Precisely how difficult the transition is, from an autocratic to a parliamentary regime, can be illustrated by many, also more recent, examples. For instance, Spain, which shortly after the death of Franco and the establishment of a constitutional monarchy, was shocked by an attack on the Spanish parliament by Lieutenant-Colonel Tejero on 23 February 1981. 'Everyone sit down for Christ's sake!', were the historic words with which Tejero, cocked pistol in his hand and a three-cornered hat on his head, climbed onto the speaker's chair in the meeting chamber. Tejero was part of a plot intended to overthrow the government. However, the majority of the army divisions adopted a wait-and-see attitude after parliament was held hostage, and a television appearance by King Juan Carlos, Commander-in-Chief of the army, resulted in a definite end to the attempted coup.

FIGURE 7.2   Lieutenant–Colonel Antonio Tejero Molina addresses Spanish parliamentarians, 1981 (Photo ANP/EFE)

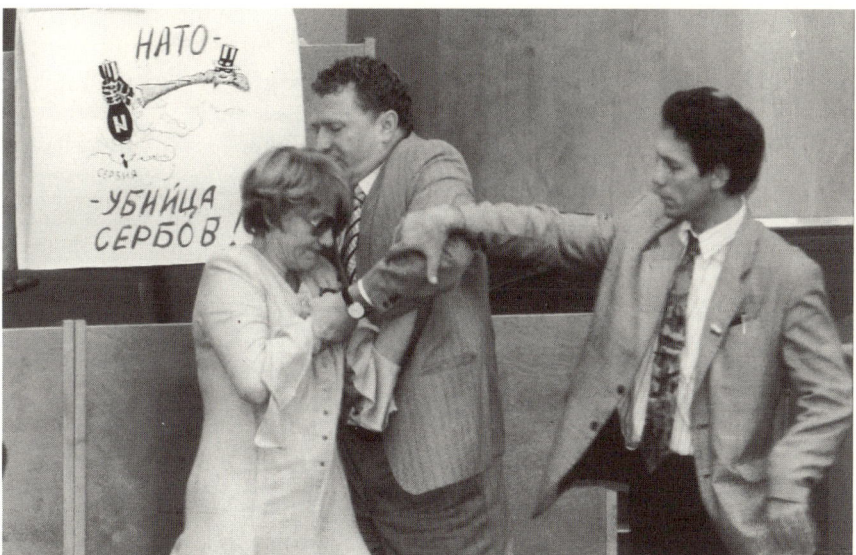

FIGURE 7.3   Vladimir Zhirinovski fights with the delegate Evgenia Tsykovskaya in the Russian Duma, September 1995 (ABC Press, Amsterdam)

Another example can be found in the recent parliamentary history of Russia. On 4 December 1992, two years after the collapse of the communist dictatorship, a physical fight took place for the first time in the Duma, the Russian parliament. Incited by a debate about voting procedure, delegates of the National Communists and the Radical Democrats started to punch each other. The majority had resolved to decide in a secret vote on several constitutional changes. In the eyes of the Radical Democrats, this decision was at odds with the code of order. Thus, several of them advanced towards the platform of the presidium. The chairman, Chasboelatov, did not succeed in restoring order and shouting, 'Defend me from these threats, protect me from these delegates', upon which the National Communist leaders advanced to remove their opposition from the platform with some force.

In the months following the rivalry between both groups became more and more enraged. On 5 June 1993 the first sitting of a Constitutional Meeting took place, summoned by Yeltsin. It was a telling blow. Using the argument that 'the code of order was already determined', Yeltsin refused to allow Chasboelatov, the Chairman of the parliament, to have the word, despite his begging for it. 'With his head submissive, Chasboelatov whispered "Five minutes". At this Yeltsin reacted and, stabbing his finger in Chasboelatov's direction, exclaimed, "The order of the day has been determined by *ukase*. This is not a meeting, this is not a *sobranje* [meeting]. This is a *sovjesjtsjene* [a word for meeting that has a more elevated emotional value like assembly]. Restrain your emotions. I will give you the word in the next plenary session". The next session was to be the last and all was then to be decided. Finally, Chasboelatov, after begging a few more times, was given the word for seven minutes. But, he did not speak for seven minutes. Rhythmic clapping silenced him, and he left, followed by fifty supporters. A little later, another Communist delegate, Yuri Slobodkin, who wished to see his own draft for a constitution dealt with, was forcefully ejected from the chamber by four presidential bodyguards. In the scuffle he lost his shoe, which he was later allowed to retrieve' (*NRC Handelsblad*, 7 June 1993). The tensions between the presidential camp and the communist-dominated parliament were to increase and, four months later, lead to a public confrontation during a revolt, which was crushed by the military.

Lately the Russian parliament, the Duma, is generally more subdued. According to the political scientist Sergei Markov of the Carnegie Centre in Moscow, this is a result of the new Constitution, which allows very limited power to the parliament. Furthermore, the members of the Duma are afraid of the government dispersing them if they go too far. The dominant opinion within the Kremlin is that a parliament is only useful as long as it does not obstruct 'necessary' reforms. 'We do not have a real democracy, but a system which is for one third democratic, for one third authoritarian and for one third anarchistic', Markov said (*De Volkskrant*, 21 June 1997).

History shows that the transition from an autocratic to a parliamentary regime is a difficult and lengthy process, which generally extends over several generations. In explanation of this, Elias has pointed out that these two forms of government represent different stages in the process of civilization (Elias, 1989, pp. 382). In an autocratic regime, individuals structure their personality by attuning it primarily to ordering and obeying. In comparison, a parliamentary regime requires a more complex and more differentiated structure of personality with a greater degree of self-control. In contrast to autocratically ruled societies, where lower level conflicts are settled by force from above, and conflicts at the highest level of command are fought out in secret, parliamentary regimes legitimize conflicts between people. Parliamentary regimes consist of rules which restrict the struggle between people to a verbal struggle, and the participants mutually acknowledge the outcome of that struggle. In comparison to autocratically regulated societies, where norms of ordering and obeying dominate, a parliamentary regime demands a higher capacity to think for oneself and a greater degree of consciousness. The transition from an autocratic to a parliamentary regime is a social learning process, in which frequent vehement conflicts and regressions occur. In most parliamentary countries, it took several generations before standards of parliamentary behaviour were generally accepted by the population.

Parliamentary integration of the lower classes by associations

In the stage of parliamentarization in which the franchise was extended to include all adults, workers' associations and labour parties came to play a crucial role. In the introduction to the French edition of *Parliamentary Tactics*, Dumont writes that the code of order of the central political meetings colours the national spirit. This code is taken over by clubs, groups and lower meetings, where people gladly adhere to the regularity which has been demonstrated to them by the grand model (Bentham, 1822, p. 18). Dumont's observation was lent support by, when large groups of people in associations, societies, political parties and stockholders' meetings began to apply parliamentary manners.

Great Britain and the United States took the lead. In *The Making of the English Working Class,* E.P. Thompson (1969) noticed that the working-class community of early nineteenth-century England was to a high degree the product of conscious working-class endeavour. Workers were organized in unions and societies which placed emphasis upon self-discipline and community purpose, especially during meetings. These meeting traditions often date from the eighteenth century:

FIGURE 7.4   Prime Minister Georges Clemenceau leaves the meeting room of the French National Assembly, while socialists sing 'The Internationale' (© G. Dagli Orti)

> Rules which survived of the Manchester small-ware weavers in the 1750s show already meticulous attention to procedure and to institutional etiquette. The committee members must sit in a certain order. The doors must be kept locked. There are careful regulations for the safe-keeping of the 'box'. Members are reminded that 'Intemperance, Animosity and Profaneness are the Pest and Vermin that gnaw out the very Vitals of all Society'. (Thompson, 1969, p. 457)

According to Thompson, these codes (sometimes in the form of model rules) were extended to ever wider sections of working people. Workers sought to insure themselves against sickness, unemployment, or funeral expenses through membership of 'box clubs' or friendly societies. 'But the discipline essential for the safe-keeping of funds, the orderly conduct of meetings and the determination of disputed cases, involved an effort of self-rule as great as the new disciplines of work' (ibid., p. 458). So the Glass-Makers' Society, founded in 1755, added fines for failure in attending meetings, for failing to keep silence when ordered, speaking together, answering back the steward, betting in the club or disclosing secrets outside the society. Due to the relatively early industrialization in England, the movement of middle-class societies partly coincided with the foundation of working-class associations. As appears from the examples of Thompson, the latter strongly elaborated on the traditions of the guilds. In the Netherlands, however, this was not so much the case, because of the time gap between the vanishing of the guilds and the emergence of the industrial workers' movement.

In the United States, however, parliamentary forms of conduct spread through large groups of the population rather early. Visiting there in the 1830s, Alexis de Tocqueville was surprised to observe this:

> No sooner you set foot upon American ground than you are stunned by a kind of tumult; a confused clamour is heard on every side, and a thousand simultaneous voices demand the satisfaction of their social wants. Everything is in motion around you; here the people of one quarter of a town are met to decide upon the building of a church; there the election of a representative is going on; a little farther, the delegates of a district are hastening to the town in order to consult upon some local improvements; in another place the labourers of a village quit their plows to deliberate upon the project of a road or a public school. Meetings are called for the sole purpose of declaring their disapprobation of the conduct of the government; while in other assemblies citizens salute the authorities of the day as the fathers of their country. Societies are formed which regard drunkenness as the principal cause of the evils of the state, and solemnly bind themselves to give an example of temperance. (Alexis de Tocqueville, 1961 Vol. I, p. 259)

He noticed a special, widespread meeting behaviour in the United States:

> To take a hand in the regulation of society and to discuss it is his biggest concern and, so to speak, the only pleasure an American knows. This feeling pervades the most trifling habits of life; even the women frequently attend public meetings and listen to political harangues as a recreation from their household labours. Debating clubs are, to a certain extend, a substitute for theatrical entertainments: an American cannot converse, but he can discuss, and his talk falls into a dissertation. He speaks to you as if he were addressing a meeting; and if he should chance to become warm in the discussion, he will say 'Gentlemen' to the person with whom he is conversing. (*ibid.*, p. 260)

This particular meeting behaviour may have been an organic element of the culture of colonist groups who are largely thrown into each other's company. Tocqueville writes that 'the citizen of the United States is taught from infancy to rely upon his own exertions in order to resist the evils and the difficulty of life; he looks upon the social authority with an eye of mistrust and anxiety, and he claims its assistance only when he is unable to do without it' (p. 198).

In continental Europe association is often seen as 'a weapon which is to be hastily fashioned and immediately tried in the conflict. A society is formed for discussion, but the idea of impending action prevails in the minds of all those who constitute it. It is, in fact an army; and the time given to speech serves to reckon up strength and to animate the courage of the host, after which they march against the enemy' (ibid., p. 203). These different practices reflect different stages of state formation and parliamentarization. Tocqueville may have had in mind (post)revolutionary France in particular, since in England, the meeting standards were more similar to those in the United States:

> In a country like the United States, in which the differences of opinion are mere differences of hue, the right of association may remain unrestrained without evil consequences. Our inexperience of liberty leads us to regard the liberty of association only as a right of attacking the government. The first notion that presents itself to a party, as well as to an individual, when it has acquired a consciousness of its own strength is that of violence; the notion of persuasion arises at a later period, and is derived from experience. The English, who are divided into parties which differ essentially from each other, rarely abuse the right of association because they have long been accustomed to exercise it. In France, the passion for war is so intense that there is no undertaking so mad, or so injurious to the welfare of the state, that a man does not consider himself honoured in defending it at the risk of his life. (ibid., p. 204)

Tocqueville saw a close connection between parliamentarization and the development of meeting behaviour. He called universal suffrage as perhaps 'the most powerful of the causes that tend to mitigate the violence of political associations in the United States. In countries in which universal suffrage exists, the majority is never doubtful, because neither party can reasonably pretend to represent that portion of the community which has not voted. The associations know, as well as the nation at large, that they do not represent the majority.' He continued:

> The means that associations in Europe employ are in accordance with the end which the propose to obtain. As the principal aim of these bodies is to act and not to debate, to fight rather than to convince, they are naturally led to adopt an organisation which is not civic and peaceable, but partakes of the habits and maxims of military life. They also centralise the direction of their forces as much as possible and entrust the power of the whole party to a small number of leaders. (ibid., p. 205)

This last observation could be the beginning of an analysis of the emergence of workers' parties. Some of the military meeting habits and manners observed by Tocqueville were maintained or reintroduced in radical socialist and communist parties in the nineteenth and twentieth centuries. With the decline of communism in East Europe and the transformation of communist countries into more democratic societies, relics of military-agrarian meeting manners such as carrying and electing by acclamation and forced consensus were also becoming obscure in the government and political parties of these countries, as well as in communist parties elsewhere in Europe.

National integration of the lower classes by means of associations occurred everywhere in the western world, although at different times and various paces. It often was promoted by enfranchisement. For instance, in the Netherlands this process, which reached a peak with the institution of the universal suffrage for men in 1918 and for women in 1919 after several extensions of the franchise in the nineteenth century, took place gradually and more peacefully than in many other western countries. Several circumstances may help to explain this: there already existed a parliamentary infrastructure, and freedom of association and meeting at the relatively late moment industrialization accelerated and a working class arose in the Netherlands; the magnitude and power of the Dutch workers' movement were limited; and, the degree to which the social groups which were already represented in parliament were prepared to make concessions. The process of national and parliamentary integration by the working class developed in a unique manner, which is referred to as 'pillarization' (Lijphart, 1968; Ellemers, 1984). It reflected and continued the decentralized and egalitarian aspects of the Dutch state.

Alongside the long tradition of tolerance within the upper class, there has also been, in the Netherlands, a long tradition of religious dogmatism, particularly among the people who took the position of the doctrines of the Synod of Dort. Many of them belonged to the lower middle class of small shopkeepers, craftsmen, barge skippers, fishermen, farmers and lowly officials. Those people started to form groups and to strive for 'sovereignty in one's own circle'. In the latter half of the nineteenth century this led to the establishment of their own church, and their own political and cultural organizations. The manner in which these Calvinistic people organized themselves, locally, regionally and nationally, served as a model for other groups in the population, particularly for the Catholics. Broad layers of the population were organized into mutually competitive, philosophical or ideological sections or 'pillars', which presented at the most a challenge to the upper class but never a threat. The segmented integration of the working class, led by people who, in imitating the old meeting class, were prepared to negotiate and make compromises, made a hefty contribution to the national integration of the working class and the parliamentarization of class struggles, free from any great, violent conflicts. The groups, who were represented in the central administrative apparatus, were less concerned about loss of power and prestige through the admission to parliament and the government of representatives of the lower classes segmented in blocks than the upper classes in countries which were confronted with a united workers' front.

The organization of the population within 'pillars' dominated by confessional groups and finally containing all the facets of social life, not only contributed to the acceleration of the 'modernization process' in the period from 1870 to 1920, but also to the stagnation of this process in the first part of the twentieth century (Stuurman, 1987, p. 266). After 1920 the 'pillariza- tion' of the society acted more as a brake on social mobility than offering any assistance. In 1950 the Netherlands lagged behind 'the majority of other highly developed countries of the Atlantic world regarding industrialization, urbanization, demographic characteristics, and secularization' (ibid., p. 264). Around 1960, when the Netherlands began to close this gap, there began a process of 'de-pillarization'.

The pillarization has been written about, interpreted, explained, and judged in various ways. However, what is not disputed is that the national integration of the lower classes largely occurred through associations or clubs. In all of the studies about pillarization, clubs are given a prominent position, whether pillarization is interpreted as 'the totality of strategies to maintain, resurrect, or construct, with the use of modern organizational and political techniques, a confessional hegemony in separate societal areas', or as 'the emancipating from a discriminated position with the introduction of new ways of social administration'.[4] In his dissertation, in which he investigated the local differences between the processes of 'pillarization' and 'de-pillarization', P.J.M. Pennings (1991) commented that associations had been 'of crucial importance for the process of "pillarization"', as they 'functionally infiltrated on a supra- local level and allowed the possibility of mass mobilization' (p. 219). Club life developed as 'an answer' to the social problems which arose due to industrial- ization, urbanization and nationalization, and the accompanying loss of the old forms of society based on neighbourhoods and family ties.

Three stages can be distinguished in the development of workers' associations (Abma, 1962). The first stage concerned the establishment of independent local societies; the second stage, the commencement of ways of co-operation between societies at regional and national levels; and the third stage, the organization of new local societies from regional and national levels (Kuiper, 1972, p. 116). The two initial stages developed during the wave of industrialization from 1870 to 1920, and the second stage developed during the subsequent period of stagnation which lasted until about 1950. In the second and third stages, manuals appeared for the establishment and administration of societies. These manuals will be dealt with in the next chapter.

Associations were the means by which broad layers of the population realized fresh opportunities for power, which had developed during the process of industrialization. The increase in the number of recognized societies occurred at about the same rate as the increase in the number of enfranchised and the increase in the number of members in the Dutch parliament who did not stem from the aristocracy or the patricians. This relationship can be explained by viewing societies as organizations in which large groups of people have learnt to meet in a parliamentary manner and, as such, have developed a new parliamentary elite.

Societies, to which limited or incorporated companies can also be included on the basis of historical and legal agreements, can be seen as the parliamentary offspring of the eighteenth-century societies and clubs which had lost much of their original, political and educative functions with the political unification and centralization of the Netherlands, and the admission of representatives from wealthy middle classes to the central state meetings (Mijnhardt, 1983, p. 93). An important difference between these organizations was that the older societies promulgated agreement by instinct between the members, while matters by the new associations were more consciously based on agreement about political, cultural, and economic aims (Fassaert, 1987, pp. 61–4). These differences imply that the conduct in the nineteenth-century associations was more businesslike and more democratic, and the mutual discussions and decisions had a more central position. And, finally, the nineteenth-century associations were distinct in that they possessed a more formal character; that is, the legal power of the internal rules of conduct through recognition by the government. In the first part of the nineteenth century, the law for societies was legally enacted. For this, the main regulations of parliamentary meetings were taken as the standard, for example, by the previously mentioned statutory regulation of the right of association and meeting around 1850. Thus, there appeared in the Civil Code the regulation that every member of an association had equal rights regarding voting and that the decision should be taken by majority. Furthermore, this law also states that a society can act as a corporate body with a set name and a set administration, after the government had recognized it by approving the statutes and regulations which covered the aim, the foundation, the composition, and the remaining rules of the society. Societies whose intentions, or actual activities, were aimed at civil disobedience, law breaking, assault, tainting morals or interfering with anyone practising their rights, were forbidden (Articles 2 and 3).

In the course of the nineteenth and twentieth centuries, the meeting manners of societies were further parliamentarized. This is evident in the manuals for societies which appeared at the beginning of the century. These books contain models of statutes and common regulations, in which stipulations appeared concerning the election and function of the administration, the chairman's duties, the order of speaking, the proposing of regulations, and the amending of administrative proposals.

Prior to such manuals, the organization of the population into associations was totally dependent upon information verbally communicated. Thus, it is clear that, from the outset, the organizational activities of the leaders of the workers movement were powerfully dominated by the transmission of the rules of societies and parliamentary meetings. Numerous people learnt the conduct of meetings along elementary parliamentary lines in societies; a learning process accompanied by many conflicts and difficulties. The application of these rules required a form of self-control with which many of the lower classes were unfamiliar. One example of this should suffice, given the range of this book.

At the end of the nineteenth century, meetings as conducted by the societies were something unknown for many Catholic workers. Instructions about conduct in societies and meetings can be found on practically every page of the collected talks, letters, and articles of Alphons Ariëns, organizer of Catholic workers in the two decades around 1900 (Roes, 1982). Many of his talks consisted of a sort of public lesson in society and meeting techniques, and many of his letters and articles consisted of short instructions for the establishment and administration of societies:

> We must have respect for the opposition. It is not only impossible that several hundred people all think alike within a society, it is even good to have opposition. Because an Administration frequently makes mistakes and when the Administration is never called to book, then we would lurch from one mistake to the next. Therefore, the Administration and the majority should still respect the words of the opposition, because those words could prove beneficial. Hence, do not laugh when someone speaks; absolute liberty should reign; we should uphold the law. On the other hand, the opposition should also remain respectful. (Roes, 1982, p. 170)

> You have to have strong regulations, adhered to by all, superiors and inferiors; . . . If you are the chairman, ensure that you are present in time to open the meeting; come prepared on the platform, and show that you are capable of leading. If you are the secretary, use your pen, ensure that you are ready with your business. (*ibid.*, pp. 401–2)

The efforts made by leaders such as Ariëns to teach workers meeting conduct was part of a more embracing 'campaign to civilize', which was noticeable during the industrialization process. This has been characterized by Ali de Regt and other figurational sociologists as the whole of the conscious attempts by enlightened bourgeoisie, clerics and leaders of the workers' movements to direct the workers' behaviour into the form desired by the leaders, by promoting their own behaviour as the example (De Regt, 1984, pp. 136–42). These sociologists have neglected the fact that the learning of meeting conduct has been an important aspect of the intellectual and moral elevation of the proletariat from their position of poverty, sickness, and ignorance.

Party formation, 'oligarchization' and parliamentarization

In the second stage of the process of parliamentarization, the enfranchised increased step by step by widening the census and the increase in welfare. This ratified the movement where people with their own (ideological) vision on national issues, like the subsidizing of special education and social legislation, joined together in national associations to fight for extension of the franchise, draft parliamentary programmes and appoint parliamentary candidates. In a competitive struggle to win voters and to expand their influence on state administration, social groups forced each other into formations of like-minded people: political parties.

Political parties based on a principle, ideal, or belief, with a political programme stemming from this, are relatively recent phenomena. The eighteenth-century English philosopher, Hume, was probably the first to comment that there were two different sorts of factions or parties present in the English parliament: one based on its 'own interests', the other based on 'principles'. He wrote, that 'parties from principle, especially speculative principle, are known only to modern times and are, perhaps, the most extraordinary and unaccountable phenomenon that has yet appeared in human affairs' (quoted in Tromp, 1993, p. 276). Modern parties often combine both aspects: gaining benefits for their leaders and followers as well as realizing a political programme. They form a sliding scale. Thus political parties in the United States are aimed towards gaining benefits, while socialist parties in Europe are more orientated on realizing (items of) a programme.

The emergence of ideologically based political factions and parties was part of the development of increasingly complex and intangible networks that mutually dependent people developed with each other. With this, it became clearer that societal processes and events could not be reduced to decisions by individual people or groups, and that another, less personal manner of speaking and thinking was necessary to understand and regulate the changes in the relationships between people. Amid the less tangible societal processes, people sought to grasp explanations which did not directly emanate from individual people. In close association, two types of orientations developed: social scientific and religious ideological ones. The former developed from studying social processes 'using an approach analogous to that of the older sciences, as internally consistent, largely self-regulating and relatively autonomous, functional nexuses'. The latter approach developed from seeking orientations 'to relatively opaque social situations with the aid of relatively impersonal but emotionally charged social belief systems and ideals. These are all the more satisfying because they usually promise immediate relief for all social ills and sufferings, or even a complete cure in the near future' (Elias, 1978, p. 69). In the competition between politicians to gain the favour of the voters, parties developed which were aimed at a national future. In these parties, there reigned a strict tendency to view the present and the past with a specific ideal of the future in mind. Distinct from these political groups, scientific societies arose which, in mutual rivalry, strove towards a more factual interpretation of society as it had been. In respect to organized political groups, the autonomy of these societies has been relatively small, at least smaller than the autonomy exercised by physics societies. Generally, the two types of social orientation are less distinguishable from each other than, for example, astronomy and astrology.

The process of political party formation is to be considered as an example of the relative autonomy of societal development in respect to the intentions and plans of people. Just as states came into being in a competitive struggle for land and land control, parties have formed in a 'blind' competitive process to win the favour of voters and decisive power over the state. 'They entered the political arena with the pretension of making themselves superfluous as a party by eliminating potential opposition, and by persevering with their vision of how society should be constructed. Party pluralism resulted from the fact that no single party succeeded in attaining its original object. Thus, they were forced to endlessly compete with each other to win the voters' favour' (Tromp, 1993, p. 277). And so the generally accepted definition of a modern, political party became this: 'Any political group that presents at elections, and is capable of placing through elections, candidates for public office' (Sartori, 1976, p. 64).

Political parties are the parliamentary successors of groups taking up arms in their struggle for power. Their emergence is characteristic of a certain stage in the monopolization and centralization of organized violence and the process of parliamentarization. As long as the monopolies of physical force were unstable and vulnerable and a relatively homogeneous and co-opting societal group had control of the state administration, party formation remained limited to changing coalitions of individuals and groups in the central meetings. Political formations, which could be designated as parties, arose in a number of western countries since, with the extension of the number of enfranchised, the distance between voters and elected increased as did the need for an organization to keep both groups in touch with each other. The first political parties in the modern form had begun to emerge in Britain at the end of the eighteenth century. Initially they were called Tories, Whigs and Radicals. After the Reform Act of 1832, the Tories transformed into the Conservative Party and the Whigs together with the Radicals became the Liberal Party, which remained powerful up until the First World War. The term 'Liberal' had made its first appearance in Spain when it was used to denote the promoters of the anti-monarchical Cadiz Constitution of 1812. Through the writings of Bentham it spread to Britain and then to France.

As the democratic system which was more or less modelled on Britain spread, there developed a conviction that political parties were the instruments best adapted to political struggle. That assumption was to find startling confirmation in Marxist and especially Leninist analysis, and also in the 1917 Revolution, which made the Communist Party the instrument through which the working class could first win, and then administer, power. At this point, the debate shifted: the question was no longer, as in the nineteenth century, whether there should be political parties, but whether the party system should be pluralist or monolithic. (Mény, 1994, p. 49)

Party formation often originated from, or was promoted by, dissatisfaction with the policies of the ruling monarchs. 'Liberal' oppositions arose striving for a constitutional administration. However, there was little of a mutual, longer term programme or political loyalty among these old 'Liberals'. Furthermore, this was not in line with the 'Liberal' vision that considered individual freedom to be central, and that parliament was a forum where the elected could bombard each other with arguments in order to reach the best solutions to the problems. Party organization was rejected because this would break through the interpersonal ties of the voters and the elected in a district. Despite their 'ideology', Liberals gradually organized themselves into parties in order to resist the 'conservative' and other parties which had sprung up in reply to them. In the Netherlands, the first to establish a party were orthodox Protestants. They organized a national political association as a result of dissatisfaction with the Liberals' education policy: the Anti-Revolutionary Party. This name has no European equivalent, and it can be considered characteristic of the relatively advanced meeting regime of the Dutch Protestant churches. The formation of the orthodox Protestant party increased the pressure on other groups, like Catholics and Liberals, to organize themselves as social 'pillars', that is to say along the lines of ideological principles and political programmes.

The party formation process, which was promoted by a sequential extension of the number of enfranchised and the consequent weakening of the personal ties between the electors and the elected, accelerated with the entrance to parliaments of representatives of socialist movements, which started in Germany and Sweden in the last quarter of the nineteenth century. The development, in which the socialist movement of radical opponents to 'civilian parliamentary democracy' changed into a parliamentary opposition not to be ignored, was a difficult and lengthy process, associated with difficult internal strife, divisions, and retributions. In the middle of this development, Robert Michels wrote his study *Zur Soziologie des Parteiwesens in der modernen Demokratie* (1910, 1924). Based on the history of the labour movement (namely the German and Italian labour movements), he supports the proposition that every organization, even the most anti-oligarchic and most democratic like the socialist parties and unions, produced their own elite. This he terms as 'the iron law of oligarchization'.

Michels' attempted to demonstrate that the 'democratic' framework of organizations such as parties and unions, within which general meetings were the highest deciding authorities, gave no guarantee against the accumulation of power in the hands of a small group of leaders. To explain this, he pointed out the tendency of individuals in a leadership position to use their extra authority and their advantage regarding information to make themselves popular and indispensable, and to the tendency of the 'masses' to revere the self-aware leaders rather than to criticize them, and thus allow themselves to be forced into a passive, subservient role. 'Just like the democratic leaders developed into party autocrats, the rebellious mass changed into docile membership' (van Doorn, 1969, p. 19). According to Michels, the most important impulse to the process of oligarchization was the mounting need for organization. The multiplying of functions and duties, the internal division of labour and the growing need for specific professionals made it possible and necessary that the leaders extended the power in respect to the members. The centralization of power into the hands of a small group was strengthened by the necessity for being able to act quickly and flexibily in the struggle with other rival organizations. 'Thus, the organization of the means for attaining a goal became a goal in itself' (Michels, 1970, p. 348). The iron law of oligarchization was applicable to every organization, including the state, according to Michels. He considered democracy as an illusion of the young; oligarchization and democratization as stages in an endless circle.

This summary does not do justice to Michels' detailed study, subsequent to which, it has frequently been pointed out that the socialist movement did not actually start its development from a democracy and result in an oligarchy. Initially, the movement was merely centred around a number of charismatic individuals, and it gradually developed into a stabler organization which shaped the conditions for the attainment of various socialist aims. Michels did not study political parties in general, but early forms of parties from an early and immature political system, such as existed in Germany and Italy around the turn of the century. The Dutch sociologist, Bonger, has commented, 'Michels should not write about the oligarchic malady of democracy but about "the healing of childhood ills"' (van Doorn, 1969, p. 33).

Elaborating upon this criticism, it could be said that the process described by Michels represented a stage in the parliamentarization of the workers' movement and the working classes. The moment the socialist movement attained a social basis in society and the charismatic leaders were replaced by elected leaders, the processes described by Michels came into operation; processes leading to changes in and the transferring of their aims, and oligarchization. All things considered, the changes in their aims indicated acceptance of parliament as the central arena for the attainment of socialist ideals and the recognition of other parties as parliamentary rivals; the transference of their aims pointed to the spreading of the number of meetings and meeting levels within the party; and oligarchization pointed to the differentiation of incidental and more professional meeting participants, by which the party representatives in parliament became the central leaders.

The now unstoppable formation of a societal upper class of rival party leaders represented a break in 'the circulation of elites', which had occurred for centuries in military, agrarian societies. In parliamentary societies, there existed a top layer of people, who were afforded power and prestige by their position within the increasingly complex network of meetings, and who distinguished themselves from others primarily due to their capacities for holding and participating in meetings. This parliamentary upper layer was extended, replenished, and replaced by those from below at a faster rate than the noble upper layer had been replaced in an agrarian society. The leaders of parliamentary, industrial societies, who were tied to broader layers of the population via numerous meetings, had limited freedom for manoeuvre compared to leaders of military–agrarian societies. With the increase in the number of administrative and meeting levels and the development of a moderate, more open rivalry between and within political parties, the organization of society came to correspond less and less to the division 'leaders' and 'masses', which formed the basis of Michels' hypothesis.

In the process of political party formation, parliamentary meeting activity has acquired the character of a battle of words between parliamentary divisions of political parties or factions. As society became more complex, as the number of national functions grew, and as more population groups became involved in the national decision-making processes and began to organize themselves into political parties, parliamentary meetings increased in number, diversity and complexity. The changes in the power and dependency relationships between the represented and their representative figurations (society and parliament) allowed, and made it necessary, once more to pay some attention to matters such as: who speaks when, in which order, how often, for how long, and in which manner; what may not be said or done; and, how would the rules for speaking be maintained and through which sanctions. The reconsideration of these matters led to a further increase, refinement, and sharpening of what was requisite or forbidden in parliament.

Regularities in the dynamics of meeting

The increasing precision in the division and recording of addresses is an illustration of a phenomenon which demonstrates an 'iron' regularity that could be viewed as a 'law' or a regularity in the dynamics of meeting. It can be reduced to the following: meeting participants force each other into nuancing and differentiating their behaviour, particularly their use of language, as they represent more people, and have to take into consideration more people in their discussions and decisions. Thus, as parliament developed from a structure bearing the character of a closed 'debating club' of like-minded notables into a public 'arena' where representatives of diverse social groups fought verbally for power, property, and prestige, the participants in the struggle were obliged to be aware of, and control their behaviour more closely, particularly their manner of speaking and their use of language. Similarly, this can be illustrated by the example that fifty pence more or fifty pence less per month makes little difference to an individual on benefits, but a huge difference to the government's financial budget; greater still as more people are dependent upon benefits.

Thus, as in many other parliaments, in the Dutch parliament conditions covering the duration of budgetary addresses are adopted in the code of order. This was done for the first time in 1914. The precise quota restrictions and division of speaking times were left to the chairmen of the factions in the 'senior assembly'. However, as a rule, it was proposed that 'during general discussions concerning the budget and its details, the length of address may not exceed forty-five minutes per member' and the responses not longer than ten minutes. During general budgetary discussions by the Ministry of War and the Navy, the maximum duration should actually be one hour; an exception which reflected the relative weight of military expense within the state budget at that time (about 35 per cent). Since 1914 the length of an address concerning the budget was determined and rationed, more closely and to an increasing degree (to within thirty seconds) according to the distribution of party seats in the Dutch parliament (Pippel, 1950, pp. 349–63). In September 1993, during a general debate, the factions comprising one person were granted an address of seven and a half minutes in the first round.

In parliamentary meetings, gestures and words have acquired a greater significance as more people came to be dependent upon the decisions of these meetings. Within the meeting pyramids of large social units, such as states, institutions, and companies, these regularities can still be observed: the higher the level of the meeting, the higher are the requirements for behaviour control and the use of language. This is more applicable for meetings which are more public than those which are more closed. This was ascertained by Dutch politicians and businessmen several years ago, when they participated in each others' meetings as a 'practical'. One member of parliament commented: 'Every step was followed and every word was heard . . . similar control factors are much less overt in a company and that makes practice much simpler' (van Engen, 1985, p. 38). Likewise, a businessman commented that, in his practice, he had learnt that a politician sometimes had to present his position in stages, because he needed to be in line with the thinking processes of his supporters and he did not wish to incite any unnecessary confrontations. 'A politician does not only take into consideration how something comes over, but how it comes over at that precise minute' (van Engen, 1985, p. 40). Moreover, the television broadcasting of debates has increased pressure on politicians to choose their words carefully.

Another illustration of this trend is the more accurate noting of what is covered in the Dutch parliament. From 1815, after the close of each meeting, the minutes were made on the basis of the notes made by the clerk of the parliament. These notes which covered the incoming and outgoing correspondence, the different points of view and the decisions (not the text of the addresses) were read out at the start of the subsequent meeting, after they had been approved of by the parliament, transferred into a registry, and signed by the chairman and the clerk. As the plenary meetings of the Second Chamber of the Dutch parliament were, in principle, public, reports were regularly published in the national press. These reports 'could not claim to be exhaustive, while the comprehensiveness of the reports of the various meetings was unequal' (Pippel, 1950, p. 298). In the 1840s, with the growth in power of the Dutch parliament, there was an increased need to publish a comprehensive and continuous view of what was dealt with in parliament. In 1874 it was decided 'to regularly publish comprehensive reports of the meetings in a series of separate supplements in the *Staatscourant* [State Journal] followed by the bills, reports, government responses, and incoming and outgoing correspondence dealt with in Parliament' (*ibid.*). Three of the editors of this paper wrote an 'analytical' report, in which the addresses that the members had in writing were reported extensively. In the view of the members of parliament, this report often left much to be desired. It was decided in 1849 to publish those matters covered in the meetings of the States-General, faster and more comprehensively, by using stenographers to record the addresses. From that time onwards a word-for-word report has been made by stenographers in the service of the States-General which bears the title *Hansard of the Dutch States-General*. In 1853, in order to supervise the stenographic service and the publication of the report within 24 hours of the close of a meeting, a regulation and a committee for stenography in both Chambers of the Dutch Parliament were brought into being. In 1921, the *Hansard* was adopted as the official report of the meetings of the Chamber(s). The business section of the *Hansard*, that is, everything except the text of the addresses, remained the duty and responsibility of the clerk and, from then on, was presented at the clerk's department during the first hour of the subsequent meeting, and approved during the course of the meeting. In the 1930s it became possible to replace unparliamentary, disrespectful comments in the *Hansard*, or to remove them entirely by order of the chairman and with the agreement of the committee for stenography.

In the process of the pacification of the societal rivalry for power, property, and prestige, the sensitivity to denigrating expressions, verbal threats, accusations, expressions of anger and aggression, and everything reminiscent of domination and humiliation, became keener in central meetings. Likewise, what was requisite and forbidden with regard to these items became more detailed, more inclusive, and more tightly controlled. These changes came about in waves, which were closely associated with the entrance of new layers of society to parliament. Similar to what occurred during previous extensions of the franchise, parliamentary conduct was firstly formalized and tightened during the period when the organized workers' movements stepped into the parliamentary arena. Several illustrations of this follow.

Fearing serious disturbances to order after the entrance of communist representatives to parliament, the Dutch parliament decided in 1919 to extend the disciplinary authority of the chairman (van Raalte, 1958, p. 170; Coopman, 1939, pp. 123–4). In the Code of Order, a stipulation was added which enabled the chairman to deny entrance to the parliamentary Chamber to a member who hindered the proceedings of parliament; a day for the first offence, longer for any repetition. The idea for this regulation was taken from parliamentary practices in other countries, where chairmen had already acquired greater authority in order to prevent incidents, chaos and obstruction. In a juridical dissertation from 1914, W.J. Couturier argued for an extension of the disciplinary stipulations of the Dutch parliament. He wrote that the Dutch Houses of Parliament were indeed praised in Auguste Reynaert's comparative study of the history of parliamentary discipline (1884) for their 'freedom without having to be reined, reasonableness without affectation, calmness without weakness, moderation, proprieties, and their seriousness and courtesy during debate'. However, in recent years 'a decline in the level of parliamentary morals' could be observed in the Netherlands (Couturier, 1914, p. 54). Moreover, there were 'grounds' to fear that the level would decline further. Although the Netherlands did not 'have any differences in nationality, from which sprang the fiercest obstructions in the British and Austrian Parliaments, here other causes could be equally as good as those elsewhere in achieving this effect'. The author was making reference to the general franchise, which 'also brought representatives into the representative body who were less-civilized than those who the elected representatives had previously had authority over', and to the sharpened class distinction and the extension of state concerns which overloaded parliament such that 'the members usually missed the necessary time to calmly study the bills in hand and to prepare their discussions thoroughly, and were frequently overtired and consequently irritated; all bad conditions for a calm and business-like handling of the proceedings' (*ibid.*, p. 55).

The development which actually unfolded was the exact opposite to what Couturier so much dreaded. As more societal groups entered parliament and the parliamentarization of the competitive struggle advanced, tensions outside parliament declined and the debates within parliament became calmer and more businesslike, although not lineally.

With the entrance to parliament of the National Socialist Movement in 1934, the Code of Order was changed such that a member who disturbed order or used unseemly language, whether previously admonished or not, could be ordered to silence, or excluded from the meeting for one day. From that time onwards, the chairman had the authority to silence a member who 'appeared to be assenting to illegal procedures in some way or other' or to exclude the offending member from further debate. The third decision included the introduction of the condition that, when a member is admonished by the chairman for using unacceptable language, he should be given the opportunity to take back the offending words or to rephrase them, and that, if the member makes use of this opportunity, the offending words would not be reported in the stenographic report. When the member did not make use of this opportunity, this became reason sufficient to remove the word from him. This latter condition is responsible for a list of unparliamentary expressions, termed 'cadavers'. By comparing these 'cadavers' and the expressions which caused speakers to be called to order in the beginning of this century, an impression can be gleaned of the changes in the standards of (un)parliamentary language, in the standards of 'reasonable or polite expressions' or the 'rules of verbal reasonableness', which have developed during the national integration of the workers and other subordinated groups.

An ex-clerk of the Dutch parliament has summarized the disapproved expressions which members of the Chamber hurled at each other during the period from 1908 to 1922: cynic, whippersnapper, political poisoner, yapping dog, spinning top, dishonest, dirty, dismal junk plunger, unscrupulous, shameless, mucky pup, gangleader, gilded hooligan, perjurous sirs, barbarians, impudent, idealistic nonsense, Indian warcries, nonsense, twaddle, rubbish, lies, crime, joke, demagogy, mystification, monkey house, inanity, unfair politics, rotten business, false information, distortions, insinuations and swindle (Hoekstra, 1984, p. 13). The following 'cadavers' or unparliamentary expressions from the last 25 years have been collected by the journalist D.J. Hoekstra: twist, barmy, bloody hell, rabble-rouser, scoundrel, the minister is not tired – simply inactive, impolite, demeaning for parliament, nitwit. The collection of unparliamentary expressions from the last few decades is noticeably more meagre than those from the first few decades of the century.

If these expressions are taken into consideration, then it is evident that practically all the recent 'cadavers', collected by Hoekstra, had something to do with 'lying'. Here follows a few examples: 'That also in our circle, Mr Lubbers cannot be taken as a specialist in political honesty', 'not a word of truth', 'untrue', 'in contradiction to the truth', 'dishonest', and 'lies'. Also, the question as to whether 'someone speaks the truth, the whole truth, and nothing but the truth', was termed inappropriate. The word 'lying' was replaced by 'untruth', 'incorrectness', and 'in contradiction to the truth'. The comment 'bare lies' was altered to 'I have seldom seen the opposite of the truth phrased so precisely', and 'he's lying' became 'he's walking a tightrope when it comes to the truth'.

It is significant that, nowadays, particularly the use of the word 'lies', and variations upon it, is considered to be inappropriate. The huge sensitivity to just this sort of accusation is the reverse of the more exact and more empirical way of speaking and deciding about people, towards which the unplanned process of extending and differentiating the chains of actions, and increasing mutual dependence between more people, compels society. With the decline in power differences and tensions between social groups within Dutch society, the mutually anticipated self-control increased, and parliamentary language became less personal and more businesslike. With this, the official rules covering what may or may not be expressed in a debate have become more flexible; in contrast, the informal rules have become tighter. Some expressions which previously, when there were large power differences, were considered accusatory or demeaning by certain groups, and thus banned from parliament for precisely this reason, have acquired a less weighty significance and are now permitted. This concerns words such as nonsense and hypocritical, and probably also words such as spinning top, distortion, twaddle, joke, cynic and mystification. Other expressions, such as Indian warcries, whippersnapper, gilded hooligan, barbarians, dismal junk plungers, political poisoner, unscrupulous and Pharisees have not been used for decades in the Dutch parliament. During the process of national integration, these have got a more painful and more shameful impact, just like comments such as 'deformed church', 'then the inkpots go through the Chamber', or similar challenges to a duel.

A characteristic aspect of the development of parliamentary conduct in the last few decades in the Netherlands is the changed attitude towards interruptions. In 1909 the chairman of the Second Chamber commented about interruptions: 'Whoever has the word is frequently stimulating and there could well be a sort of discussion or even a dispute developing from it' (Pippel, 1950, p. 334). The regulations of the Chamber forbade interruptions with the stipulation: 'A speaker may not be disturbed in his address unless he has to be reminded to comply to the Code of Order'. In the 1970s a condition was added that allowed the chairman to permit interruptions. This change in attitude may be explained by the desire to modify the rather dull meeting style of the Dutch parliament, but it may also be an expression of a more embracing and unplanned, long-term process which results in forms of conduct becoming less formal. This process, referred to as 'informalization', has been summarized by Cas Wouters as follows: 'As the do's and don'ts enclosed in the good old manners became less wide-ranging, less detailed and less rigid, the obvious expectations that people held regarding each others' and their own self-control became more extensive, more detailed, and more rigid' (1990, p. 54). With the parliamentarization of increasingly larger parts of the population of nation states, the mutual fear and the sharpness of the debate between representatives of different classes and groups diminished. Meeting manners in general became more easy. Using international meeting manuals, it is possible to trace this process of informalization more closely and within a larger area.

CHAPTER 8

THE PROFESSIONALIZATION
OF MEETING MANNERS

Manuals for associations and meetings[1]

While 'conversing' and 'speaking in company' remained the subjects of etiquette books or general books of manners, a literary genre developed totally focused upon meeting manners. This development occurred as the monopolies of force and taxation became more public and as society became industrialized. There are many indications that, after the demise of court society and the sharper distinction between private and professional lives, etiquette books came to be written particularly by and for women, whereas meeting manuals were written more particularly by and for men. Women had been excluded from all more or less official meetings, probably since the beginning of the military-agrarian society. Opportune use is made of this fact in a parody of a manual for societies and meetings, which appeared in the Netherlands in 1962 and which marked the end of the first stage in the development of the Dutch meeting manuals genre. In the foreword of this work, it was stated:

> This book is actually a mirror; or put in a better way, a pocket distorting mirror. Party functionaries, weighty advisors, local council members, secretaries of wrestling clubs or middle-class cartels, and the president-commissioner of a dozen lucrative enterprises should not take umbrage. They alone will only recognise others and never themselves. Here, those who always remain at home, those lonely spouses of all those important people, will finally get to see what 'he' actually perpetrates or refrains from, all that time that he's gone again. (Wolff and Wessum, 1962)

Since the emergence of the parliamentary-industrial society women are successfully acquiring the right to attend political and an increasing number of other powerful meetings. However, this is a slow process. Even today, one does not often see women in political and business summit conferences and meetings. Old beliefs and prejudices still seem to be alive, although they are no more expressed as explicitly as they were in a Dutch meeting manual of 1961:

> Therefore I can have little respect for those administrations which do not enter a debate to attain a victory, but only round up possible friends as a herd of voters to support the administration. Generally, a number of ladies then show up at the meetings. An ominous sign! (Posthumus Meyjes, 1961, pp. 28 and 29)

If one can speak of a leeway or organizational disadvantage for women in relation to men, it was, and still often is, in the sphere of meetings. This impressive fact deserves more attention from students of social sciences in general, and in particular from researchers in the field of linguistic differences between women and men in particular (see Deborah Tannen, 1986, 1994). The monopolization of official meetings by men and the long exclusion of women from these meetings may help to explain the historical and still-existing, gender gap. Questions which arise are: To what extent does this historical development explain the margin between informal and formal meetings and meeting behaviour? To what extent has typically masculine (speech) behaviour developed and been preserved in meetings? To what extent is men's language in fact just 'meeting language'?

As a means of communicating the prevailing ways of conduct to lower layers of the population, the genre of meeting books is a direct progression from the court etiquette books. The relationship between both genres is apparent from the many passages similar to both books, in which the readers were instructed to curb anger and aggression, to avoid threatening, giving offence, and making accusations, and to present their own opinion in a quiet, pleasant, friendly and careful manner, so that the discussion remained free from arguments, quarrels, shouting and other incidents; in short, those conflicts which tended towards bodily confrontation. The fact that writers of books on meeting manners continually refocus upon regulating this precise aspect of behaviour, is a reminder that the act of meeting is a more 'civilized' way of dealing with societal conflicts and tensions. Above all, the meeting rules and norms serve to regulate tensions between participants; in the sense that a flame is prevented from flaring up, but also that it is prevented from becoming so weak that it no longer gives any heat or light. In this chapter, an attempt will be made to trace some main trends in the development of the genre of meeting manuals. This investigation is exploratory; an initial attempt at a sociological approach to this genre.

In the national bibliographies of the United States of America, Great Britain, Germany, France and the Netherlands, Gerard Bos and I noted

FIGURE 8.1   The meeting of the future? (Blenks Groupware, Liempde)

approximately 800 titles, including reprints up until 1990, which qualified as meeting manuals or textbooks. Grouping these titles by their country of publication, the figures were as follows: 50 per cent American, 10 per cent British, 20 per cent German, 15 per cent Dutch and 5 per cent French.[2] The first titles appeared some 100 years ago. Given the number of translations and quotations, it is clear that the writers have influenced each other to an increasing degree. The various national series can be considered together as a single literary genre.

Besides manuals and textbooks, other educational tools to communicate meeting manners and rules have emerged since the decline of court society. Such tools are regular lectures at schools and universities, audio-visual courses, and various training programmes. The books are merely a shadow of the enormous amount of activity geared to impress desirable meeting behaviour on younger generations and other groups of 'outsiders', in the process of establishing themselves. Nevertheless, it should be kept in mind that a lot of modern meeting textbooks were developed within the framework of training programmes.

The fact that, in many countries, a large number of similar meeting manuals were published, is a clear indication that these countries began to differ less and less from each other in the degrees and ways of meeting during the period of industrialization. Every parliamentary, industrial society has a series of meeting manuals and textbooks, which can be considered as vehicles by which the dominant meeting manners (the meeting manners of the dominant groups) spread. Figure 8.2 contains the figures of the annual number of prints and reprints of American, Dutch and German meeting manuals and gives an initial impression of the progress of this genre.

In the development of the genre, two phases can be distinguished. The first phase comprised manuals which covered the etiquettes of national parliaments as models for political assemblies at lower levels, and for meetings of clubs and shareholders. The second phase comprises textbooks in which more attention is paid to those manners and customs which should be (and already are) observed in meetings and negotiations of managerial boards and companies. This divide occurred around the 1950s. From about 1960 onwards, there was a spectacular increase in the number of such textbooks, not only in Dutch and German, but especially in English.[3]

During the parliamentarization of the lower classes politicians, administrators, lawyers and other professionals (in some countries earlier than others) began to write manuals about parliamentary conduct in meetings of shareholders, local councils, public administrative boards and societies of various kinds (political, literary, scientific, benevolent and religious). The American series of parliamentary meeting manuals contains about 250 editions and reprints, and the English series contains about 50, as does the German series. The Dutch series of parliamentary meeting manuals consists of about 15 different books, which have been reprinted twice on average. As far as it is possible to ascertain, the French language lags way behind in this trend with only a few publications. The American series, which can be found in their national bibliography under the entry 'parliamentary practice' and 'public meetings', is not only the largest of this series, but also the longest running and the most continuous. In the United States, from the middle of the last century up until the present, manuals have been published for the 'everyday' use of parliamentary rules. However, in the last two decades this number has rapidly decreased (see Figure 8.3). Within a few decades of Jefferson writing his manual, (see ch. 7) the formation of societies began to create an increasing need for a body of rules adapted to the requirements of non-legislative organizations. Adjustments were necessary because, differing from a legislative body, the sessions of an ordinary local society rarely lasted for longer than one meeting of two or three hours, the quorum in a voluntary society had to be much less than the majority of the members if the organization were to function, and the business in a local society was less far-reaching and less complex, so that no standing committees were required.

The first author who attempted to meet the procedural needs of the United States' growing number of voluntary societies and local councils was Luther S. Cushing, clerk to the Massachusetts House of Representatives and a noted lawyer. In 1845 he penned a small book entitled *Manual of*

Parliamentary Practice: Rules of Proceedings and Debate in Deliberative Assemblies.
Although this was the first manual for 'assemblies of every description, but
more especially for those which are not legislative in their character', it has
not become the standard work in this field (*Robert's Rules of Order*, 1981,
pp. xxxv–xxxvi). This honour falls to *Robert's Rules of Order*, penned by
Major Henry Martin Robert, an engineering officer in the US army who
was also very active in church and civic organizations. While serving as a
major in San Francisco, he discovered great disparity and conflict about
parliamentary procedures. 'Under these conditions, confusion and
misunderstanding had reached a point where issues of procedure consumed
time that should have gone into real work of the societies', he wrote (*Robert's
Rules of Order* 1970, Introduction, p. xxxvii). Thus he conceived a plan to
compile a work on parliamentary law:

> Based, in its general principles, upon the rules and practice of Congress, but
> adapted, in its details, to the use of ordinary societies. Such a work should give
> not only the methods of organising and conducting meetings, the duties of officers
> and names of ordinary motions, but should also state systematically in reference
> to each motion, its object and effect; whether it can be amended or debated; if
> debatable, the extent to which it opens the main question to debate; the
> circumstances under which it can be made, and what other motions can be made
> while it is pending. (*Robert's Rules of Order*, 1880, Preface)

The first edition of 4000 of this manual appeared in 1876, 1000 of which
Robert sent to parliamentarians, educationalists, legislators and church
leaders throughout the country, at his own expense (*ibid.*, p. xii). This
edition was sold out within four months. A second edition published later
in 1896 increased the size of the book by sixteen pages, and changes and
additions in a third edition in 1893 added 26 more pages. The first complete
revision, published in 1915, was the product of three years of the original
author's full-time effort. This edition, *Robert's Rules of Order Revised*, had
less than one-quarter of its content taken directly from the previous edition
of 1893. The revision and expansion were largely the result of hundreds of
letters from all over the country, submitting questions on parliamentary law
arising in organizations. In 1970, a new revision of the book was published.
'Almost ten years, and perhaps more work than on all six previous editions
combined, have gone into the preparation of *Robert's Rules of Order Newly
Revised*', the new author, Sarah Corbin Robert, wrote in the preface (1970,
pp. xxi–xxv). The three editions of the Pocket Manual by 1915 had totalled
more than a half million copies. In 1970 a total of 2,650,000 copies had
been printed. The 1981 edition listed 3,400,000 copies in print. The last
major revision, the ninth, appeared in 1990. According to the present

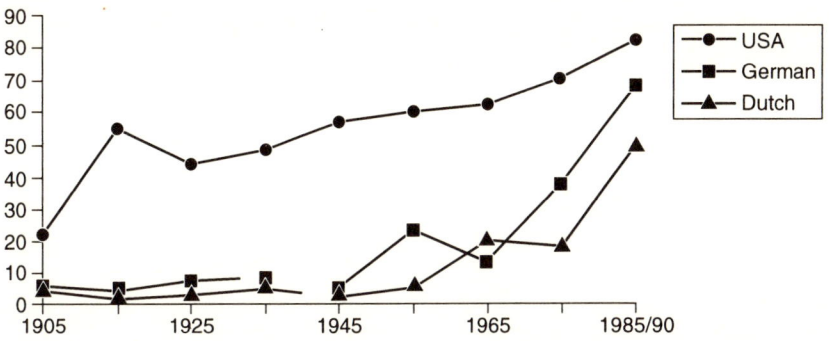

FIGURE 8.2 Number of (re)prints of North American, German and Dutch meeting textbooks and manuals

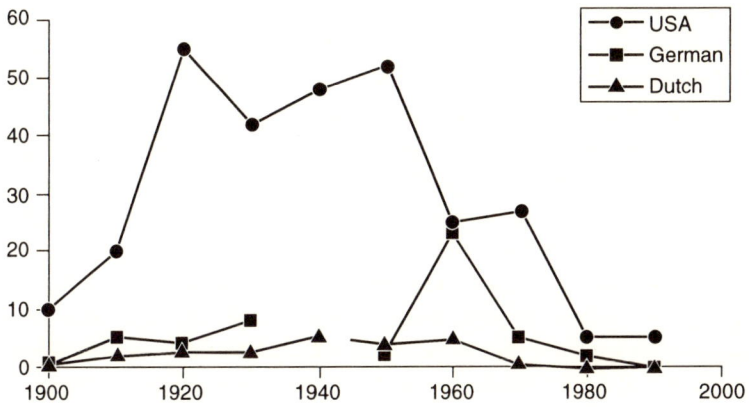

FIGURE 8.3 Number of prints and reprints of parliamentary manuals in the United States, Germany, and the Netherlands

publisher, Addison-Wesley, more than 4,450,000 copies of the book had been sold by 1997.

In retrospect, Cushing's and Robert's manuals were the beginning of a long-running, continuous American series of manuals for parliamentary practice. Robert's manual is the core of the American series. It can be used to get an idea of these series in their entirety, covering questions such as the summoning to a meeting, the opening, the quorum, the creation of an agenda, the introduction of business, the assignment of the floor, the handling and submission of motions, propositions and amendments, the formation of boards and committees, the ways of deciding and voting and the way of taking minutes.

Both the content and style of the parliamentary manuals are predominantly formal. Thus, the manner which speakers should take and leave the floor is specified in the following manner:

> Before a member can make a motion or address the assembly upon any question, it is necessary that he *obtain the floor*, that is, he must rise and address the presiding officer by his title, thus: 'Mr. Chairman,' who will then announce the members name. Where two or more rise at the same time, the Chairman must decide who is entitled to the floor, which he does by announcing that member's name. In making his decision he should be guided by the following principles. (*Robert's Rules of Order*, 1880, pp. 20–1)

It is interesting to see how this passage has been changed. About 100 years later, it ran as follows:

> To claim the floor, a member rises at his place when no one else has the floor, faces the chair, and says, 'Mr. President', or 'Mr. Chairman', or 'Madam Chairman', or whatever is the chair's proper title. If the member is entitled to the floor at the time, the chair recognises him – normally by announcing, as applicable, the person's name or title, or the place or unit that he represents. This member then has the floor and can remain standing and speak. If only one person is seeking the floor in a small meeting where all present know and can clearly see one another, the chair can recognise the member merely by nodding to him. . . . If two or more rise at about the same time, the general rule is that, all other things being equal, the member who rose and addresses the chair first *after the floor was yielded* is entitled to be recognised. (*Robert's Rules of Order*, 1970, pp. 24–5)

One hundred years later the instructions are more extensive and more attention is paid to informal (situations in) meetings. The new, more differentiated, rules obviously give a chairperson more grasp than the former, simpler, cruder, and less precise ones. As shall be seen later in this chapter, this change represents a general trend in the development of meeting manners books.

In Germany and the Netherlands, the stream of manuals which concentrated upon the use of parliamentary manners started a decade later than it did in the United States. It was interrupted during the national-socialist administration when a ban on meetings was in force. In Germany this was from the start of the 1930s until the end of the Second World War; in the Netherlands, it was during the German occupation from 1940 to 1945 (refer to Figure 8.3). The first attempts to introduce parliamentary ways of conduct are to be found in manuals intended for the establishment and administration of societies, and limited or incorporated companies. Gradually, meeting conduct began to occupy a larger part of these manuals, and instruction books appeared, which were entirely dedicated to meetings along parliamentary lines. In the Netherlands in the 1960s, and in Germany in the 1980s, the entire parliamentary series appeared in a wave of other types of meeting instruction books. These books will be investigated further in the next section of this chapter. The growth of parliamentary manuals in Germany was prominent during the 1950s, the decade of the restoration of parliamentary democracy in that country.

The first German manuals date from the 1880s and bear titles such as *Rules for a Parliamentary Arrangement of Societies* and *How to Direct Societies and Meetings*. Several were entirely dedicated to (the chairing of) meetings of societies. Of these early meeting manuals, some were characterized by a personal, somewhat capricious style. Thus, in *How do I Chair a Meeting? A Manual for Administrators of Societies* (1897), the author who was a 'teacher and administrator in a military society' writes:

> In general the chairman has to take care of good order during the meeting, as is also legally required. All disturbances by hissing, whistling, making noise, etcetera should be suppressed by the chairman. Many societies have special bylaws to inflict a fine upon such members or, if necessary to expel them from the society. I, for one, would not make use of fines many times, but would immediately decide to expel such dubious elements who did not pay their fines and harmed the society. To call such people to order would only miss the mark. (A. Karst, 1897, p. 19)

Other German manuals were more solid and characterized by a rather impersonal style, much like *Robert's Rules of Order*. An example is *Wie leitet man eine Versammlung? Handweiser für Vorsitzender (How to Chair a Meeting? A Manual for Presidents)* (1893, 1908), penned by 'a member of the German Reichstag'. That is all we know about the author. The instructions show greater expertise and detachment by its author. For instance:

> More than anything else, the chairmen has to be impartial and, although elected by the majority, be nevertheless ready to represent the minority: he must be particularly attentive to defending the rights of the minority against the majority and not to curtail its speaking time and its freedom of speech. (1908, p. 26)

After the enfranchisement of all adults, and political parties were generally accepted, the content and style of the manuals changed somewhat. More often, authors exercised professions such as (law) teacher and journalist. Their manuals were intended for meetings of the lower classes and had a more anecdotal character than their predecessors. One of these is *Ich bitte ums Wort zur Geschäftsordnung!* (*I Ask Permission to Speak about the Regulations*) (1930), written by E. Paquin, university teacher and political editor at the Reichstag and the Prussian Landtag. From this concise handbook, the following passage about the way the chair should treat long-winded and incessant talkers, serves as an illustration:

> A chairman wringing his hands, told me that a member of his society had managed to talk sixty times in one and the same meeting! Another non-stop talker succeeded thirty-five times. This is a lot of nonsense. One has to manage this in the following manner: when in a meeting such things happen, let the assembly make one of the following decisions: 1. nobody is allowed to speak more than twice about a subject, the second time no longer than half the time of the first period . . . 2. if someone spoke five times in one and the same meeting, the sixth time the chair is to ask the assembly whether this person should be allowed to take the floor again. (This might seem draconian but it will undoubtedly help the speaker to restrict himself to the essence of the matter). 3. if some members are repeatedly trying to be the first to take the floor, the chair is allowed to rearrange the speakers' list in such a way that the candidates will speak first by turns. (Paquin, 1930, p. 22)

After the national-socialist administration and the Second World War, when parliament was actually abolished and a ban on association and assembly was in force, Germany went through a period of re-parliamentarization, when a lot of meeting manuals were published. Often, authors were university scholars of (parliamentary) law and history. However, representatives from other disciplines had already started to dabble in the genre. An illustration of this developmental stage is given in the manual *Ich bitte ums Wort* (*I Ask Permission to Speak*) (1960) by Professor Dr Dr Maximilian Weller, who had previously written a bestseller about rhetoric. Weller's manual can be considered a milestone of the German series. It is the first German compilation of scattered knowledge of juridical, psychological-tactical and rhetorical aspects of formal meetings. This comprehensive book, which comprises almost 400 pages, is one of the last German manuals explicitly modelled on parliamentary conduct although, in the introduction, the author refers to a great variety of different meetings including business conferences. The aim of the book is described as follows:

> The principles which you employ deliberating, have eventually to be described entirely and with systematic thoroughness; the customary laws and rules in this field have to be laid down in writing, so as that individuals who want to be active in any administration do not need to laboriously collect rules, techniques, customs, unwritten laws and common practices all over again. . . . Point of reference of this book has been the code of order of the German parliament. (Weller, 1960, p. 9)

Regarding the treatment of long-winded and incessant talkers, Weller recommends his readers to limit the allotted speaking time and let no one speak more than three or, at most, four times on a subject. It is preferable that the chair asks the assembly permission to apply this rule at the very beginning of the meeting. Then the proposal will certainly be adopted by a majority. But if the speaking time has not been previously allotted, the chairman has a number of options if a speaker continues to talk in an irrelevant and boring way:

> The chairman may look at his watch manifestly, then pass the speaker a note with a reminder, and when this still does not work, interrupt and give him a very short time to finish his speech. He is not allowed to exceed the time span with just one second, otherwise he will be closured. This should be said by the chairman courteously and with an expression of regret, but unrelentingly, according to Bismarck's motto: 'courtesy until the last step to the gallows, but hanging will take place anyway'. (Weller, 1960, p. 193)

The first parliamentary phase of the German series of meeting manuals shows many similarities to that of the Dutch series. In the Netherlands, between 1897 and 1963, fifteen different books were published, in which it was described how participants should conduct themselves in meetings. The first attempts to present parliamentary ways of conduct are to be found in manuals intended for the establishment and administration of societies and shareholders' meetings. Some of these manuals (often written by civil servants) are very formal, whereas others are rather informal and more personal. Thus, in *Hoe richt ik een vereeniging op?* (*How do I Start an Association?*) the author, J.M.I.A. Simons, starts with the description of a fictitious meeting in which an association is established. Every step of the formation process is concluded with a relevant (meeting) lesson. Gradually, meeting conduct began to occupy a larger part of these manuals, and instruction books appeared, which were entirely dedicated to meetings along parliamentary lines. In 1934 there appeared the *Handboekje voor secretarissen van verenigingen en voor directeuren en commissarissen van naamloze vennootschappen* (*Manual for Secretaries of Societies and for Directors and Commissioners of Companies*), the most frequently reprinted Dutch manual for the establishment and administration of societies and limited companies. It was written by C. Weststrate and G.H.A. Grosheide, a lawyer and a law professor. The content and style are rather formal and impersonal and do not principally differ from those of the majority of the English and German parliamentary manuals.

Also in 1934 the first fully specialized Dutch meeting manual *Een vergadering leiden* (*Chairing a Meeting*) was published, penned by the publicist and radio broadcaster, Dr P.H. Ritter jr. Ritter covered the same series of official rules which other writers of parliamentary manuals had done. However, the way in which he did this was somewhat exceptional. Ritter referred to a meeting as 'a small society in which, just like every society, a number of practical norms must be adopted, so as not to descend into chaos' (p.15). He particularly understood parliamentary manners as falling under these norms. Such were quorum regulation, the constructing and applying of the agenda, the opening, the taking of minutes, the calling to order when digressing from the subject, the number of times the word may be given concerning a subject, the way of submitting and the order of dealing with motions and amendments, the confirmation of a personal fact, the voting procedure, the interruptions, the adjournment of the debate, the suspension of the meeting, the interruptions to order, the regulation to stand while speaking, the maintenance of order and the allocation of speaking times. In covering these themes, Ritter regularly referred to the regulations of the Dutch parliament, British parliamentary practice, and the standard procedures employed by local councils.

In Ritter's manual old instructions are revitalized. Thus according to Ritter, it frequently occurred that individuals presented long-winded, unclear, overcomplicated and presumptuous arguments:

> The essence of meetings is that everyone gets a turn to speak, stands up, addresses oneself to the chairman, and can attach a cachet of truth and decorum to a sometimes highly ridiculous speech. It is a matter of satisfying personal vanity. It makes the members more important than they are and they can talk with a weighty authority, which already has very little connection to the bare content of their speech. (pp. 35–6)

In such cases the chairman should intervene 'courteously': 'The best thing the chairman can do is to use a little humour. If he gets those who laugh on his side, he has won the case'. Ritter wrote in a more lively manner and made it quite clear that he had experienced it all personally. In this respect his book is somewhat comparable to that of the German author Paquin, although Ritter writes in a more personal and, especially more humorous, sometimes ironical, manner. Anyway, both manuals were aimed at broad layers of the population, both authors had a journalist background and wrote in a more anecdotal manner than their predecessors.

Ritter focuses upon the possibility of rising socially by chairing a society or another board which held meetings at predetermined times. As far as I am aware, Ritter's manual was the first in which this connection, between competence in meetings and the opportunity for societal success, was made explicit. The back cover of the work contains the statement that participation in meetings was 'a way towards a prominent position' and the recommendation 'allow your capability as chairman to develop further and the masses under you will elevate you'. The book begins thus: 'In these times we are so very much focused upon each other that when we attempt something, in nine out of ten cases, it means working co-operatively with others. Co-operation always leads to assembling and in very many cases to holding meetings. A meeting has to be chaired. Who will hold this function? Automatically, the eyes of all those present turn towards the man who took the initiative. Before he has realized, he has the chairman's gavel in his hand' (p. 2).

The outlines of the American, German and Dutch series of parliamentary manuals are convergent. The first authors were practising politicians, lawyers and administrators of societies or they came from a legal or political background. Later, authors also were teachers or journalists. Every one of them wrote primarily for (potential) administrators, especially presidents of societies, local councils, committees, and shareholders' meetings and, secondly, for 'ordinary' members. Generally, there is a legal character to the instructions and the explanations of them, although the authors usually promise to do their utmost to make 'no profound, legal pronouncements', but in 'the simplest way possible' answer the many practical questions which come up in club life – in discussing and voting, in drafting an agenda and taking minutes and in administrative practice. On reading the instructions as to how to hold a meeting, it is apparent that these have largely been borrowed from national parliaments, although not every title is as obvious in this respect as the subtitle of *Ich bitte ums Wort zur Geschäftsordnung!* (*I Ask Permission to Speak about the Regulations*). This subtitle runs: 'the rules of correctly chairing meetings by the most far-reaching imitation of parliamentary customs and practices'.

Differences between the national series largely run parallel to differences in the speed and the nature of the various national processes of parliamentarization. Thus the relatively late start of the Dutch series is connected with the process of 'pillarization': the peculiar way in which the lower classes were integrated within a national framework. As pointed out in the previous chapter, these classes were organized along denominational and ideological lines by leaders from bourgeois and middle-class families, who were familiar with the basic parliamentary rules. They often taught their followers orally how to behave in a parliamentary manner. The slightly rough tone which is found in some German manuals, and the particular attention to possible violent breaches of the peace which one more generally finds in German manuals, reflect the relatively late parliamentarization of the upper classes and the rather sharp class differences which existed as a consequence of long military dominance.

As far as meeting is concerned, national differences in behaviour and habits can be explained by the diverse ways in which meeting problems were solved in the central assemblies. Thus, Major Henry M. Robert noted in the introduction to his manual that:

The practice of the National House of Representatives should have the same force in the United States as the usages of the House of Commons have in England, in determining the general principles of the common parliamentary law of the land; . . . to avoid the serious difficulties always arising from a lack of definiteness in the law, every deliberative assembly should imitate our legislative bodies in adopting Rules of Order for the conduct of their business. (Roberts, 1970, p. 14)

It is to be expected that meeting manuals themselves have promoted certain national divergences in parliamentary rules and practice.

National variants in parliamentary behaviour notwithstanding, the similarities are more striking. In all manuals, there are the same type of instructions as in Bentham's book *Parliamentary Tactics* in respect to the expression of moods, emotions and affects. A central question is how to control aggressive impulses, feelings of hostility, passions and passing impulses. At this the chairperson is presented as the embodiment of 'the social constraint towards self-constraint' (Elias). Attention is focused upon the duties of the chair. These are officially to open the session by calling the members to order, to announce the business before the assembly in the order in which it is to be acted upon, to conduct the discussions, to make sure that the speakers do not digress onto subjects not on the agenda, to close the discussions at an appropriate time and to state and to put the vote if one is to be held, to announce the result of the vote, and to officially close the meeting. Another main duty of the chair is the maintenance of order:

> To restrain the members, when engaged in debate, within the rules of order; to enforce on all occasions the observance of order and decorum among the members, deciding all questions of order and to inform the assembly when necessary, or when referred to for the purpose, on a point of order or practice. (*Robert's Rules of Order*, 1880, p. 101)

One of the most difficult (and from a 'civilizational' point of view, most interesting) tasks of the chair is dealing with disorder. More attention was given to this task as the genre developed. This is obvious in *Robert's Rules of Order*. Compared to what is mentioned on this topic in the newly revised edition of 1970, sparse and careful words are dedicated to it in the 1880 edition. Apparently, in this edition preserving order was not an issue then. It became increasingly more urgent with the parliamentary mingling of more different layers of the population as a consequence of the expansion of the franchise:

> The chairman has to conduct the meeting according to parliamentary rules. It is up to him that the debates take place in correspondence to the values of the meeting and the society. He should admonish disturbers of the peace and professional wranglers, keep the quiet and not permit inappropriate interruptions and noise so as to jeopardise the smooth proceeding of the meeting. (Paquin, 1930, p. 8)

The chairman is authorized and obliged to call to order members who misuse the right to speak by employing unparliamentary expressions; when this produces no result, he is authorized and obliged to remove the right to speak from those concerned. He is authorized and obliged to ask or order those to leave who seriously misbehave in one way or another. (Weststrate and Grosheide, 1934, p. 67)

In dealing with any case of disorder in a meeting, the presiding officer should always maintain a calm, deliberate tone – although he may become increasingly firm if a situation demands it. Under no circumstances should the chair attempt to drown out a disorderly member – either by his own voice or the gavel – or permit himself to be drawn into a verbal duel. If unavoidable, however, proper disciplinary proceedings to cope with immediate necessity can be conducted while a disorderly member continues to speak. (*Robert's Rules of Order*, 1970, pp. 539–40)

Compared to the first and second quotation, the third one represents a more psychological approach of meeting problems, which has become characteristic for the genre in the last half of this century. A work which heralded this change was Ritter's manual. His most important lesson for chairmen was: 'Before you control others, you must control yourself'. The chairman had to imprint this maxim 'on his memory with illuminated letters'. Worded differently, this motto was repeated several times in the book. For instance, under the heading 'The chairman is impartial' it was stated: 'Whoever is incapable of bringing himself under control does not have the right to maintain order in a meeting. And, as a rule, he will not succeed in this, if he so tries' (p. 3). For a chairman, self-control was of the utmost importance, as:

Experience demonstrates that every meeting has the tendency to adjust its behaviour to the behaviour of the chairman. The chairman is the example for the meeting. And, in the majority of cases, the meeting reflects this example in its behaviour and its attitude. Apparently, without any reason, a meeting becomes boisterous, drowsy, or nonchalant, when the chairman is not involved with heart and soul and not only for show. And if the chairman becomes moody, he totally loses any authority over the meeting. (p. 29)

Under the heading 'incidents', Ritter (1934) covers the 'conflicts between members who momentarily forget that a meeting is a working entity and not a club where personal opinions can be fought out' (p. 37). If those speaking exclusively address themselves towards the chairman, the chance for conflicts to develop is lessened:

Whoever addresses the chairman, addresses the entire meeting and not just one single member. If the chairman maintains this practice, the chance of moody personal outbursts becomes immediately much smaller. Thus, the chairman does not tolerate members talking amongst themselves. . . . In spite of these preventative measures, a meeting can become heated and an interruption can act as a spark to the powder. . . . If the personal insults continue, then it is time to suspend the meeting, if only for several minutes. Then, behind the scene, the chairman can attempt to set the conflict to the side. (p. 38)

However, it is better to act before the meeting takes place. In preparing for a meeting, it could prove useful to the chairman if he were to visit the members at home, so that he knew 'the angle they were coming from' and so 'could prevent clashes during the meeting itself':

Many a person, who cannot be convinced to grant a concession about what he considers to be a matter of principle in front of a meeting, is much less adamant at home, over a cup of tea and a cigar, and prepared, without relinquishing his principles, not to place such a heavy emphasis on the matter, so that the meeting can complete its business without restraint. (p. 7)

All authors of parliamentary meeting manuals emphasized in turn that a chairman is expected to 'stand above the parties', to 'be objective towards everything which comes up in the meeting', and to 'maintain the law of the meeting'. Or, as Ritter put it: 'The chairman is the Authentic Decision-maker for all matters which are not dependent upon assessments, but upon the clarification of facts' (pp. 3 and 15). Furthermore, he should know 'all matters concerning order and procedure like the back of his hand':

An experienced secretary, who scribbles warnings or reminders on a notebook to pass secretly onto the chairman, is undoubtedly an extremely useful person. But a good chairman can do without him. He should not practice casually letting his gaze fall onto warnings but, on the whole, he should practice not having to rely on this. (p. 4)

As mentioned earlier, Ritter's manual is characterized by a personal and stylish approach to holding meetings. In subsequent parliamentary manuals, the existing rules and customs are generally presented in an anonymous and relatively legalistic manner, such as 'if a speaker uses offensive or unseemly expressions, or he disturbs the order in any way whatsoever, then the chairman calls him to order'. From 1960 onwards, within the whole genre of meeting manuals, a more differentiated approach to holding meetings became accepted. Attention was now focused on the arrangement and conduct of meetings of small groups of administrations, committees, management teams and (local) governments. This shift of attention from large, legislative and deliberative assemblies with emphasis on formal manners towards smaller meetings with emphasis on informal manners included a similar shift from the duties of the chairman towards the duties of all participants. These alterations reflect more embracing societal changes, in which holding meetings extended enormously over practically every area of the society, and meetings and meeting behaviour became more varied, more informal and more businesslike.

Meeting textbooks as modern chronicles

In the latter half of the twentieth century, a new sort of meeting manual appeared. One of the common characteristics of these books, which were usually presented as 'textbooks', was that they had been written from a social psychological perspective. They paid less attention to the formal manners and codes evolved in parliamentary practices than to informal manners; those which largely developed in administrative and company meetings and international conferences.

This new trend started in the United States, where the publication of manuals for 'parliamentary procedure' and 'public meetings' slowly began to decline in the 1940s and 1950s in favour of manuals for holding 'business meetings', 'management conferences', 'international conferences', and 'negotiations'. One of the most influential books in this genre was *Successful Conference and Discussion Techniques* by American Professor of Speech, H.P. Zelko, which was published in 1957. This book was revised in 1969 and renamed *The Business Conference: Leadership and Participation*. It is the classic of this type of book, translated into many languages such as German, Japanese and Dutch, and frequently reprinted; for example, in the Netherlands it has been reprinted thirteen times in the period from 1963 to 1993. This book is frequently referred to in this chapter.

In Germany, the number of manuals published for holding *Versammlungen* (assemblies) has sharply declined since the start of the 1960s (to none after 1983), while the number of manuals for *Konferenztechnik* (conference techniques), and particularly *Verhandlungstaktik* (negotiation tactics) increased considerably. Since 1963 in the Netherlands, no manuals have appeared in which only official parliamentary conduct is covered.

In the new meeting manuals, attention is mainly paid to the informal, not legally established rules which individuals employ or should employ in various sorts of meeting, particularly in professional and business meetings. This is already apparent from simply looking at the titles of the new American meetings textbooks: *How to Run a Sales Meeting* (1944), *Conference Leadership in Business and Industry* (1945), *Conference Guide to Basic Management Training* (1947), *Right Way to Conduct Meetings, Conferences, and Discussions* (1948), *Management Conferences; How to Run Them* (1947), *How to Plan Meetings and Be a Successful Chairman, Make Your Staff Meetings Count* (1953), *How to Hold Better Meetings* (1958). Later textbooks, European as well as American ones,

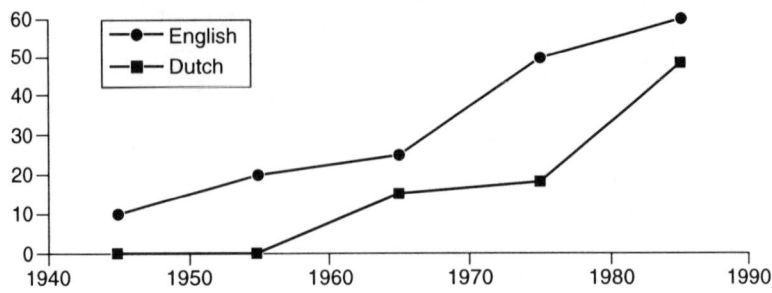

FIGURE 8.4   Number of prints and reprints of social psychological meeting manuals which have appeared in Dutch and English until 1990

have titles in the shape of 'modern meeting techniques', 'meeting and discussing', 'directed meeting methods', 'effective meeting methods', 'meeting and negotiating' and 'better business conferences'. For example, from the Dutch series it is evident that the majority of the books are primarily focused upon meetings of work organizations, and have been written for particular professional categories, such as managers, members of boards of directors, salesmen, teachers and students. Other books cover meetings in a more general sense and are intended for a broad reading public or for certain social groups and categories, such as women, members of the Reformed Church, the elderly, and those drawing social benefits. Yet again others focus upon minute taking, and there is even a manual which covers the specific difficulties of holding a meeting with people with a physical handicap.

In the Netherlands until 1990, there were about 90 editions (prints and reprints) of social psychological manuals in total; 50 different titles excluding books dedicated to the noting of the minutes.[4] In Germany, about 120 editions have appeared, in France about 50, and in the United States and the United Kingdom about 150, cautiously estimated. To give an impression of the quantitative development, the number of the second-generation books of meeting manners which have appeared in English and Dutch is given in Figure 8.4.

In this chapter, quotes will be taken from several trend-setting, often reprinted and translated books. Some were first published in the United States (especially Zelko 1957, 1969 etc. and Dunsing 1978 etc.), others in Germany (Rüdenauer 1980, 1982 etc.) and the Netherlands (especially Mastenbroek 1984, 1987, 1992 etc.). Together these books give a reliable impression of the second stage of the international genre of meeting manuals. Attention is focused on common aspects and general trends.

The arrival of social psychological, mainly company-focused meeting manuals, and this genre's explosive take-off in the 1970s and 1980s are closely related to changes in the competitive relations between states and between societal groups within states, by which the business and professional worlds became more meeting orientated, and holding meetings rapidly became more businesslike. The first new-style meeting manuals appeared in the United States in the 1940s, when collective labour agreements were made and social security was introduced. This occurred with the enlargement in scale of companies and the growing influence of the school of human relations, which considered the (informal) relations between people in companies as primary. These books were translated and imitated in European countries in the 1950s and 1960s, when a rapid expansion of co-ordinating functions took place with the pacification of the relations between European countries, the increase in international (economic) transactions, and the expansion and increase in scale of organizations. During this period, businesses remained:

> Largely national, and business success, as far as profits and sales were concerned, was translated into the growth of investments and employment in those countries in which the businesses had established their head office. . . . The expansion of businesses made the managers and owners of these businesses more dependent upon their employees. In contrast, employees were less dependent on their employers due to the strong growth in wages and employment. (N. Wilterdink, 1993, p. 24)

As far as meetings are concerned, these developments were translated into a rapid and largely unanticipated extension of the number of meetings and meeting levels, not only *within* but also *between* states and companies. One saw the development of meeting units, such as NATO and Warsaw Pact, the establishment of the United Nations and the arrival of continental-scale consultation and negotiation centres like the European Community for the economic regulation of developments in areas such as agriculture, trade, industry, and transport. Within states, the consultations rapidly multiplied between different administrative levels (local, regional and national), and the decision-making processes became less transparent and more difficult to control for the elected representatives and the central administrators.

Likewise, within businesses and other work organizations, an enormous expansion took place as regards the holding of meetings. In his research *Work and Authority in Industry* (1956), Reinhardt Bendix pointed out that, since the 1930s and 1940s, a rapid and largely unforeseen increase had taken place in the number of meetings and meeting levels in American companies: 'Weekend meetings for middle management and supervisors, evening dinner meetings, regular staff meetings at all levels' (Bendix, 1974, p. 321). In 1957, Zelko wrote: 'We have come face to face with the fact that the work scene is a part of the total social and democratic environment of a democracy, no less important as a medium for the discussion process than the legislative hall or the club meeting. . . . Since the work environment strikes so close to the well-being of all of us, we might examine more fully the part that discussion plays in the business world of today' (1957, p. 7). The rapid, unplanned increase in meetings and meeting levels in work organizations of various kinds has prompted, in consideration of costs, the search for more efficient and more effective meeting manners. This search began in the United States in the 1940s. Zelko reported that:

> Business and industrial organisations, and government agencies, have so well recognised the uses and values of the conference method that training in conference leading has become a major training objective. Of some 150 companies and government agencies in one major survey, more than 65 per cent said that they had in operation conference training programs to equip supervisors to hold conferences. Among the many outstanding programs are those conducted by Esso Standard Oil, Johnson & Johnson, General Electric, du Pont, International Harvester, General Motors, many government agencies, and a host of others. (1957, p. 11)

The oldest written business source about meetings, to which Zelko (1957) refers, is *Conference Leadership Training*. It was published in 1947 by the training centre of Esso Standard Oil Company in New Jersey. Whether or not this was the first business publication about meetings in the United States remains a question (and a point to consider in later research).

One of the first European companies to review meetings from the point of view of costs was the Dutch multinational chemical company, AKU, later to be known as Akzo Nobel NV. In 1958, a little over ten years after the Esso publication in the United States, this company published a pamphlet entitled *Efficient Meetings*, which started with the words: 'The AKU is probably not the only enterprise where meeting has slowly become a problem. There are so many meetings that one wonders, "Are they all really necessary?". A far weightier question is that of the purpose of the meeting, even when the necessity for the meeting is obvious.' Referring to the results of previous research into meetings in 100 Dutch companies, the writers of the pamphlet point out that 'after the Second World War, there began a steep rise in the number of organized company discussions within the enterprises. This growth was gradual, but it did develop in almost all of the researched companies, showing the strongest growth in the largest companies'. In the pamphlet was a short report about the effort that AKU had exerted to streamline meetings within the concern of making them more efficient. All the chairmen and secretaries of the operating workgroups and committees were called together to make them aware of 'the costs that AKU meetings carried', and then to get them to discuss in groups the possibilities for shortening the time spent in meetings by holding meetings that were more directed. The suggestions and comments which came from these group discussions were, after a forum discussion, written as *A Guide to Meetings* (Sweers & Deffelen, 1958). The *Guide* covers questions and complaints, such as: Why is there not a good agenda? Why do I get bogged down with all sorts of matters which I would have preferred to have had a chance to think about beforehand, or which I would have preferred to make my mind up about after consulting my colleagues? The preparation is frequently insufficient, so there is no chance for a fruitful discussion. The detailing of the points on the agenda is frequently too brief and unclear. The chair is no good: in discussions speakers digress from the subject; several people talk at the same time; the participants speak or put their points unclearly; the topic is only relevant to a small section of those attendant; the meeting does not come to any conclusion, and everyone goes home without really knowing what had been decided about any specific point.

A recurring complaint emanating from the group discussions was the deficient way in which meetings were chaired, while 'whether a meeting expired to be good or bad depended, on many occasions, on how the chairman conducted the meeting'. The pamphlet reiterated that 'the question of training chairmen was so incredibly important simply because chairmen of company discussions were nearly always chosen mainly due to their position in the hierarchy of the company and not so much for their ability as a chairman'. The *Guide to Meetings* gives guidelines as to the participation, the invitation, the organizing of an agenda, the preparation, the chairing, the questioning, the use of language, the coming to a conclusion, the arguments for and against the cases, the taking of the minutes and the follow up. There follows a few comments made about this: 'Do not allow the discussion to become emotional; prevent anyone (including yourself) monopolizing the discussion.' And: 'Phrase emotionally laden words in a "neutral" manner, which simplifies an objective assessment of the reasoning and its actual worth becomes more evident.'

These instructions for 'civilized' behaviour demonstrate that the duties of company managers had moved from directing the distribution of tasks and checking how they were carried out to chairing and attending meetings in which representatives from various departments and administrative levels discussed and determined future projects and the issues accompanying it. When previously a boss had directed the distribution of tasks, this was now done by holding a team meeting chaired by a director or manager. Executive and meeting skills began more and more to coincide, which implied that those higher placed had to have more consideration for the wishes and feelings of subordinates, and that they had to have more control over their tendency towards self-elevation, and also that those lower down the ladder could give better expression to their feelings and wishes.

During the accelerated development of meeting activities in the past 50 years, all sorts of difficulties and problems arose which psychologists began to investigate. A new scientific community was developing: that of social psychologists, and other researchers from 'the small group'. Initially in the United States, and then in Europe, individuals emerged from the ranks of these specialists, who systematically sought for solutions to problems which went hand in hand with the increased meeting contacts between people of different societal classes and groups. The solutions they found were spread by manuals and training sessions in which people discussed and decided on how to arrange and hold meetings (i.e. meetings about meetings). The research referred to by the new meeting specialists was generally conducted 'in a manner analogous to research in the physical sciences, such that certain factors are held constant whilst others are varied to observe what actually occurs in a certain discussion' (Koekebakker, 1956, p. 7). Therefore, the research reports by social psychologists, and the statements and the lessons in the meeting manuals which are based upon them, can be considered as modern chronicles, as contemporary historiography (Gergen, 1973). They report the manners which contemporary western people, originating from the middle and higher classes, employ during meetings, and the solving of the problems which are encountered.

However, this is not the whole story. In comparison to their juridical predecessors, who more or less only passed on what was common at higher meeting levels, there was more elbowroom for social psychologists to introduce their own 'scientific' insight and rules. The altered power and dependency relationships can explain the fact that, as relative outsiders, they could, with approval of the management, concern themselves with meetings within companies and other work organizations and could function as go-betweens or referees by appealing to 'psychological universals'. Writing about Socrates' search for moral truth in his study, *Nihilism and Culture*, Goudsblom comments that whenever the distance between people, based on suspicion, enmity, and hierarchical relationships, actually becomes smaller, and individuals start to be involved in frequent contact with dissenters, 'a need arises for some mutual understanding, common points of departure, and possibly for a higher truth which cancels out the original differences of opinion' (1977, p. 183). Seen from this point of view, the development and spread of the new, social psychological approach to meetings and meetings behaviour can be explained as an expression of an acceleration in social integration. In this process groups of people with different opinions and societal backgrounds have to get along with each other, and the need grows for 'generally applicable principles to which all opinions could be subjected' (*ibid.*).

An upper class of professional chairmen

The upper classes of the industrial countries in Europe and North America have not become more clearly distinguished in anything than they have in their meeting behaviour. The everyday work of politicians and civil servants is dominated almost entirely by discussing, deliberating, negotiating and deciding in groups. If they do not actually participate in meetings, they are preparing the meetings or processing the results of them. Many, especially those at the top, have to live under extreme 'meeting pressure'. When Eisenhower was president of the United States, it was only after he had had two heart attacks that he received permission from his advisors for one meal per week free from meetings. The remainder of his extremely long working days was practically entirely full with activities concerning meetings, conferences, and other group discussions.

In European countries, holding meetings has received sharp stimulation with the formation of the European Community. At the top of the national meeting pyramids new meeting fora have been erected, from the European Council and the Council of European Unity to the European Commission and the European Parliament and all the accompanying, continuous, official discussions. Politicians, ambassadors, diplomats, civil servants, and others directly involved with the European integration process, are under extremely high pressure as far as meetings are concerned. In the Council Buildings in Brussels everyday, 3000 to 4000 officials from national capitals attend meetings (Fiona Hayes-Renshaw and Helen Wallace, 1997, p. 70). And that only concerns meetings of one European entity, the Council of Ministers.

In all western industrialized countries, company managers have begun to allocate more and more time for meetings. The higher the individual is in the hierarchy, the more the number of meetings. Research from the start of the 1960s among chief executives in the United Kingdom and the Netherlands indicates that members of boards, chief executives and departmental heads of huge, large and medium-sized concerns spend 30 to 50 per cent of their time in all sorts of meetings (Luijk, 1963, pp. 7, 69). Several hundred directors from primarily private Dutch companies were asked how much time they generally spent on meetings during courses into meeting practices given by myself between 1995 and 1997. According to their own reckoning, those managing companies of fewer than ten personnel spent at least 10 per cent of their time preparing, executing and concluding meetings, while those managing organizations with more than 500 personnel spent up to 75 per cent (sometimes even more) of their working time on these activities. In his survey of research into what managers actually do, as well as in his own research into the work of five chief executive officers in large organizations, Mintzberg points out that, in the United States at the start of the 1970s, nearly 60 per cent of a manager's time was spent in meetings. Schwartzmann quoted the researchers McCall, Morrison, and Hannan, who concluded that 'meetings consume more of a manager's time than any other activity' (1989, p. 56). Above all, from research, it seems that managers consistently underestimate the time they spend in meetings, whereas they consistently overestimate the time they spend reading and writing. This may be seen as an example of Elias's observation that people of this highly individualized society are inclined to overestimate thinking above speaking (Elias, 1991, p. 65). Group activities are usually lower valued than individual ones. Bargiela-Chiappini and Harris, who wrote a comparative study about meetings in a large Italian-British telephone company, concluded that meetings were the essence of managerial practice and the corporate communication process. They wrote:

> A link could be established between the consistency in understimating time spent on meetings and the implicit and explicit expressions of scepticism or boredom vis-à-vis this practice registered during our company visits. This consideration may become an important one when trying to understand the role played by meetings in situations of strategic and/or cultural change, where high levels of uncertainty are counterbalanced by an increase in the number of meetings at all company levels in order to maintain a semblance of status quo. (1997, p. 30)

It is possible to go a step further in one's explanation of the reason why meetings have become a grind and are often associated with boredom and dullness. In present organizations, meetings often seem to have similar functions as etiquette had in the French court society, as described by Norbert Elias (1969). Courtiers gathered on set places and at set times to perform specific acts according to exact rules. They bitterly complained about these useless rituals, but went through them again and again. The court etiquette endured as a 'ghostly *perpetuum mobile*' because of the current power relationships between the most important social groupings. The slightest modification of a ritual might have been interpreted by a group or faction as an attempt to upset the shaky social power balance. In the same way contemporary 'organization men' seem to be socially fated to meet and to meet again with the same colleagues on set places and at set times to perform similar acts every time. In our society, power, status and property are largely being distributed in and through meetings to an unprecedented degree. Whoever is not a professional sportsperson, artist, film star, pop star or entrepreneur on a boom market and yet is willing to advance societally, has hardly any option but to climb the meeting ladder in a (large) organization.

Meetings lend themselves very well to exploring, describing and explaining alterations in the (power) relationships between and within social groups. It is possible to form a sharper picture of the social stratification in our society by studying who how often hold meetings with each other, in what manner and about what items they are talking and deciding, how some meetings determine the agendas of other meetings, etc. Boden writes: 'Meetings are the proper arena of organizational activity for management, locating and legitimating both individual and institutional roles. Indeed, the world of work may appropriately be divided into those organizational members who routinely attend meetings and those lower-echelon members whose duties tie them to the clerical desk or factory floor' (Boden, 1994, p. 81). However, there are many corporations in which workers at the lowest organizational levels have to attend regular meetings to talk about their daily tasks and evaluate them. Such is, for instance, the case in many Japanese companies. In France, Germany, the Netherlands, Belgium, Scandinavia and many other European countries, work organizations are often legally obliged to establish elected workers councils with parliamentary-like functions.

The time that a person spends meeting and preparing meetings is closely connected to the number of people that he or she has under his 'span of control'. Thus, in an enquiry conducted in a middle-sized distribution company by the author, it appeared that the amount of working time spent on meetings rose from a few per cent on the shop floor to a good 50 per cent at the highest management level. This trend is noticeable in all of the industrialized state societies. Thus, it appears from a series of American research that 'as one moves up the organizational hierarchy, the time spent in meetings increases' (Schwartzman, 1989, p. 57). With reference to this, the comment was made that 'this may be punishment for advancement in the system' (ibid.). However, this fact should be taken more seriously. Meetings fulfil different functions at every hierarchical level for the participants. Thus, in 1959, Melville Dalton commented in his study, *Men Who Manage*, that in meetings one sees the interplay of formal and informal systems in organizations.

> Right down the hierarchy one finds meetings a stage for exploratory skirmishes; for making authoritative hints to those moving too fast in one direction; for studies of faces and inflections; for catching slips and checking on pre-meeting tips, etc. The formal meeting is a gallery of fronts where aimless, deviant, and central currents of action merge for a moment, perfunctorily for some, emotionally for others. All depart with new knowledge to pursue variously altered, but rare the agreed courses. (Dalton, 1957, p. 227)

Conferences of various kinds have become important meeting places in (work) organizations. In large organizations, personnel are also 'assessed' regarding their behaviour during meetings. Due to personal capacity in meetings, someone may be seen in a favourable light, and thus has more chance for promotion and rising within the hierarchy. In consideration of this, it is somewhat surprising that professionals, in depicting organizations, for the most usually disregard meetings. To obtain a practically more adequate representation of an 'organization', it is insufficient to only look at the (hierarchical) relationships between individuals. These are just some examples of relevant questions that come up when one puts meetings and meeting behaviour in the centre of organization studies. Organization is normally treated as something concrete, as a thing, but in fact, it is a social activity and process. Who thinks of 'organizing' instead of organization soon enough comes across meetings. Thus, studying meetings and meeting behaviour is a strategic means of approaching the dynamics of organization. Studying the complicated regimes of meetings in which, and by which, an organization is continually shaped would be more important. How have these networks been structured, layered, and subdivided? In which direction have they developed and how did the accompanying meeting manners and the meeting behaviour change at different levels? How did meeting activities change when an organization grew or shrank; if the external market became more dynamic and more complex, or even more stable and simpler? Oddly enough, so far, little use has been made of the possibility to study and enlighten organizations by answering such questions, save attempts by Schwartzman (1989), Boden (1994) and Bargiela-Chiappini and Harris (1997) and some other ethnomethodologists. However, none of these authors crosses the threshold of 'hodiecentrism' (see Epilogue).

Also noteworthy are some older studies. One of them is *Work and Authority in Industry* by Reinhardt Bendix. In this book, which appeared for the first time in the 1950s, Bendix commented that with the spread of meeting activities in companies, an upper layer of 'moderate businessmen' had emerged; 'even-tempered when others rage, brave when others fear, calm when others are excited, self-controlled when others indulge' (Bendix, 1974, p. 332). Also, others have pointed out that the management of large industrial concerns had moved from consisting of owners–cum–capitalists, usually the founders of the concern, to consisting of a new group of managers who had gained a position in the company due more to their abilities than to their possession of stocks (Heilbroner, 1977, p. 140). William M. Whyte (1957) has designated these changes as the arrival of the 'organization men'. He wrote:

> For a young man on the make there is no better vehicle than the conference way. Where fifty years before he might have to labor unseen by all but his immediate superior, now via the conference he can expose himself to all sorts of superiors across the line of command. Given minimum committeemanship skills, by an adroit question here and a modest suggestion there, he can call attention to himself and still play the game. (William H. Whyte, 1957, p. 152)

Around the turn of the century, the sociologist, Thorstein Veblen (1953) had already advanced the idea of 'organization men' in his proposal that a leisured class would form an idle class of company owners, which would leave the practical operation of the firm to a 'soviet of engineers'. In a study of 1941, James Burnham predicted both a managerial revolution in which company directors would take over the authoritative power concerning the means of production and the division of wealth from the owners–cum–capitalists, and that politicians would lose more and more power to official bureaus and their directors. Fifty years on, it can be stated that no 'revolution of directors' has taken place , but that a professional meeting regime had established itself in states and companies. As the number of meetings and meeting levels within and between states spread enormously, a new upper layer formed, consisting of managers who delegated, co-ordinated, and controlled functions by means of meetings in which they were more often *primi inter pares* than they were 'commanders' or directors.

In his explanation of the changes which occurred in the attitudes, performance and ideas of managers of American companies since the 1930s, Bendix focused attention upon a notable correspondence with the process of courtization of warriors which was outlined by Elias:

> I suggest that the changeover from the idealisation of the 'strenuous life' to the idealisation of 'human relations' may be an adaptation of a similar kind. The manners commended by the personnel experts of modern American industry certainly facilitate the co-operation which management requires, much as the commendation of polite manners facilitated peace at the Royal Court. . . . The calm eyes which never stray from the other's gaze, the easy control in which laughter is natural but never forced, the attentive and receptive manner, the well-rounded, good-fellowship, the ability to elicit participation and to accomplish change without upsetting relationships, may be so many devices for personal advancement when the man is on his way up. (Bendix, 1974, p. 335)

The ability and the attitude, which, according to Bendix, are characteristic of 'moderate businessmen' or managers, developed during the mainly unplanned spreading of meeting activities and negotiations in, and between, complex company organizations, by which people from the lower levels of the population and women could take part in meetings. In a summary of the historical, psychological study entitled *Anger*, Peter Stearns and Carol Zisowitz-Stearns commented:

> From the late 1920s into the 1950s, American corporations devoted attention and expense to retraining sessions for foremen, in order to replace bullying style, and to personality tests in order to winnow out ill-tempered candidates in the first place. . . . Secretaries, male and female, were now probed not just for honesty and reliability – the late nineteenth century clerical virtues – but also for temper control. (1993, p. 59)

Such behaviour demands can be found over and over again in meeting manuals; the following examples are illustrations of this:

> Your physical listening manner should be animated and expressive. Listeners as well as speakers can be animated. Animation should show in your face, in your

eyes, and in your physical bearing. . . . Sloughing in a chair, leaning on elbows, supporting chin on hand, or playing with a pencil are not the habits of a good listener. (Zelko, 1969 (1957), pp. 137–8)

People should always have the impression that there is seated the man who undoubtedly has control of the meeting. You do not give this impression if you are nervously looking around. In contrast, it is of the most paramount importance that you CALMLY LOOK AT the people in the meeting. . . . Obviously, you have to divide your attention. Never fix onto a person or specific object, but let your focus STRAY. (Dekker, 1969, pp. 8, 9)

You must know your physical state as well as possible; that you know when you are having one of your 'good' days or one of your 'bad' days. Your conference partners will be no different. When you know that they are having one of their strong or weak moments, you can adjust your conference tactics accordingly. (Rüdenauer, 1982, p. 946)

The ideal is an attitude that is relaxed, yet alert, at the same time. Try to get your presence to radiate a 'we' feeling, in the sense of 'how do *we* sort this *out* together'. (Mastenbroek, 1993, p. 50)

The societal significance of the forms of conduct which were developed in company meetings and other work organizations has increased even more with the extension of the international market, the growth of world trade and capital exchanges and the expansion of companies. Nico Wilterdink has pointed out that since the 1970s 'directors of large enterprises and owners or managers of large amounts of capital were more detached from their nation and, due to this, were less dependent on the employees and the government of a particular national society' (1993, p. 27). With the 'strengthening of interdependencies in international relations and the weakening of national interdependencies' employees and national governments have become more dependent upon large enterprises and executives and not vice versa (*ibid.*, p. 28). This increase in power, which was demonstrated by an enormous rise in the incomes of directors and owners of large companies, is in direct contrast to the simultaneous struggle towards less hierarchical organizations in which more and more duties are delegated to relatively small business units that work as independently as possible and which are, furthermore, simultaneous meeting units. It is to be expected that, with production processes becoming more complicated and more vulnerable in social as well as material respect, this latter trend will continue and, with progressive integration at continental and worldly levels, will be a hindrance to further increases in income differences (*ibid.*, p. 35).

In conclusion, it can be said that ability in applying company-like or businesslike meeting manners has become much more significant for having a chance for societal success in terms of income, power and prestige. Both the development of meeting regimes of work organizations, and the increased chance for societal advancement via meeting activities, are the circumstances for the continuous growth in the supply of company-directed meeting manuals and the increasing public interest in such books since the 1950s and 1960s. The development of the meeting behaviour of executives and company directors can be considered as a phase in the formation of a new upper class who were compelled to consider more aspects of more people in order to maintain their position of power. Viewed from this perspective, the second-generation meeting manuals were the vehicles which passed on the central forms of conduct and manners of the new upper class in particular. From this series of books, one can expect to gain more insight into changes in the relationship between power and behaviour.

Psychologization and sociologization of meeting behaviour

Experimental research in the field of the small group was the area of science which first used meetings on a relatively large scale as 'testing grounds' for a variety of theoretical models, and as an activity for research into phenomena such as the power of groups and group norms to determine the behaviour of members; leadership style and its effects on group productivity and member satisfaction; interpersonal power and the effect of social networks on communication within groups; co-operation and conflict in groups; and structural effects such as group size, room size and interpersonal proximity on group performance and productivity (Schwartzman, 1989, p. 50).

Social or group psychologists were primarily interested in meetings in order to study the nature of groups as a general phenomenon and to develop more effective ways to study groups. In an article on meetings, published in 1960, group psychologist Professor J. Koekebakker pointed out:

> A blossoming of types of discussions after the Second World War, which obligated many of adjustments. In companies, there were nuclei, executive boards, staff meetings, and many internal forms of talks. In club life, activities were federated, co-ordinated, and internally differentiated and, through this, came countless people and countless meeting tables. In the administrative world of lesser and higher governments, plans were laid, laws were prepared, and reorganisations were planned and, through this, new large groups entered into meeting activities. By no means everyone who participated in this blossoming of meetings was ready for fulfilling a similar societal function. Generally, neither one's ambition nor one's training were directed at meetings. Thus, those involved were not spared the frustrating introduction period. And the technique of meeting irregularly, which

necessarily characterised these poorly manned committees, etcetera, offered insufficient opportunity to learn professional meeting conduct well. (1960, p. 153)

Posing the question whether 'the participants' satisfaction with meetings could be raised by a greater adherence to the meeting rules by chairmen and assessors', Koekebakker delves into 'the psychological backgrounds of the difficult procedure for cultivating good meeting habits'. He points out that meeting problems which are due to a training deficit could be helped by studying modern manuals for meeting and discussion techniques and by participating in courses in meetings; those which 'particularly took root in circles of industry' where, bearing in mind a rise in returns from meetings, great value was attached to 'efficient communication and clear discussions' (pp. 154–5). Then he named several training methods developed in the United States. They were directed at becoming conscious of 'more deeply ankered processes and hidden motives which played a role in meeting activities' and on the enlargement of the 'safety of the group' or the 'focus of the group', through which the participants in meetings and discussions were charged with 'seeing through the facade of group activities and to learn to feel what is going on behind the scenes as regards feelings, expectations, and disappointments' (p.156). In such group training all sorts of emotions, intentions and tactics come to light which are pushed aside in the normally functioning committee. People learn 'to understand why people at certain stages can not progress further, branch off at a tangent, are threatened to be dominated by certain members. Every member discovers for himself, often precisely through the great openness, however much he can misjudge the situation, apply certain tactics himself, block others' (ibid.).

This change is an example of the 'emancipation of the emotions', that Wouters thought characteristic of the process of informalization which accelerated in the 1960s:

> In the status competition, the control of emotions and self-knowledge acquired a heavier influence in respect to other criteria such as background, education, profession, and income. The fine line between forms of conduct . . . were made greater: the number of acceptable and respected behavioural and emotional variations and nuances increased between the boundaries of continuing and shutting up, and between the extremes of being too direct (rude) and too cautious (shy). (1990, p. 173)

At the end of his article, Koekebakker investigates further the meaning of the phenomenon of the 'hidden agenda' or the operation of a tacit aim. He points out that meeting behaviour is pre-determined for a large part and becomes highly complicated by absent 'third parties', upon whom the meeting participants are dependent:

Lack of co-operation, obscurity in ways of expressing, hesitancy, etcetera, are a number of the symptoms through which the invisible 'third parties' behind the scenes become knowable. There exists a heavy propensity to leave tacit these side-motives. And the obscurity which therefore develops through this makes good discussions and the striving towards solutions extremely difficult. Clashes in interest are simply little appreciated in our society. And the 'agreement to disagree' is a stage difficult to reach in the present-day pattern of discussions. (p. 158)

According to Koekebakker, people in groups' training can learn the role of the invisible men, and to recognize the clash of interests which they represent, and to bring them into the light and win over their 'conflict anxiety', so that people see the existing opposition 'realistically':

Without doubt, more conscious experience in and with groups teaches people to be able to handle more conflicts and to be more creative in finding solutions than they tend to consider possible. Generally, this means problematic delving into areas where the weight becomes unbearable. But this difficult preparation is the actual price that people have to pay for a society in which everyone is able to follow any direction as much as they please as their right. (Koekebakker, 1960)

These latter passages highlight the fact that meeting activities not only demand more self-knowledge but also more social knowledge or awareness about the more and more complicated societal 'game' in which the meeting takes place. In other words, meeting activities and writing about them have become not only more 'psychological' but also more 'sociological'. Koekebakker's article bears witness to a rapid extension in the number of meetings and levels of meetings, which was coupled with both an increase in pressure during meetings to take more people into consideration, and with a greater opportunity to express feelings, expectations and disappointments. These developments can be interpreted as an expression of the accelerated processes of integration and differentiation, during which the power differences between social groups diminished. While life became safer and more prosperous for many, opportunities for emotional outbursts and threats diminished, the fear of conflicts lessened and mutually anticipated self-control increased. These socio-psychological changes can also be observed in the meeting books genre.

The last Dutch parliamentary manual *Verenigen en vergaderen* (*Societies and Meetings*) appeared in 1963. The authors, J. Boer and A. Hijmans, refer to 'a pervasive dissatisfaction with the way in which the activities of coming together and meeting are generally conducted in contemporary society' (p. 7). They point out that 'at all levels of the complicated present-day society at local, provincial, national, and extremely heavily at international level like the EEC, entirely different types of meeting practices developed than were common in traditional in associations':

These are directed towards tentative exploration, through researching objections that have been made, and through closely distinguishing between what can and what can not be altered in the opinions thus far contributed, to determine the limits within which discussion, co-operation, or co-ordination appears possible. . . . This way of conversing and discussing, which is apparently necessary at all levels in today's complicated world, is far removed from the strongly rational straightforward meeting technique, which has survived in its old form from associations, where people met to take decisions with a majority of fifty percent plus one!! Fundamentally these new types of meeting are definitely no less democratic than the old tried and trusted types. Predominantly they bear witness to a refinement in methods, which had become necessary in the complicated world of today. Sometimes apparently irreconcilably opposing opinions can be brought together without compulsion and with complete respect for mental freedom. (pp. 100–1)

Shortly after, the international genre of meeting manuals was deeply affected by the development of these new meeting practices. This was most obviously expressed by the fact that informal meeting rules and codes took over the central position of the formal parliamentary rules. Zelko (1969) explained this as follows:

Parliamentary procedure and motions should be avoided in reaching decisions in most conferences. Parliamentary procedure is the most formal method a group can use, and conference process is based primarily on informal methods. Some informal conference processes do involve controls, but not in the rigorous and exacting sense that prevails under parliamentary procedure. . . . Parliamentary procedure imposes a degree of formality on the conduct of the discussion which does not allow for the informality, spontaneity, and permissiveness we strive for in the conference and in other types of informal discussion meetings. . . . Members should feel free to speak up and make contributions at any time, without recognition by the chair or first indicating their desire to speak. This allows for free spontaneous exchange of ideas approaching the informality of conversation and interpersonal relations. . . . The conference-room objective is to find the will of the group while keeping group unity, as much as possible without identifying the minority, and while giving the greatest possible atmosphere for free and informal participation. (Zelko, 1969 (1957), pp. 162–3)

The most important difference between formal and informal meetings, as seen by Zelko and others, refers to the manner of turn taking; to the extent to which turn taking is directed by and restricted through the chairperson. In more formal meetings, 'speaker selection depends on the chairperson, who has both rights and obligations in relation to the assembled members and the purpose of the meeting. The Chair attends to the agenda, taking points of order and information, guiding both discussion and speaker order, and generally maintaining order and temporal pacing' (Boden, 1994, p. 86). In more informal meetings, the way in which members take their turns and make it possible for others to take theirs (asking questions, soliciting advice, clarifying issues, expounding opinions, creating and resolving conflicts), bears closer resemblance to the manner in which people usually take turns during everyday conversations:

> Your interpersonal relationship with each other member differs little from any ordinary day-to-day contact, but conference relationships are multiplied and made more complex because of all the cross currents and the pyramiding of feelings and reactions that can develop in a group. One who has developed an understanding of and liking for people, who has a friendly and sympathetic attitude in his general dealings with others, and who habitually respects the thoughts and feelings of others will find that all these attributes are applicable in the conference. (Zelko, 1969 (1957), p. 129)

The replacement of formal parliamentary rules with more informal businesslike meeting manners can at first be examined further with the help of a Dutch meeting manual, entitled *Mr. Chairman . . .* (1962). Besides the usual explanation of the parliamentary rules, this transitional book contains a part written by the political scientist, W. Langeveld. He approached meeting activities in a manner which has finally become typical for the whole international genre. Not surprisingly his article drew its inspiration from recently published American literature concerning group dynamics and meeting techniques. It is largely a summary and application of the new ideas and ideals carried out in this socio-psychological literature. Furthermore, there is much reference to relevant German literature. Not being a very original work, it represents the state of affairs within the international genre of meeting manuals at the beginning of the 1960s.

As is to be expected, it is not the application of the official parliamentary procedures that is central in Langeveld's approach, but the informal rules of group talks and group discussions. According to the author, associations need to find outcomes where everyone agrees by means of discussions in small groups called 'talk-work groups'. The groups should not be larger than twelve to fifteen people who preferably sit in a circle around a table, so that the chairman can maintain visible contact with all of the members:

> Discussion is actually necessary before a group makes a decision – and meeting is therefore necessary and useful providing the talks are kept as short as possible and everyone has the actual feeling that during the discussion something is being 'done'. To be able to attain this, anyone who leads the meeting in any way has to be cognisant of the techniques which are applicable in the 'talk-work group'. (p. 120)

The author considers group discussions to be exceptionally applicable for administrative meetings of associations. 'An administrative meeting aims to reach certain results by a discussion where everyone comes to an agreement.' An administration does not need to debate, but to discuss:

> In a debate, everyone gives their opinion about a certain matter – whether or not from the perspective of one's philosophy of life – and a decision is taken by majority. In a discussion, people work their way towards each other. It is precisely in an administration that voting has to be avoided as much as possible. Talking should continue until there is agreement. The chairman is the go-between in this. (pp. 122–3)

Langeveld focused attention more upon the forms of conduct in administrative and committee meetings than upon those in general assemblies. This change of focus was closely related to the increase in social mobility and the expansion of associations, through which the number of administrative duties rose greatly, the composition of the administrative personnel changed faster, and members of the administration were increasingly recruited from more varied societal classes. Due to these changes, administrations were compelled to take notice of more aspects of societal life and to hold their meetings in a more businesslike manner. The following recommendations by Langeveld also refer to this.

According to Langeveld, 'every problem should be put in such a way that it creates the impression of coming from outside the group; that is to say, as business-like, objective, and impersonal as possible' (p. 123). For every item on the agenda, the chairman should make a introduction which 'outlines the matter clearly and simultaneously starts the discussion' (p. 126). Then the chairman should 'regulate the discussion', when 'he should be continuously aware that a discussion can take place at three levels in turn: the level of the duty itself, the level of the group, and at a personal level'. The main level of the 'talk-work group' concerns the level of the duty itself. But, to manage a 'duty-orientated talk' it is necessary 'that the situation is good on both of the other two levels. If there are any tensions, then the group's energy shifts to a group or personal level. The problems which are present must be solved before there can be any further progress with the matter' (p. 127). The chairman 'continually samples the mood of the group and possibly attempts to uncover any tensions that have remained hidden. Through his capacity to chair a meeting, these should be unburdened without causing any damage' (p. 128).

In comparison to meeting activities, as presented in the other manuals for associations, Langeveld's approach to meetings requires a greater degree of self-knowledge, a more active position from the participants, a greater capacity to empathize with the feelings and thoughts of others, and more nuances and more flexibility in the control of feelings and behaviour:

At the start of the discussion, it will perhaps be necessary for the chairman to maintain for a while the central position that he occupied during the introduction. Generally, he will be asked for more information by the members. With the members already in discussion, feelings of aggression and sympathy, disinterest and enthusiasm, dislike and antipathy, develop. The leader of the discussion attempts to maintain the group's balance and to prevent certain feelings getting the upper hand. He conducts the meeting and ensures that everyone participates as much as possible. . . . Gradually, the talks lift off. The discussion is no longer conducted exclusively via the chairman, but the members exchange ideas reciprocally, obviously not starting with pacts 'just between ourselves', and the chairman does not need to continuously intervene whenever someone takes the word. There is a clear working exchange between the members; there is a unique group mood and opinions are now formed. (pp. 128–30)

The development of the 'talk–work group' is part of the process to make meetings less formal. By becoming less formal, more problems become discussible, rules become less rigid and less stringently taken into consideration, more attention is paid to emotional aspects, and the stipulations in meeting manuals have less the character of what is strictly obligated and what is forbidden.

The impressions which participants had of each other became 'more psychological'. This is indicated, among other things, by the typology of meeting participants which likewise originated 'from the practice of many American discussion leaders'. He refers to the talker, the twister, the helper, the scatterbrain, the rebel, the mistaken affiliate, the provoker, the stammerer, the unknown and the silent one. In describing these 'types', he indicates 'how the chairman can approach them in a cautious way' (pp. 135–9). The writers of the old-style manuals generally only distinguished two sides, the majority and the minority, government and opposition. Any attention paid to individual meeting participants was limited. For example, Ritter refers only to 'modest' and 'rude' members; *Robert's Rules of Order* refers only to official meeting functions as 'presidents', 'elected officers' and 'committee members', while the German Paquin speaks of 'long-winded and non-stop talkers', 'disturbers of the peace' and 'professional wranglers'.

Types of meeting participants are found in all later meeting manuals. Frequently a distinction is made between types who hinder the discussion and types who aid the discussion. Usually authors assign to the first category of meeting participants: the know-alls, the arrogant, the negative person, the aggressive person, the waffler, the long-winded person, the silent person, the timid and the favourite topic holder. To the second category of meeting participants, authors assign: the organizer, the critical thinker, the animator, the reconciler, the constructor and the helper. Other writers make other distinctions, sometimes using comparisons to certain animals. In a more advanced version of types of meeting participants, which is often used in most recent manuals, variations in behaviour, such as silence, assistance, leadership, distrust and anger, are no longer considered to be characteristics of particular meeting participants, but as 'types of contributions members of a group make'. For instance, Zelko wrote,

> Every individual is not a 'typical' participant, and all do not fit into the same mold. Observation does indicate that there tends to be an approximate balance in most meetings between questions, answers, and reactions among the remarks made. In a democratic discussion process, we do not want all remarks to be positive, for we know the value of opposing and questioning remarks in shaping the best conclusions and decisions. The important thing, as far as positive and negative remarks are concerned, is to avoid intense conflict and great tension when argument develops. (Zelko, 1969, p. 127)

Such views bear witness to becoming more conscious of the dynamics of meetings. Another example is the meeting etiquette proposed by Edward de Bono. In order to 'avoid useless discussions and escalations of opposite viewpoints' de Bono distinguished six different 'manners of thinking' and coupled these to certain goals and stages of a meeting. In his manual *Six Thinking Hats* (1985), he pointed out that a white hat refers to thinking in terms of facts and numbers, a red hat refers to emotive thinking, a black one to negative, a yellow one to positive, a green one to creative and a blue one to detached thinking. Consciously choosing one of these, imaginary, 'thinking hats', meeting participants bend their mind to just one specific way of thinking and talking. According to de Bono, his method makes meetings more conciliate, more productive, more transparent and easier to conduct. His meeting etiquette is used in various big companies and multinationals, especially in East Asia and the United States. This is an instance of the recent expansion of business meetings and businesslike meeting manners on a worldwide scale.

As is evident from the meeting manual genre, not only the typology of meeting participants, but the entire manner of approaching meeting activities has been further developed in the last 50 years. Attention has shifted from general deliberative assemblies to more differentiated, namely professional and business meetings; from formal rules to informal codes; from debating to discussing; from majority decisions to consensus; from the attitude of parties, administration, and opposition to the behaviour of individual meeting participants; and from a chairman's function to the duties of ordinary meeting participants. This shift of attention can be substantiated by several quotes from meeting manuals.

The shift from formal to informal manners has been mentioned and elucidated earlier. Another more striking example is:

Robert's Rules of Order. Such rules are necessary in some kinds of large groups assembled to make decisions or recommendations. And they are required in legally constituted meetings. But in small groups, the ponderous procedures involved stymie human interaction and the flow of creativity. The rules stimulate a legalistic and mechanical way of thinking. (Dunsing, 1978, p. 29)

The shift in accent from large to small meetings and from formal to more informal meeting codes, is to be considered as an expression of the expansion and further differentiation of meeting regimes and meeting behaviour, which requires a greater impute from one's own thoughts and knowledge. Thus, it is no longer expected that the chairman mainly watches over and applies the procedures, but that he varies his leadership according to the type of meeting and knows how to control tensions and conflicts neutrally and smoothly, based on his own insight and feelings. 'Above all, the conference leader must be resourceful, systematic yet flexible, compassionate, and ready to use his own judgement rather than relying on fixed rules, mechanics, or techniques' (Zelko, 1969 (1957), p. 119).

Courteous behaviour (see the next quote) and a joke as a rapid diversion for aggressive feelings among the participants can, as before, prove useful to him. The second quote that follows emphasizes the paramount psychological approach of the chairman compared to the predominantly legalistic approach which characterized the first stage of the genre:

At the fixed time, the chairman will open the meeting. . . . Latecomers should be made to feel that they should have been on time providing this is done in a fault-finding way. . . . Prince Bernhard, who is an excellent chairman, said to a latecomer in a charming tone; 'Good afternoon sir, excuse us for starting already; we are at item three on the agenda. (Scheurer, 1969, p. 53)

The chairman's authority does not rest on the fact that he is the leader or the boss, but on the fact that he exercises a specialist function, just as his discussion partners. . . . It is his job to create a pleasant, stimulating and motivating discussion atmosphere. . . . A good chairman has self-confidence. He accepts himself including his weaknesses knowing that no one is perfect. Therefore, every one may make mistakes, including the chairman. Adopting this basic attitude, the chairman has much patience, radiates peace and quiet, is open to others and has sympathy for his discussion partners. In this manner he generates respect and sympathy. (Rüdenauer, 1982 (1980), p. 21)

Attention has shifted from chairman to participants. Everyone is considered to be responsible for good order and fair turn distribution. With this shift and the arrival of a less formal way of 'controlling order' by the chairman, the way in which a point of order is raised, has also been 'informalized':

Make or suggest making internal summaries or transitions if the leader is not doing these well, in order to keep the organisation of the discussion clearly before the group. (Zelko, 1969 (1957), p. 139)

In a meeting things are getting heated, there prevails a tense atmosphere. The chairman is so busy with the content and progress of the discussions that he does not notice it. . . . Any member that actually does notice it, can tactically help the chairman to avoid an outburst. (Knepper and Kamphuis, 1973, p. 135)

If the leader vacillates and exerts weak leadership, you may begin to 'take over' the meeting without portfolio. You can get closure on discussion, sharpen goals, call for a decision, and track group progress simply by doing it and overriding lesser voices. (Dunsing, 1978, pp. 102–3)

You can help the chairman in the exercise of his duties. For instance, 'I suppose to first define the subject, before beginning to discuss it', 'That seems to be a misunderstanding. You probably mean . . .', 'In my view the question of Mr./Mrs. B has not been answered yet'. When you dash to the help of the chairman, you do not have to ask permission to speak. (Rüdenauer, 1982 (1980), p. 27)

Generally, writers of meeting manuals point out the relationship between the degree of informality and the size of the meetings. They show a preference for meetings not larger than twenty people:

In the ideal case, a discussion between five to seven people without a chairman is very well possible. Good discussions partners are able to guide a discussion towards a commonly agreed goal and simultaneously create a productive discussion climate. (Rüdenauer, 1982 (1980), p. 29)

By calling an entire group of 30 to 40 people together to analyse a problem and to suggest a plan of action, the leader hopes to avoid insulting anyone and is assured of the support of others. But because the group is too weighty to get into action, the participants become opposed to each other when the unavoidable misunderstandings and unrealistic use of time stands in the way of any efficient business (due to the size of the meeting). (Dunsing, 1978, pp. 16–17)

It has become usual to give instructions as to the form and placing of tables and chairs, and also about the seating arrangements:

The most appropriate arrangement of table and chairs (including the shape of the table) should be considered in relation to each particular groups. Conferences are most successful when all members see each other face to face. If the group is small enough, this can best be accomplished at a round table which induces informality and tends to bring the leader into the group itself. (Zelko, 1969 (1957), p. 81)

Being able to see and hear easily is affected by the structure of the room and its furnishings. A working meeting of three to ten people is obviously unsuited to a 'theatre seating' arrangement – chairs in rows, one behind the other. The next worst possible arrangement occurs in a planned meeting room that's similar to what is called a 'boardroom'. The room is usually long and narrow. Dominating most of the space is a dark, ponderous wood table shining and smelling of lemon polish. As if this weren't 'heavy' enough, it's further buttressed by dark wall panelling, overstuffed chairs, and perhaps some paintings of glowering admired leaders (Dunsing, 1978, p. 55).

All of those present must be able to see each other well. The chairman should have a good view of the whole group. The participants should not sit too close together and should have enough room on the table for their papers. By placing name cards, the seating arrangements can be arranged beforehand if desirable. (Rüdenauer, 1982, p. 97)

In a later edition of Zelko's book, a comment has been added to the last-mentioned of his quotes, which points out that more significance is attached to the choice of furniture and the seating arrangements as the meeting becomes more precarious and more important: 'The Paris peace talks on the Vietnam War are an example of a struggle to have each participant and delegation appear equal and "integrated" (the final decision was to use a large round table).'

Considering what was written about the establishment of the British parliament and the States-General of the United Dutch Provinces in Chapter 6, it is noticeable that writers of meeting manuals generally consider a round or oval table to be the best solution, whereas the common parliamentary establishment, such as the British House of Commons, consider it as the worse choice (for example, Rüdenauer, 1982, p. 97). This advice fits the long-term trends by which people meet, and should meet, more and more peacefully and increasingly on an equal footing, and parliamentary meeting manners lose some of their model functions in favour of the more businesslike meeting manners of (global) companies.

Meeting tables, pejoratively described by Dunsing in the last quoted passage, have become the outstanding symbols of power in our industrialized world. In 1996 the photographer, Jacqueline Hassink, published the book *The Table of Power*, containing pictures of the boardroom tables of 21 of the largest European industrial companies (nineteen other companies refused to admit photographers to their board rooms for different reasons). Among them are Akzo Nobel NV, BASF AG, Daimler-Benz AG, ENI SpA, Philips

Electronics NV, Renault SA, Siemens AG, Unilever NV, Volkswagen AG. The pictures are accompanied by detailed information about size, material, designer and price of the table, the room in which it is standing, the usual table arrangement (seats of the president and the other members of the board) and some economic key figures of the company. In an epilogue, Henri Peretz points out that, indeed, 'all the table-tops shine impeccably. They are made of several kinds of wood. Warm colours predominate. The size of the table-tops is proportionate to the number of participants' (p.18). The usually oval tables are original designs, save one. 'The oval shape allows for a central point upon which all eyes can converge and which may be occupied by the president.' Just like their older brothers, the dining tables, meeting tables vary greatly according to social class, nationality and generation. 'The globalization of companies, the development of a complex hierarchy at the top and the ever stronger presence of financial power, entails a group of decision-makers located at the heart of a permanent structure. They are therefore invited to sit periodically at the tables of power' (p. 14). Another remarkable observation is, that the boardrooms are usually situated 'on the top floor of a recent building and have large bay windows, as if to show its dominance of the city or the immediate surroundings'. Older relatives of the meeting tables of big companies are the tables of (national) governments. Most of these tables are situated in richly decorated rooms in old, respectable buildings. They are at least just as much, often even more original, impressive and solemn. In sum, the tables of the current meeting classes and the earlier-mentioned book of photographs itself once more draw attention to how closely power and behaviour are related. The social development of power and interdependency relationships between people have compelled them to increasingly develop their meeting behaviour. Gradually and in the long run, chairing and attending meetings have become the pre-eminent route to power, income and status.

In comparison to their mainly juridically schooled predecessors, the writers of modern meeting manuals attach more value to holding discussions and striving towards a consensus than debating and voting. About debating and discussing:

> Debate is not discussion in the true sense, for there is no attitude of inquiry and reflective thinking about what is the best solution. The debater has made up his mind in advance, and he does all he can to advance and defend his point of view with no thought to being 'won over' by his opposition. The terms 'opposition' and 'opponent(s)' are quite common to debate. The good discussion participant rarely regards other participants as opponents even though he may be in disagreement with their points of view from time to time as the discussion progresses. (Zelko, 1969 (1957), pp. 233–4)

Debating is thinking *against* each other; on the other hand, the true group discussion should be to think along *with* each other. . . . Democratic group discussion requires a totally different, more objective attitude from the participants, who want to understand the others better, show more propensity to examine their own opinion in the light of their conference partners, and be prepared to ultimately review it. (Roels, 1967, p. 13)

And concerning voting and the struggle for a consensus:

Voting should be avoided in most conferences where group agreement is to be reached, unless it appears absolutely necessary. Voting tends to crystallize opinion and harden positions: it emphasizes the majority and minority rather than the whole group. . . . This tends to emphasize a spirit of advocacy and contention rather than the spirit of reflective inquiry and open-mindedness that we strive for in a discussion. (Zelko, 1969 (1957), pp. 161–2)

Rules relying on decision by vote create a win-lose atmosphere in which the defeated group (which may contain only one member less than half of the group) focuses on plots to get even. All responsibility devolves on the leader and the winning group, as the losers say. 'O.K., you win. Now try to make it stick.' The act of voting itself allows for glossing over many salient points and may smother budding views with potential. (Dunsing, 1978, p. 29)

After a well-guided discussion, decisions should regularly be made by common consent. This is because the participants will consider the results as their personal achievement and no one feels persuaded, taken by surprise, washed over or put under pressure. (Rüdenauer, 1982 (1980), p. 133)

Consensus is necessary in a small team, where the members are mutually responsible for certain regulations. It does happen that a team will not strive for a consensus for less weighty decisions; the search for a broadly accepted solution would cost too much time. People strive for a consensus only for fundamental decisions. (Schermer, 1991, p. 103)

Debating and voting decline. They support and promote the formation of parties on the basis of belief, ideals or philosophies of life, and increase the chance of violent, hostile, and aggressive feelings being expressed and the outbreak of arguments, which hinder an open and businesslike discussion based on facts. The second generation of meeting manuals most clearly deviates from the first with the ban on debating and voting on the basis of already-made viewpoints and the advocacy to talk to each other and to decide on the common future in a 'frank' and 'businesslike' manner. The continuity of manners and meeting manuals is demonstrated in particular by the fact that arguing and quarrelling were strongly ill-advised:

> The important thing, as far as positive and negative remarks are concerned, is to avoid intense conflict and great tension when argument develops. (Zelko, 1969 (1957), p. 128)

> Avoid emotional reactions and keep the discussions business-like and 'to the point'. As much as possible, stimulate the other party also to guard against an emotional approach. Do not get unnecessarily irritated, but remain calm, and act with propriety and friendliness at all times. (Luijk, 1966, p. 53)

> Proposals of other participants should be approached businesslike, pragmatic, and if possible, positive. They must be formulated in such a manner that the addressed person does not feel challenged or takes offence. On the contrary, the party concerned must be motivated to collaborate on the improvement of his proposal. (Rüdenauer, 1982 (1980), p. 31)

> Stop intimidation, direct and indirect. Those with bigger jobs, bigger bodies, and/or bigger mouths often lean on others to get their way. It works in football, war, and rush-hour traffic. In meetings, however, it blocks a lot of good ideas. 'Bigger' does not equal 'brighter' – a fact that the meeting leader should keep bringing up as necessary. (Dunsing, 1978, p. 112–13)

> Try to reach a stage of 'peaceful coexistence' if 'co-operation' does not (yet) seem possible. If the opposing views develop into open conflict, try to administer to these conflicts and, if possible, solve them. (Schermer, 1991, p. 151)

The instructions which appear in modern meeting manuals are largely intended to answer the question as to how the individual meeting participant and the productivity of the meeting could be increased, given the prevailing balance of power within the meeting unit. The central question is: how can someone submit their own opinion powerfully and purposefully without having this lead to violent conflicts and feelings of animosity? However, the modern meeting manuals advocate a less anxious attitude with regard to conflicts than the parliamentary, juridical manuals. People should allow themselves and others more opportunity to express their feelings (carefully and differentially). Expression of emotions should not be taboo. Weeping, screaming, being angry, are allowed in certain situations and on certain conditions, At least they should not give other participants a fright:

> Meeting leaders and participants must bear in mind that encouraging the expression of feelings will free the flow of thoughts – and suppressing or ignoring them will

filter, distort, or block thoughts. Our feelings come from basic human needs that, though now and then openly discussed, are infrequently served in meetings – or anywhere else in organisations, for that matter. (Dunsing, 1978, p. 41)

Conflicts are nothing negative. They point to problems and challenge to think of creative changes. We can consider conflicts in society as safety valves. (Rüdenauer, 1982 (1980), p. 77)

One can also try to uncover the background to the argumentative manner of conduct with each other and to see if anything can be done about it. And do not be confused by tears or shrill voices or shouting matches. It is also possible to talk to emotional people if you do not bypass their emotions. . . . Naturally, one must prevent such an emotional debate hindering the further progress of the meeting. (Schermer and Wijn, 1983, p. 158)

Feelings cannot go unrecognized and ignored in negotiations. It is also unnecessary. Feelings stimulate people into action. Feelings partially express opinions in negotiations. It is said: 'feelings are facts'. Facts must be given a place in the meeting tactics by naming them. (Ponsioen, 1988, p. 23)

Such observations and instructions reflect an informalizing process: as the power relationships became less unequal, people began to be less threatened by those feelings and behaviours, which had been loaded with anxiety and shame in earlier stages of social and psychological development in relation to tensions between social groups, classes and sects (Wouters, 1990). The controlled expression of feelings of anger, disappointment and aggression were acceptable to a certain degree in meetings on the basis of an increase in the reciprocally anticipated self-control.

In the altered attitude towards debating and voting, the expression of feelings and the starting of arguments come down to the fact that the lessening of the power differences between the classes, sexes and generations, made it necessary and possible for people to take into consideration more aspects of themselves and others in the discussions and decisions about the common future. The ideal of equality is considered of paramount importance in the modern meeting manuals. Meeting manuals propagate a way of meeting, through which people allow differences regarding age, sex, education and position to have as little influence as possible in the judging of what someone says:

Sometimes men think that women do not go deeply enough into the problem at hand; women are of the opinion that men generally talk in such theoretical terms that they are not quickly able to come up with any practical solution. Naturally, this difference in mentality is not applicable to every man and every woman. But it is for the leader of a mixed company to ensure that people accept each other not only officially but in actual fact. This means that people should, as far as possible, give each other a free rein in their approach according to their own nature. If one of the women present begins to talk without formally asking for the word, then there should be no ado made about this. (Scheurer, 1969, p. 21)

Not infrequently, participants completely orientate their behaviour towards what they think their boss expects from them, even though this attitude damages the results of the talks. Therefore, invite as few participants as possible who are too dependent and who possess hardly any administrative capabilities. (Rüdenauer, 1982, p. 96)

It is important that the more powerful participants value and respect the less powerful participants, and that they does not misuse their position to belittle others. . . . The ever-present differences in professionality or capability can cause the necessary controversy, with the consequence that people, sometimes, pay more attention to the combat than to the content of the quarrel. (Schermer and Wijn, 1983, p. 24)

The civilizing process has made people psychologically more sensitive and in some respects more vulnerable. Some authors of meeting textbooks encourage their readers to make use of this sensitivity and express certain feelings consciously and tactically in order to 'attract attention and improve the quality of one's meeting life':

Be a cantankerous participant. Squeak and chirp, complain or yell 'bull' until you shift the tide of things or until others stop and say, 'OK loudmouth, we'll take the time to look at what we're doing here'.
    Cry. It doesn't matter whether you're a man or a woman. Crying feels good when it's genuine, and it might get you the attention you want.
    Fall out of the chair or fall asleep, or both. (Dunsing, 1978, p. 103)

As people have become more 'civilized' (or grown older), they may feel quickly ashamed or embarrassed when others express emotions in a way, which they had often painfully learned to control in their childhood.

Much socio-psychological research into meetings was directed towards finding the relationship between the speed at which a group found a solution to a given problem, the presence of a more or less directive leadership style, and the satisfaction felt by the members of the group. Research results indicated that 'the productivity of a group generally was relatively low when the structure of the communication allowed no central figure to be prominent, but that the satisfaction of the members of the group was exceptionally high' (Koekebakker, 1956, pp. 7–8 and 10). This 'democratic dilemma' has become one of the central problems covered in business-directed meeting textbooks. Zelko comments:

> Theoretical conclusions drawn from such research suggest that small groups should operate in a 'democratic' and 'permissive' climate with minimum control by the leader. There is an obvious difficulty here. The degree of freedom or permissiveness suggested in theory is not normally possible in the business setting. It is for this reason that the practised business-man or professional, considering the use of the conference for a specific situation or problem, is faced with a problem. . . . The practical solution is to strike a balance. The democratic process must be controlled according to the situation and the judgement of the leader and group. (1969 (1957), p. 23)

In conclusion, it can be said that the changes in the meeting manual genre from a parliamentary-juridical approach to a psycho-sociological approach indicate a growing insecurity with regard to what belongs in a meeting and what does not belong in a meeting. 'The ambivalent character of the relationships between people has become clearer and become to be seen more as a psychological phenomenon, and there has been both an increase in the tension between impulses and the control of those impulses within oneself, and the attention to emotions and the regulation of those emotions' (Wouters, 1990, p. 51). This change was closely connected with the decline in the direct threat of war, and the lesser risk of poverty, sickness, and ignorance, the lessening the power differences and the decline of societal tensions and oppositions within states

As security, prosperity and social mobility rose, and more people were compelled to hold meetings, the party-political and socio-economic contrasts have lost their edge. The struggle towards revolutionary changes by advocates from lower classes of the population ebbed and, with it, the anxiety of the established groups has decreased about both people from these classes, and for the behaviours and feelings that were associated with these classes. People from different classes, from both sexes, and from more varied ages, began to meet each other more often and more regularly at higher levels of meeting than previously. In these meetings, they could express their feelings more freely (within the limits fixed by the balance of power). It became less dangerous for one's position and prestige to do so, and it was reciprocally expected that the necessary self-control would be employed and there would be no misbehaviour. As the social tensions and ideological contrasts declined, the picture that meeting participants formed of each other became more 'psychological' and more 'sociological'; in other words, more variegated and freer from brief emotions, and more tuned to the power and dependency relationships between people. After the establishment of the parliamentary norms and rules in the social habitus of people, and with the further reduction in the risks of being conquered and humiliated, a more differentiated regulation of behaviour and emotions became possible and necessary. In a recent meeting manual, W.F.G. Mastenbroek describes these changes in a sharp and short manner:

> More and more people are compelled to negotiate through the altered power and dependency relationships in the networks which they are part of. The most recent stage in this development is that we have been compelled towards a flexible and informal style of negotiating; a style which fits well into the relationship pattern of greater mutual dependency. Therefore, we were compelled into informal behaviour. Such an informal style provided advantages and quickly became prevalent over a more cautious and formal style. Differentiation and the blending of activities score over and above any awkward performances. (Mastenbroek, 1992, p. 103)

A more business-like meeting language

Meetings and negotiations in and between companies and other organizations extended, people from the middle and lower classes moved to higher levels of meeting, and more women began to take part in meetings. During these processes the pressure increased on people to take into account more of the wishes and feelings of more people, and more aspects of their own personality, in meetings. Central to this trend is the obligation to refer to oneself and others in a businesslike manner. This is testified by the recommendations which meeting manuals offer concerning the use of appropriate language:

> If you start out by calling the other person 'foolish', 'ignorant', or 'utterly lacking in common sense', you are insulting him, and he likely to send back an equally strong reply. Moreover, you are attacking the man rather than his point; this is one of the best ways to destroy good human relations. . . . As you take up someone else's point, do it in a pleasant manner; try to avoid such words as 'disagree' in stating your own position. (Zelko, 1969 (1957), p. 135)

> Negative comments may not be personal. . . . With comments such as 'you have been negligent', 'it is your fault that', 'due to mistakes in your department', and 'as a result of your stupidity', the person being addressed has been confronted on a socio-emotional level and has to defend himself. Due to such, there is much arguing and quarrelling without getting a step closer to the solution to the problem. (Rüdenauer, 1982, p. 48)

> Stop sarcastic exchanges and other zip-zaps among participants. The game 'Gotcha', which keeps everyone either on guard or off balance, is not designed

to encourage the release of creative energy or to stimulate problem-solving activities.

Stop the 'Blame' game. If you don't, the entire meeting may turn into a session of Pin the Tail on the Dummy' – a futile, time-wasting exercise. Instead of engaging in a 'Who-Done-It' hunt, try finding out *what* is wrong and how to fix it. (Dunsing, 1978, p. 112)

Providing tactical information during negotiations is permissible; presenting false facts, in other words, lying, is never permissible! One's credibility would be lost for years. (Mastenbroek, 1985, p. 24)

Lacking better argumentation, some people use quite consciously faulty reasoning to persuade others to agree with the speaker. . . . 'That is incredibly stupid, mean, ungenerous, sharp.' The other is condemned or applauded, but what actually for? What was the content of his argument? . . . 'It is clear that . . .'. 'Naturally, it is such that . . .'. 'It is logical that . . .'. It is implicit that one who is in agreement with this is judged to be as thick as a plank. But is it so obvious, so natural, so logical? Just ask once for an explanation. (Schermer, 1991, p. 87)

The language which is forbidden is rude and sarcastic remarks, swear words, threatening language, cursing, blaming, negative personal comments and lies. The modern meeting manuals hardly deviate from the parliamentary manuals on this point. The last two quotations actually point to a noticeable difference. With the decline in appreciation of political parties based on belief, philosophy of life, principles or other non-testable notions, comments which place the speaker themselves or their proposals in an implicitly or explicitly favourable light are no longer acceptable. With this, it is quite apparent that there have been increases in societal pressure during meetings to suppress (megalomaniac) fantasies, and to speak about people in a more distanced manner. This development also includes the large rise in the number of manuals directed towards keeping minutes, which leads to an accurate and businesslike reporting of what was said and decided in the meeting:

The report should be business-like, in the sense of being free from emotionality. When feelings and emotional comments have to be registered, then it is up to the minute-taker to use the appropriate language. Then it should not be written, for example, that the chairman could hardly utter his words with his tear-choked voice, commemorated someone, but that 'the chairman commemorates with several sensitive words'. (Van Reen, 1975, p. 3)

The socio-psychological meeting manuals which spread the forms of conduct and codes of behaviour which were mainly developed in meetings within work organizations, reflected an increasing societal pressure towards a less personal and less 'idealistic' way of talking about the communal future. At the same time counter-trends can be observed, which might be interpreted as 'controlled decontrolling of controlled emotions', Elias's original definition of what later would be referred to as informalization (Wouters, 1990, p. 36):

> The note taker is often instructed to soften the tone of things. The 20–minute battle between two department heads about which department should bear the cost of a recent repair will be reported as follows: 'A brief discussion of appropriate accounting procedures affecting repair charges was held.' Not entirely wrong, but entirely useless. (Dunsing, 1978, p. 76)

Dunsing's message is not to be afraid of fighting out conflicts and expressing emotions, even in the minutes. This indicates a relaxation of meeting etiquette and a reduction of the gap between formal and informal (meeting) behaviour. While the number of meetings and meeting levels gradually extended, attending meetings lost much of its exclusiveness and some formal meeting manners, which primarily developed as a means of power and distinction for the social upper crust, lost significance. Instead, meetings were making greater demands on one's own initiative and feeling of responsibility. This trend has become more prominent with the expansion of meeting regimes to continental and global levels.

Negotiating European and global meeting regimes[5]

In the last decades, the attention paid to 'negotiating' had risen in the meeting manual genre. For instance, in Germany alone, from 1970 to 1990, 80 meeting manuals about *Verhandeln* (negotiating) were published, and 53 of these were published after 1980. Negotiating is written about as the way in which interest groups or parties try to find solutions, which are more or less acceptable to all parties. Negotiating is a way to come to decisions in meetings where the application of the majority rule is neither possible nor desirable. For example, because there are two people or parties, or because the participants differ enormously with respect to their chances for power or their possibilities to exercise pressure over each other.

Negotiating demands more from the personal thoughts and knowledge of the participants than those ways of meeting where a regulation is valid, a chairman acts as 'guardian of the social constraint to self-constraint', and a majority can finally make the decision. Often, negotiations are seen as a form of conduct which takes a middle course between 'fighting' and 'co-operating'. It is considered as a type of meeting in which the character of the reciprocal dependency between the parties participating in the conflict means that neither of them can realize their wishes or aims without the agreement or the co-operation of the other; with the impracticability of the majority rule, both parties do not exclude the application of more than verbal means of battle. Often in meeting manuals, it is not made clear what is exactly meant by this. In practice, the meaning of 'fighting' changes with shifts in power and dependency relationships. Thus, 'fighting' has another meaning within states than 'fighting' has in the relations between modern European states, or within the less stable units of offence and defence in fifteenth century Europe or certain parts of contemporary Africa. The same remains valid for 'co-operation'. In the present industrial society, in practice, 'co-operation' mainly comes down to discussing and deciding with each other about the common future in a relatively peaceful way and following certain institutionalized rules. In military-agrarian societies 'co-operation' more often meant the use of canons of orders and obedience.

With the arrival of modern states and the organization of national welfare rather peaceful meeting and negotiating behaviour has spread to numerous areas of society. Abram de Swaan (1979) pointed out that canons of ordering and obeying in the social behaviour of lovers, married couples, parents and children have been replaced by negotation manners, which developed particularly in companies concerned with caring and providing services. The difficulties for conduct and perception which were brought about by the historical shift from ordering to negotiating have become the field for professionals like psychotherapists, organizational advisors, and social scientists, who provide 'the terminology and the models by which these difficulties in perception and conduct are to be expressed and experienced and treated (by them) as problems' (De Swaan, 1979, p. 19). Many who wrote manuals for negotiating and meeting in the last decades are from these and related professional groups.

The recent extension in negotiating in public and private life was able to take place under the condition of a relatively high level of violence control within and between national states and a, resulting, corresponding level of mutually expected self-control. The common regulation of societal changes has developed in the direction towards an increasingly wider continuum of variations of meetings, of which negotiating is one end. The further development of this variant seems to be dependent upon a continuing pacification in the struggle for power, prestige and wealth and the development of meeting regimes and meeting behaviour at continental and global levels.

The entire continuum from fighting to co-operation including negotiating is subject to constant change. Negotiations within states are under more and stricter, mutually accepted rules than negotiations between states; negotiations within companies are under more rules than negotiations between companies. War can be the ultimate means of pressure in cases of state representatives negotiating; if employers' organizations and employees' organizations

FIGURE 8.5A
Peace Conference
of Ryswick: The
Meeting Room of the
Ambassadors of France
(Atlas Van Stolk,
Rotterdam)

FIGURE 8.5B
Peace Conference
of Ryswick: The
Meeting Room
of the German
Imperial Electors
(Atlas Van Stolk,
Rotterdam)

FIGURE 8.5C
Peace Conference
of Ryswick: The
Meeting Room of
the Representatives
of the Allied Powers
(Atlas Van Stolk,
Rotterdam)

negotiate, 'fighting' means at the most a strike and a lock-out. In comparison to negotiating in pre-parliamentary states or between parliamentary states, negotiating within parliamentary states has more the character of co-operation.

In many cases, negotiating gradually developed into a more regular and regimented form of meeting, discussing and deciding as the negotiating units became more dependent on each other. During such processes, there often arose new possibilities for meeting and negotiating at lower levels. An example of this was the parliamentarization of the struggle between employers' organizations and employees' organizations at national level. This process promoted an increase in meeting activities and a decrease in issuing orders and practising obedience within companies. Another example was the development of meeting units which represented and strengthened the interdependencies in social relations on continental and global scales. In this part of the world, there was an increase in the interest in negotiating not only between national state governments but also between representatives of companies and other organizations from different countries. In the absence of fixed rules and customs at this level, people were compelled to employ forms of discussion and decision-making which made greater demands on their own initiative and feeling of responsibility.

On the political front, national meetings in which elected representatives take decisions by majority vote have lost significance with respect to more-embracing meetings such as those of the European Council of Ministers and the Security Council of the United Nations in which national (government) representatives make agreements on the basis of compromise and unanimity. The growing significance of continental and global, negotiation-like meetings is closely related to the strongly increased social interdependencies in military, economic and ecological areas. The globalization of the economy and the risk of large-scale wars and ecological disasters force individual states to discuss closer co-operation and implementation of policy. The new tensions and problems which arise in this process tend to result in generally elected and more adequately functioning assemblies at the higher levels of integration.

However, this is not a linear process. The rise of more-embracing meeting regimes is characterized by accelerations and reversals. With every step forward social tensions grew and new problems had to be solved. An example of this is the formation of the European Community. To understand this process it may help to recall to mind the formation of the Dutch Republic in the sixteenth and seventeenth centuries as described in Chapter 6. This historical process of integration shows some remarkable parallels with the formation of the European Community, besides many differences of which the absence of generally elected parliaments is the most important one.

Characteristic of both processes of integration is the differentiated use of decision-making procedures varying between unanimity, qualified majority and simple majority. This variety reflects the presence of two conflicting

FIGURE 8.6   Preparatory meeting of the European Commission, presided over by Jacques Santer, 1995 (European Commission, Brussels)

tendencies: further integration on the basis of increasing dependency and preservation or even extension of regional autonomy. In the Dutch case as well as in the contemporary European case we see markets expanding in a politically fragmentated situation or a tardy process of political centralization (Kapteyn, 1996). Co-operation between political units was not enforced by use or threat of organized violence by one of these units, but by enlightened self-interest in a (cold) war against a common enemy. Integration was not enforced by mutual use of force of arms but resulted from negotiations and decisions in peaceful meetings. The decision-making processes were complicated by the fact that the constituent parts, the provinces and national states respectively, were not proportionally represented in the central meetings with regard to their actual power and population. Thus, lobbying, manipulating, and coming to agreements in informal gatherings and in the corridors were necessary tools of the more powerful members to assert their potentiality.

The administration of the Dutch Republic as well as the European Community developed as a pyramid of meetings set up from the bottom. In the first case, municipal meetings appointed delegates to represent them in provincial meetings and those sent delegates to the central intersection of meetings, the States-General. In the second case, meetings of national governments appoint delegates to represent them at central European level, the Council of the European Union (council of ministers) and the European Council (council of heads of states and government and foreign ministers). This model of power delegation from the bottom allows the employment of a small number of civil servants at central level. Most of the meeting holders at central level are in the pay of the meeting units on behalf of which they speak. Thus, the number of 15,000 men and women in the service of the European Community itself is smaller than that of a medium-sized European town.

In the Dutch Republic, there was a strong tendency to wander away from the instructions and the mandates of the principals, with the result that the central meetings gained independence. The central meeting holders tended to show more consideration for each other and the representatives of competing states and federations than for their principals. The potentiality of the last mentioned revealed itself rather indirectly: in the attempts of the central meeting holders to side-track them as much as possible and to keep them under control. In the European Community, such tendencies are decreased and slowed down by the presence of generally elected national parliaments and, in an increasing degree, the European Parliament.

Another example of the structural similarity of both historical processes is the textual character and the confidentiality of summit meetings. Just like the States-General, the European Commission spent a lot of time discussing draftings. The procedure is as follows. Two or more members are debating, the others listen, apparently to be persuaded by one of the debaters. Everyone uses high-sounding arguments, but is looking for the hidden (national) interests at the same time. Finally, a compromise has to be reached by finding an acceptable, multi-interpretable, wording. Frans Andriessen, who was European Commissioner, Dutch Minister of Finance and commissioner of a number of multinationals, called the European Commisson the great master of formulation. According to him, formulation takes much more time in these meetings than in those of national governments or boards of directors because of the greater complexity, bigger ambiguity and more varied interests of the discussion items. Here again we see the working of the 'iron' regularity in the dynamics of meeting, formulated in Chapter 7: meeting participants force each other into nuancing and differentiating their behaviour, particularly their use of language, as they represent more people, and have to take into consideration more people in their discussions and decisions.

Confidentiality played an important role in politics during the Republic. The same is true in the European Community, although in a decreasing degree. The ministers of the Council of the European Union and the members of the European Council made decisions in secret meetings. Elected bodies such as national parliaments and the European Parliament were not able to keep an eye on them and exercise supervision over them. Minutes were kept confidential. According to their employment contract, European civil servants were not allowed to speak with others about their work. This situation has changed since the Treaty of Amsterdam of 1997, which regulates the public nature of official European documents, the votes and the motivation of them by the ministers of the European Council. National parliament and press are now able to find out the positions of their ministers in Brussels. The European Parliament was empowered into co-legislator besides the Council.

Linguistic diversity often makes mutual talks difficult, especially in meetings. A similar problem existed at the beginning of the Dutch Republic. The populations of the various Low Countries such as Flanders, Brabant, Holland, Limburg and Friesland spoke different vernaculars. Deputees of the States-General spoke in French with each other. As we have seen, this changed during the Revolt, when new groups and representatives of lower classes gained admittance to the central meetings. On 7 March 1582 the States-General decided that, 'henceforth, the decisions will be in the language of the Netherlands' (Japikse, 1918, p. 320). This decision can be considered as a major step in the development of a national language, the 'Standard Dutch'.

The number of languages in administrative European meetings, such as the European Commission, was restricted from eight to five. The European Parliament still is a tower of Babel. Verginie Mamadouh (1995) pointed out that the members of the European Parliament are unfamiliar with each other's languages. This is one of the most important reasons why this assembly is relatively powerless compared to the Council of the European Union and the European Commission. Members of the European Parliament do not easily get admittance to the press and the authorities of foreign member countries. Second, deliberation, discussion and debate in Parliament are seriously impeded by the fact that eleven languages are spoken. In this situation interruptions in parliamentary sessions are actually impossible and jokes drop dead. Solving these problems by a simple resolution as the Dutch States-General did 400 years ago, is unthinkable. In present-day Europe, three or four different languages fight for priority. It might be that the admittance of Middle and East European countries to the Community cause such urgent problems that the number of official parliamentary languages will be restricted. The next step may be the gradual development of a common European language: 'Standard European', probably a sort of continental European English.

This linguistic process is an aspect of the gradual development of an European meeting regime by the extension of transnational meetings and the amalgamation of national meeting manners and customs into generally accepted meeting standards to fall back on in dubious cases. This development can be further investigated by studying the etiquettes of European institutions as the European Council, the European Commission and the European Parliament. For instance, the meeting manners of the European Parliament and its predecessors were dominated by south

European, especially French, practices until the beginning of the 1970s. According to Florus Wijsenbeek, a long-standing member of the European Parliamentary Committee on Standing Orders, Credentials and Immunities, there was a shift to north European standards after 1973, when the United Kingdom, Denmark and Ireland joined the European Parliament. The British members started cheering and booing which made the debates more lively. Others imitated this behaviour, but in comparison to the British parliament it remained limited due to the use of different languages. Another example of changing meeting manners is the trend to separate more sharply between lunches and formal talks. Gradually, the European Community is developing its own amalgam of meeting rules and manners as it grows in number and power.

The process of economic and political integration is strongly promoted by the rise of private and public European organizations. Every day, we hear of combinations and take-overs of companies in the world of insurance and banking, car industry, press and publishing trade, accountancy and consultancy and almost any other line of business or branch of trade and services. The emergence of bigger companies requires new facilities and organization structures, such as European business units, European boards of directors and European workers' councils. Club life is also subject to an accelerated process of scaling-up to continental level. More and more national clubs and associations of all kinds, varying from technical and medical research groups, to trade unions, sports federations and numerous other branches, lines and disciplines of human activity make the plunge from a half-fastened co-operation to a single integrated European organization with a transnational committee and administration.

All those forms of integration involve a strong increase of conferences, conventions and congresses to talk and decide about the common future. According to the Union des Associations Internationales in Brussels the number of external, international meetings in Europe has doubled since the beginning of the 1980s. The coming together of people from societies with various traditions has made them more conscious of their mutual identities, similarities and differences in thinking and acting. During meetings one is forced to take each other into consideration to a greater extent, to assimilate with each other and to soften and narrow (national) differences in standards of behaviour. In contemporary Europe, traditional differences and sharp contrasts are being transformed into cultural variations and local colour.

Besides pubs, dance, football matches, restaurants, hotels, beaches and other tourist attractions, conferences, congresses and assemblies of companies and clubs pre-eminently offer opportunities for people of different countries to get to know each other. Etiquettes and manners in meetings are stricter and more compelling than those on tourist spots. Meetings require more self-discipline. Words and gestures require more precise attention, while the need for mutual understanding and consideration is greater. That is exactly why meetings strongly promote the development of common etiquettes and languages. They are the trail-blazers of contemporary, continental and global integration processes.

Knowledge of each other's customs, habits and particular practices and the genesis of them is necessary in order to push out frontiers and clear barriers on the road to further civilization and more efficient and succesful co-operation. The need of such knowledge is being reflected by a rapidly growing stock of international etiquette books. In these, information about common and different national negotiating and meeting styles is communicated.[6] One finds comments and references like this:

French see meetings as an opportunity to state viewpoints rather than to make a decision. French like to 'sniff' a bit first in order to find out to whom they are speaking. They talk about everything under the sun and adopt a playful attitude towards the agenda. (V. Merk and M.J. Browaeys, 1992, p. 100)

Germans are technical and factual in negotiations. Your proposals should be concrete and realistic, presented in an orderly and authoritative manner. Beyond normal courtesies, do not bother with efforts to establish personal relationships – Germans remain aloof until business is complete. German contracts are detailed. (Lennie Copeland, 1985, p. 234)

British contributions tend to be pragmatic and realistic. They may not always be supported with hard fact, offering opinion and assertion for discussion rather than proposals for adoption or imposition. Their predilection for humour may relieve tense or tedious moments, but it can also be regarded as trivialising. They are the least likely to lose interest or temper. (John Mole, 1995, p. 223)

The *Dutch* have a similar approach to the British in terms of seeking a common resolution instead of imposing one, preferring the practical to the theoretical and using humour to defuse conflict and tedium. Their contribution will be brutally frank. (John Mole, 1995, p. 223)

Traditionally, the *Italians* are sly, qualified, tenacious, purposeful and patient negotation partners. They like the foil, not the sabre. They resolutely refuse threats during negotiations. (Heinz Commer, 1990, p. 119)

The use of emotion can be very persuasive in business deals but like coercion, it must be used with care. It tends to be employed in *Mediterranean* areas but seldom used in northern *Europe* or the *Far East*. If emotions are involved, try to control them without allowing yourself to become too stressed. (Catherine K. Leuz, 1996)

Most meetings begin with some small talk, a few minutes in *Europe* or *Japan*, but much longer in the *Arab world, China, South America or Africa*. Personal subjects (family, politics, money, religion) should be avoided, as well as particularly sensitive subjects, which vary by country. Generally the rule is to follow the lead of the host. When in doubt it is safe to talk about weather, sports, local non-political events or local sources of national pride, such as architecture. (Lennie Copeland, 1985, p. 31)

Processes of social integration are accompanied by counter-movements. Old and familiar patterns of behaviour do not disappear or lose impact in a trice. It takes time, costs trouble and may bring along intensified competition and struggle, especially when certain groups gain power and status at the cost of others. Collective consciousness raising and alerting of mutual differences are part of integration processes. Periods of accelerated cultural integration alternate with periods during which supposed advantages of national differences are reinforced and enlarged upon.

Within the multinational IBM, all employees have to speak English and call each other by their first name in official company meetings. In a German office of IBM this was done, but during coffee breaks employees immediately fell back into German terms of address such as 'Sie', 'Herr X', 'Frau Y', 'Herr Doktor Z'. Even when people are full of peaceful intentions and well-informed about each others customs their encounters can be painful. It is well-known that Indians open presents only in the absence of the giver. A western manager visited his colleague in India. They exchanged presents. Both wanted to be polite and considerate. The westerner did not open the present he received from his collegue but put it away for later. His Indian host also wanted to be polite and immediately opened the present he received. Such experience is saliently represented by the cartoon of a Japanese businessman ready to shake his hand in welcome with a western visitor who is bowing like a Japanese. These and other, more serious misunderstandings, as much as the rise of international (meeting) manners books, belong to the lengthy processes of social integration, which are characterized by accelerations, stagnations and reversals.

CHANGING MEETING BEHAVIOUR AS AN ASPECT OF CIVILIZING PROCESSES

Social scientists on meetings

One of the main aims of this study was to make a contribution to the further development of the civilizing theory and sociology in general. This book concludes, therefore, with some thoughts on the significance of meetings and meeting manners for that theory and the importance of studying meeting activities for a better understanding of people and societies.

Many of the meeting manuals which have appeared in the last decades open with the assurance that nowadays people meet more and in a different way than previously, and explain this difference in a sociological way by pointing out that society has changed in various respects. For example, Zelko indicated the necessity to hold business conferences a result of 'the increasing realization and feeling of all people that they are a more closely knit society in the world at large, in the nation, the community, and among social groups' (1957, p. 8). He regarded the increased significance of meetings as an aspect of a world-wide communication revolution: 'We need to step back from the setting of this dynamic phenomenon of modern business life, the small group around the table in the cooperative deliberative effort called a conference. We need to observe the world around us and realize that it is the world that is "in conference"' (1963, p. 4). In a textbook of a Dutch television course from 1979, it is stated that: 'In our society there is a growing need for purposeful meeting and discussion techniques', of which 'the origin lies in a number of developments in modern society', such as 'raising of the standards of living and an advancing process of democratization, . . . the increase in scale and the growth of organizational connections, as well as the increased mobility of modern man' (p. 7). In the last revised edition of his book *Negotiate*, Mastenbroek has traced the development of negotiating as 'an increasing differentiation in behavioural reactions and emotions', which closely corresponds with 'the development of wider networks with more intensive and more symmetrical, mutual dependencies' (1992, pp. 103 and 96).

Writers of meeting manuals do what sociologists have generally not done: they formulate sociological hypotheses about meeting activities. In comparison to lawyers and psychologists, sociologists so far have contributed little to understanding of meeting activities. There have been attempts at a sociological approach to meeting activities by some nineteenth-century researchers, such as Alexis de Tocqueville and Herbert Spencer. Tocqueville's work was referred to earlier. He frequently compared meeting practices in the United States with those in Europe. For example, in consideration of the fact that political meetings in many Western European countries, namely France, other than in the United States, were dominated by aristocrats, he commented:

> Each of them enjoys high established rank in his own right, and the position that he occupies in the assembly is often less important in his eyes than that which he fills in the country. This consoles him for playing no part in the discussion of public affairs and restrains him from too eagerly attempting to play an insignificant one.
>
> In America it generally happens that a representative becomes somebody only from his position in the assembly. He is therefore perpetually haunted by a craving to acquire importance there, and he feels a petulant desire to be constantly obtruding his opinion upon his fellow members. (Toqueville, 1945, Volume II, pp. 94–5)

In *Principles of Sociology*, Herbert Spencer gave an account of the first stages of 'political evolution' by using the meeting manners of 'primitive peoples', which he extracted from proto-anthropological descriptions by missionaries and explorers. Spencer established no school of sociological thought about this point.

For many generations of sociologists, meeting activities seem to have been considered in the same way as has been in the period prior to the appearance of the Magdenburg hemispheres: the omnipresent pressure of the phenomenon did not lead them to the idea that it had mass and could be weighed. In the nineteenth and twentieth centuries, ideologies and theories, which dominated the accounts of society as it was, and as it should be, meetings were not activities to be paid much attention to. The adherents to the liberal, socialist, and conservative models of society focused their attention more on the market, the class struggle, and the historically grown consensus, respectively, as the most important forces or 'mechanisms' which (should) determine the development of society and the acting of people (Goudsblom, 1977, pp. 157–66). The majority of them actually left out meeting activities. A pertinent example was Karl Marx's account of the socialist society after capitalism had been conquered by the workers. Marx saw a society in which nobody had an exclusive activity, but everybody could qualify in whatever direction they wished, society organized general production and, precisely due to this, gave the chance to hunt in the mornings, to fish in the afternoon, to husband animals in the evening and, after dinner, to offer criticisms for as long as desired without ever having been a hunter, a fisherman, a shepherd or a critic (1969, vol. 3, p. 33). The absence of meeting activities in socio-logical models of society can partially be explained by the fact that workers in Marx's time were excluded from central political meetings. As workers gained power, they and many others saw that they were obliged to discuss and decide among themselves and with others about the societal future, more often and more regularly. The societal rising of the working class during the industrialization of society was coupled with an enormous extension in meeting activities, as much in 'capitalist' countries as in countries which termed themselves 'socialist' or 'communist'. For example, in the Former Soviet Union, a broad and unique system of meetings developed. The Russian writer, Alexander Zinoviev, was inspired by it to write the following satirical passage in his book *The Yawning Heights*:

> What on earth is a meeting anyway? An extremely important discovery of civilization, Neurasthenicus says. The highest form of social democracy for the individual who finds himself on the lowest rung of the social hierarchy. When the complete '-ism' is established, then humanity will start a new cycle of development which will be rounded off by the metamorphosis of the entire society into a permanent meeting. And in the subsequent stage, society will develop so that it changes into a permanent presidium of a meeting. And finally, into an honourable presidium. . . . Although the practice of it is overwhelming, there is not yet a science concerning itself with the phenomenon of meetings (we will just term it meetingology). (Zinoviev, 1979, 1981, p. 630)

Differently from how Marx had anticipated, society has developed in the direction of a 'society' in which the members meet about 'the general production' in the mornings, afternoons and evenings. Class struggle has largely been translated into meeting activities.

The unplanned and unanticipated development of meeting behaviour has also sealed the societal fate of the other two great ideological schools of thought of the nineteenth century. The working of the 'market mechanism' has become more dependent upon negotiations and meetings; the 'invisible hand' of Adam Smith is the entirety of unpredictable and unexpected results of meetings and negotiations. The historically developed consensus has more and more come to consist of decisions from earlier meetings.

With the growth of meeting activities, the need for expansive theories about the (desired) societal development has been replaced by the need for more factual information about society. There is an increasing demand for more detailed and more accurately ordered social facts which can serve as weapons for those people who, on behalf of social groups, struggle with words about the future in meetings. As more social facts became available, this battle of words acquired a less principled and a more pragmatic character. Forced to use a more 'reality-adequate' approach of society, meeting participants became more dependent on researchers and the results of empirical research.

Social-scientific institutions began to operate as delivery firms for social facts about societal life within national states, the most powerful meeting units. The increasing mutual dependency between social-scientific communities and national meeting communities involved new methodological and theoretical problems for the former. In the competition for information about society there originated research techniques such as surveys by which national data could be gathered, and ideals such as 'freedom from value judgements' by which scientific communities tried to distance themselves from meeting participants. As social-scientific research became more dependent on money and assignments, shared out by national meetings, social scientists began to direct their attention more to the comings and goings of powerful meeting participants. Their ideas of society were modelled upon the largest meeting units, of which they were a part, their approach to society became more today centred, the scope of their theories was restricted, and their understanding acquired a more static and absolute character (according to Goudsblom, 1977).

In the 1960s, when social psychologists almost completely replaced lawyers as the writers of meeting manuals, many sociologists were in the grip of the 'harmony model' and the 'conflict model'. The advocates of the first model concentrate particularly upon socialization, social control, and other processes which could explain how the social system remained in balance. The advocates of the conflict model were more focused on phenomena such as demonstrations and strikes, under the supposition that social conflicts cause 'social changes' – something which the harmony model advocates could not explain. For the advocates of the conflict approach, a meeting was an affirmation of the status quo (Marcuse's 'repressive tolerance'); for the advocates of the harmony approach, it was a threat to the stability of society and the historically developed consensus. In actual fact, meeting is a mixture of harmony and conflict, be it without the use of physical violence. W.F.G. Mastenbroek expressed this thought in a meeting manual for works councils:

> Mainly we see a mixture of more harmonious and more conflicting discussions. It is hard to be otherwise because administrators and works councils have as many communal interests as different ones. For both, it is important to continue the discussion in as good an atmosphere as possible. (Mastenbroek, 1985, p. 10)

Anthropologists maintained an interest in meeting behaviour. A recent theoretical handling of anthropological research on meeting manners can be found in the previously referred to study, *Democracy and Despotism in Primitive*

Societies (1986) by the political scientist, Ronald Glassman. Another recent example is the study *The Meeting. Gatherings in Organizations and Communities* (1989) by the anthropologist Helen B. Schwartzman. Her approach is more static than that of Glassman who formed an idea of the changes in meeting behaviour during the transformation of hunter-gatherer societies into horticultural and herding societies.

Schwartzman focuses on meetings in the United States. She juxtaposes her research at an American mental health organization with anthropological research in non-western societies to examine the significance of meetings in American society. By comparing the forms and functions of meetings in a variety of 'cultures' she develops a view on meetings contrary to the common assumption, at least in the western world; that meetings are a 'tool' for making decisions, solving problems, and resolving conflicts. She points out that decisions, problems and conflicts are tools for creating more meetings, while organizations and communities need meetings to present the organization as an entity to their members. Schwartzman regards meetings as Emile Durkheim did in his study *The Elementary Forms of the Religious Life*. The general conclusion of this study is that 'religious representations are collective representations which express collective realities; the rites are a manner of acting which take rise in the midst of the assembled groups and which are destined to excite, maintain or recreate certain mental states in these groups' (Durkheim, 1965 [1915], p. 22). The source of religion and morality is in the 'collective mind of society' and not inherent in the 'isolated minds of individuals'. In shaping this collective mind meetings are of the utmost importance:

> There can be no society which does not feel the need of upholding and reaffirming at regular intervals the collective sentiments and the collective ideas which make its unity and its personality. Now this moral remaking cannot be achieved except by the means of reunions, assemblies and meetings where individuals, being closely united to one another, reaffirm in common their common sentiments. (*ibid.*, p. 475)

For Durkheim 'there is something eternal in religion which is destined to survive all the particular symbols in which religious thought has successively enveloped itself' (*ibid.*, p. 474). Just like Durkheim's approach to elementary forms of religious life, Schwartzman's approach to forms and functions of meetings is essentially static. She is not studying how these forms and functions have been developed step by step in long-term processes, but is rather looking for eternal or unchanging elements by comparing meetings in a variety of societies with each other. Her work is not embedded in a long-term theory of social dynamics. In this respect, it is not really different from the older, juridical and social psychological approaches to meeting activities.

Recently, meetings have become items for ethnomethodologists and conversation analysts. Examples of their books are *The Business of Talk. Organizations in Action* (1994) by Deirdre Boden, *Managing Language. The Discourse of Corporate Meetings* (1997) by Francesca Bargiela-Chiappini and Sandra J. Harris and the German study *Arbeitsbesprechungen* (1997) (Work Conferences) by Christoph Meier. The authors stress the central position of meetings in organizational and societal life:

> Meetings are where organisations come together. They . . . remain the essential mechanism through which organisations create and maintain the practical activity of organizing. They are in other words *the* interaction order of management, the occasioned expression of management-in-action, that very social action through which institutions produce and reproduce themselves. (Boden, 1994, p. 81)

> To insist on *sense-making* is to acknowledge its fundamental role in the interpretation of organizational disorder where meetings perform the function of public fora that enable individuals to confront and adjust to multiple realities, i.e. weave the threads of interpersonal and social coherence. (Bargiela-Chiappini and Harris, 1997, p. 57)

None of these authors crosses the threshold of hodiecentrism. Trying to 'analyse' meeting behaviour, they focus exclusively on the here and now and on meeting adults. This, somewhat 'narcissistic', approach seems to follow from the central and useful, ethnomethodological notion that everyday human action should be treated 'as a topic in its own right'. However, that is not necessarily so. As has been demonstrated in this study, a developmental approach makes it possible to treat meeting processes as a topic in their own right, and at the same time, treat them as tracks of larger social processes, which on their turn can explain changes in meeting standards and behaviour. From a long-term, comparative perspective on meetings and meeting behaviour, it is possible to make a 'diagnosis' of the meeting manners of people and societies in different ages and different developmental stages. As previously mentioned, our attention was drawn to the emergence of an upper class of professional meeting participants, who forced each other into nuancing and differentiating their behaviour, as they had to represent more people in their discussions and decisions. The behaviour standards of this upper class functioned as models for new generations and lower classes, who imitated and modified these standards, as they rose socially. From a short-term perspective such regularities in the dynamics of meeting activities are far more difficult, if not impossible, to detect. The corresponding theories are limited means for social orientation in a globalizing world. They do not tell us anything about the structure and the direction of the processes in which standards of meeting behaviour take shape and what we may expect of the meeting standards and behaviour of people of other societies.

For instance, let us look at the following 'hot items' of ethnomethodological and conversation-analytical research: turn taking during meetings and openings and closings of meetings.

Turn taking in general is seen as 'perhaps the most fundamental unit of social action. It provides a simple, economic and extraordinary efficient way of allocating activities across any number of participants. In the process, it creates the rhythms of daily life, from the formal public rituals and ceremonies of ancient religious and national states to the most intimate of human intercourse' (Boden, 1994, p. 66). The essential features of this model are that: one speaker speaks at a time; number and order of speakers vary freely; turn size varies; turns are not allocated in advance but also vary; turn transition is frequent and quick; there are few gaps and few overlaps in turn transition. According to Boden the structure of the turn-taking mechanism is modified in meetings and on conference calls, but 'the core of organizational communication remains this simple, reciprocal and self-organizing system' (*ibid.*, pp. 72–3). The model takes specific shape and direction as meetings are more formal:

> In informal meetings, talk most approximates the conversational turn-taking model, with the general exception that long turns are expectable. . . . In formal meetings, on the other hand, turn-taking may be characterised as a rather distinct departure from the interactional dictates of the basic model, since . . . turn allocation, transition, and even duration are overtly managed by the chairperson functioning as a kind of central switching situation for the meeting. (*ibid.*, p. 99)

This might well be true, but intercultural research indicates that such divergences especially depend on the differences in power and status between the meeting participants. For instance, studying British and Italian management meetings, Bargiela-Chiappini and Harris observed meeting behaviour conflicting with the basic turn-taking model. They concluded that 'turn-taking dynamics (in terms of both length and number of turns) are clearly related to the *status* of the individuals and they are therefore taken to be indicators of power.' They also observed that the participants with explicit and visible status and power both interrupt and are interrupted more frequently, while less powerful speakers rarely interrupt and are interrupted. They suggested that interruptions in management meetings often seem to function as a taken-for-granted means of reaching agreement in task-oriented discourse (1997, pp. 202–3).

This study of the long-term development of meetings and meeting behaviour indicates that turn taking in meetings is closely connected with the power and dependency relationships of the larger figuration the meetings are part of. Thus, the differences between formal and informal meetings, and between the meeting manners of more and less powerful participants, were much larger in military-agrarian and those other societies where the dependency relationships between people are more asymmetric and the identification circles are smaller, than in those of the contemporary highly developed societies studied by ethnomethodologists. In the long run, meeting activities and behaviour changed in a particular direction together with human society at large. There is no reason to believe that this long-term process has come to an end. It can be further examined by looking at the way meetings usually were, and are, opened and closed.

Bargiella-Chiappini and Harris observed that:

> The meeting can be said to commence when the predetermined chair, or the person from the group (with its approval), initiates the opening of the proceedings. From this moment on, that individual takes on the specific role of chair and becomes invested with the unconditional power of opening and closing the meeting. Thus, the openings and closings are the most rule-governed stages of meetings: no other participant is allowed to carry them out without committing a noticeable breach of conventions. (1997, pp. 537–8)

Boden calls the openings 'structured sequences', which 'embody a variety of critical organizational issues'. The presence or absence of specific members is critical in the accomplishment of any opening, she writes. 'Openings bracket out the busy workday while bracketing in the local meeting membership – into the interaction order and the organizational tasks at hand' (Boden, 1994, p. 90). In our society openings usually consist of premeeting by informal conversation, checking the formal or informal quorum and a sentence such as 'let's get started' or 'let's call the meeting to order' or just a single word like 'right' or another 'attention-attractor' (Atkinson, Cuff and Lee,1978, p. 135). Above, it has been pointed out that the long-term changes in the Western European ceremonies of opening and closing meetings were closely linked to the monopolization of organized violence and the pacification of daily life. On the basis of this study, it can be expected that, also, in other less pacified societies, openings and closings will take more time, be more ritualistic, and more dependent on the presence of some powerful leaders, who are able to establish and maintain the holy meeting peace. The tendency, or the compulsion, physically to fight out differences of opinion is relatively strong in societies that are both barely centralized and strictly stratified. As differences in power decrease, and reciprocal expectations of self-control increase, the opening formula will be de-ritualized and shortened.

Rationalization

Another theme of recent ethnomethodological research into meetings is concerned with meeting behaviour as an 'incremental and local process for the enactment of everyday organizational rationality' (Boden, 1994, p. 178). This ethnomethodological notion points to a question which, from a longer term perspective, can be put as follows: to what extent does the development of meeting behaviour present and represent a historical process of 'rationalization'? Norbert Elias emphasized that processes, such as the civilizing process, are not planned, intended, or foreseen by people, although they do presume intentions, plans and actions of people:

> From the interweaving of countless individual interests and intentions (whether tending in the same direction or in divergent and hostile directions) something comes into being that was planned and intended by none of these individuals, yet has emerged nevertheless from their intentions and actions. And really this is the whole secret of social figurations, their compelling dynamics, their structural regularities, their process character and their development; this is the secret of sociogenesis and of relational dynamics. (Elias, 1994, II, p. 389)

When considering the significance of the statement that intentions, plans and actions of different people interweave with each other, then meeting activities quickly come to mind. Goudsblom called this passage 'paradigmatic'; 'the "secret" alluded to belong to the category of what Thomas Kuhn would call the "fundamental problems"' (Goudsblom, 1977, p. 148; 1987, pp. 27–38). The paradigmatic meaning of the last passage will increase if it is explicitly added that society's development in the direction of increasingly larger interdependent networks has been coupled with the development of meeting behaviour, the activity through which people more consciously make communal aims and plans.

The development of meeting activities can be considered as an aspect of the long-term process of social interweaving, which, on closer research can clarify Elias' statement that 'the blind dynamics of men intertwining in their deeds and aims gradually leads towards greater scope for planned intervention into both the social and individual structures – intervention based on a growing knowledge of the unplanned dynamics of these structures' (Elias, 1994, p. 445). Meetings, in which people talk with each other about changes in their mutual relations and decide what they are to do, are 'nodal points' of plans and intentions of individual people. The development of meeting behaviour can be considered, and further investigated, as a process in which people constrain each other towards control of their mutual relations and thus also of themselves, by orientation to ever-longer, more permanent, and more differentiated chains of action.

Thus, the development of meeting activities can also be seen as an aspect of the 'rationalization' of human behaviour. This process of 'rationalization', or rather the development of 'thinking' and 'conscience formation' is not a change within a separate sphere of 'ideas' or 'thought' and does not involve

solely a change of 'knowledge', a transformation of 'ideology' or the content
of consciousness, but a change of the whole human make-up, in which ideas
and habits of thought are only a single sector. 'We are here concerned with
changes in the whole personality throughout all its zones, from the steering
of the individual by himself at the more flexible level of consciousness and
reflection to that of the more automatic and rigid level of drives and affects.
And to grasp changes of this kind, the pattern of thought summoned to mind
by the concepts of "super-structure" or "ideology" is not enough' (Elias,
1994, p. 486). Processes of rationalization developed in relation to the tensions
and conflicts between different functional and other groupings, and must be
seen as psycho-social processes without an absolute beginning point, just like
the more encompassing civilizing process. In view of the spurt of rationality
which appeared in the late Middle Ages, Elias wrote:

> This often-noted historical rationalisation is not something that arose from the
> fact that numerous unconnected individual people simultaneously developed from
> 'within', as if on the basis of some pre-established harmony, a new organ or
> substance, an 'understanding' or 'reason' which had not existed hitherto. What
> changes is the way in which people are bonded to each other. This is why their
> behaviour changes, and why their consciousness and their drive-economy, and,
> in fact, their personality structure as a whole, change. The 'circumstances' which
> change are not something which comes upon men from 'outside': they are the
> relationships between people themselves. (Elias, 1994, p. 480)

The idea that the spurt in the direction towards more rational behaviour was
exclusively connected to rising bourgeois functions has been resolutely ruled
out by Elias. He refers to his sketch of the tendencies towards rationalization
in the camp of the courtly aristocracy; and also the court nobility is not to be
considered as the 'originator' or 'inventor' of more rational thought. The
spurt of rationality was an aspect of the entirely altered field of tensions of
mutually competing states, and clerical, aristocratic, bourgeois and other
groups within them. The institutionalizing of more regulated forms of
competition, of holding discussions and making agreements about the
communal future, and the rationalization of the modes of conduct of certain
groups of people, can be considered as different aspects of the same societal
process. The pacification of society demanded and demands continuing
refinement of the art of meeting.

In his final publication, *The Symbol Theory*, Elias further investigated
speaking, thinking and knowing as three specifically human activities, based
on socially standardized sound patterns. It is hard to keep them apart. All three
activities are concerned with the handling of symbols. 'People who speak
send messages to others by means of sound-waves articulated in accordance
with the models of a communal language, knowledge of which they expect

to share with potential receivers of the messages' (Elias, 1991, p. 65). Furthermore, people learn to think by 'internalizing' speaking. In western society, Elias argues, 'attention is often focused exclusively on acts of thinking, performed in silence and perhaps in solitude by a single person, while even today, acts of thinking by way of discussions, of thinking in groups, are frequent events. Children are more inclined than adults to think aloud. In fact, thinking in silence and without any overt form of speaking has to be learned' (*ibid.*). With this fits Boden's opinion that much of the literature on decision 'making' 'depends on cognitive models of individuals, whereas what seems to be needed are interactional models of people "thinking out loud" – *together*' (Boden, 1994, p. 85). The neglect of attention paid to the development of meeting behaviour by western social scientists may be explained by the customary overestimation of thinking above speaking. A meeting provides for a disciplined way of talking or thinking aloud together about chains of human actions and networks of human relationships. To an important degree, thinking about people in multiples was formed and directed in, and by, meetings.

This orientation function of meetings is very similar to the function of social sciences. In both cases, they concern speaking, thinking and writing about people in multitudes, about groups, social figurations or societies of people. There is a relationship between the development of meeting activities and that of social sciences which requires explanation. Thus, it can be established that the development of social sciences in the nineteenth century coincided with the development of national parliaments, and social scientific research has been intensely focused on solving problems of having inadequate information, which came up in those meetings where decisions had to be made about large numbers of people. The need for more empirical information about people and society by meeting participants was one of the most important stimuli for the rise and growth of the social sciences. Numerous sociologists, economists, psychologists, urban and rural planners and social demographers worked, implicitly or explicitly, to meet the demands of meeting participants, and provided the material upon which decisions could be taken in meetings. The short-term perspective which has come to dominate social science can also be explained by the large involvement of social scientists by powerful, topical meetings of states, companies and other figurations.

The accelerated development of meeting behaviour in the latter half of this century has formed the backdrop to the social-scientific debate about 'the end of the ideology' which was practised in the 1950s and the beginning of the 1960s in the United States in particular and which has since been resurrected after the introduction of Francis Fukuyama's (1989) essay entitled 'The End of History?' One of the first publications in which the end of the ideology was indicated was the book *Political Man* by Seymour Martin Lipset (1960). He propounded his argument as follows. Now that workers have been emancipated and are totally equal citizens, the conservatives have accepted the welfare state, and the democratic left has realized that the state is not able to do everything, political conflicts about the division of the societal product have a restricted and businesslike character and those problems which previously were seen as matters with a mainly political and ideological character have become defined as social technical problems which could be solved with the help of social science.

With the demise of communism and the rise of worldwide parliamentarization, the 'end of the ideology debate' acquired a global character. Thus, Fukuyama declared that, with the collapse of the Soviet Empire, there was no longer any universal ideology which could take on the struggle against liberalism. The liberalism, which Fukuyama so broadly defined that all parliamentary movements from conservatism to democratic socialism were included, will be the only remaining political ideology left to spread further over the world (Tromp, 1993, pp. 252–3).

Many observations and assertions which have played, and still do play, a part in these debates can be explained as aspects of the increasing societal pressure to regulate society in meetings and through discussions and agreements. This largely unplanned and unforeseen process was 'advanced' by the accelerated differentiating of social activities and the corresponding increase in co-ordination functions and problems. The ideology debates illustrate that this process is not fully understood yet.

Taking the view that social scientists have the task of extending the understanding of the 'unplanned dynamics' of society by means of distancing themselves, then studying the ways in which the plans and intentions of increasingly more people intertwining with each other (i.e. the ways people hold meetings) is of the utmost relevance. Understanding the ways in which people have tried to plan their common future is a condition for the development of a more realistic and more adequate depiction of the way in which people change.

Activities through which individuals control their behaviour, more or less consciously, have increasingly become functions of the meetings through which people control their relationships. Elaborating on the concept 'self control' or 'I-control' the concept 'we-control' can be considered. Just as elementary energy in every person is controlled by thinking and conscience, society is controlled by meetings in which people (in consideration of many links during the interpretation of the interests and intentions of others) discuss and make decisions about the future society. Housed in statutes, minutes and law books, many of these decisions disappear from the consciousness of people but remain operative as a sort of conscience, a 'we-conscience'. Just as the personality structure has altered in the course of the civilizing process by the development of the I-control functions: thinking and conscience. Thus the structure of the relationships between people has changed by the development of we-control functions: discussing and observing the agreements made. Meeting behaviour, thinking, and activating conscience are aspects of one and the same process.

In *The Civilizing Process*, Elias (1994) showed that the self-control functions, thinking and conscience, of adults within state societies of Western Europe have become more differentiated and more stable, less permeated by drives and affects which, more and more, were seen as threatening, shaming, and painful. It has already been shown that, by studying meetings, not only the I-control functions, but also the we-control functions, have become more differentiated, more constant, and more controlled, and less 'permeated' by violent contests and physical contacts, stormy outbursts, impulsive decisions, and collective fantasies. While regulating figurations by meeting activities, people have become more dependent on more reality-adequate information of society in the long run. That is to say: information about the regularities in the dynamics of human society.

The development of meeting regimes and meeting behaviour

As we have seen in this study, many codes and manners we employ in meetings today have been developed as standardized solutions of regularly recurring problems. In a long-term, collective learning process, some of these solutions were handed on, almost unchanged, from generation to generation, while other ones disappeared or were changed together with the functions they had for the group, nation, class, gender or any other social grouping employing them. We may speak of 'functional continuity' in the first case and of 'functional change in structural continuity' in the second case. These formulations are borrowed from biology. One of Darwin's first critics, George Mivart, asked how natural selection can explain the incipient stages of complex structures, like wings or eyes, that can only be used in much more elaborate form. Stephen Jay Gould put the problem as follows: 'If complexity precludes sudden origin, and the dilemma of incipient stages forbid gradual developments in functional continuity, then how can we ever get from here to here?' (1991, p. 143). After all, it is impossible to fly with 2 per cent of a wing. According to Gould, Darwin worked out an adequate and interesting resolution. He suggested that 'if incipient stages originally performed a different function suited to their small size and minimal development, natural selection might superintend their increase as adaptations for this original role until they reached a stage suitable for their current use' (*ibid.*). This conversion from one function to another is referred to as 'functional change in structural continuity'.

The development of meeting behaviour can be partly explained with the help of these originally biological notions. An example of 'functional continuity' is the development of the agenda. Composing, in advance, a

FIGURE E.I   Delegates observe a moment of silence on the opening of the 52nd session of the General Assembly of the United Nations, 16 September 1997 (UN/DPI Photo by Eskinder Debebe)

relatively fixed list of items for a meeting, probably originated in ancient Greek city councils, passed on to the meetings of the Roman Empire and medieval church, developed further in the court society, found its way to estates parliaments and spread to ever more sectors of society. During this journey the agenda requirements were gradually modified until the present day, when listing the items of a meeting has to conform to new standards of variation and pleasant tension. Other manners and procedures developed as a result of functional change in structural continuity. Many of them, such as opening and closing ceremonies, largely functioned as a means of power and distinction for social upper classes, and were altered in a more practical sense when constraints on the upper classes and pressure from lower classes increased. Another striking example is the development of the chairman's gavel. This attribute, used to open the meeting, close a debate, restore order or confirm a decision, descends from a fighting axe with two sharp blades, which was used in folk meetings to execute lawbreakers and chop off limbs or pieces of cloth from those who violated meeting rules and broke the holy peace of a meeting. The sharp axe has gradually become a blunt hammer while its functions for the meeting conductor and the assembled group changed in a particular direction. This instance of functional change in structural continuity is to be regarded as a metaphor for what happened to meeting behaviour in general: in the long run,

Features of societal stages	Features of dominant meeting standards	Features of necessary self-regulation
Agrarian Small, vulnerable, unstable, territorial monopolies	Incidental, martial, masculine coarsely regulated, ritualistic, sectional	Less embracing, unsteady, rather undifferentiated, hardly predictable, enforced of organized violence
Industrializing Larger, less vulnerable, more stable, territorial monopolies of organized violence	Regular, more peaceful, elite more regulated, solemn, fairly particularistic	More embracing, steadier, more differentiated, more predictable, stiff,
(Post)industrial Development in direction of more effective, transnational monopolies of organized violence	Development in direction of continuous, generally peaceful common, increasingly varied, more informal, global	Development in direction of all embracing, steady, highly differentiated, generally predictable, smoother

Processes go on   Processes go on

FIGURE E.2   Stages in the development of meeting behaviour in Western Europe

it has become more 'polite' and 'civilized: more peaceful, more differentiated, more regular, more democratic, more informal and smoother.

In the long-term, unplanned or 'blind' process of civilizing meeting behaviour, several phases can be discerned. About meeting behaviour in the earliest stages of human development we do not know very much with any certainty. Nevertheless, it is possible to form a plausible idea of the meeting regimes of pre-historic societies by 'reasoning back' on the basis of archaeological and anthropological material and empirically controlled regularities in the dynamics of meeting. So, it is possible to say that meeting regimes in small, pre-agrarian, relatively egalitarian societies of hunters and gatherers probably had the characteristics of a 'campfire democracy'. People usually met around a fire, eating, drinking, chatting, singing, making music, dancing, doing some manual work, resolving conflicts and planning common actions. Between these activities there were no sharp boundaries. Although the meeting regime was to a great extent dominated by adult men, the other group members, women and children, could also exert important influence on the course and outcome of the decision-making process. The relatively large predominance of men was based on their greater physical strength and their arms monopoly. In fact, except when hunting, the use of weapons was rare. As long as the number of people in relation to the available open land remained small, and groups could avoid each other, aggression remained limited to skirmishes. Presumably, previous to the assumption of a monopoly of arms by men, women had played at least an equally important role in the plans of action.

Features of subsequent stages in the development of meeting behaviour in Western Europe are sketched in Figure E.2.

The origin and spread of agriculture and husbandry were coupled with cultural divergence and social differentiation. Between societies, the cultural differences increased and within societies, different social classes developed between which the differences in behaviour and power grew. The trend towards social stratification, or the dividing of people into higher and lower classes with respectively more and less access to power, possessions, and status, can be considered as a common characteristic of a settled agrarian society. This characteristic had a specific shape. In practically all agrarian societies the possession of weapons, that had long been a monopoly of adult males, became monopolized by specialized warriors and they became the ruling class. Other social groups were usually insufficiently able to resist the organized force of the warriors. Their job or function made them vulnerable to physical force, and allowed them neither the time nor the means to defend themselves. They became dependent upon warriors who could protect them against other warriors. The domination by warriors formed a common structural characteristic of developed agrarian societies, which can then also be generally characterized as military-agrarian societies.

The common structural characteristic of agrarian societies, the dominance of warriors, manifested itself in the development and spreading of formal, martial rules of meetings and manners. This development was initially due to the 'spiral of wars' by which larger numbers of people were compelled to act as one body. Waging war demanded, from the able-bodied men in particular, activities such as training boys for defence, the selection of leaders, the discussion and announcement of the strategy to be followed, the court-martialling and punishing of warriors, deliberations about surrender or truce, and the division of seized goods and conquered land. For this purpose warriors issued commands and orders which they sanctioned by harsh physical punishment. Due to permanent warfare or threats of war, the martial meeting rules acted as an example for others.

Threats of war, and waging war itself, forced people to organize themselves into units of offence and defence led by warriors who could protect them against the organized violence of other warriors. Through pressure from above, by imitation, and resulting from habit, the meeting manners of warrior councils spread and the participation in meetings became strongly dependent upon military power and military considerations. In such a way, women, children, and initially also non–able-bodied men were excluded from the central meetings of survival units and from many other meetings. Until long after the Middle Ages, unrelenting rules forbidding women to take part in meetings of courts of justice, guilds, churches and towns, remained valid.

The trend in the direction of the militarization of meetings was coupled with opposition from the non-military population. This opposition worked in the direction of a further differentiation of manners in meetings. The importance of warrior councils as a general model for meetings decreased. The functions of meetings expanded from concerning the administration of the law, preparations for war, and the establishment of peace, to controlling taxation, water boards, trade, industry, social services, and many other activities and problems stemming from the extension and differentiation of the chains of actions. With the concentration of people, meetings became centralized in special violence-free areas and separate buildings. The increase in the division of labour was accompanied by the arrival of more specialized meetings, in which various meeting styles developed, directed toward specific problems, functions, and possibilities of the various classes of farmers, craftsmen, priests and warriors. Within the larger military, religious, political and economic associations people had to simultaneously learn to speak and decide about the future of more people. The stratification of people had the consequence that some people met more than previously and decided for many, while others met less and were compelled to obey the decisions taken usually outside their knowledge, by small groups of rulers.

In comparison with later developments, the most striking characteristics of the meeting manners of the medieval, agrarian societies were the limited number of psychological nuances to be found, and their limited degree of complexity. Corresponding to the relatively short and little differentiated series of transactions, the high level of danger, and the large divisions in power in the society dominated by warriors and priests, the tendency to solve problems by discussion and agreement was, in general, relatively weak. Most people assembled infrequently, often only when they were directly threatened from outside or by some higher authority. Meeting behaviour was regulated by a limited number of rules which permitted quite a large amount of elbowroom for the expression of either belligerent or excessively congenial emotions. In cases of tensions and conflicts, personal decisions played a large role; the more powerful the person, the larger the role.

The undocumented rules of meeting behaviour of the agrarian societies gradually altered as the balance of power between members of the local communities changed. This occurred more swiftly and more radically in times of war, uprisings, epidemics, floods and other events that made deep inroads into the social life of the local communities. The new or altered rules were part of an oral 'tradition', passed from generation to generation, which often differed widely between districts or regions. The rules of thumb which were used to regulate mutual tensions and co-ordinate actions, were neither strict nor impersonal. Their application and functioning were dependent upon both the changeable personal emotions and decisions of the powerful. Prior to state formation, the legitimacy of the standards of behaviour were mainly determined by the degree of direct force that people exercised over each other in face-to-face situations; they changed faster and were more strictly tied to the power relationship of that specific moment.

When warriors became more dependent upon non-military groups who supported them in their rivalry against other warriors, units of offence and defence were created, within which the tendency and compulsion to control social tensions by discussion and agreement increased, to the detriment of the more martial strategies for controlling conflicts. The warriors were compelled to concern themselves with problems other than those of military co-ordination and had to adjust themselves to the meeting manners and customs of upcoming groups; first mainly the bishops, later urban representatives and, sometimes farmers and water boards. The war council became insignificant as a model for meetings and the predominant meeting standards became more refined. Examples of this can be seen in the greater possibilities to express divergent personal opinions, the decision making by majority vote, and the signing and registering of decisions. With the continuing differentiation of meetings, and the merging of the meeting manners of warriors and upcoming groups, meeting standards arose which, in comparison with previous standards, prompted greater and more differentiated self-control, and allowed a more detached idea of the changing relations between people.

As long as the monopolies of violence remained vulnerable and unstable, holding meetings remained limited and it only obtained some degree of naturalness within small societal upper layers. As long as many people were strongly inclined to settle a dispute or difference of opinion by coming to blows or by armed combat, the necessity for holding a meeting was relatively limited and meetings maintained a highly ritualistic character. The meeting rules were determined to a large extent by external threats, by fear of suffering through warfare or natural disasters, and the fear of punishment at the hands of those in a more powerful social position. Both the prohibited and prescribed meeting rules were concerned with the abstinence from tempestuous violence for the duration of the meeting, until the appearance of rules which, in the pre-state, and early state, stages of co-existence in the Europe of the Middle Ages, were so widespread and generally accepted as to suggest a family resemblance between meetings.

Compared to later developments, there was little discussion and argumenta-tion. Ecclesiastical meetings mainly consisted of praying and performing religious rituals. For the most part, many secular meetings consisted of swearing oaths, reciting 'thing' incantations and indulging in bouts of eating and drinking. Activities used as a means to obtain decisive answers for the question of how to proceed were: trials employing bodily injury; man–to–man fights where men cursed, wounded, or killed each other; dreams; loud screaming; collective hymn singing; communal catcalling; spontaneous flashes of the imagination; and other highly affective behaviour. Agreements were frequently undocumented, but orally endorsed by sworn oaths, meals and prayers.

It was only during the period of state formation, when organized violence was monopolized over extensive areas and a small number of monopolies came to dominate the rest, that more groups and layers of the population came to participate in meetings and sanctioned rules of conduct were created. The emerging meeting regimes of new, dominant groups, presumed and demanded, greater and more differentiated self-restraint. While previous meeting regulations contained numerous stipulations referring to disruptions to order, such as fighting, shouting, drunken talk, knife pulling, glass throwing and bearing arms, the new meeting rules were more concerned with regulating verbal battles, and made greater demands upon an individual's capacity for thinking and his 'conscience'. Although everyday social intercourse was still far from peaceful, the more violent aspects of society were excluded from the prescribed meeting behaviour, more than they were in the previous period. The meeting rules were not formulated as worldly wisdom or practical requirements for social behaviour, but rather as ethical norms or laws of God, and learnt as 'semi–automatic functioning impulses of conscience'.

As conflicts and tensions between states and classes and groups within states lessened, conditions became more favourable for the individual learning processes of how to hold and attend meetings. The rules became more self-evident. This development accelerated during the process of industrialization and the formation of nation–states, when more people were forced to consider the results of centrally held verbal struggles and the decisions prescribing the 'dos and don'ts', to which they could be forced to comply by the use of organized violence. One of the resulting developments was the gradual standardization of manners in meetings or the diminishing of differences in the ways of meeting between groups within nation states. As more layers of the population, by means of their chosen representatives, took part in the struggle for the control and the use of the organized violence, the central meetings were precisely those places where different meeting manners smelted together to become new standards of meeting behaviour.

In the last two centuries, industrial societies have developed into differentiated, multi–layered, meeting units which, in turn, are constituents of continental and worldwide units. The number of meetings and meeting levels in the areas of politics, economics and culture, and almost everything else has increased enormously. More than ever before, opportunities for societal success have become dependent upon an individual's competence and experience in talking and decision making about the common future. The upper level of industrialized society was, and increasingly is, shaped in and by meetings which require a relatively large, precise, constant and smooth self-constraint of expressions of affects and emotions.

Whoever wishes to rise in present-day society has to climb the meeting ladder. Every rung higher carries with it the consequence of holding and making discussions and decisions more frequently and more regularly with others, about lengthier, more enduring and more differentiated chains of actions. Manners and habits pass continually faster from above to below and in an increasing degree from below to above. As the contrasts in meeting behaviour between social groups diminished, the variations and nuances in the way in which meetings are held increased. Meeting manners have spread to family life with the increase in power opportunities for women and young people. Family members have obliged more often and more regularly to discuss and negotiate their relationships. With the entrance of more women into the labour force, marriage has developed from a male-dominated institution towards an institution composed of more equal partners, who largely have to negotiate their personal interaction rules themselves, more frequently have to discuss their problems. After an exile of thousands of years, women are successfully reconquering the right to attend political and an increasing number of other powerful meetings. However, this process is slower than often is desired.

In increasingly more organizations, both men and women of all ages and of all classes gather more often and more regularly in order to talk and decide on more and more aspects of their common future. Learning how to participate in meetings has become an important part of the rearing and education of the young. Whoever wants to participate in society with some degree of success needs to know and be able to apply elementary meeting rules, and to have mastered the type of language spoken in meetings. Pressure increased in meetings for people to take more into account the wishes and feelings of more people, and more aspects of their own personality. Central to this trend was the obligation to refer to oneself and others in a businesslike manner. Comments which placed the speakers themselves or their proposals in an implicitly or explicitly favourable light were less acceptable. With this, it was quite apparent that there had been increases in the societal pressure during meetings to suppress (megalomaniac) fantasies, and to speak about people in a more distanced manner. In meetings, mutual fear between of representatives of different classes and groups diminished. Meeting manners in general became more easy and informal.

The meeting regime currently in use has been developed under conditions of a relatively high level of violence control and a corresponding level of mutually expected self-control. The continuum of the communal regulating of societal changes has developed in the direction towards a continuum of variations of meetings, of which negotiating is one. The further development of this variant seems to be dependent upon a continuing pacification of the struggle for power, prestige and wealth and the development of meeting behaviour at continental and global levels.

Final remarks

In this study, we have seen that the course and the content of the Western European civilizing process, in the last millennium, have been strongly influenced by the development of national meeting regimes. Today national meeting regimes are losing significance in favour of relatively quickly emerging continental and global meeting regimes. The changes accompanying this shift in balances of power may make people feel uncertain and anxious and cling to old habits. What possibilities do we have to direct or influence these processes?

The current networks of interwoven meetings, in which decisions are made on the future of unprecedented large numbers of people, are very complex and cannot be clearly surveyed even by the most gifted participants. It is increasingly difficult, as an individual or as a single meeting unit, to channel the decision-making process in a desired direction, although there is no lack of effort through manipulation and lobbying or even using violence to do precisely this. As the continentalization and globalization of markets and state functions go on, the processes that result from the interweaving of decisions of a large number of less unequal meeting units, will even more strongly structure the thinking and acting of every single meeting unit. More people will more often be confronted with the relatively autonomous course of social processes. This development will offer sociologists and other social scientists new opportunities.

According to Elias sociologists are or should be 'destroyers of myths'. By factual observations, they endeavour to replace myths, religious ideas, metaphysical speculations and all unproved images of social processes with theories, that is, testable, verifiable and correctable by factual observation (1978, pp. 50–70). For sociologists, meetings are important resources of knowledge. They may be considered as 'proto-sociological regimes'. Because meeting is an engaged and disciplined manner of speaking and thinking about multiples of people, meeting participants are to be regarded as 'worldly sociologists'. The difference between people as professional sociologists and as meeting participants is that the former stand with their back to the future and primarily reason in view of empirically based theories, while the latter stand with their back to the past and primarily reason with their thoughts directed to the future. Both groupings are dependent on each other, to an unequal extent. Meeting participants decide on the research budgets of the social sciences, but at the same time, they are dependent on sociological research results which enable them to confer more adequately and more meticulously about the complex social reality. The paradox of social scientists is that they have to destroy the myths of the present meeting classes (and possibly exasperate them), in order to get research budgets from this upper layer. It is part of the duty of sociologists to destroy the myths of the meeting classes. Not that they did not do anything in this field, but they can do it more consciously, more accurately and more methodically, and become more successful. More distance from the meeting classes is necessary and possible through studying meetings and meeting behaviour from a long-term perspective.

The most important weapons of the meeting class are words, which are preserved in the form of minutes. These verbal mummies, the relics of the meeting class, are to be considered as an extremely strategic research field for those who want to the sharpen the picture of long-term changes in the relationship between social ideals and social facts, between language and social reality. In what words and terms did successive generations of dominant groups depict society? What societal changes and goals did they aim at? What, in fact, happened to their plans? From this long-term perspective, what does the meeting behaviour and language of the present upper classes look like? A lot of work still has to be done.

It is to be expected that the processes of differentiation and integration will continue. In many aspects, increasingly larger groups of people will become more interdependent. The degree to which this development will be coupled with an increase in the use of organized violence is increasingly more conditional upon the way in which people speak and decide about the chains of actions which they develop with each other. One of the conditions for the increase in safety, welfare, and quality of life is a further refinement of our meeting manners which makes possible the development of a more distanced, more representational, meeting language. With the help of this we can focus more adequately on the dynamics of society. Nowadays, in discussing and deciding about the common future, great value is attached to economic regularities. In meetings, there is a strong tendency to speak in metaphors which have been borrowed from business meetings and the economic sciences which are focused upon them. Using economic terms in the language of meetings can be considered as attempts to make the relatively complicated chains of actions, by which people have become tied to each other over great distances, clearer and more manageable. To be able to administer and control complex societal developments, it is just as necessary to take into account more aspects of society in the discussions and decisions about the future than only the economic aspect. More research into the way and the direction in which long-term processes, such as the development of meeting behaviour, have occurred and still occur, can extend our understanding of the unplanned dynamics of society and contribute to a further development of meeting behaviour and meeting language, and thus to a more civilized society.

NOTES

CHAPTER 1   **Meeting Behaviour and Civilization**

1   There is at least one exception, which is actually very significant. It concerns a Dutch etiquette book by Godefroy Boot from the beginning of the seventeenth century. Extensive attention will be paid to this book in Chapter 6.
2   Elias has actually not completely traced how 'speaking behaviour' is handled in courtly etiquette books. It is precisely this part of etiquette books which has most in common with meeting manners.

CHAPTER 2   **The Development of the Concept of Meeting**

1   Cf. Elias: 'Mathematical concepts can be separated from the group which uses them. Triangles may be explicable without reference to historical situations. Concepts such as "civilization" and *Kultur* are not' (Elias, 1994, p. 6). As a rule, although there is a greater level of synthesis in the concepts used in physics than everyday concepts and those used in the social sciences, the explanation of all concepts becomes easier when the history of their development is considered.
2   E. Verwijs and J. Verdam, 1907, Vol. VIII, pp. 1721–1730; *Woordenboek der Nederlandse Taal*, Vol. 19, pp. 1863–1906; P. Weiland, 1810, pp. 139–40.
3   Refer to *Woordenboek der Nederlandse Taal*, Vol. 19, pp. 1863–1906.
4   *Weekblad van het Regt*, 1871, Nos 3386 and 3387, p. 3.
5   Refer to *Woordenboek der Nederlandse Taal*, Vol. 19, pp. 1863–1906. Likewise, the Van Dale dictionaries dated 1872.
6   Refer to F. Brunot, *Histoire de la langue française des origines à 1900*, Vol. IX, Tome 2, Paris, 1913, p. 761.
7   Refer to Sir James A.H. Murray, *A New English Dictionary on Historical Principles*, *Vol. I*, Oxford, 1908, pp. 503–4.
8   Refer to *Der Grosse Duden, Etymologie*, Mannheim, 1963, p. 698.

9   This quotation is taken from Dalloz and Colliard, 1975, p. 627; concerning the right to meet in England: P. Mousset, 1931 and M. Baffrey, 1937; in Germany: W. Müller, 1973; and in France: Dalloz and Colliard, 1975.

10 Sir James A.H. Murray, *A New English Dictionary on Historical Principles, Vol. VI*, p. 306.

PART II   Meetings in Military–Agrarian Societies

1   Glassman's 'ideal type' description of the 'campfire democracy' agrees mainly with the image of those political processes in societies comprised of hunters and gatherers which Johnson and Earle have outlined from a different, archeological-anthropological perspective in their study *The Evolution of Human Societies* (1987) and, also, with what anthropologists have recently observed in societies of hunters and gatherers (Leacock and Lee, 1982; Silberbauer, 1982; Woodburn, 1980, 1982).

2   Generally, the trends referred to took place in conjunction, but not always as a unilineal process: 'In individual societies and in exceptional times, these trends sometimes underwent a drastic interruption or even a reversal but, for humanity as a whole, they advanced in conjunction in the same direction for a long period. If one of the five trends stagnated or reversed, it nearly always happened in conjunction with the other trends' (Goudsblom, 1992, p. 81).

CHAPTER 3   The Militarization and Demilitarization of Meetings

1   My knowledge about the 'things' of the Middle Ages stems mainly from the following literature: Ganshof, 1981; Kossman-Putto, 1982; Monté ver Loren, 1982; Planitz, 1971; M. Weber, 1978.

2   The Frankish battle-axe, known as the *Francisca* was particularly renowned in Western Europe. If one takes into consideration the contents of graves from as far back as the Merovian period, this throwing axe, which was described in the early literature of the Middle Ages as a double-sided axe, must have been single-bladed. Up until the eighth century, for as long as the Frankish army was mainly a foot army, it was a formidable weapon, used both as boomerang and fighting weapon in man-to-man combat.

3   Thus, in the so-called *Annals of Metz*, it is written that the Frankish army approved a proposition by a commander-in-chief in the year 690 by rattling its weapons and shouting (Maleczek, 1990, p. 90).

    The old Norwegian word for 'approval' is *vàpnatak* (rattling weapons), the old Anglo-Saxon word is *waepengetaec*. J.F. Verbruggen wrote that the Normans still recognized this custom in the tenth and eleventh centuries: 'Three hundred warriors were prepared to fight and die with their leader William. United, they appeared before him, swore their allegiance, and promised their loyalty and support. Then, following Danish custom, they all clashed their lances against each others'. This custom . . . served to ceremoniously strengthen the armed brotherhood in exceptional circumstances' (1954, p. 141).

4 Minorities, who either tried to extract themselves from unacceptable decisions by staying away from a meeting or were too tenacious in holding a deviant opinion, risked combat with the strongest and most powerful, and a lecture from them if they lost the fight. In the chronicles of Bishop Thietmar van Merseburg, dated approximately 1000, it is written that, on the lower reaches of the Oder, the Liutizi people had unanimously to agree on the execution of an undertaking. If, in a meeting, a fellow countryman opposed such decisions, he received several blows with a stick and, if he openly demonstrated resistance outside the meeting, all his worldly goods were burnt and totally destroyed or, dependent on his rank, he was fined a certain sum of money in a plenary meeting (Thietmar von Merseburg, *c.* 1000, Chronicles VI, 25).

5 'Kings and lawyers may not have felt the need to legislate against feud and private settlements of disputes . . .; what they could do instead was absorb the feuding process and its analogues into their own institutional structures, by making these available for the conduct of conflict at all levels' (Davies and Fouracre, 1986, p. 240).

6 Gosses, 1941; Slicher van Bath, 1949, 1960; Siebs, 1933; Wiarda, 1818; Wichers, 1965. Also refer to the section on farmers' republics, later in this chapter.

7 With the establishment of an effective dominion within the old Roman province of Gaul, the Merovingians built on the remains of the Roman territorial divisions and state organization. The Gallo-Roman and the Frankish episcopate, originating from the senator nobility, played a large role in this process (Hannig, 1982, p. 50). The continuity between the Roman and Frankish administration initially seems to come from the fact that the borders of the dioceses were largely equivalent to those of the Roman-Gallic *civitates* (Hannig, 1982, p. 66).

8 The most important difference between the Frankish councils before, and after, the appearance of the meeting code, which was influenced by the West Gothic *Ordines*, lies in the liturgical ritual in which the councils were cloaked. In the early part of the Merovingian period, there probably existed only the beginnings of a similar ritual (Barion, 1963, pp. 55–61, in particular, p. 57). A few differences might have existed with regard to the rules of the deliberations and the decision-making processes. These rules were already generally employed in the central and regional political meetings of the late Roman Empire (according to Gelzer, 1907; Batiffol, 1913 and 1919; Sohm, 1892; Barion, 1963 and Sieben, 1979). For criticism of the old legal approaches of the Merovingian and Carolingian councils see Hannig, 1982, p. 153ff.

9 Hincmarus drew this sketch of court administration in 882. He based it upon an older, lost manuscript written by Adalhard de Corbie in 826. Hincmarus gave a somewhat idealized picture of what he had observed during his youth, but 'the bare bones . . . provide useful information' (Mckitterick, 1988, p. 79).

The quotations were translated from the German. Refer to Hincmarus, *De ordine Palatii*, in *Monumenta germaniae historica, fontes iuris germanici antiqui*, Thomas Gross (ed.), Rudolf Schieffer, Hannover, 1980, Hahnsche Buchhandlung, p. 82ff, chs. VI–VII, 466–635.

10   For the Carolingian court, there was some sort of educational literature written for the sons of the great warriors of that court. One example of this is the *Manuel pour mon fils* by a lady who wrote under the alias Dhuoda (Pierre Riché (ed.), Paris, 1975, Les éditions du Cerf). In this manual, it is written that a young man had to learn from others that he should offer advice to the monarch: 'L'un peut y apprendre de l'autre, s'il veut, l'humilité, la charité, la chasteté, la patience, la mansuètude, la modestie, la sobriété, la prudence et toutes les autres vertus, avec le zèle du bien.'

11   In the main, the following observation is based in particular on the work of Van der Linden (1978, 1982). Furthermore, the following works were referred to: Van Dam, 1989; Galjé, 1963; Fockema Andreae, 1934, 1952; Beekman, 1905, 1907.

12   To get a first-hand account of the functioning of the Athenian city meetings, the classic masterwork of Thucydides, *The Peloponnesian War* is recommended. For a classic overview of the development of the Athenian city establishment, *The Athenian Constitution* by Aristotle can be consulted. Refer further to: Botsford, 1909; Finley, 1983; Hansen, 1983; Larsen, 1949, 1955; Mommsen, 1888; Staveley, 1972; Soltau, 1880; Taylor, 1966.

13   According to Blockmans, 1986, 1987. My knowledge of the guild meetings and their history is based, in particular, upon the work of Akkerman (1962, 1971), Coornaert (1948) and Planitz (1940, 1971).

14   Remnants of the toasting and feasting ceremonies could still be seen in the fifteenth century in the meetings of the Flemish towns, by which the 'senior bailiff' of the host town served 'attendance wines'. Remnants of this could still be seen in the seventeenth and eighteenth centuries in both the meetings of the Dutch United East India Company, and in the New Year's meetings of the Dutch town councils (Prevenier, 1961, pp. 136–7; Smit, 1957).

15   At the start of the Spanish ecclesiastical councils in the Middle Ages, questions were asked which are reminiscent of questions concerning security (refer to Chapter 5, note 5).

16   The English word *majority*, borrowed from the French, appeared for the first time in the dictionary at the end of the seventeenth century and, in the course of the eighteenth, became the standard expression. In 1691 it carried the meaning 'greater in number' and, in 1743, it carried the meaning 'majority of votes' (*A New English Dictionary on Historical Principles*, Oxford 1908, Bd VI, Vol. II, p. 59).

   In French, the concept *majorité* first carried the meaning 'majority in number' in a letter by Voltaire (dated 24 July 1790). In 1789 it appeared for the first time in dictionaries with the meaning 'majority of votes' (*Grand Larousse de la langue française*, Tome IV, Paris 1975, p. 3178 f.).

   In Germanic languages, the word *Mehrheit* was used for the first time in a Dutch-German dictionary, dated 1719, having the meaning of 'the majority of votes' (Friedrich Kluge, *Etymologisches Wörterbuch der deutschen Sprache*, 20 Aufl., Berlin 1967, p. 471). Carrying this meaning, it became popular through the writers Klopstock, Möser and Schiller (eighteenth century), although they used it in a restricted sense (Jakob and Wilhelm Grimm, *Deutsches Wörterbuch*, Bd. VI, Leipzig 1885, p. 1896; Johann Cristoph, *Grammatisch kritisches Wörterbuch der Hochdeutschen Mundart*, 3. Bd. Vienna 1811, p. 151; Schiller, Friedrich, *Demetrius*, 1. *Akt*, Verse 468 ff).

In Dutch, the concept *meerderheid* was already used from about 1600 with the meaning 'majority of votes', probably as a translation from the French 'supériorité' or 'pluralité'. In 1719 it was adopted in the New High German as Mehrheit (Jan de Vries, *Nederlands Etymologisch Woordenboek*, Leiden 1971, published by E. J. Brill, p. 433).

In this century much has been written about the history of the majority decision. Historical research into this phenomenon originated during the struggle for the introduction of general voting rights, at the start of this century. Since that time it has remained a point of interest for historians. There follows a selection from writings about making decisions with the majority vote: F. Elsener, 1956, 1969; C. Engel and C. Borrmann, 1991; A. Esmein, 1907; O. von Gierke, 1915; W. Heun, 1983; A.M. Honoré, 1978; L. Konopczynski, 1930; M. Kopp, 1959; J.A.O. Larsen, 1949; C. Leclercq, 1971; H. McClosky, 1949; L. Moulin, 1958; H. Pirenne, 1930; J.R. Pole, 1966; U. Scheuner, 1973; W. Starosolskyj, 1916.

CHAPTER 4 The Courtization of Meetings

1 In the main, I have taken his interpretation of the meetings of estate parliaments from: Blockmans, 1978; Brokken, 1982; Gilissen, 1965; Van de Kieft, 1964; Kokken, 1991; Koenigsberger, 1971; Prevenier, 1961; Uyttebrouck, 1975; Uytven, 1976; Wellens, 1974.

2 The first edition of the *Colloquia* appeared in 1529 in Basel. Initially, the work was not reprinted often, probably due to the dismissive attitude of the Catholic church. During and after the Reformation, it became a frequently read book; in the seventeenth century it was published in eleven languages (Spierenburg, 1981, p. 18).

3 Baelde distinguished four stages: introduction, discussion, decision, and implementation (1965, pp. 131–49). In practice, there was hardly any distinction made between discussing and deciding, as is also apparent from Baelde's own description.

4 When towns met on their own initiative, the invitations were issued by one or several of them, and they did not consist of a command but rather a friendly request.

5 According to Tracy (1990): 'One has the impression that the pressures of war-time finance were including local authorities at various levels – from village elders to the States of Holland – to presume to act on behalf of their constituencies in new ways, and to find a new, corporate language to express the powers they claimed. For if Holland was indeed a body, there would be no question of the States' right to act in ways by which all Hollanders would be bound' (1990, p. 36).

PART III   Meetings During the Transition from an Agrarian to an Industrial Society

1   Compare to Elias, 1939, II; Tilly, 1990; and Blockmans, 1974, 1978, 1987.
2   Refer to Spierenburg, 1977 and 1978.
3   In a study dated 1947, H. A. E. van Gelder defended the notion that the Calvinist Church, in particular, represented those people who originated from the middle and lower classes of the urban population who, from way back (also by means of the guilds) attempted to show resistence to the ruling nobility. This interpretation was criticized later by Roorda (1971) and more strongly by Th. van Deursen (1974), according to whom the higher classes also played an important role in in the Calvinist Church. Heinz Schilling has pointed out that these authors based their conclusions on research from three successive stages. Van Gelder's research concerned the last decades of the sixteenth century, Van Deursen's the first half of the seventeenth century, and Roorda's the third quarter of the seventeenth century. Schilling expressed his suspicion, and affirmed this before the church council of Leiden, that there was a development over time which accounted for the opposing theories of the three afore-mentioned authors (Schilling, 1980, p. 420).

CHAPTER 5   The Emergence of a Protestant Meeting Order

1   According to Schilling, 1980, p. 391: as far as origin and function is concerned, this Presbyterian organization is totally urban. The line runs from Zurich, via Basel and Strasbourg, to Geneva and the Dutch towns.
2   Refer, for example, to Calvin's *Institutio Christianae Religionis*. The author put his hand to this work for the last time in 1559. Different from Luther, Calvin founded the organization of the church upon Biblical examples and considered it to be valid for any country at any point in time. Calvin held the opinion that the 'people' should play an important role in the choice of their church leaders and the interpretation of the religion. The choice of a leader was actually 'the choice of God', but it had to be 'prepared' by church ministers. They had to propose two candidates, from which the church members chose one by raising their hands, as was the practice for choosing magistrates in the ancient Greek people's meeting which was the example for early Christian communities.
3   The synodal character of the church order was emphasized in the last article of the church order of Emden, in which it was determined by general consensus, that the preceding stipulations were determined 'in such a fashion that, if in the interests of the church something else would be required, they could and should be altered, increased, or decreased, but that no individual church was at liberty to do this. All churches should apply themselves to demonstrating their support until something else was ordained by a synod' (Plomp, 1971, p. 90).
4   Refer to the meeting regulations of the church council of Monnickendam, dated from 1600 to 1642 (Van Deursen, 1974, Appendix III, pp. 375–8); the regulations and the practices of the Wallonian congregation of Amsterdam (Roodenburg,

1990, pp. 109–10); and the regulations and the practices of the Friesian synod and classes of the seventeenth and eighteenth centuries (Cuperus, 1916, pp. 13–16 and 34–46).

5   Hyperius also wrote that, in olden times, a bishop opened the meeting with a set prayer, and then the chairman or another bishop delivered an 'admonishing speech'. After this, somebody acting in the name of the bishops proclaimed that whoever it did not concern, or whoever had been sent with a mandate, should leave the synod immediately. Possibly these rules, which Hyperius borrowed from the councils of Toledo, were a Christian variation of the procedure in the 'thing' and the 'security questions', by which those who could not concur to the 'peacefulness of the thing' had to leave the meeting (refer to Chapter 3, note 15).

CHAPTER 6   The Formation of the First Meeting Class in Europe

1   For Rotterdam, refer to Van Belle, c. 1740; for Amsterdam: Bontemantel, 1897; and in general: De Bruin, 1991, pp. 200–14.

2   Refer to De Jong, 1985, pp. 40–6; Prak, 1985, pp. 43–9; Kooymans, 1985, pp. 34–7.

3   Published by M. Gachard, *Actes des Etats Généraux des Pays-Bas*, 1576–1585, Tome 1 (6 September 1576–14 August 1568), Brussels, 1861, pp. 440–1.

4   Information concerning the use of the chairman's gavel is hard to come by. However, this requisite was in use from the beginning of the seventeenth century in the meetings of the States-General. This appears to be the case from the afore-mentioned passage in *The History of the Reformation* by Gerard Brandt, in which the treatment of the Remonstrants in the meeting of the States-General was mentioned.

    Another example, this time from the eighteenth century, is: On 19 May 1744, the Registrar of the States, François Fagel, noted in his personal report that the representative, Bergsma (who was thought to have exchanged matters of provincial interest with private individuals) pursued a question by the Grand Pensionary and 'at the sounding of the President's gavel, said that he was allowed to speak in just the same manner as the Grand Pensionary' (Japikse, 1964, p. 113).

5   Refer to the Council of State, Van Deursen, 1964, 1981 and Fontaine, 1954.

6   Concerning the VOC, refer to Gaastra, 1989, 1991 and Klerk de Reus, 1894.

7   Japikse, 1861, p. 440. In previous motions in the same year, there was also mention of an increase in tasks which prompted the making of regulations. For example, this motion proposed on 20 March: 'Sur ce qu'il auroit pleu à Messieurs pour accélérer la dépeche des requestes et aultres affeires qui en grand nombre journellement se présentent' (Japikse, 1915, p. 156).

8   The original reason for the prohibition on consulting guilds should be seen not so much as a sign of the consolidation of the regent's power, but more as a manifestation of the insecurity of the new governors, who feared that the population would abandon the struggle against the Spanish. This fear did not apply for the Orange-orientated, strictly anti-monarchist Calvinist churches,

which were also not affected by the prohibition on participation (according to Schilling, 1980b, p. 245).

9   Literally, it is stated: 'Tous aultres seront tenuz seoir et demourer en leur places, chascun à son reng, à paine d'estre reprins de leur incivilité: sur quoy ledict président aura regard que soit bien observé.'

10   Refer to C.E. Dijkstra, 1974/75 and C. Pauw, 1956. The former covers the armed conflict between Groningen and the Oldambt of 1648, and the latter covers the later, less violent, bickering between town and country representatives, who together had to conduct the administration of the province (cf. Hofstee, 1937).

11   The manual continues thus: 'The regulations from 1815–1851 contain a condition that every member, without having to justify his reasons, was at liberty to let it be noted in the minutes that he had not been in agreement with an adopted decision. With the proposal, made in 1852 by the committee for the revision of the regulations, it was registered that the condition referred to, which was from "a time when, not as now, the names of the members who voted for or against appeared in the minutes of the session, and when the official report of the outcome of the votes was not regularly made known in the pro-government newspaper", could be dropped as pointless. So, it came about' (Pippel, 1950, pp. 366–7).

12   In the 1700s, the political elite consisted of just less than 1200 people, 45 per cent of whom originated from Holland (De Bruin, 1991, p. 214). Together with the governors of the churches and the water boards, they formed an upper crust of several thousand people. If one takes the percentage of enfranchised as a measure of political involvement, then England had the higher figure for approximately that period (1715): 15 per cent of the adult male population had voting rights. In the Netherlands, the percentage was identical with the number of those actively involved in administration, therefore, much lower (Schilling, 1980b, p. 247).

13   In the eighteenth century the army of the Dutch Republic consisted of approximately 40,000 mercenaries in permanent service. Forty to 60 per cent of these possessed Dutch nationality. Ten per cent of the officers were of noble descent; of those highly placed officers (excluding the technical units such as artillery, engineers and the trench diggers) only one-third were of middle-class origin (Zwitser, 1991).

14   According to Fockema Andreae, 1961, p. 107; Spierenburg, 1973, p. 73 and 1981, p. 21.

15   Temple, 1978 (1673), p. 97. Remarkably enough, 150 years after Temple, Alexis de Tocqueville commented similarly about the inhabitants of the state whom he considered to be the least aristocratic and the most democratic of that particular time.

PART IV   Meetings in Industrializing and Industrialized Societies

1 Literature on this topic can be found in J.Th.J. van den Berg, Weesp, 1983.
2 For instance, in the Netherlands in 1995 there were approximately 10,000 works councils, which met at least six times annually. Between 90,000 and 100,000 people are members of these councils. With total observance of the law, there should be approximately 20,000 works councils with 200,000 members.

CHAPTER 7   Development and Spread of Parliamentary Manners

1 Around the turn of the century the first comparative studies of parliamentary codes of order appeared (Reynaert, 1884; Moreau and Delpech, 1906). This branch of science gradually spread. The study of parliamentary meeting regulations has become an international specialism with its own research institutes, periodicals and archives. This development has been powerfully stimulated by the arrival of international, political and parliamentary co-operation, such as the European Parliament and the Inter-Parliamentary Union.
2 While writing this chapter, I was unable to obtain the English version of Bentham's work. The oldest version of the book to be found in the University Library of Amsterdam is the second print of the authorized French translation, dated 1822. In this translation, there is a long introduction by the co-author, E. Dumont.
3 Crane Brinton wrote in his book *The Jacobins*, 'Language is sometimes a most treacherous guide for the historian. It might seem that, since the French borrowed the word "club" from England, they borrowed the thing as well; and essayists have often brought forward this detail to help contrast the ease and frequency with which the Anglo-Saxon creates all sorts of voluntary groups and the social poverty of the Frenchman, with only the family between himself and the state. But any attempt to discover the origins of the Jacobin clubs will soon show that this sort of association was quite indigenous to eighteenth century France. It is not unlikely that a Frenchman spoke of "le club", when he might have spoken of "le cercle", "la chambre" or "la société", much as the English might say "rendezvous" for "appointment" or "assignation", because it sounded distinguished and a trifle romantic' (Brinton, 1930, p. 10). Whatever one might think of this, the important point is that the French borrowed the word 'club' from the English and the English the term 'rendezvous' from the French and not the other way around. In England, opportunities for the middle classes to organize and express themselves were much greater than in the absolute monarchies like France.
4 Refer to Stuurman, 1987, p. 267; Kuiper, 1972, pp. 37–8. There is a recent survey of interpretations and opinions about the process of 'pillarization' in Pennings' study (1991, pp. 2–33).

CHAPTER 8　The Professionalization of Meeting Manners

1　I have conducted a large part of the research in conjunction with Gerard Bos. The titles of the meeting manuals were found under the entries *(manual of) parliamentary practice, (conduct of) meetings* and *conference* in the American bibliography, *meeting, business procedure* and *management* in the English bibliography, *Versammlung, Verein, Konferenz* and *Verhandeln* in the German bibliography, *association, réunion, discussion,* and *animation* in the French bibliography and *verenigingstechniek, vergaderen* and *vergadertechniek* in the Dutch bibliography.

　　We were able to obtain the most complete picture from the Dutch section. The list of meeting manuals mentioned in the Appendix has been extracted from *Brinkmans Catalogus* and supplemented by using the central catalogues of the Koninklijke Bibliotheek in The Hague and the Openbare Bibliotheek in Amsterdam. The number of editions of the various books is not known to us. If the average number is taken to be approximately 3000 to 4000 per edition, then just under half a million meeting manuals would have been published.

2　I have not estimated the number of different books from the non-Dutch section. A reprint is counted as a separate book here.

3　In the Dutch version of this book, in the Appendix to Chapter 8, I listed the entire Dutch section of meeting manuals (Van Vree, 1994, 1996). As yet, no lists exist of such series in other countries. The lists of American, English, French, and German titles which the researchers have compiled are incomplete and not entirely trustworthy. The titles can only be checked in situ in local libraries, just as for most of the books. This is a task to be performed by indigenous sociologists.

4　The important points of the international series were found by comparing bibliographical data and some key words of the Dutch, English/American, and German series. Key books are books which were edited more than once and translated into at least one other language. As far as the main points are concerned, the Dutch series can be considered as representative of the international genre as a whole. The writers of Dutch meeting manuals frequently refer to related foreign literature. And, what is more, authoritative non-Dutch meeting manuals, such as the book by Zelko, are translated into Dutch and, being part of the Dutch series, have heavily influenced other ones.

5　I am grateful to Frans Andriessen and Florus Wijsenbeek for their useful information about European integration.

6　The number of international 'etiquette books' for managers and international negotiation books is large. It is possible to gain an impression of it by surfing the World Wide Web.

BIBLIOGRAPHY

Abma, E. (1962) 'Verenigingen in verleden, heden en toekomst, *Drift en koers. Een halve eeuw sociale vernieuwing in Nederland*, Assen.

Akkerman, J.B. (1959, 1961) 'De heilige wieg van het recht', *Themis*.

Akkerman, J.B. (1971) 'Schets van de rechtshistorische betekenis van het gildewezen', *Tijdschrift voor Rechtsgeschiedenis*, XXXIX (**39**).

Antoine, Michel (1970) *Le conseil du Roy sous le règne de Louis XV*, Geneva.

Aristoteles (1984) *The Athenian Constitution*, Harmondsworth.

Atkinson, M.A., E.C. Cuff and J.R.E. Lee (1978) 'The recommencement of a meeting as a member's accomplishment', in Jim Schenkein (ed.) *Language, Thought and Culture*, New York.

Baelde, M. (1965) *De Collaterale Raden onder Karel V en Filips II (1531–1578)*. Verhandelingen van de Vlaamse Academie voor Wetenschappen, Letteren en Schone Kunsten van België, Klasse der Letteren, Vol. XXVII, 60, Brussels.

Baelde, M. (1967) 'Edellieden en juristen in het centrale bestuur der zestiende eeuwse Nederlanden (1531–1578)', *Tijdschrift voor Geschiedenis*, 80.

Baffrey, Michel (1937) *Le droit de Réunion en Angleterre et en France*, Paris (dissertation).

Bargiela-Chiappini, Francesca and Sandra J. Harris (1997) *Managing Language. The Discourse of Corporate Meetings*, Amsterdam/Philadelphia.

Barion, Hans (1963 [1931]) *Das fränkisch-deutsche Synodalrecht des Frühmittelalters*, Amsterdam.

Barker, Alan (1997) *How To Hold Better... Meetings*, London.

Baron, Hans (1970) 'Calvinist ideas of resistance grew from civic experience', in *Calvin and Calvinism: Sources of democracy?*, Lexington.

Bartlett, Robert (1986) *Trial by Fire and Water. The Medieval Judicial Ordeal*, Oxford.

Batiffol, Pierre (1913) 'Le Règlement des Premiers Conciles Africains et le Règlement du Sénat Romain', *Bulletin d'ancienne Littérature et d'Archéologie Chrétiennes*, 3.

Batiffol, Pierre (1919) 'Origines de Règlements des Conciles', *Etudes de Liturgie et d'Archéologie Chrétienne*, Paris.

Beekman, A.A. (1905, 1907) *Het dijk- en waterschapsrecht in Nederland vóór 1795* (2 vols), The Hague.

Belle, van (c. 1740) *Methode in 't houde van de vroedschap*. Gemeente Archief Rotterdam, Oudarchief, 806.

Bendix, Reinhard (1974 [1956]) *Work and Authority in Industry*, Berkeley, London.

Bentham, M. Jeremy and Etienne Dumont (1822 [1816]) *Tactique des Assemblées Législatives* (2nd edn), Paris. First German translation (1817) *Taktik oder Theorie des Geschäftsganges in deliberirenden Volksversammlungen*, Erlangen.

Berg, J.Th.J. van den (1983) *De toegang tot het Binnenhof: De maatschappelijke herkomst van Tweede-Kamerleden 1849–1970*, Weesp.

Bergsträsser, Ludwig (1967) 'Die Entwicklung des Parlamentarismus in Deutschland', in Kurt Kluxen (ed.) *Parlamentarismus*, Köln/Berlin.

Bleker, H. (1984) *Na(ar) goed overleg*, Deventer.

Blockmans, W.P. (1974) 'Typologie van de volksvertegenwoordiging in Europa tijdens de late Middeleeuwen', *Tijdschrift voor Geschiedenis*, 87.

Blockmans, W.P. (1978) *De volksvertegenwoordiging in Vlaanderen in de overgang van middeleeuwen naar nieuwe tijden (1384–1506)*, Brussels.

Blockmans, W.P. (1986) 'Vertretungssysteme im niederländischen Raum im Spätmittelalter', in *Der Ost- und Nordseeraum, Hansische Studien*, 8, Weimar.

Blockmans, W.P. (1987) 'Princes conquérants et bourgeois calculateurs', in *La Ville, la Bourgeoisie et la Genèse de l'États Modernes XIIe–XVIIIe siècles*, Paris.

Blondel, Jean and Ferdinand Müller-Rommel (1997) *Cabinets in Western Europe*, Basingstoke.

Boden, Deirdre (1994) *The Business of Talk. Organizations in Actions*, Cambridge, USA.

Boden, Deirdre (1995) 'Agendas and Arrangements: Everyday Negotiations in Meetings', in Alan Firth (ed.) *The Discourse of Negotiation: Studies of Language in the Workplace*, Oxford.

Boer, J. and Hijmans, A. (1963) *Verenigen en vergaderen*, The Hague.

Bono, Edward de (1985) *Six Thinking Hats*, Key Poorter Books.

Bontemantel, Hans (1897) *De regeeringe van Amsterdan soo in 't civiel als crimineel en militair (1653–1672)* (2 vols), The Hague.

Boot, Godefroy (1623) *Eene Burgherlijcke Onderrechtinghe*, Amsterdam.

Bor, Pieter (1635) *Oorspronck, begin ende vervolgh der Nederlandsche Oorlogen*, Amsterdam.

Botsford, George Willis (1909) *The Roman Assemblies*, New York.

Brake, Wayne P. te (1988) 'Violence in the Dutch Patriot Revolution', *Comparative Studies in Society and History*, 30.

Brakel, S. van (1908) *De Hollandsche Handelscompagnieën der Zeventiende Eeuw*, The Hague.

Brandt, Gerard (1704) *Historie der Reformatie en andere kerkelijke geschiedenissen in en omtrent de Nederlanden* (vol. 3), Rotterdam.

Brasart, Patrick (1988) *Paroles de la Révolution. Les assemblées parlementaires 1789–1794*, Paris.

Brinton, Clarence, Crane (1961 [1930]) *The Jacobins*, New York.

Bruges, Galbert of (1960 [1127]) *The murder of Charles the Good, count of Flanders* Translated from the Latin with an introduction and notes by James Bruce Ross, New York.

Bruin, G. de (1991) *Geheimhouding en verraad. De geheimhouding van staatszaken ten tijde van de Republiek (1600–1750)*, The Hague.

Buntinx, J. (1950) 'De instellingen van de vorstendommen tot het eind van de twaalfde eeuw', *Algemene Geschiedenis der Nederlanden*, Vol. II, Utrecht.

Burnham, James (1961 [1941]) *The Managerial Revolution*, Harmondsworth.

Callières, F. de (1716) *De la manière de négocier avec dles souvereins*. Paris. English translation: H.M.A.Keens-Sope and K.W. Schweizer (1983), *The art of diplomacy*, Leicester.

Cameron, Euan (1991) *The European Reformation*, Oxford.

Casa Giovani della (c. 1558) *Galateo*. Dutch translation (1715) *Galateus of welgemanierdheid*, Amsterdam.

Christophersen, A.J. (1969) 'The provincial assembly of the three Gauls in the Julio-Claudian period', *Historia*, 17.

Coenen, J.M.A. (1986) *Graaf en grafelijkheid. Een onderzoek naar de graven van Holland en hun omgeving in de 13de eeuw*, Utrecht (dissertation).

Commer, Heinz (1990) *Richtige Umgangsformen, erfolgreiche Verhandlungsmethoden und optimale Geschäftsbeziehungen in allen Ländern der Welt*, Düsseldorf.

Coopman, I. (1939) *Bescherming van het Parlement*, Amsterdam (dissertation).

Coopmans, J.P.A. (1983) 'Het Plakkaat van Verlatinghe (1581) en de Declaration of Independence (1776)', *Bijdragen en Mededelingen betreffende de Geschiedenis der Nederlanden*, 98.

Coornaert, E. (1948) 'Les Ghildes Médiévales (Ve-XVIIIe siècles)', *Revue Historique*, CXCIX.

Copeland, Lennie (1985) *Going International*, New York.

Courtin, Antoine de (1671) *Nouveau traité de la civilité qui se pratique en France, parmi les honnestes gens*. Paris. Dutch translation (1733) *De Hoofsche Wellevendheid en Loffelijke Welgemanierdheid*, Amsterdam.

Couturier, W.J. (1914) *Handhaving van de Orde in Parlementaire Vergaderingen*, The Hague.

Cuperus, S. (1916) *Kerkelijk leven der Hervormden in Friesland tijdens de Republiek*, Vol. 1, Leeuwarden; Vol. 2 (1920) Leeuwarden/Groningen.

Cushing, Luther S. (1845) *Manual of Parliamentary Practice: Rules of Proceedings and Debate in Deliberative Assemblies*, Massachusetts.

Dagverhaal der handelingen van de Nationale Vergadering representeerende het volk van Nederland (1796) The Hague.

Dale, van (1984) *Groot Woordenboek der Nederlandse Taal*, Utrecht/Antwerpen.

Dalloz, Précis and Claude-Albert Colliard (1975) *Libertés Publiques*, Paris.

Dalton, Melville (1959) *Men Who Manage*, New York.

Dam, Petra van (1989) *Bestuur en Beleid in het Moeras. Het Hoogheemraadschap van Rijnland in de Vijftiende Eeuw*, Leiden.

Dann, Otto (ed.) (1981) *Lesegesellschaften und bürgerliche Emanzipation. Ein europäischer Vergleich*, Munich.

Davies, Wendy and Paul Fouracre (1986) *The Settlement of Disputes in Early Medieval Europe*, Cambridge, London, New York.

Deininger, Jürgen (1965) *Die Provinziallandtage der Römischen Kaiserzeit*, Munich and Berlin.

Dekker, J.B. (1969) *Ik open de vergadering. Een geprogrammeerde instructie*, Alphen a/d Rijn.

Dekker, Rudolf (1982) *Holland in beroering. Oproeren in de 17de en 18de eeuw*, Baarn.

Dekker, Rudolf (1988) 'Getrouwe broederschap: Organisatie en acties van arbeiders in pre-industrieel Holland', *Bijdragen en Mededelingen betreffende de Geschiedenis der Nederlanden*, 13 (**103**).

Deursen, Th. van (1964) 'De Raad van State en de Generaliteit (1590–1606)', *Bijdragen tot de Geschiedenis der Nederlanden*, XIXII.

Deursen, Th. van (1974) *Bavianen en slijkgeuzen, Kerk en kerkvolk ten tijde van Maurits en Oldenbarnevelt*, Assen.

Deursen, Th. van (1981) 'De Raad van State onder de Republiek van 1588–1795', in H. de Schepper *Raad van State 450 Jaar*, The Hague.

Diderot, Dennis (1982) *Voyage en Hollande*, Paris.

Dijkstra, C.E. (1974/5) 'De Oldambten tegen de Stad – een vruchteloze strijd', *Groningse Volksalmanak, Historisch Jaarboek voor Groningen*, Groningen.

Dillen, J.G. van (1970) *Van Rijkdom en Regenten. Handboek tot de Economische en Sociale Geschiedenis van Nederland tijdens de Republiek*, The Hague.

Doorn, J.A.A. van (1969) Foreword to Dutch translation of Robert Michels' Political Parties: *Democratie en organisatie*, Rotterdam.

Dronkers, J. and S. Hillege, (1995) 'Studentencorps en elite in Nederland', *Amsterdams Sociologisch Tijdschrift*, 21 (**4**).

Duke, Alastaire (1990) *Reformation and Revolt in the Low Countries*, London.

Dumont, Etienne (1951) *Souvenirs sur Mirabeau, et sur les deux premières assemblées législatives* (rev. edn), Paris.

Dunsing, Richard, J. (1976-77) 'Meetings in General', *Supervisory Management*, New York.

Dunsing, Richard, J. (1978) *You and I have Simply to Stop Meeting This Way*, New York.

Durkheim, Emile (1965 [1915]) *The Elementary Forms of the Religious Life*, London.

Durkheim, Emile (1966) *The Rules of Sociological Method*, New York. Translation from *Les Règles de la Méthode Sociologique* (1895).

Eijk, Inez van (1983) *Hoe gedraag ik me en blijf ik toch mezelf*, Utrecht.

Elias, Norbert (1939) *Über den Prozess der Zivilization*, Vol. 2, Bern.

Elias, Norbert (1956) 'Problems of involvement and detachment', *British Journal of Sociology*, 7. Extended version (1987): *Involvement and Detachment*, Oxford.

Elias, Norbert (1969) *Die höfische Gesellschaft*, Darmstadt. English translation (1983) *The Court Society*, Oxford.

Elias, Norbert (1978) *What is Sociology?*, London.

Elias, Norbert (1984) *Über die Zeit*. Frankfurt. English translation (1992) *Time. An Essay*, Oxford.

Elias, Norbert (1989) *Studien über die Deutschen*, Frankfurt a.M. English translation (1996) *The Germans: Power Struggles and the Development of Habitus in the Nineteenth and Twentieth Centuries*, Oxford.

Elias, Norbert (1991) *The Symbol Theory*, London.

Elias, Norbert (1994) *The Civilizing Process. The History of Manners and State Formation and Civilization*, Oxford, Cambridge.

Elias, Norbert and Eric Dunning (1986) *Quest for Excitement*, Oxford.

Ellemers, J.E. (1984) 'Pillarization as a process of modernization', *Acta Politica*, 19.

Elsener, Ferdinant (1956) 'Zur Geschichte des Majoritätsprinzips (Pars maior und Par sanior), insbesondere nach Schweizerischen Quellen', *Zeitschrift für Rechtsgeschichte Kanonische Abteilung*, 73.

Elsener, Ferdinant (1969) 'Das Majoritätsprinzip in konfessionellen Angelegenheiten und die Religionsverträge der schweizerischen Eidgenossenschaft vom 16. bis 18.

Jahrhundert', *Zeitschrift der Savigny-Stiftung für Rechtsgeschichte. Kanonische Abteilung*, 66.

Engel, C. and C. Borrmann (1991) *Vom Konsensus zur Mehrheitsentscheidung: EG-Entscheidungsverfahren und Nationale Interessenpolitik nach der einheitlichen Europäischen Akte*, Bonn.

Engen, Paul van (1985) *De Gescheiden Wegen van Parlement en Onderneming*, The Hague.

Erasmus, Desiderius (1529) *Colloquia*, Basel.

Esmein, A. (1907) 'L'unanimité et la majorité', *Mélanges H. Fitting*, Vol. I, Montpellier.

Evenhuis, R.B. (1965) *Ook dat was Amsterdam*, Amsterdam.

Fassaert, R.R.H. (1987) 'Vereniging en verandering', *Volkskundig Bulletin*, 13.

Finley, M.I. (1983) *Politics in the Ancient World*, Cambridge.

Floehr, Ralf (1984) *Ordnung ist die halbe Rede*, Krefeld.

Fockema, Andreae S.J. (1934) *Het hoogheemraadschap van Rijnland, zijn recht en zijn bestuur van den vroegsten tijd tot 1857*, Leiden.

Fockema, Andreae S.J. (1952) *Studiën over waterschapsgeschiedenis*, Leiden.

Fockema, Andreae S.J. (1961) *De Nederlandse staat onder de republiek*, Amsterdam.

Fontaine, P.F.M. (1954) *De Raad van State, zijn taak, organisatie en werkzaamheden in de jaren 1588–1590*, Groningen.

Franken, M.A.M. (1980) 'De diplomatie der Staten-Generaal in de tweede helft van de zeventiende eeuw', in C.B.Wels (ed.) *Vaderlands Verleden in Veelvoud*, Vol. II, The Hague.

Fruin, Robert (1984) *Tien jaren uit de 80-jarige oorlog*, Dieren.

Fukuyama, Francis (1989) 'The End of History?', *The National Interest*, Summer.

Fürst, Max (1924, 1928, 1930) *Rede-, Debatte- und Versammlungstechnik*, Marburg.

Gaastra, S. (1989) *Bewind en Beleid bij de VOC*, Zutphen.

Gaastra, S. (1991) *De geschiedenis van de VOC*, Zutphen.

Gabriëls, A.J.C.M. (1989) *De Heren als Dienaren en de Dienaar als Heer*, Leiden (dissertation).

Gachard, M. (1861) *Actes des États Génereaux des Pays-Bas, 1576–1585*, Brussels.

Gadant, J.W.M. (1904) *Blikken in het kerkelijk en gemeentelijk leven onzer vaderen*, Oudewater.

Gallé, P.H. (1963) *Beveiligd Bestaan. Grondtrekken van het middeleeuwse waterstaatsrecht in Z.W. Nederland en hoofdlijnen van de geschiedenis van het dijksbeheer in dit gebied (1200–1963)*, Delft.

Ganshof, François Louis (1947) *Geschiedenis van de Middeleeuwsche Instellingen*, Books III and IV, Gent.

Ganshof, François Louis (1965) *Frankish Institutions under Charlemagne*. Translation (1970) by Bryce and Mary Lyon, New York.

Ganshof, François Louis and G. Berings (1981) 'De staatsinstellingen in de Karolingische tijd', in *Algemene Geschiedenis der Nederlanden*, Part I, Haarlem.

Ganshof, François Louis and D.P. Blok (1981) 'De staatsinstellingen in de Merowingische tijd', in *Algemene Geschiedenis der Nederlanden*, Part I, Haarlem.

Geer, J.L.W. de (1838) *Antecedenten. Orderglement van de Staten-Generaal (Tweede Kamer) 1815–1837*, The Hague.

Gelder, H.A.E. van (1947) *Vrijheid en onvrijheid in de Republiek*, Haarlem.

Gelder, H.A.E. van (1960) 'De Nederlandse Staten en het Engelse Parlement in verzet tegen vorstenmacht en gevestigde kerk', *Mededelingen van de Koninklijke Academie voor Wetenschappen, Letteren en Schone Kunsten van België, Klasse der Letteren*, Vol. XXII, Brussels.

Gelzer, H. (1907) 'Die Konzilien als Reichsparlamenten', *Ausgewählte kleine Schriften*, Leipzig.

Gergen, Kenneth J. (1973) 'Social psychology as history', *Journal of Personality and Social Psychology*, 26 (2).

Geyl, P. (1948) *Geschiedenis van de Nederlandse stam*, Part 1, Amsterdam.

Geyl, P. (1956) 'De Bataafse revolutie', *Bijdrage voor de Geschiedenis der Nederlanden*, 11.

Gierke, Otto, von (1915) 'Über die Geschichte des Majoritätsprinzipes', *Schmollers Jahrbuch für Gesetzgebung, Vertretung und Volkswirtschaft im Deutschen Reiche*, Leipzig.

Gilissen, J. (1965) 'Etats Généraux des Pays de par deçà', *Assemblées d'États*, Leuven/Paris.

Glamann, Kristof (1981) *Dutch–Asian Trade 1620–1740*, The Hague.

Glassman, Ronald M. (1986) *Democracy and Despotism in Primitive Societies* (2 vols), Millwood, New York, London.

Gorski, Philip S. (1993) 'The Protestant Ethic revisited: disciplinary revolution and state formation in Holland and Prussia', *American Journal of Sociology*, 99 (2).

Gosses, I.H. (1941) *De organisatie van bestuur en rechtspraak in de landschap Drenthe (tot den tijd der Republiek)*, Groningen/Batavia.

Gosses, I.H. (1946) 'Met meerderheid van stemmen', *Verspreide Geschriften*, Groningen/Batavia.

Gosses, I.H. and N. Japikse (1947) *Handboek tot de Staatkundige Geschiedenis van Nederland*, The Hague.

Goudsblom, J. (1967) *Dutch Society*, New York.

Goudsblom, J. (1974) *Balans van de Sociologie*, Utrecht/Antwerpen. English translation (1977) *Sociology in the Balance. A critical Essay*, Oxford.

Goudsblom, J. (1977 [1960]) *Nihilisme en Cultuur*, Amsterdam.

Goudsblom, J. (1979) 'De Nederlandse samenleving in ontwikkelingsperspectief', *Symposion*, 1/2. English translation (1978) 'Dutch Society in Developmental Perspective'. Paper presented at the 9th World Conference of Sociology, Uppsala.

Goudsblom, J. (1980) *Nihilism and Culture*, Oxford.

Goudsblom, J. (1986) 'Morele beesten. Notities over moraal', *De Gids*, 149 (3).

Goudsblom, J. 1987 *De Sociologie van Norbert Elias*, Amsterdam.

Goudsblom, J. (1988 [1964]) 'Het Algemeen Beschaafd Nederlands', *Taal en sociale werkelijkheid*, Amsterdam.

Goudsblom, J. (1992a) *Vuur en Beschaving*, Amsterdam. English translation (1992) *Fire and Civilization*, London/New York. Reprint (1994) Penguin Books.

Goudsblom, J. (1992b) *Het civilisatieproces in Europa*, W.A. Bonger-lezingen, Amsterdam.

Goudsblom, J., E.L. Jones and S. Mennell (1989) *Human History and Social Process*, Exeter. Rev. edn (1996) *The Course of Human History: Economic Growth, Social Process, and Civilization*, New York/London.

Gould, Stephen J. (1991) *Bully for Brontosaurus*, Harmondsworth.

Grever, John Henry (1973) *The Making of Foreign Policy Decisions in the United Provinces, 1660–1668*, Los Angeles (dissertation).

Groenveld, S. and H.L.Ph. Leeuwenberg (ed.) (1979) *De Unie van Utrecht, Reeks Geschiedenis in Veelvoud*, 6, The Hague.

Groskamp-Ten Have, Amy (1945) *Hoe hoort het eigenlijk?*, Amsterdam.

Haeften, Olga van (1936) *Manieren. Wenken voor wie zich correct wil gedragen*, Amsterdam.

Hagendijk, Rob (1980) *Het studentenleven. Opkomst en verval van de traditionele studentenkultuur*, Amsterdam.

Hannig, Jürgen (1982) *Consensus Fidelium, frühfeodale Interpretationen des Verhältnisses von Königtum und Adel am Beispiel des Frankenreiches*, Stuttgart.

Hansen, Mogens (1983) *Herman The Athenian Ecclesia*, Copenhagen.

Hart, Marjolein C. 't (1989) *In Quest for Funds. Warfare and State Formation in the Netherlands, 1620–1650*, Leiden (dissertation).

Hassink, Jacqueline (1996) *The Table of Power*, Amsterdam.

Hatsell, John (1781) *Precedents of Proceedings in the House of Commons*, London

Hayes-Renshaw, Fiona and Helen Wallace (1997) *The Council of Ministers*, Basingstoke, London.

Heilbron, Johan (1990) *Het ontstaan van de sociologie*, Amsterdam.

Heilbroner, Robert L. (1962) *The Making of Economic Society*, New Jersey. Dutch translation (1977) *De ontwikkeling van de economische samenleving*, Utrecht.

Hendriks, J. (1971) *De emancipatie van de Gereformeerden*, Alphen aan den Rijn.

Heringa, Jan (1961) *De eer en hoogheid van de staat*, Groningen.

Hermans, Jules (1996) *Uitgerekend Europa. Geschiedenis van de Europese integratie*, Amsterdam.

Heun, Werner (1983) *Das Mehrheitsprinzip in der Demokratie. Grundlagen, Struktur, Begrenzungen*, Berlin.

Heyden-Hermesdorf, E.J.J. van der (1965) *Aantekeningen bij de geschiedenis van het oude vaderlandse recht*, Nijmegen, Utrecht.

Hillege, Serafine and Meindert Fennema (1992) 'Studentencorpora en elitevorming', *Amsterdams Sociologisch Tijdschrift*, 19 (**1**).

Hincmarus 'De ordine palatii', (1980 [882]) *Monumenta Germaniae Historica, Fontes Iuris Germanici Antiqui III*, Hannover.

Hobbes, Thomas (1651) *Leviathan*, London.

Hoekstra, D.J. (1984) *Een minister–president verkoopt nooit leugens. Onparlementair taalgebruik*, Dieren.

Hofstee, E.W. (1937) *Het Oldambt*, Groningen.

Holland, Garry (1984) *Running a Business Meeting*, New York.

Honoré, Antony M. (1978) 'Die menschliche Gemeinschaft und das Prinzip der Mehrheitsregel', *Recht und Gesellschaft. Festschrift für Helmud Schelsky zum 65. Geburtstag*, Berlin.

Hoofsche Welleventheid en Loffelijke Welgemaniertheid (1733) Jacob Graal, Amsterdam.

Hooft, C.P. (1871) *Memorieën en adviezen*, Part I, Utrecht.

Hooft, C.P. (1925) *Memorieën en adviezen*, Part II, H.A. Enno van Gelder (ed.), Utrecht.

Huizinga, Johan (1973) *Herfsttij der Middeleeuwen*, Groningen.

Huizinga, Johan (1982 [1912]) 'Uit de voorgeschiedenis van ons nationaal besef', *Verspreide opstellen over de geschiedenis van Nederland*, Alphen aan den Rijn.

Huntington, Samuel P. (1993) *The Third Wave. Democratization in the Late Twentieth Century*, Norman, London.

Hyperius, D. Andreus (1610) 'Tractaat over het houden van een synode', *Vande Ordre int beroepen ende beleydinge der jaerlijcksche Synoden*, Amsterdam.

IJnzo IJnzonides, H. (1939) *Het recht van Vergadering*, Zwolle.

Japikse, N. (1915–1970) *Resolutieën der Staten-Generaal van 1578–1609*, 's-Gravenhage.

Japikse, N. (1916) 'De Staten-Generaal van 1576', *Bijdragen voor Vaderlandsche Geschiedenis en Oudheidkunde*, Fifth Series, Part III, The Hague.

Japikse, N. (1964) 'De Staten-Generaal in de achttiende eeuw', *Vijfhonderd jaar Staten-Generaal*, S.J. Fockema Andreae and H.Hardenberg (eds), Assen.

Jellinek, G. (1905) *Das Pluralwahlrecht und seine Wirkungen*, Dresden.

Johnson, Allen W. and Timothy Earle (1987) *The Evolution of Human Societies*, Stanford, California.

Jong, J.J. de (1985) *Met goed fatsoen. De elite in een Hollandse stad, Gouda 1700–1780*, Hollandse Historische Reeks, V, The Hague.

Kaajan, H. (1914) *De pro-acta der Dordsche Synode in 1618*, Rotterdam (dissertation).

Kapteyn, Paul (1996) *The Stateless Market*, London, New York.

Karst, A. (1897) *Wie leite ich eine Versammlung?*, Minden.

Kendall, Willmoore (1950) 'Prolegomena to any future work on majority rule', *The Journal of Politics*, 12.

Kennedy, Michael L. (1982) *The Jacobin Clubs in the French Revolution. The first years*, New Jersey.

Kernkamp, G.W. (1894) 'De droogscheerderssynode', *Geschiedkundige opstellen ter ere van Dr. H.C.Rogge*, Leiden.

Kieft, C. van de (1964) 'De Staten-Generaal in het Bourgondisch-Oostenrijkse tijdvak', *Vijfhonderd jaar Staten-Generaal*, S.J. Fockema Andreae and H. Hardenberg (eds), Assen.

Klamer, Arjo (1990) *Verzuilde Dromen*, Amsterdam.

Klerk de Reus, C.G. (1894) 'Geschichtlicher Überblick der administrativen, rechtlichen und finanziellen Entwicklung der Niederländisch-Ostindischen Compagnie', *Verhandelingen van het Bataafs Genootschap van Kunsten en Wetenschappen*, Part XLVII, The Hague, Batavia.

Kluit, A. (1882) *Historie der Hollandsche Staatsregeling tot aan het jaar 1795*, Part I, Amsterdam.

Kluxen, Kurt (1983) *Geschichte und Problematik des Parlamentarismus*, Frankfurt am Main.

Knepper, J.A. and J. Kamphuis (1973, 1982) *Gespreks- en vergadertechniek*, Groningen.

Knight, Greg (1993) *Parliamentary Sauce. More helpings of parliamentary invective*, London.

Knippenberg, Hans and Ben de Pater (1988) *De eenwording van Nederland*, Nijmegen.

Koenigsberger, H.G. (1970) 'Calvinists and Catholics Both Organized Revolutionary Parties', *Calvin and Calvinism, Sources of Democracy*, Lexington.

Koenigsberger, H.G. (1971) 'The States of the Netherlands before the Revolt', *Estates and Revolutions. Essays in Early Modern European History*, Ithaca, London.

Koenigsberger, H.G. (1977) 'Dominium regale or dominium politicum et regale? Monarchies and parliaments in early modern Europe', *Human Figuration. Essays for Norbert Elias*, Amsterdam.

Koekebakker, J. (1956) *Vergaderen en Discussiëren*, The Hague.

Koekebakker, J. (1960) 'Vergaderen of versudderen', *Maandblad voor de Geestelijke Volksgezondheid*, May.

Kokken, H. (1991) *Steden en Staten. Dagvaarten van steden en Staten van Holland onder Maria van Bourgondië en het eerste regentschap van Maximiliaan van Oostenrijk (1477–1494)*, Hollandse Historische Reeks 16, The Hague.

Konopczynski, Ladislas (1930) *Le Liberum Veto. Etude sur le développement de principe majoritaire*, Paris.

Koopman, Paul and Jeroen Pool (1992) *Management en besluitvorming in organisaties. Een strategisch perspectief*, Maastricht.

Koopmans, J.W. (1990) *De Staten van Holland en de Opstand. De ontwikkeling van hun functies en organisatie in de periode 1544–1588*, Hollandse Historische Reeks 13, The Hague.

Kooymans, L. (1985) *Onder regenten. De elite in een Hollandse stad, Hoorn 1700–1780*, Hollandse Historische Reeks 4, The Hague.

Kopp, Max (1959) *Die Geltung des Mehrheitsprinzips in eidgenössischen Angelegenheiten vom 13. Jahrhundert bis 1848 in seiner Bedeutung für die alte Eidgenossenschaft*, Winterthur.

Kossman-Putto, J.A. (1982) 'Bestuur en rechtspraak tussen Eems en Schelde circa 1100–1400', *Algemene Geschiedenis der Nederlanden*, Part 3, Bussum.

Krumrey, Horst-Volker (1984) *Entwicklungsstrukturen von Verhaltensstandarden*, Frankfurt am Main.

Kuiper, Dirk Theodoor (1972) *De Voormannen. Een sociaal-wetenschappelijke studie over ideologie, konflikt en kerngroepvorming binnen de gereformeerde wereld in Nederland tussen 1820 en 1930*, Meppel.

Langeveld, W. (1962) *Mijnheer de voorzitter*, Amsterdam.

Larsen, J.A.O. (1949) 'The origin and significance of the counting of votes', *Classical Philology*, XLIV.

Larsen, J.A.O. (1955) *Representative Government in Greek and Roman History*, Berkeley.

Leacock, Eleanor and Richard Lee (1982) 'Introduction', *Politics and History in Band Societies*, London, New York.

Leclercq, Claude (1971) *Le Principe de la Majorité*, Paris.

Lemaire, C. (1977) 'Het Nederlands en de Nederlandse literatuur van Bourgondische inspiratie onder Karel de Stoute', *Karel de Stoute*, P. Cockshaw, C. Lemaire and A. Rouzet (eds), Brussels.

Leuz, Catherine, K. (1996) 'The Art of Negotiation Tactics That Works', *Business Review*, 11 (**4**).

Liebermann, F. (1913) *The National Assembly in the Anglo-Saxon Period*, New York.

Lijphart, A. (1968) *The Politics of Accommodation: Pluralism and Democracy in the Netherlands*, Berkeley.

Linden, H. van der (1978) *Zeventuig. Waterschap en waterschapsrecht in beknopt historisch perspectief*, Deventer.

Linden, H. van der (1982a) 'Een nieuwe overheidsinstelling: het waterschap circa 1100–1400', *Algemene Geschiedenis der Nederlanden*, Part 2, Bussum.

Linden, H. van der (1982b) 'Geschiedenis van het waterschap als instituut van waterstaatsbestuur', *Het waterschap, recht en werking*, Deventer.

Lipset, Seymour Martin (1963 [1960]) *Political Man. The Social Bases of Politics*, New York.

Lis, Catharina and Hugo Soly (1992) 'Beter een goede buur dan een verre vriend. Buurtschap en buurtleven in Westeuropese steden aan het eind van het Ancien Régime', *De Kracht van de Zwakken. Studies over arbeid en arbeidersbeweging in het verleden. Opstellen aangeboden aan Theo van Tijn bij zijn afscheid als hoogleraar Economische en Sociale Geschiedenis aan de Rijksuniversiteit Utrecht*, Amsterdam.

Lis, Catharina and Hugo Soly (1993) 'Neighbourhood social change in West European cities, sixteenth to nineteenth centuries', *International Review of Social History*, 38.

Lith, P.A. van der (1895) *Verboden verenigingen*, Leiden (dissertation).

Locke, John (1693) *Some Thoughts Concerning Education*, London.

Locke, John (1696) *Some Thoughts Concerning Reading and Study for a Gentleman*, London.

Loening, E. (1878) *Geschichte des deutschen Kirchenrechts: II Das Kirchenrecht im Reiche der Merowinger*, Strassburg.

Luijk, H. (1963) 'How Dutch executives spend their day', *How the Executive Spends His Time*, London.

Luijk, H. (1966) *Doelmatig vergaderen*, Alphen aan den Rijn.

Luursen, Lidi (1964) *De gulden regels der wellevendheid in woord en beeld*, The Hague.

McClosky, Herbert (1949) 'The fallacy of absolute majority rule', *The Journal of Politics*, 11.

Mckitterick, Rosamon (1983) *The Frankish Kingdoms under the Carolingians, 751–987*, London.

McNeill, Wiliam H. (1963) *The Rise of the West. A History of the Human Community*, Chicago.

McNeill, Wiliam H. (1976) *Plagues and Peoples*, New York.

McNeill, Wiliam H. (1983) *The Pursuit of Power*, Oxford.

McNeill, Wiliam H. (1996) *De excentriciteit van het wiel en andere wereldhistorische essays*, Amsterdam.

Mahlmann, Regina (1991) *Psychologisierung des Alltagsbewusstseins. Verwissenschaftlichung des Diskurs über Ehe*, Opladen.

Mak, Geert (1991) *Reportages uit Nederland. De geschiedenis in meer dan honderd ooggetuigenverslagen*, Amsterdam.

Maleczek, Werner (1990) 'Abstimmungsarten. Wie kommt man zu einem vernünftigen Wahlergebnis?', *Wahlen und Wählen im Mittelalter. Vorträge und Forschungen*, Sigmaringen.

Mamadouh, Verginie (1995) *De talen in het Europees Parlement*, Amsterdam.

Mann, Michael (1984) 'The autonomous power of the state', *Archives Europèennes de Sociologie*, XXV.

Mann, Michael (1986) *The Sources of Social Power. A history of power from the beginning to AD 1760*, Cambridge, New York.

Marx, Karl (1969) *Die Deutsche Ideologie*, Karl Marx and Friedrich Engels Werke, Part 3, Berlin.

Mastenbroek, W.F.G., G.C. Ezerman and P. Straaten van (1985) *Macht en onmacht in de overlegvergadering*, Alphen a/d Rijn.

Mastenbroek, W.F.G. (1984, 1987, 1992) *Onderhandelen*, Utrecht. English translation 1989 *Negotiate*, Oxford.

Mastenbroek, W.F.G. (1991) 'The development of negotiating skills', V.A. Kremenyuk (ed.) *International Negotiation: Analysis, Approaches, Issues*, San Franscisco.

Mastenbroek, W.F.G. (1993) *Conflict Management and Organization Development. An expanded edition*, Chichester, New York.

Mastenbroek, W.F.G. (1995) 'The development of negotiating skills: Struggling with violence, deceit, arrogance and humiliation', *International Organizational Development Association Journal*, 3.

May, Erskine (1848) *Treatise on The Law, Privileges, Proceedings and Usage of Parliament*, (20th edn, 1983) London.

Mee, Charles L. (1993) *Playing God*, New York.

Meier, Christoph (1997) *Arbeitsbesprechungen. Interaktionsstruktur, Interaktionsdynamik und Konsequenzen einer sozialen Form*, Opladen.

Mennell, Stephen (1985) *All Manners of Food. Eating and Taste in England and France from the Middle Ages to the Present*, Oxford.

Mennell, Stephen (1992) *Norbert Elias. An Introduction*, Oxford, Cambridge.

Menting, C.L. (1976) . . . *hij is in vergadering*, Deventer (dissertation).

Mény, Yves and Andrew Knapp (1994) *Government and Politics in Western Europe. Britain, France, Italy, Germany*, Oxford.

Merk, Vincent and Browaeys, Marie-Joëlle (1992) *Frankrijk*, Groningen.

Meyers, A.R. (1975) *Parliaments and Estates in Europe to 1789*, London.

Michels, Robert (1970 [1910]) *Soziologie des Parteiwesens*, Stuttgart. Dutch translation (with a foreword by J.A.A. van Doorn) (1969) *Democratie en Organisatie*, Rotterdam.

Mijnhardt, W.W. (1978) 'Veertig jaar cultuurbevordering: Teylers Stichting', *'Teyler' 1778–1978, Studies en bijdragen over Teylers Stichting n.a.v. het tweede eeuwfeest*, Haarlem.

Mijnhardt, W.W. (1983) 'Het Nederlandse genootschap in de achttiende en negentiende eeuw', *De Negentiende Eeuw*, 2, Leiden.

Mijnhardt, W.W. (1984) 'Het nut en de genootschapsbeweging', *Om het Algemeen Volksgeluk*, W.W. Mijnhardt and A.J. Wichers (eds), Edam.

Mintzberg, Henry (1980 [1973]) *The Nature of Managerial Work*, London.

Mole, John (1995) *Mind Your Manners. Managing business cultures in Europe*, London.

Mommsen, Theodor (1888) *Handbuch der Römischen Alterthümer*, Part III, Leipzig.

Monté ver Loren, J.P.H. de and J.E. Spruit (1982) *Hoofdlijnen uit de ontwikkeling der rechterlijke organisatie in de Noordelijke Nederlanden tot de Bataafse omwenteling*, Deventer.

Moreau, F. and J. Delpech (1906) *Les règlements des Assemblées Législatives*, Paris.

Moulin, L. (1958) 'Sanior et maior pars', *Revue historique de Droit Français et Étranger*, 4th Series, Vol. XXXVI, Paris.

Mousset, Paul (1931) *Les Meetings, Essai sur les Caractères Politiques et Jurifiques de la liberté de Réunion en Angleterre*, Paris (dissertation).

Müller, Werner (1973) *Wirkungsbereich und Schranken der Versammlungsfreiheit, insbesondere im Verhältnis zur Meinungsfreiheit*, Munich (dissertation).

Muller, P.L. (1872) *De Staat der Vereenigde Nederlanden in de jaren zijner wording (1572–1594)*, Haarlem.

Murris, R. (1925) *La Hollande et les Hollandais au XVIIe et au XVIIIe siècles vus par les Français*, Paris.

Myers, Fred R. (1986) 'Reflections on a meeting: structure, language, and the polity in a small society', *American Ethnologist*, 13.

Nierop, H.F.K. van (1984) *Van ridders tot regenten. De Hollandse adel in de zestiende en zeventiende eeuw*, Dieren.

NRC Handelsblad (June 7 1993). Dutch newspaper, Rotterdam.

Oestreich, Gerhard (1972) 'Zur parlamentarischen Arbeitsweise der deutschen Reichstage unter Karl V (1519–1556)', *Mitteilungen des Österreichischen Staatsarchivs*, 25, Horn.

Oud, P.J. (1982) *Honderd Jaren*, Assen.

Oudendijk, Johanna Katharina (1937) *Een cultuurhistorische vergelijking tusschen de Franse en de Engelsche parlementaire redevoering*, Utrecht (dissertation).

Oulmont, Charles (1974 (1911)) *Les débats du clerc et du chevalier dans la littérature poètique du Moyen-Age*, Geneva.

Overvoorde, J.C. and J.G.Ch. Joosting (1897) *De gilden van Utrecht tot 1528. Oude vaderlandsche rechtsbronnen*, The Hague.

Paquin, E. (1930) *Ich bitte ums Wort zur Geschäftsordnung*, Velbert.

Pauw, Cornelis (1956) *Strubbelingen in stad en lande*, Groningen.

Pennings, P.J.M. (1991) *Verzuiling en ontzuiling: de lokale verschillen*, Kampen.

Petyt G. (1689) *Lex Parliamentaria, or a treatise of the Law, etc. of the Parliaments of England*, London.

Piët, Susanne (1990) *Overleg, vergaderen en onderhandelen. Hand- en oefenboek voor een effectieve en efficiënte communicatie*, Groningen.

Pippel, J.G. (1925, 1950) *Het Reglement van Orde van de Tweede Kamer der Staten-Generaal, zijn geschiedenis en toepassing*, The Hague.

Pirenne, H. (1930) 'Les origines du vote à la majorité dans les assemblées publiques', *Revue Belge de philologie et d'histoire*, Brussels.

Planitz, Hans (1940) 'Kaufmannsgilde und städtische Eidgenossenschaften', *Zeitschrift der Savigny-Stiftung für Rechtsgeschichte*, Germanische Abteilung, 60, Weimar.

Planitz, Hans (1954) *Die deutsche Stadt im Mittelalter*, Graz, Cologne.

Planitz, Hans (1971) *Deutsche Rechtsgeschichte*, Graz, Cologne.

Ploeg, T.J. van der (1978) *Het burgerlijk recht en de vrijwillige organisaties*, Deventer.

Plomp, J. (1971) 'De kerkorde van Emden', *De synode van Emden, Oktober 1571*, D. Nauta, J.P. van Dooren and O.J. de Jong (eds), Kampen.

Pole, J.R. (1966) 'The emergence of the majority principle in the American Revolution', *Études sur l'histoire des Assemblées d'États*, Paris.

Pollard, A.F. (1964 [1920]) *The Evolution of Parliament*, New York.

Ponsioen, Marjan (1988) *Onderhandelen. Van belangenverschil tot overeenkomst*, Leiden.

Posthumus Meyjes, W.C. (1961) *Jaarvergadering en jaarverslag*, Laren.

Prak, M.R. (1985) *Gezeten Burgers. De elite in een Hollandse stad, Leiden 1700–1780*, Hollandse Historische Reeks 6, The Hague.

Prak, M.R. (1992) 'Een verzekerd bestaan', Ambachtslieden, winkeliers en hun gilden in Den Bosch (ca. 1775)', *De Kracht van de Zwakken. Studies over arbeid en arbeidersbeweging in het verleden. Opstellen aangeboden aan Theo van Tijn bij zijn afscheid als hoogleraar Economische en Sociale Geschiedenis aan de Rijksuniversiteit Utrecht*, Amsterdam.

Prevenier, W. (1961) *Vergaderingen van de Leden en de Staten van Vlaanderen (1384–1405)*, Brussels.

Prins, W.F. (1964) 'De Restauratie (1814–1848)', *500 jaar Staten-Generaal*, S.J. Fockema Andreae and H. Hardenberg (eds), Assen.

Prinz, Friedrich (1971) *Klerus und Krieg im früheren Mittelalter, Untersuchungen zur Rolle der Kirche beim Aufbau der Königsherrschaft*, Stuttgart.

Pursch, Günter (1980) *Parliamentarisches Schimpfbuch*, Frankfurt am Main.

Raalte, E. van (1939) *Het recht van vereniging en vergadering in Nederland*, Alphen aan den Rijn.

Raalte, E. van (1958) *Het Nederlandse Parlement*, The Hague.

Rabus, Pieter (1684) *Samenspraken van Desiderius Erasmus*, (2nd edn, 1697) Amsterdam.

Reen, J. van (1975) *Vergaderingen prepareren en notuleren*, The Hague.

Regt, Ali de (1984) *Arbeidersgezinnen en beschavingsarbeid*, Meppel.

Reinalter, Helmut (ed.) (1993) *Aufklärungsgesellschaften*, Frankfurt am Main, Berlin, New York.

Rentes de Carvalho, J. (1982) *Waar die andere God woont*, Amsterdam.

Resolutien van de Staten van Holland en Westvriesland.

Reynaert, Auguste (1884) *Histoire de la Discipline parlementaire*, Paris.

Rich, Pierre (1975) *Dhuoda, Manuel pour mon fils*, Paris.

Ritter, P.H. (1934) *Een vergadering leiden*, The Hague.

Robert, Henry M. (1880) *Robert's Rules of Order*, (rev. edn (1970) Sarah Corbin Robert) Glenview, Illinois.

Roels, Renaat (1967 (1974)) *Discussiëren en vergaderen*, Groningen.

Roes, Jan (1982) *Toespraken, brieven en artikelen van Alphons Ariëns, 1887–1901*, Bronnen van de katholieke arbeidersbeweging in Nederland, Baarn.

Rogge, C. (1796) *Tafereel van de geschiedenis der jongste omwenteling*, Amsterdam.

Romein, Jan and Annie Romein (1977) *De Lage Landen bij de zee*, Amsterdam.

Rompaey, J. van (1980) 'Het ontstaan van de Grote Raad onder Filips de Goede', *Miscellanea Consilii Magni*, Amsterdam.

Rompaey, J. van (1981) 'Hofraad en Grote Raad in de hofordonnantie van 1 jan. 1467', *Recht en instellingen in de oude Nederlanden tijdens de Middeleeuwen en de nieuwe tijd*. Liber Amicorum Jan Buntinx, Leuven.

Roodenburg, Herman (1990) *Onder Censuur: de kerkelijke tucht in de gereformeerde gemeente van Amsterdam, 1578–1700*, Hilversum.

Roorda, D.J. (1971) *Partij en factie*, Groningen.

Rowen, Herbert H. (1970) 'Management of Estades in the Seventeenth Century: John de Witt, the States of Holland and the States General', *Representative Institutions in theory and practice. Studies presented to the international commission for the history of representative and parliamentary institutions*, Vol. XXXIX, Brussels.

Rüdenauer, M. (1980) *Durchsetzungsvermögen in Besprechungen und Konferenzen, Technik, Taktik, Psychologie*, Kissing.

Sacks, Harvey, Emanuel A. Schelgloff and Gail Jefferson (1974) 'A simplest systematics for the organization of turn-taking for conversation', *Language*, 50.

Sartori, G. (1976) *Parties and Party Systems. A Framework for Analysis*, Cambridge.

Schama, Simon (1977) *Patriots and Liberators. Revolution in the Netherlands 1780–1813*, London.

Schaper, J.H. (1933/35) *Een halve eeuw van strijd* (2 vols), Hilversum.

Schermer, Klaas (1991) *Effectief Vergaderen*, Stichting Teleac, Utrecht.

Schermer, Klaas and Marcel Wijn, (1983 (1992)) *Vergaderen en onderhandelen*, Alphen aan den Rijn.

Scheuner, Ulrich (1973) 'Das Mehrheitsprinzip in der Demokratie', *Rheinisch-Westfällische Akademie der Wissenschaftler. Vorträge*, Opladen.

Scheurer, J.H. (1969) *De techniek van het vergaderen*, The Hague.

Schilling, Heinz (1980a) 'Calvinistische Presbyterien in Städten der Frühneuzeit – eine kirchliche Alternativform zur bürgerlichen Repräsentation?', *Städtische Führungsgruppen und Gemeinde in der werdende Neuzeit*, W. Ehbrecht, Cologne, Vienna.

Schilling, Heinz (1980b) 'Religion und Gesellschaft in der calvinistische Republik der Vereinigten Niederlande', *Kirche und gesellschaftlicher Wahl in deutschen und niederländischen Städten der werdenden Neuzeit*, Franz Petri, Cologne, Vienna.

Schmid, J.J. von (1970) 'Spinoza's staatkundige verhandeling in de ontwikkeling van de staatsleer', *Mededelingen XXVI vanwege het Spinozahuis*, Leiden.

Schneider, Reinhard (1977) 'Mittelalterliche Verträge auf Brücken und Flüssen', *Archiv für Diplomatik*, 23.

Schöffer, I. (1964) 'Naar consolidatie en behoud onder Hollands leiding', *500 jaar Staten-Generaal*, S.J. Fockemae Andreae and H. Hardenberg (eds), Assen.

Schotel, G.D.J. (1841) *Kerkelijk Dordrecht, eene bijdrage tot de geschiedenis der vaderlandsche hervormde kerk sedert het jaar 1572*, Utrecht.

Schröter, Michael (1985) *'Wo zwei zusammen kommen in rechter Ehe'. Sozio- und psychogenetische Studien über Eheschliessungsvorgänge vom 12. bis 15. Jahrhundert*, Frankfurt am Main.

Schwartzman, Helen B. (1989) *The Meeting. Gatherings in Organizations and Communities*, New York, London.

Schutte, G.J. (1985) 'A subject of Admiration and Encomium. The history of the Dutch Republic as interpreted by non-Dutch authors in the second half of the eighteenth century', *Clio's Mirror Historiography in Britain and The Netherlands*, Zutphen.

Seret, G. (1910) *Het voorzitterschap in de Staten-Generaal*, Amsterdam (dissertation).

Sheppard, Pamela and Bénédicte Lapeyre (1993) *Meetings in French and English*, London.

Shetter, William (1987) *The Netherlands in Perspective. The Organization of Society and Environment*, The Hague.

Sickel, Wilhelm (1888) 'Die merowingische Volksversammlung', *Mitteilungen des Instituts für Geschichtsforschung*, Vol. 2.

Sieben, Hermann Josef (1979) *Die Konzilsidee der Alten Kirche. Konziliengeschichte Reihe B: Untersuchungen*, Paderborn.

Siebs, Benno Eide (1933) 'Grundlagen und Aufbau der altfriesischen Verfassung', *Untersuchungen zur deutschen Staats- und Rechtsgeschichte*, 144.

Silberbauer, George (1982) 'Political process in G/wi bands', *Politics and history in band societies*, Eleanor Leacock and Richard Lee (eds), London, New York.

Simons, J.M.I.A. (1914) *Hoe richt ik een vereeniging op?*, Amsterdam.

Slicher van Bath, B.H. (1949) *Herschreven Historie*, Leiden.

Slicher van Bath, B.H. (1960) *De agrarische geschiedenis van West-Europa (500–1500)*, Utrecht.

Slingelandt, Simon van (1784) *Staatkundige geschriften*, Amsterdam.

Smit, J. (1957) *Een regentendagboek uit de achttiende eeuw*, Assen.

Smith, Thomas (1673) *Het Parlement van Engeland, met het Sitten en de Macht van het selvige*, Amsterdam (translation of part of *De republica Anglorum* (ca. 1560)).

Sohm, Rudolf (1892) *Kirchenrecht. Vol. I: Die geschichtlichen Grundlagen*, Leipzig.

Soltau, Wilhelm (1880) *Über Entstehung und Zusammensetzung der altrömische Volksversammlungen*, Berlin.

Spencer, Herbert (1974 (1876)) *The Evolution of Society*, Chicago, London.

Spierenburg, Pieter (1973) *Het proces der civilisatie in Nederland*, Amsterdam.

Spierenburg, Pieter (1977) 'The Northern patriciate during the revolt of the Netherlands: a "Zweifrontenschicht" in the sixteenth century', *Human Figuration. Essays for Norbert Elias*, Amsterdam.

Spierenburg, Pieter (1978) *Judicial Violence in the Dutch Republic. Corporal punishment, executions and torture in Amsterdam 1650–1750*, Amsterdam.

Spierenburg, Pieter (1981) 'Elites and Etiquette', *Centrum voor maatschappijgeschiedenis*, Vol. 9, Rotterdam.

Spierenburg, Pieter (1991) *The prison-experience. Disciplinary institutions and their inmates in early modern Europe*, New Brunswick, London.

Spinoza, Benedictus de (1677) *Tractatus Politicus*, Amsterdam, English translation 1975, *A Theologico-Political Treatise and A Political Treatise*, New York.

Spoormans, Huub (1988) *Met uitsluiting van voorregt. Het ontstaan van de liberale democratie in Nederland*, Amsterdam.

Standing Orders of the States of Holland, 19th February 1585.

Staveley, E.S. (1972) *Greek and Roman Voting and Elections*, London.

Stearns, Peter N. (1993) 'Girls, boys, and emotions: redefinitions and historical change', *Journal of American History*, 80 (1).

Stearns, Peter N. and Carol Zisowitz-Stearns (1986) *Anger. The Struggle for Emotional Control in America's History*, Chicago, London.

Steffani, Winfried (1967) 'Amerikanischer Kongress und deutscher Bundestag – ein Vergleich', *Parlamentarismus*, Köln, Berlin.

Stolk, Bram van and Cas Wouters (1983) *Vrouwen in tweestrijd*, Deventer.

Starosolskyj, Wolodymyr (1916) *Das Majoritätsprinzip*, Leipzig.

Stützel-Prüsener Marlies (1993) 'Lesegesellschaften', in Helmut Reinalter (ed.) *Aufklärungsgesellschaften*. Frankfurt d.M.

Stuurman, S. (1987) 'De Nederlandse staat tussen verzuiling en moderniteit', *Balans en perspectief, visies op de geschiedwetenschap in Nederland*, Groningen.

Swaan, A. de (1976) 'De mens is de mens een zorg: over de verstatelijking van verzorgingsarrangementen', *De Gids*, 139 (1/2).

Swaan, A. de (1979) *Uitgaansbeperking en uitgaansangst. Over de verschuiving van bevelshuishouden naar onderhandelingshuishouden*, Amsterdam (lecture).

Swaan, A. de (1988) *In Care of the State: The Social Dynamics of Public Health, Education and Income Maintenance in Western Europe und the United States*, Oxford.

Sweers B.M. and E.M. Deffelen, (eds) (1958). *A.K.U. Guide to Meetings*.

Tannen, Deborah (1986) *That's Not What I Meant!*, New York.

Tannen, Deborah (1994) *Talking from 9 to 5*, New York.

Taylor, Lily Ros (1966) *Roman Voting Assemblies*, Ann Arbor.

Temple, William (1978 [1673]) *Observations upon the United Provinces*, .

Thompson, Craig R. (1965) *The Colloquies of Erasmus*, Chicago, London.

Thompson, E.P. (1969) *The Making of the English Working Class*, Harmondsworth.

Thorson, Thomas, Landon (1961) 'Epilogue on absolute majority rule', *Journal of Politics*.

Thucydides (1986) *De Peloponnesische oorlog*, Amsterdam.

Tilly, Charles (1990) *Coercion, Capital and European States, AD 990–1990*, Cambridge.

Tilly, Charles (1993) *European Revolutions, 1492–1992*, Cambridge, Massachussets.

Tocqueville, Alexis de (1961 [1835]) *De la démocratie en Amérique, Complete Works*, Vols 1 and 2, Paris. English translation (1945) *Democracy in America*, New York.

Tracy, James D. (1985) *A Financial Revolution in the Habsburg Netherlands. Renten en Renteniers in the County of Holland, 1515–1565*, Berkeley, Los Angeles, London.

Tracy, James D. (1990) *Holland under Habsburg Rule, 1506–1566*, Berkeley, Los Angeles, London.

Tromp, Bart (1993) *De wetenschap der politiek*, Leiden.

Tukker, C.A. (1965) *De classis van Dordrecht van 1573–1609*, Leiden.

Tumin, M. (1982) 'The Theory of Democratic Development', *Theory and Society* 11.

Uytven, R. van (1976) 'Vorst, adel en steden: een driehoeksverhouding in Brabant van de twaalfde tot de zestiende eeuw', *Bijdragen tot de Geschiedenis*, 59 (3–4).

Uytven, R. van (1980) 'Stadsgeschiedenis in het Noorden en Zuiden', *Algemene Geschiedenis der Nederlanden*, Part 4, The Hague.

Valentine, Herman (1976) *Parliaments of the World*, Berlin, New York.

Veblen, Thorstein (1953 [1899]) *The Theory of the Leisure Class*, New York.

Verbruggen, J.F. (1954) *De krijgskunst in West-Europa in de Middeleeuwen (IXde tot begin XIVde eeuw)*, Brussels.

Vis, J.J. (1989) 'Over Parlementen' *Volkeren Vertegenwoordigd*, The Hague.

Volkskrant (de) (June 21 1997). Dutch newspaper, Amsterdam.

Voss, Ingrid (1987) *Herrschertreffen im frühen und hohen Mittelalter*, Cologne.

Vossestein, Jacob (1997) *Dealing with the Dutch*, Royal Tropical Institute, Amsterdam.

Vrankrijker, A.C.J. de (1934) *In andermans ogen*, Utrecht.

Vrankrijker, A.C.J. de (1938) 'Overstemming en Submissie', *Historisch Tijdschrift*, 17.

Vree, Wilbert van (1994a) *Nederland als vergaderland. Opkomst en verbreiding van een vergaderregime*, Groningen.

Vree, Wilbert van (1994b) 'De Nederlandse vergadercultuur in vergelijkend perspectief', *Negotiation Magazine*, VIII (4).

Vree, Wilbert van (1997) 'De mythe van de vergaderstand', *Alles Verandert. Opstellen voor en over J. Goudsblom*, Amsterdam.

Vree, Wilbert van (1997) 'Meetings, Manners and Civilization' *Paper for Norbert Elias Centenary Conference*, Amsterdam 1997.

Vree, Wilbert van (1998) 'An upperclass of professional chairmen', *Paper presented to the 14th EGOS Colloquium*, Maastricht.

Vree, Wilbert van and Gerard Bos (1989) 'Vergaderen, verhoofsing en parlementarisering', *Amsterdams Sociologisch Tijdschrift*, 16 (**3**).

Vries, J. de (1973) 'On the modernity of the Dutch Republic', *Journal of Economic History*, XXXIII.

Vries, J. de (1984) *European Urbanization*, London.

Waitz, Georg (1953) *Deutsche Verfassungsgeschichte*. Vol. 1: *Die Verfassung des deutschen Volkes in älterer Zeit*; Vol. 2 (1953): *Die Verfassung des fränkischen Reichs*; Vol. 3 (1954): *Die Verfassung des fränkischen Reichs*,

Walther, H. (1920) *Das Streitgedicht in der Lateinischen Literatur des Mittelalters*, Munich.

Walzer, Michael (1970) *The Revolution of the Saints*, New York.

Warren, F.M. (1907) 'The council of Remiremont', *Modern Language Notes*, 22.

Weber, Heinrich (1962) *Die Reichsversammlungen im ostfränkische Reich 840–918. Eine entwicklungsgeschichtliche Untersuchung vom karolingische Grossreich zum deutschen Reich*, Würzburg (dissertation).

Weber, Max (1972 (1922)) *Wirtschaft und Gesellschaft*, Tübingen.

Weber, Max (1978 (1922)) *Economy and Society* (2 vols), Berkeley.

Weber, Max (1988 (1920)) *Gesammelte Aufsätze zur Religionssoziologie*, Vol. I, Tübingen.

Weekblad van het Regt, no.3386/3387 (1871).

Weidemann, Margarete (1982) *Kulturgeschichte der Merowingerzeit nach den Werken Gregors von Tours* (2 vols), Mainz.

Wellens, R. (1974) 'Les États genénéraux des Pays-Bas des origines à la fin de Philippe de Beau (1464–1506)', *Anciens Pays et Assemblées d'États*, LXIV.

Weller, M. (1960) *'Ich bitte ums Wort'*, Düsseldorf.

Weststrate, C. and G.H.A. Grosheide (1934, 1935, 1937, 1949, 1952, 1955, 1965) *Handboekje voor secretarissen van verenigingen en voor directeuren en commissarissen van naamloze vennootschappen*, Alphen aan den Rijn.

Whyte, William H. (1957) *The Organization Man*, New York.

Wiarda, Tilemann Dothias (1818) *Von den Landtagen der Friesen in der mittleren Zeiten bei Upstalboom*, Leer.

Wichers, A.J. (1965) *De oude plattelandsbeschaving. Een sociologische bewustwording van de 'overherigheid'*, Wageningen.

Wie leitet man eine Versammlung? Handweiser für Vorsitzenden (1893, 1908) Berlin.

Wie leitet man Vereine und Versammlungen? (1908) Leipzig.

Wilterdink, Nico (1993) *Ongelijkheid en interdependentie*, Groningen (lecture).

Windmuller, John P. and C. de Galan (1979) *Arbeidsverhoudingen in Nederland* (2 vols), Utrecht.

Wolff, L.J.B. and Wessum (1962) *Voor- en tegenzitters. Van ingekomen stukken tot brokken*, Laren.

Wood, Ian (1986) 'Disputes in late fifth- and sixth-century Gaul: some problems', *The settlement of disputes in early medieval Europe*, Wendy Davies and Paul Fouracre (eds), Cambridge, London, New York.

Woodburn, James (1980) 'Hunters and gatherers today and reconstruction of the past', *Soviet and Western Anthropology*, Ernest Gellner, New York.

Woodburn, James (1982) 'Egalitarian Societies', *Man, New Series*, 17 (**3**).

Wouters, Cas (1990) *Van minnen en sterven*, Amsterdam.

Wouters, Cas (1995) 'Etiquette Books and emotion management in the 20th century'. Part I: 'The integration of social classes', *Journal of Social History*, 29 (**1**) (September); Part II: 'The integration of sexes', *Journal of Social History*, 29 (**2**) (December).

Zahn, Ernest (1989) *Regenten, Rebellen en Reformatoren. Een visie op Nederland en de Nederlanders*, Amsterdam.

Zee, G. van der (1962) *1000 Jaar Harderwijk, Kerk en Bethel*, Harderwijk.

Zelko, H.P. (1957, 1963) *Succesful Conference and Discussion Techniques*, New York.

Zelko, H.P. (1969) *The Business Conference: Leadership and Participation*, New York.

Zinoviev, Aleksander (1979) *The Yawning Heights*, New York. Dutch translation (1981)

Zöllner, Erich (1970) *Geschichte der Franken, bis zur Mitte des 6. Jahrhunderts*, Munich.

Zwaan, Ton (1982) 'One step forward, two steps back. Tumin's Theory of Democratic Development: A Comment', *Theory and Society*, 11.

Zwitzer, H.L. (1991) 'De militie van den staat', *Het leger van de Republiek der Verenigde Nederlanden*, Amsterdam.

INDEX